줄리정 불법 IELTS Writing Task II

Juli Jung's Immutable Law for IELTS Writing Task II

2015년 5월 15일 초판 1쇄 인쇄
2025년 2월 24일   3쇄 인쇄

지은이   줄리정

발행인   홍은경
발행처   SUNNY SUNDAY www.sunnysunday.co.kr
주소   경기도 성남시 분당구 성남대로 343번길 12-2, B301호
전화   070-8972-0816
성우   Alex Jensen, Katie Aitken
삽화   홍진실
디자인·인쇄 디자인온 designon1010@naver.com

ISBN 979-11-953898-3-4 13740

※ 책값은 뒤표지에 있습니다.
※ 잘못된 책은 구입처에서 교환하여 드립니다.
※ 이 책은 저작권법에 의하여 보호를 받는 저작물이므로 무단 전재와 무단 복제를 금합니다.

Academic / General 공통

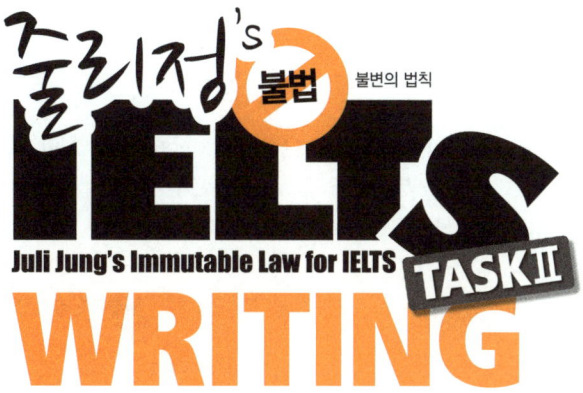

줄리정 지음

BBC 앵커 출신 영국인 성우가
녹음한 MP3 파일 무료 제공
sunnysunday.co.kr
blog.naver.com/iloveielts

H Publishers Co.

추천서

효과적인 아이엘츠 시험 준비의 시작과 끝!

줄리정 선생님을 한번이라도 만나본 사람이라면 그녀의 샘솟는 에너지와 아이엘츠 시험 준비생 개개인에 대한 진심 어린 애정에 깜짝 놀랄 것입니다. 아이엘츠 시험을 면밀히 연구하고 그 간의 온라인 오프라인을 아우르는 전문성과 경험으로 녹여낸 이 책이야말로 효과적인 시험 준비의 시작과 끝이 될 것입니다.

_ **최현경** 주한영국문화원 IELTS 시험센터 팀장

아이엘츠의 보증수표, 7.0의 기적을 일상처럼 일으키는 줄리정 선생님!

줄리정 선생님의 강의를 듣는다는 것은 곧 아이엘츠 보증수표를 거머쥔 것이다. 첫 시험에서 7.0을 획득하는 기적을 일상처럼 일으키는 줄리정 선생님의 노하우와 열정의 집합체인 본 도서 '불법 아이엘츠'가 현재 점수가 몇점이든 단기간에 목표 점수로 이끌어주는 최고의 길잡이가 되리라 확신한다. 시원스쿨랩을 처음 시작할 때 가장 모시고 싶었던 줄리정 선생님께서 본서로 아이엘츠 명가 시원스쿨랩에서 혼신을 다해 강의하신 명품 인강은, 단연코 줄리정 선생님에 대한 과거 수많은 아이엘츠 수험생들의 찬사를 훨씬 뛰어넘는 짙은 감동을 줄 것이다.

_ **양홍걸** 시원스쿨 대표이사

아이엘츠의 여왕, 줄리정이 만든 아이엘츠 고득점을 위한 바이블

Juli has taken the IELTS market by storm with her passion and drive. She has a unique ability to make language learning both fun and practical, and if you do what she says, your English will improve along with your IELTS score! For those reasons, I would certainly recommend her to my Korean friends.

_ **알렉스 젠슨** 前 BBC 앵커, 現 TBS 교통방송 진행자

줄리정불법아이엘츠 Writing 학습법

Step 1 — 빈출 문제
최근 몇 년간 아이엘츠 시험에 자주 나온 문제들을 주제별로 수록하였다. 영어로 된 문제를 혼자 힘으로 해석해 보고 필자의 해석과 비교해 보자. 모든 빈출 문제에 대한 에세이를 작성하는 것은 현실적으로 불가능하지만, 문제를 정확하게 해석할 수 있고, 그 내포하는 의미까지도 파악할 수 있어야 한다. 반드시 모든 빈출 문제를 사전 없이 해석할 수 있는 실력을 갖춘 후 시험에 응시하자!

▼

Step 2 — 브레인스토밍 🎧 MP3
라이팅이 두려운 이유는 영어를 못해서일까? 아이디어가 없어서일까? 이 질문에 대해 90%가 넘는 학생들은 후자를 이유로 꼽았다. 객관식 시험에 익숙한 한국 학생들이 장문의 글을, 그것도 짧은 시간 안에 영어로 작성하기란 결코 만만치 않다. 따라서 필자는 '줄리정불법아이엘츠VOCA'에 수록한 단어와 표현들을 바탕으로 라이팅에 그대로 쓸 수 있는 문장을 영작 연습으로 구성하였다. 반드시 충분한 영작 연습을 통해 단어와 표현을 익힌 후 실전 문제로 넘어가자! 영국인 성우가 녹음한 MP3를 듣고 따라하는 연습도 놓치지 말 것!

▼

Step 3 — 실전문제
라이팅은 수학 공식이다. 뜬금없는 소리처럼 들릴지는 모르나, 이 책의 공식에 맞춰 에세이를 최소 5개 이상 작성한 학습자라면 필자의 말을 저절로 이해할 수 있게 된다. 실전문제는 6가지 단계에 맞춰 작성되었고 각 단계마다의 고유한 공식이 있다. 가령 서론은 2문장으로 쓰고, 본문은 3단계로, 결론은 유형별 템플릿에 맞춰서 작성하고… 이러한 공식을 익히면 금세 에세이에 대한 자신감이 생긴다. 이 책의 Sample Answer는 캠브리지 시리즈에서 자주 나오는 표현과 너무 어렵지 않으면서도 점수 향상에 도움이 되는 단어를 바탕으로 논리적으로 작성되었고 에세이 수준은 8.0 이상이다.

▼

Step 4/5 — 불법 Review & 불법 포인트 정리
실전 문제에서 각 단계 작성 요령을 충분히 익힌 후, 불법 Review와 불법 포인트 정리를 통해 복습까지 충분히 마친다면 어떤 주제의 에세이도 두렵지 않다.

Contents

Chapter 01

IELTS란?

1. IELTS 기본 정보

1-1. IELTS 시험 종류	12
1-2. IELTS 시험 응시 방법, 접수, 응시료	12
1-3. IELTS 시험 장소	13
1-4. IELTS 시험 당일 준비물 및 입실 절차	13
1-5. IELTS 시험 시간표	14
1-6. IELTS 성적	14
1-7. IELTS 채점 기준	15
1-8. IELTS vs TOEFL 점수 환산표	15

Chapter 02

Writing 작성요령

1. Writing Tips!

1-1. 채점기준	18
1-2. Writing 6.0 달성을 위한 필수조건	19
1-3. 시간분배와 작성순서 : Task 2 (35min) → Task 1 (20min) → Correction (5min)	19
1-4. Task 1은 170 단어 정도, Task 2는 270~300 단어 정도로 작성한다	20
1-5. Task 1은 4 단락으로, Task 2는 4~5 단락으로 작성한다	20
1-6. 중요하지만 쉽게 고칠 수 있는 문법적 오류를 확인한다	21
1-7. 슬랭을 쓰지 않는다	22
1-8. 단락이 바뀔 때만 한 줄을 띄어 쓴다	23
1-9. IELTS 시험은 IELTS 기출 단어로 준비한다	24
1-10. 한국인들이 가장 빈번히 저지르는 문법적 실수를 줄인다	24

2. Writing Task 2

2-1. 각 유형별 전략	25
2-2. Task 2 서론, 본론, 결론 작성 공식	49

Chapter 03

주제별 Writing Task II 🎧 MP3

Day 1. Family 가족	61
Step 1 빈출문제	61
Step 2 브레인스토밍	62
Step 3 실전문제	65
Step 4 불법 Review	77
Step 5 불법포인트 정리	78
Day 2. Growing Up 성장	79
Step 1 빈출문제	79
Step 2 브레인스토밍	80
Step 3 실전문제	83
Step 4 불법 Review	95
Step 5 불법포인트 정리	96
Day 3. Health & Food 건강과 음식	97
Step 1 빈출문제	97
Step 2 브레인스토밍	98
Step 3 실전문제	101
Step 4 불법 Review	113
Step 5 불법포인트 정리	114
Day 4. Lifestyles & Leisure Activities 생활방식과 여가활동	115
Step 1 빈출문제	115
Step 2 브레인스토밍	116
Step 3 실전문제	119
Step 4 불법 Review	131
Step 5 불법포인트 정리	132
Day 5. Student Life 학교(학생) 생활	133
Step 1 빈출문제	133
Step 2 브레인스토밍	134
Step 3 실전문제	137
Step 4 불법 Review	149
Step 5 불법포인트 정리	150
Day 6. Communication 의사소통	151
Step 1 빈출문제	151
Step 2 브레인스토밍	152
Step 3 실전문제	155
Step 4 불법 Review	167
Step 5 불법포인트 정리	168
Day 7. Travelling & Transport 여행과 교통	169
Step 1 빈출문제	169
Step 2 브레인스토밍	170
Step 3 실전문제	173
Step 4 불법 Review	185
Step 5 불법포인트 정리	186

Contents

Day 8. Past & History 과거와 역사 — 187
    Step 1 빈출문제 — 187
    Step 2 브레인스토밍 — 188
    Step 3 실전문제 — 191
    Step 4 불법 Review — 203
    Step 5 불법포인트 정리 — 204

Day 9. Natural Environment & Wildlife 자연환경과 야생동식물 — 205
    Step 1 빈출문제 — 205
    Step 2 브레인스토밍 — 206
    Step 3 실전문제 — 209
    Step 4 불법 Review — 221
    Step 5 불법포인트 정리 — 222

Day 10. Earth & Space 지구와 우주 — 223
    Step 1 빈출문제 — 223
    Step 2 브레인스토밍 — 224
    Step 3 실전문제 — 227
    Step 4 불법 Review — 239
    Step 5 불법포인트 정리 — 240

Day 11. Building & Design 빌딩과 디자인 — 241
    Step 1 빈출문제 — 241
    Step 2 브레인스토밍 — 242
    Step 3 실전문제 — 245
    Step 4 불법 Review — 257
    Step 5 불법포인트 정리 — 258

Day 12. IT(Information Technology) 정보기술 — 259
    Step 1 빈출문제 — 259
    Step 2 브레인스토밍 — 260
    Step 3 실전문제 — 263
    Step 4 불법 Review — 275
    Step 5 불법포인트 정리 — 276

Day 13. Shopping & Party 쇼핑과 파티 — 277
    Step 1 빈출문제 — 277
    Step 2 브레인스토밍 — 278
    Step 3 실전문제 — 281
    Step 4 불법 Review — 293
    Step 5 불법포인트 정리 — 294

Day 14. International Relations & Urbanisation 국제관계와 도시화 — 295
    Step 1 빈출문제 — 295
    Step 2 브레인스토밍 — 296
    Step 3 실전문제 — 299
    Step 4 불법 Review — 311
    Step 5 불법포인트 정리 — 312

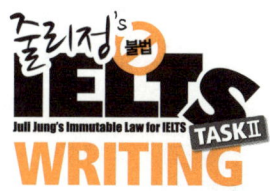

Day 15. **Environmental Pollution** 환경오염 — 313
- Step 1 빈출문제 — 313
- Step 2 브레인스토밍 — 314
- Step 3 실전문제 — 317
- Step 4 불법 Review — 329
- Step 5 불법포인트 정리 — 330

Day 16. **The Energy Crisis** 에너지 위기 — 331
- Step 1 빈출문제 — 331
- Step 2 브레인스토밍 — 332
- Step 3 실전문제 — 335
- Step 4 불법 Review — 347
- Step 5 불법포인트 정리 — 348

Day 17. **Economy & Business** 경제와 산업 — 349
- Step 1 빈출문제 — 349
- Step 2 브레인스토밍 — 350
- Step 3 실전문제 — 353
- Step 4 불법 Review — 365
- Step 5 불법포인트 정리 — 366

Day 18. **The Government & Law** 정부와 법 — 367
- Step 1 빈출문제 — 367
- Step 2 브레인스토밍 — 368
- Step 3 실전문제 — 371
- Step 4 불법 Review — 383
- Step 5 불법포인트 정리 — 384

Day 19. **Mass Media, Movie & Play** 대중매체, 영화와 연극 — 385
- Step 1 빈출문제 — 385
- Step 2 브레인스토밍 — 386
- Step 3 실전문제 — 389
- Step 4 불법 Review — 401
- Step 5 불법포인트 정리 — 402

Day 20. **Art** 예술 — 403
- Step 1 빈출문제 — 403
- Step 2 브레인스토밍 — 404
- Step 3 실전문제 — 407
- Step 4 불법 Review — 419
- Step 5 불법포인트 정리 — 420

Chapter
01

IELTS란?
IELTS (International English Language Testing System)

IELTS는 International English Language Testing System의 약자로 국제 공인 영어능력 평가시험이다. IELTS(www.ielts.org)는 미국, 영국, 호주, 캐나다, 뉴질랜드 등 영어권 국가로 유학, 취업, 이민을 희망하는 사람들을 위한 시험으로 영국문화원(British Council), IDP : IELTS Australia와 케임브리지 대학 산하 영어평가 연구소(Cambridge Assessment English)가 공동으로 개발, 관리, 운영하고 있다.

1989년부터 시행되어 현재는 전 세계 140여 개 국 1,600여 개 센터에서 운영되고 있으며 매년 수백만 명의 수험자가 응시하는 큰 규모의 시험이다. 2019년을 기준으로 350만 명 이상이 응시하였으며, 이는 전 세계 TOEFL 응시자보다 많은 숫자다. 미국식 영어를 배우는 우리나라에서는 IELTS 시험이 이제야 활발하게 알려지고 있지만, 전 세계 인구의 3분의 1을 차지하는 중국과 인도에서는 TOEIC, TOEFL 응시자보다 IELTS 응시자가 압도적으로 많다. 국내 응시자 규모 또한 최근 5년 동안 1만명 이상 증가하며 빠르게 성장하고 있다.

1
IELTS 기본 정보

1-1. IELTS 시험 종류

1) Academic Module
영어권 국가에서의 학사 과정, 혹은 국내외 다양한 국가에서의 석사, 박사 등의 과정에 지원하는 사람들이 준비하는 시험으로 고등교육에 필요한 학문적인 영어 의사소통 능력에 중점을 둔다.

2) General Training Module
영국, 호주, 뉴질랜드, 캐나다 등 영연방 국가로의 이민을 계획하거나 이러한 국가에서 중등교육, 전문 주립대 입학, 직업 연수를 받으려는 사람들을 대상으로 하는 시험으로 그 사회에서 직업을 구하고 생활을 지속하는 데에 필요한 기본적인 영어 의사소통 능력에 중점을 둔다.

※ 이 책 '줄리정불법아이엘츠 Speaking'은 아카데믹과 제너럴 공통이다.

1-2. IELTS 시험 응시 방법, 접수, 응시료

문제지가 주어지고 연필로 답을 적어서 제출하는 지필 시험 방식(IELTS on paper)과, 개별 모니터와 헤드폰으로 문제를 보고 들은 후 마우스와 키보드로 답을 작성하는 컴퓨터 시험 방식(IELTS on computer) 중 하나를 선택할 수 있다. 단, 두 가지 방식 모두 Speaking 시험은 원어민 시험관과 1:1 대면 방식으로 진행되며, 응시하는 국가나 시험장에 따라 실시간 온라인 화상 면접 형태로 Speaking 시험(Video-Call Speaking)을 진행하는 곳도 있다. 지필 시험은 한 달에 4회(토요일 3회/목요일 1회), 컴퓨터 시험은 한 달에 약 50회 진행으로 더 자주 응시할 수 있다. 아이엘츠 시험의 주관사인 영국문화원과 IDP의 접수 사이트를 통해 온라인 접수가 가능하고, 주관사나 시험장별 문제나 난이도의 차이는 없다. 시험 등록 시 허용되는 신분증은 여권이 유일하므로 되도록 유학 기간을 다 포함할 만큼 유효 기간이 넉넉히 남은 여권을 꼭 준비하도록 하자. 응시료는 2024년 1월 기준 아래와 같으며, 신용 카드와 계좌 이체의 결제 옵션이 있다.

응시료	Regular IELTS on paper/computer	29만9천원
	IELTS for UKVI on paper/computer	33만3천원
주관사 별 접수사이트	영국문화원 www.britishcouncil.kr/exam/ielts	
	IDP ielts.idp.com/korea	

1-3. IELTS 시험 장소

서울, 경기뿐만 아니라 인천, 대전, 대구, 광주, 부산, 제주 등 거의 전국에서 아이엘츠 시험을 응시할 수 있다. 대학 및 대형 어학원 등을 고사장으로 사용하고 있다.

1-4. IELTS 시험 당일 준비물 및 입실 절차

1) 고사장에서는 아래 명시된 물품만 허용된다.

① 허용 물품

연필/샤프, 지우개, 유효한 여권과 이 여권의 사본 1부 (신분증은 모든 과목의 시험이 끝날 때까지 반드시 지참한다.)

② 금지 물품

허용되는 것 이외 모든 것. 대표적으로, 가방, 커피, 물을 제외한 음료수, 휴대전화, 스마트 기기, 모든 종류의 시계, 블루투스 이어폰, 볼펜, 형광펜, 필통, 무릎 담요, 모자, 목도리, 장갑 등이 있다.

2) 입실 절차 (지필, 컴퓨터 동일)

1-5. IELTS 시험 시간표

과 목	시 간 (Briefing부터 Listening까지 휴식 시간 없이 진행된다.)	문제 개수	비 고
Briefing (시험안내)	8 : 50 ~		답안 작성 시 주의사항 등 시험 전반에 대한 간략한 안내
Writing (쓰기)	9 : 10 ~ 10 : 10 (총 1시간)	2개의 Task Task 1은 150 단어 이상 Task 2는 250 단어 이상	점수 비중이 높은 Task 2부터 작성해야 고득점을 받는다.
Reading (읽기)	10 : 20 ~ 11 : 20 (총 1시간)	3개의 Passage 각 Passage당 13~14문제 총 40문제	1시간 안에 문제도 풀고 답안지도 작성해야 한다. 시간이 부족하기 때문에 1번부터 순서대로 풀지 말고, 주관식 등 쉬운 문제부터 골라서 먼저 푼다.
Listening (듣기)	11 : 30 ~ 12 : 10 (총 40분 : 리코딩 30분 +답안 작성 10분)	4개의 Section 각 Part당 10문제 총 40문제	리코딩이 끝나면 답안 작성을 위한 추가 10분이 주어진다.
Break (휴식)			
Speaking (말하기)	13 : 00 ~ 18 : 00 (총 11~14분)	3개의 Part 원어민 시험관과 1:1 인터뷰	추가 접수자는 일요일에 Speaking 시험을 치를 수도 있다.

※ 시험 종료 후에도 답안을 작성하는 응시자들이 매 시험마다 있는데 이러한 행위는 부정행위로 간주되어 실격 처리된다. 따라서 시험관이 시험 종료를 알리면 필기구를 책상에 올려 놓은 후 손을 책상 아래로 내려야 한다.

1-6. IELTS 성적

IELTS의 점수 산출은 각 과목의 점수를 0~9점으로 매기고 0.5점 단위로 채점한다. 0점은 시험에 응시하지 않은 경우이고 9점은 만점이다. 총점은 각 과목의 점수를 더한 후 4로 나누어서 반올림한다.

Listening	Reading	Writing	Speaking	Overall Band Score	CEFR* LEVEL
6.5	7.5	7.0	6.0	7.0	C1

※ CEFR (Common European Framework of Reference) : 유럽 언어의 구사 능력을 표준화 해 둔 공통 기준으로 한 사람이 가진 언어 능력을 6개 등급으로 구분해 두었다. 가장 낮은 A1 부터 A2, B1, B2, C1, C2까지 올라가며, 언어 구사 능력을 상세히 기술해 놓은 Can-Do Statement가 특징이다.

즉, 6.5+7.5+7.0+6.0 = 27이고 이것을 4로 나누면 6.75, 이 점수를 반올림하면 7.0이 된다.

4과목의 점수를 더해서 4로 나눈 평균 값	6.0	6.125	6.25	6.375	6.5	6.625	6.75	6.875	7.0
Overall Band Score	6.0	6.0	6.5	6.5	6.5	6.5	7.0	7.0	7.0

1-7. IELTS 채점 기준

아래의 표는 IELTS 본부 사이트(www.ielts.org)에서 발표한 채점 기준으로 현재의 채점 기준이라고 볼 수 있다. 특히 Academic과 General Training Reading의 맞은 개수에 따른 점수 산정이 다른 것을 눈여겨봐야 하는데 비교적 난이도가 낮다고 여겨지는 General Training이기 때문에 더 많은 문제를 맞혀야 높은 점수를 얻을 수 있다.

Band Score	Listening	Academic Reading	General Training Reading
5	16~22	15~22	23~29
6	23~29	23~29	30~33
7	30~34	30~34	34~37
8	35~39	35~39	38~39

※ 위 과목은 총 40문제가 출제되며, 응시자들이 주로 목표로 하는 점수대만 표기하였다.

1-8. IELTS vs TOEFL 점수 환산표

IELTS	IBT TOEFL
7.5~9.0	113~120
7.0	100
6.5	90~91
6.0	79~80
5.5	69~70
5.0	59~60
4.5	49~50
4.0	39~40
3.5	29~30

Chapter

02

Writing 작성요령

IELTS WRITING 시험구성

- 총 2 문제 : Task 1 (그래프 분석)과 Task 2 (에세이)
- 총 소요시간 : 1시간
- 작성도구 : 연필 혹은 샤프 / 지우개 사용
- Task 1은 150 단어 이상 작성, Task 2는 250 단어 이상 작성

1
Writing Tips!

1-1. 채점기준

Task Response or Achievement 논점에 맞게 글 완성하기	문제에서 요구한 방향과 범위를 벗어나지 않고 논점에 딱 맞게 글을 썼는지에 대한 평가이다. 예를 들어 '공공장소에서의 흡연을 금지해야 하는가?' 라는 문제에 대해 담배가 인체에 미치는 영향에 대해서만 중점적으로 기술한다면, 이것은 '담배가 인체에 미치는 영향에 대해 논하라' 는 문제에 대한 에세이가 되므로 감점이 크다. 또한 Task 1과 Task 2 모두 단어 수 요건에 맞춰서 시간 내에 완성하지 못했다면 큰 감점 요인이 된다.
Coherence and Cohesion 논리적으로 일관성 있게 글쓰기	기술한 내용이 출제된 문제의 답으로서 적합한지에 대한 평가이다. 생각이나 정보 등을 논리에 맞게 일관성 있게 쓰고 대명사, 접속사 등을 적절하게 사용할 수 있어야 한다. 가령 위에 언급한 내용과 반대되는 의견을 제시하는 상황에서 but 대신 and를 쓴다면 감점 요인이 된다.
Lexical Resources 아카데믹한 단어 사용하기	출제된 문제와 관련된 아카데믹한 단어를 얼마나 다양하고 정확하게 사용하는지에 대한 평가이다. 예를 들어 '올라가다' 라는 단어를 표현할 때 increase만 여러 번 반복하기보다는, go up, rise, boost, boom, grow 등으로 다양한 표현을 적절하게 사용하는 것이 좋다. 또한 슬랭을 사용하면 감점 요인이 된다.
Grammatical Range and Accuracy 문법에 맞게 정확하게 글쓰기	응시자의 문법과 어법 능력을 평가하는 항목이다. 얼핏 보면 IELTS에는 문법 시험이 없는 것처럼 보일 수 있지만 Listening, Reading의 주관식 답안에서부터 Writing, Speaking까지 모든 과목에 문법 실력을 체크하는 항목이 포함되어 있다. 특히 관사, 수 일치, 시제, 이 세 가지 사항만이라도 꼼꼼히 체크하면 상당수의 문법적 실수를 줄일 수 있다.

1-2. Writing 6.0 달성을 위한 필수조건

1) 1시간 내에 Task 1과 Task 2 모두 작성한다.

단, Task 1은 150 단어 이상, Task 2는 250 단어 이상 반드시 작성한다. 만약 Task 2의 결론을 작성하지 못했다면 아무리 글을 잘 써도 5.0을 넘기 어렵다.

2) 논점에 맞게 작성한다.

문제를 정확하게 읽고 문제에서 요구하는 틀과 범위에 맞춰서 논리적으로 작성한다.

3) 구조에 맞게 작성한다.

일반적으로 Task 1은 4단락, Task 2는 4~5단락으로 작성한다. 문제 유형에 맞춰 단락을 나눈다.

4) 수준 높은 아카데믹한 단어를 사용한다.

IELTS 기출 단어를 중심으로 사용한다. 같은 단어를 여러 번 사용하는 것을 피하고, 다양한 동의어를 사용하여 작성한다.

5) 문법에 맞게 쓴다.

IELTS 시험에는 문법 과목이 따로 없지만, Writing은 문법에 맞게 글을 작성해야 한다. 따라서 글을 모두 작성한 후에는 반드시 스스로 교정할 수 있는 시간을 남겨두어야 한다. 이 때 특히 대부분의 한국 응시자들이 취약한 관사, 수 일치, 시제 등을 집중적으로 확인한다.

1-3. 시간분배와 작성순서 : Task 2 (35min) → Task 1 (20min) → Correction (5min)

Writing은 한 시간 내에 두 개의 Task를 모두 완성하는 시험이다. Task 2가 Task 1보다 배점이 더 높기 때문에 무조건 Task 2부터 글을 작성한다. Task 1부터 작성할 경우, 생각보다 Task 1을 작성하는데 시간이 지체되어 Task 2를 완성하지 못한 채 답안지를 제출하는 상황이 발생하게 되는데, 이럴 경우 매우 낮은 점수를 받게 된다. 반대로 Task 2는 완성했지만, Task 1을 중간 정도밖에 못 쓴 상황에서는 6점까지도 받는 경우가 있다. 그러므로 평소에 Task 1과 Task 2를 정해진 시간 내에 모두 작성하는 수험생이라 하더라도 시험 당일 출제된 문제에 따라 시간이 많이 소요될 수 있으므로 실제 시험에서는 반드시 Task 2부터 작성해야 한다.

또한 반드시 시험 종료 5분 전에는 스스로 correction을 해야 한다. 문법의 정확성도 평가항목이므로 55분 간 글을 완성한 후, 반드시 5분은 스스로 작성한 글의 문법적 오류를 확인해야 한다.

1시간 내에 Task 두 개를 모두 작성할 수 없다면 시험에 응시하기에는 아직 이르다. 1시간 동안 Task 1과 Task 2를 모두 작성하는 연습을 5번 정도 한 후, 최소한 90% 정도의 내용을 작성할 수 있을 때 시험에 응시해야 한다. 시험장에서 갑자기 영어가 빨리 써지는 기적은 일어나지 않는다.

1-4. Task 1은 170 단어 정도, Task 2는 270~300 단어 정도로 작성한다

Task 1은 적어도 150 단어를(at least 150 words), Task 2는 적어도 250 단어를(at least 250 words) 작성해야 한다. 이것은 각각 150 단어, 250 단어 미만인 경우에는 큰 감점이 된다는 것을 의미한다. 실제로 시험관은 단어 개수를 일일이 세어보고 단어 수가 모자를 경우 낮은 점수를 준다. 따라서 평소부터 Task 1은 170 단어 정도, Task 2는 270~300 단어 정도로 작성하는 습관을 갖는다면 실제 시험에서 단어 수를 세는데 시간을 낭비하지 않아도 단어 수가 미달되는 사태를 막을 수 있다. 간혹 수험생들 중에는 Task 2를 작성할 때, 300 단어 이상 400 단어까지도 쓰는 경우가 있는데 이는 좋지 않은 습관이다. 많이 쓴다고 해서 높은 점수를 받는 것이 절대로 아니기 때문이다. 또한 이렇게 길게 쓰면 시간 내에 글을 완성하지 못하는 큰 실수를 범할 수 있고 문법적 오류가 더 많이 생겨서 감점이 더 많아질 수도 있다.

1-5. Task 1은 4단락으로, Task 2는 4~5단락으로 작성한다

내용에 맞게 단락을 바꾸는 것도 Writing에서는 중요한 요소이다. 단락을 아예 나누지 않거나, 너무 많은 단락으로 글을 구성하는 것은 감점의 요인이 된다. 특히 문장 하나로 단락 하나를 구성하는 것은 좋은 방법이 아니다. 따라서 Task 1은 서론 / 일반적 경향 / 본론 1 / 본론2, 총 4단락으로 Task 2는 서론 / 본론1 / 본론2 / (본론3) / 결론, 4~5단락으로 작성하는 것이 적절하다.

1-6. 중요하지만 쉽게 고칠 수 있는 문법적 오류들을 확인한다

1) 대소문자 구분

문장의 첫 글자는 항상 대문자로 시작한다.

there has been a controversial issue in terms of keeping animals in a zoo. (×)
→ There has been a controversial issue in terms of keeping animals in a zoo. (○)

쉼표(,) 다음에는 소문자로 쓴다.

In modern society, People (×) → In modern society, people (○)

주어를 나타내는 'I' 와 고유명사는 문장에서의 위치와 상관없이 대문자로 쓴다.

However, i am convinced that~ (×) → However, I am convinced that~ (○)
south korea (×) → South Korea (○)
dr. smith (×) → Dr. Smith (○)
monday (×) → Monday (○)
february (×) → February (○)

2) 단수 / 복수 주어와 동사의 일치

동사의 형태는 각 주어의 특징에 따라 바뀐다. 3인칭 단수 (She, He, It, Victor, Charles…), 단수 명사(A child, A person…), 동명사(Studying, Eating…) 일 때, 동사의 형태는 일반 동사일 경우 동사원형에 s나 ~es가 붙지만, 주어가 1인칭 단/복수(I, We), 2인칭 단/복수(You), 3인칭 복수(They), 복수 명사(Children, People) 일 때는 일반동사일 경우 동사원형을 쓴다.

pupils plays (×) → pupils play (○)
the Internet play (×) → the Internet plays (○)

3) 단수 명사 앞에 관사 (a / the) 의 유무 / 복수 명사

단수 명사 앞에는 'a' 나 'the' 와 같은 관사가 있어야 한다. 복수 명사 앞에는 'a' 가 절대 올 수 없지만, 'the' 는 문맥에 따라서 올 수도 있다.

pupil (×) → a pupil / the pupil (○)
a childrens (×) → children / the children (○)

* children은 child 의 복수 명사이므로 ~s를 붙이지 않는다.
* the children은 앞에서 이미 언급한 '특정한 아이들' 을 지칭한다.

4) 축약형을 쓰지 않는다.

Speaking 시험에서는 축약형으로 말하는 것이 더욱 자연스럽지만 Writing에서는 축약형을 사용하면 감점이 된다. 참고로 축약형의 어포스트로피(apostrophe: 축약할 때 사용하는 기호,')는 사용하면 안되지만, 소유격의 어포스트로피는 사용해도 무방하다. 축약형과 소유격의 어포스트로피를 혼동하지 말자(e.g. My father's friend, 이 경우의 어포스트로피는 소유격이다.).

don't (×) → do not (○)
it's (×) → it is (○)
shouldn't (×) → should not (○)

5) 반드시 the를 필요로 하는 단어들에 주의한다.

the Internet(고유명사)
the government(한 국가에 정부는 하나이다.)
* governments라고 복수로 쓸 경우, 특정 국가의 정부들을 지칭하는 경우에는 the governments, 일반적인 정부들을 의미할 때는 governments라고 쓴다.

1-7. 슬랭을 쓰지 않는다

편한 외국인 친구와 영어로 대화하듯 Writing을 작성해서는 높은 점수를 받을 수 없다. 다음과 같은 표현들은 일상적인 회화에서는 자주 사용되지만 '시험' 영어에서는 마이너스 표현이다. 이는 Speaking 시험에서도 금물이다.

gonna (×) → going to (○)
wanna (×) → want to (○)
lots of (×) → a lot of (○)
guys (×) → people (○)

1-8. 단락이 바뀔 때만 한 줄을 띄어 쓴다

단락이 바뀔 때만 한 줄을 띄어 쓴다. 줄 간격을 두 배로(double spacing)하지 않고, 단락이 바뀌지 않는 경우에는 줄을 바꾸지 않는다.

다음은 Body 1의 일부이다.

1) 줄 간격을 두 배로 한 경우 (X)

> There might be no doubt electronic books are getting more and more popular than traditional
>
> books because of two advantages : faster access and easier handling. Firstly, the e-book is a
>
> smart tool which can access to information faster.

2) 단락이 바뀌지 않았을 때, 줄을 바꿔 쓴 경우 (X)

> There might be no doubt electronic books are getting more and more popular than traditional
> books because of two advantages: faster access and easier handling.
> Firstly, the e-book is a smart tool which can access to information faster.
> People can find useful data by clicking a mouse or typing a few key words.

3) Sample (0)

> There might be no doubt electronic books are getting more and more popular than traditional books because of two advantages: faster access and easier handling. Firstly, the e-book is a smart tool which can access to information faster. People can find useful data by clicking a mouse or typing a few key words.

1-9. IELTS 시험은 IELTS 기출 단어로 준비한다

IELTS는 영국과 호주에서 출제한 영어 시험이다. 따라서 미국식 영어 위주로 출제되는 시험의 단어를 공부하기보다는 IELTS 기출 단어를 공부해서 Writing에 적용하는 것이 유리하다. IELTS Writing을 위한 단어와 숙어를 익히기 위해서는 IELTS 기출 단어와 숙어가 정리된 책을 구입하거나 Cambridge IELTS 시리즈의 Reading과 Listening에 자주 등장하는 단어들을 정리해서 스스로의 단어장을 만들어 보는 것도 좋은 방법이다.

※ 오직 아이엘츠만을 생각한 단어집 - 줄리정불법아이엘츠VOCA

1-10. 한국인들이 가장 빈번히 저지르는 문법적 실수를 줄인다

IELTS 시험에는 직접적인 문법 문제는 없지만, 모든 과목에 문법 실력을 테스트하는 요소들이 숨어 있다. 특히 Writing 평가 항목으로 문법이 25%를 차지하기 때문에 고득점을 목표로 할수록 문법적 오류를 반드시 줄여야 한다.

아이엘츠 필수 문법은 'NEW줄리정불법아이엘츠' p.173~192를 참고하자!

2
Writing Task 2

2-1. 각 유형별 전략

Task 2에는 크게 3가지 문제 유형이 있다.

Agree or Disagree	Advantage or Disadvantage	Reason(Problem) and Solution
찬성 혹은 반대	장점 혹은 단점	이유(문제점)와 해결책
문제의 토픽에 동의하는지 동의하지 않는지를 논하는 유형	문제의 토픽에 장점이 많은지 단점이 많은지를 논하는 유형	문제의 토픽에 대한 이유(문제점)를 논하고 해결책을 제시하는 유형

1) Agree or Disagree

가장 자주 출제되는 문제 유형이다. 문제의 토픽에 대한 응시자의 의견을 묻는 문제로, 응시자는 논리적 일관성을 가지고 본인의 주장을 진술해야 한다. 이 유형에는 본인의 의견만 제시해도 되는 문제가 있고(1-1), 반드시 상대방의 의견(counter argument)도 포함시켜야 하는 문제가 있다(1-2).

(1-1) Do you agree or disagree? 당신은 동의하는가? 동의하지 않는가?

> In modern society traditional food is being replaced by fast food. This trend has a negative impact on both individuals and society. Do you agree or disagree with this statement?
>
> 현대 사회에서 전통 음식이 패스트푸드에 의해 대체되고 있다. 이러한 경향은 개인과 사회에 모두 부정적인 영향을 미친다. 당신은 이 말에 동의하는가? 동의하지 않는가?

토픽 (topic) : In modern society traditional food is being replaced by fast food. This trend has a negative impact on both individuals and society.
질문 (question) : Do you agree or disagree with this statement?

이 문제 유형은 다음과 같이 A, B 두 가지 타입으로 에세이를 작성할 수 있다. (Agree일 경우)

	A type : Agree + Agree	B type : Disagree + Agree
Introduction	두 문장 : Paraphrasing + Answering 1. 전통 음식이 패스트푸드에 의해 대체되고 있는 경향은 개인과 사회에 부정적인 영향을 미친다. 2. 나는 이 의견에 동의한다.	두 문장 : Paraphrasing + Answering 1. 전통 음식이 패스트푸드에 의해 대체되고 있는 경향은 개인과 사회에 부정적인 영향을 미친다. 2. 긍정적이라고 말하는 사람도 있지만, 나는 이 의견에 동의한다.
Body 1	**Agree 1** 부정적인 영향 1 - 개인에게 미치는 부정적인 영향	**Disagree** 긍정적인 영향 : 개인과 사회에 미치는 긍정적인 영향 (나와 다른 의견도 어느 정도 인정함.) Body 2 보다 짧게 작성
Body 2	**Agree 2** 부정적인 영향 2 - 사회에 미치는 부정적인 영향	**Agree** 부정적인 영향 : 개인과 사회에 미치는 부정적인 영향 그럼에도 불구하고 부정적인 영향이 더 크다. (내 의견을 강력하게 주장함.) Body 1보다 1.5배 정도 길게 작성
Conclusion	**Restatement** 전통 음식이 패스트푸드에 의해 대체되고 있는 경향은 개인과 사회에 부정적인 영향을 미친다는 의견에 동의한다. : Body 1 + 2의 내용을 요약하며 내 주장을 다시 한 번 강조	**Restatement** 전통 음식이 패스트푸드에 의해 대체되고 있는 경향은 개인과 사회에 긍정적인 면도 있지만, 부정적인 영향이 더 크다는 의견에 동의한다. : Body 1 + 2의 내용을 요약하며 내 주장을 다시 한 번 강조

이 에세이에서는 Agree의 경우가 '전통 음식이 패스트푸드에 의해 대체되고 있는 경향이 **부정적이다**' 라는 의견에 동의하는 것이다. 만약 긍정적이라고 생각하면 내 의견은 Disagree가 되어야 한다. 또한 개인과 사회에 미치는 영향 모두를 언급해야 한다.

A, B 두 가지 타입 중 어떤 것을 선택하더라도 점수와는 큰 관련이 없다. Agree에 대한 아이디어만 있을 경우에는 A type, Agree에 대한 아이디어도 Disagree에 대한 아이디어도 있을 경우에는 B type을 선택하는 것이 250자 이상 작성하는 데 도움이 된다. A type으로 작성할 때, 자칫 글자 수가 모자라는 경우도 발생하기 때문이다. B type으로 작성할 때 주의해야 할 사항은 간혹 상대방 의견인 Body 1이 나의 의견인 Body 2보다 길어지는 경우가 있다. 이 경우 본인의 주장이 명료하게 전달되지 않을 수 있기 때문에 Body 1은 Body 2보다 짧게 작성한다. (**Introduction + Body 1 〈 120 단어**)

결론에는 본론에서 언급한 내용을 요약해서 내 의견을 다시 한 번 강력하게 주장한다(Restatement).

*Agree or Disagree 유형에서 내 의견은 어떻게 정할까?

Agree or Disagree 유형에서 어느 쪽을 지지해야 더 높은 점수를 받을 수 있을지 고민되는 응시자가 있을 것이다.

1-1 문제를 예로 들어 보자.

> In modern society traditional food is being replaced by fast food. This trend has a negative impact on both individuals and society. Do you agree or disagree with this statement?
>
> 현대 사회에서 전통 음식은 패스트푸드에 의해 대체되고 있다. 이러한 경향은 개인과 사회에 모두 부정적인 영향을 미친다. 당신은 이 말에 동의하는가? 동의하지 않는가?

대부분의 응시자들은 개인적인 생각이나 순간적인 느낌만으로 Agree나 Disagree를 결정할지도 모른다. 하지만 이 경우, 상당수의 응시자들은 아이디어가 제한적이기 때문에 본론은 몇 줄 쓰지 못하고 글쓰기를 멈출 수 있다. 또한 B type으로 에세이를 작성할 경우, Body 1이 Body 2보다 훨씬 더 길어지는 경우도 발생한다. 이렇게 내 의견보다는 상대방의 의견을 더 많이 작성하면 글의 논지가 흐려져서 감점 요인이 될 수 있다.

따라서 먼저 브레인스토밍을 거친 후에 영어로 더 많은 내용을 작성할 수 있는 쪽으로 내 의견을 정해야 한다.

Brainstorming Note

다음 빈칸에 '전통음식이 패스트푸드에 의해 대체되고 있는 경향은 개인과 사회에 부정적인 영향을 미친다.' 라는 주장에 대한 본인의 의견을 영어로 작성해 보자.

Agree	Disagree
전통 음식이 패스트푸드에 의해 대체되고 있는 경향은 개인과 사회에 **부정적인** 영향을 미친다.	전통 음식이 패스트푸드에 의해 대체되고 있는 경향은 개인과 사회에 **긍정적인** 영향을 미친다.
- 개인 - 사회	- 개인 - 사회

Agree에 대한 아이디어가 많으면 내 의견은 Agree, Disagree에 대한 아이디어가 많으면 내 의견은 Disagree가 된다. 만약 아이디어의 개수가 같을 경우에는 부연 설명을 영어로 더 잘할 수 있는 쪽으로 내 의견으로 정하면 된다.

Agree로 내 의견을 정했다면 A type으로 작성할 경우 Body 1은 개인, Body 2는 사회에 미치는 부정적 영향에 대해 작성하고, B type으로 작성할 경우 Body 1에는 개인과 사회에 미치는 긍정적인 영향, Body 2에는 개인과 사회에 미치는 부정적인 영향을 Body 1보다 길게 작성한다.

Translation

다음 우리말을 영작해 보자.

Agree	Disagree
전통 음식이 패스트푸드에 의해 대체되고 있는 경향은 개인과 사회에 **부정적인** 영향을 미친다.	전통 음식이 패스트푸드에 의해 대체되고 있는 경향은 개인과 사회에 **긍정적인** 영향을 미친다.
1. 개인 : 나쁜 건강 상태 나쁜 건강상태라는 형태로 지불해야 하는 패스트푸드의 대가는 더 크다. 나쁜 건강 상태 : poor health 매우 큰 : significant 지불해야 하는 대가 : cost	1. 개인 : 현대인들의 성급함을 반영 제한된 시간 내에 먹고 장시간 기다리는 것을 피하고자 하는 욕구는 일이나 다른 취미에 시간을 쓰는 데 서두르는 현대인들의 성급함을 반영한다. 제한된 시간 내에 : within a limited period 취미 : pursuits (*pursuit가 복수일 경우, pastime, hobby와 동의어로 캠브리지 아이엘츠에 자주 나온다. 꼭 기억할 것!) 현대인들의 성급함 : the impatience of modern people
2. 사회 : 전통 문화를 위협 패스트푸드의 세계화가 있는데, 이것은 전통 문화를 위협한다. 패스트푸드 음식의 세계화 : the globalisation of fast food 위협하다 : threaten 전통 문화 : traditional culture	2. 사회 : 상대적으로 저렴한 비용 패스트푸드의 상대적으로 저렴한 비용 또한 저소득 사람들에게 호소력이 있어서 더 적은 사람들이 배고픔으로 고통을 겪는다. 상대적으로 저렴한 비용 : the relatively cheap cost 저소득 사람들 : lower - income individuals

Answer

Agree	Disagree
전통 음식이 패스트푸드에 의해 대체되고 있는 경향은 개인과 사회에 **부정적인** 영향을 미친다.	전통 음식이 패스트푸드에 의해 대체되고 있는 경향은 개인과 사회에 **긍정적인** 영향을 미친다.
- 개인 The greater cost of fast food in the form of poor health is significant.	- 개인 The desire to eat within a limited period and to avoid waiting too long reflects the impatience of modern people who rush to spend time on work or other pursuits.
- 사회 There is the globalisation of fast food, which threatens traditional culture.	- 사회 The relatively cheap cost of fast food also has an appeal for lower-income individuals and so fewer members of society suffer from hunger.

※ 완성된 에세이는 Day 3(p.97) 참고!

(1-2) **Discuss both views and give your own opinion.** 두 가지 의견을 논하고 본인의 의견을 제시하시오.

> Some people think governments should spend as much money as possible exploring outer space. Others argue they should spend the money for poor people. Discuss both views and give your own opinion.
>
> 어떤 사람들은 정부가 가능한 많은 돈을 우주 탐험에 써야 한다고 생각한다. 다른 사람들은 정부가 가난한 사람들을 위해 그 돈을 써야 한다고 주장한다. 양쪽의 견해를 논하고 당신의 주장을 제시하라.

토픽 (topic) : Some people think governments should spend as much money as possible exploring outer space. Others argue they should spend the money for poor people.
질문 (question) : Discuss both views and give your own opinion.

이 문제 유형은 다음과 같은 구조로 작성할 수 있다. (Others의 의견에 동의할 경우)

Introduction	**두 문장 : Paraphrasing + Answering** 1. 어떤 사람들은 정부가 가능한 많은 돈을 우주 탐험에 써야 한다고 생각하지만, 다른 사람들은 정부가 가난한 사람들을 위해 그 돈을 써야 한다고 주장한다. 2. 우주 탐도도 중요하지만 나는 정부가 가난한 사람들을 위해 그 돈을 써야 한다는 의견에 동의한다.
Body 1	**Some people의 의견** 어떤 사람들은 정부가 가능한 많은 돈을 우주 탐험에 써야 한다고 생각한다. : Body 2보다 짧게 작성
Body 2	**내 의견 (=Others의 의견)** 하지만 나는 정부가 가난한 사람들을 위해 그 돈을 써야 한다고 생각한다. : Body 1보다 1.5배 정도 길게 작성
Conclusion	**Restatement** 정부가 가능한 많은 돈을 우주 탐험에 써야 한다고 생각하는 사람도 있지만, 나는 정부가 가난한 사람들을 위해 그 돈을 써야 한다고 생각한다. : Body 1 + 2의 내용을 요약하며 내 주장을 다시 한 번 강조

Discuss both views는 양측 의견을 모두 제시하라는 말이다. 따라서 some people과 others의 입장에 대해 각각 브레인스토밍을 한 후, give your own opinion, 영어로 더 많은 아이디어를 적을 수 있는 쪽을 내 의견으로 삼고 상대방의 의견은 Body 1에, 내 의견은 Body 2에 적는다.

간혹 '양쪽의 견해를 논하고 당신의 주장을 제시하라.' 라는 지시문 때문에 먼저 양쪽 입장을 하나씩 Body 1과 Body 2에 각각 논하고 Body 3나 Conclusion에 내 의견을 제시하는 학생들이 있다. 하지만 이런 경우 내가 others 의견에 동의한다고 가정했을 때, Body 3 혹은 Conclusion에 Body 2에 작성한 아이디어를 반복하게 됨으로 삼가야 한다.

1-1. Do you agree or disagree? 유형에서는 내 의견만 제시하는 A type으로 에세이를 작성해도 무방하지만, 1-2유형처럼 Discuss both views가 문제에 제시된 경우에는 문제에서 양쪽 견해를 모두 논하라고 했기 때문에 반드시 1-1의 B type으로 양쪽 의견을 모두 작성해야 한다. 결론에는 본론에서 언급한 내용을 요약해서 내 의견을 다시 한 번 강력하게 주장한다(Restatement).

Brainstorming Note

다음 빈칸에 '정부는 많은 돈을 우주 탐험에 써야 하는지 가난한 사람들을 위해 써야 하는지' 에 대한 본인의 의견을 영어로 작성해 보자.

Some people	Others
정부는 가능한 많은 돈을 우주 탐험에 써야 한다.	정부는 가난한 사람들을 위해 그 돈을 써야 한다.
1.	1.
2.	2.

Translation

다음 우리말을 영작해 보자.

Some people	Others
정부는 가능한 많은 돈을 우주 탐험에 써야 한다.	정부는 가난한 사람들을 위해 그 돈을 써야 한다.
1. 가장 미스터리하고 매력적인 주제 이 분야보다 더 미스터리하고 매력적인 주제는 거의 없다. 매력적인 : fascinating 거의 없는 : few	1. 빈부격차 해소가 더 중요함 우주 탐사보다 더 분명하게 빈부격차를 강조하는 시도는 거의 없다. 시도 : endeavour 빈부격차 : the gap between the rich and the poor 강조하다 : highlight
2. 인류의 장기간 생존 보장 우주 탐사는 인류의 장기간 생존을 보장할 수 있다. 우주 탐사 : space exploration 보장하다 : ensure 장기간 생존 : the long-term survival 인류 : humanity	2. 삶의 근본적 개선이 더 큰 의미 우리가 사랑하는 사람들의 삶을 근본적으로 개선하도록 대신 그 돈을 사용할 수 있다면, 우리 중 누가 천문 행성 간의 연구에 돈을 쓰기를 선택할 것인지 의구심이 든다. 천문 행성 간의 연구 : inter-planetary pursuits(여기에서 pursuits은 일이라는 뜻으로 연구로 의역했다.) 의구심이 든다 : it seems doubtful

Answer

Some people	Others
정부는 가능한 많은 돈을 우주 탐험에 써야 한다.	정부는 가난한 사람들을 위해 그 돈을 써야 한다.
1. There are few subjects more mysterious and fascinating than this field.	1. There are few endeavours that highlight the gap between the rich and the poor more clearly than space exploration.
2. Space exploration could ensure the long-term survival of humanity.	2. It seems doubtful that any of us would choose to spend money on inter-planetary pursuits if we could instead use it to drastically improve the lives of our loved ones.

※ 완성된 에세이는 Day 10(p.223) 참고!

2) Advantage or Disadvantage (Positive or Negative Development)

문제의 토픽에 대한 장점이나 단점(혹은 긍정적인 발전인지 부정적인 발전인지)을 논하는 유형이다. 이 유형에는 장점이나 단점만 제시해도 되는 문제가 있고(2-1), 반드시 장점과 단점을 모두 제시해야 하는 문제가 있다(2-2).

(2-1) Is it a positive or negative development? 이것은 긍정적인 발전인가? 부정적인 발전인가?

> Young people are strongly influenced by fashion, such as clothing or hairstyle. Is it a positive or negative development?
>
> 젊은 사람들은 옷이나 머리스타일 같은 패션으로부터 영향을 크게 받는다. 이것은 긍정적인 발전인가? 부정적인 발전인가?

토픽 (topic) : Young people are strongly influenced by fashion, such as clothing or hairstyle.
질문 (question) : Is it a positive or negative development?

이 문제 유형은 다음과 같이 A, B 두 가지 타입으로 에세이를 작성할 수 있다. (Negative일 경우)

	A type : Negative + Negative	B type : Positive + Negative
Introduction	**두 문장 : Paraphrasing + Answering** 1. 젊은 사람들은 옷이나 머리스타일 같은 패션으로부터 영향을 크게 받는다. 2. 나는 부정적이라고 생각한다.	**두 문장 : Paraphrasing + Answering** 1. 젊은 사람들은 옷이나 머리스타일 같은 패션으로부터 영향을 크게 받는다. 2. 긍정적인 면도 있지만, 나는 부정적인 면이 더 크다고 생각한다.
Body 1	**Negative Development 1** 부정적인 영향 1	**Positive Development** 긍정적인 영향 : 나와 다른 의견도 어느 정도 인정함. 　Body 2보다 짧게 작성
Body 2	**Negative Development 2** 부정적인 영향 2	**Negative Development** 부정적인 영향 그럼에도 불구하고 부정적인 영향이 더 크다. : 내 의견을 강력하게 주장함. 　Body 1보다 1.5배 정도 길게 작성
Conclusion	**Restatement** 젊은 사람들이 옷이나 머리스타일 같은 패션으로부터 영향을 크게 받는 것은 부정적이다. : Body 1 + 2의 내용을 요약하며 부정적인 면을 다시 한 번 강조	**Restatement** 젊은 사람들이 옷이나 머리스타일 같은 패션으로부터 영향을 크게 받는 것은 긍정적인 면도 있지만, 부정적인 면이 더 크다. : Body 1 + 2의 내용을 요약하며 내 주장을 다시 한 번 강조

2-1 유형은 1-1 유형과 구조가 같다. 1-1이 어떤 의견에 대해 동의하는지 동의하지 않는지를 물어보는 유형이었다면 2-1은 어떤 현상에 대해 장점이 많은지 단점이 많은지(혹은 긍정적인 발전인지 부정적인 발전인지)를 기술하는 문제이다.

2-1은 Do advantages of 'TOPIC' outweigh negative effects? (문제의 '토픽'에 대한 장점은 단점을 능가합니까?) 와 같은 유형이고, 최근에는 'Is it a positive or negative development?' 라고 물어보는 문제가 더욱 자주 출제된다.

간혹 'Is it a positive or negative development?' 유형의 에세이를 쓸 때, development라는 단어 때문에 막히는 학생들이 종종 있다. '긍정적인 발전? 부정적인 발전이 뭐지?' 라는 고민에 빠져 시간을 낭비하게 되고, '내가 지금 제대로 논점에 맞게 쓰고 있는 건가' 라는 의구심을 가지며 애를 먹기도 한다. 하지만 여기서 development라는 단어는 전혀 중요하지 않다. 'Is it positive or negative?' (긍정적인가? 부정적인가?)라고 단순하게 생각하고 에세이를 작성하자.

결론에는 본론에서 언급한 내용을 요약해서 내 의견을 다시 한 번 강력하게 주장한다(Restatement).

Brainstorming Note
다음 빈칸에 '젊은 사람들이 옷이나 머리스타일 같은 패션으로부터 영향을 크게 받는 것이 긍정적인 발전인지 부정적인 발전인지'에 대한 의견을 영어로 작성해 보자.

Positive Development	Nagative Development
젊은 사람들이 옷이나 머리스타일 같은 패션으로부터 영향을 크게 받는 것은 긍정적이다.	젊은 사람들이 옷이나 머리스타일 같은 패션으로부터 영향을 크게 받는 것은 부정적이다.
1.	1.
2.	2.

Translation

다음 우리말을 영작해 보자.

Positive Development	Negative Development
젊은 사람들이 옷이나 머리스타일 같은 패션으로부터 영향을 크게 받는 것은 긍정적이다.	젊은 사람들이 옷이나 머리스타일 같은 패션으로부터 영향을 크게 받는 것은 부정적이다.
1. 매력적인 외모 최신 유행을 따르며 자신들의 외모에 관심을 갖는 젊은이들은 매력적으로 보일 가능성이 더 많다. 최신 유행을 따르며 : by following the latest fashions 외모 : appearance	1. 멋지게 보이고자 하는 강박관념 자신의 외모에 건강한 관심을 갖는 것과는 반대로, 패셔니스타와 유명인사들에게 강하게 영향을 받는 젊은이들은 타인의 눈에 멋지게 보이고자 하는 강박관념을 가지게 될 위험성이 있다. 건강한 관심을 갖다 : take a healthy interest in 반대로 : as opposed to 패셔니스타와 유명인사들 : fashionistas and celebrities 강박관념을 가지게 되다 : become obsessed with 타인의 눈에 멋지게 보이다 : look good in the eyes of others
2. 사회에 귀속감을 갖게 됨 유행은 문화의 표현이며 따라서 이는 젊은이들이 더욱 사회에 귀속감을 가지도록 할 수 있을 것이다. 문화의 표현 : an expression of culture 귀속감을 갖다 : be engaged in	2. 윤리의식 저해 젊은 사람들은 친구들을 따라잡기 위해 윤리와 타협할지도 모른다. 친구들을 따라잡다 : keep up with their peers (그들의) 윤리와 타협하다 : compromise their ethics

Answer

Positive Development	Negative Development
젊은 사람들이 옷이나 머리스타일 같은 패션으로부터 영향을 크게 받는 것은 긍정적이다.	젊은 사람들이 옷이나 머리스타일 같은 패션으로부터 영향을 크게 받는 것은 부정적이다.
1. People who take an interest in their appearance by following the latest fashions are more likely to look attractive.	1. Young people who are strongly influenced by fashionistas and celebrities, as opposed to taking a healthy interest in their appearance, are at risk of becoming obsessed with looking good in the eyes of others.
2. Fashion is an expression of culture and so it can encourage younger people to be more engaged in society.	2. Young people might even find themselves compromising their ethics in order to keep up with their peers.

※ 완성된 에세이는 Day 13(p.277) 참고!

(2-2) Discuss the advantages and disadvantages of 'TOPIC'. 토픽의 장점과 단점에 대해 논하라.

> Tourism is becoming a good source of revenue for many countries. Discuss the advantages and the disadvantages of developing this industry.
>
> 관광산업은 많은 나라들의 좋은 수입원이 되고 있다. 이러한 산업을 발달시키는 것의 장단점을 논하라.

토픽 (topic) : Tourism is becoming a good source of revenue for many countries.
질문 (question) : Discuss the advantages and the disadvantages of developing this industry.

이 문제 유형은 다음과 같은 구조로 에세이를 작성할 수 있다.

Introduction	두 문장 : Paraphrasing + Answering 1. 관광산업은 많은 나라들의 좋은 수입원이 되고 있다. 2. 이러한 산업을 발달시키는 것에는 장점도 있고 단점도 있다.
Body 1	Advantage 1 + 2 관광산업을 발달시키는 것의 장점들 : 분량 Body1 = Body 2 　반드시 2개 이상 (문제에 advantages라고 복수로 제시)
Body 2	Disadvantage 1 + 2 관광산업을 발달시키는 것의 단점들 : 분량 Body1 = Body 2 　반드시 2개 이상 (문제에 disadvantages라고 복수로 제시)
Conclusion	Restatement 관광산업을 발달시키는 것에는 장점도 있고 단점도 있다. : Body 1 + 2의 내용을 요약

　Discuss the advantages and disadvantages 유형에서 응시자들은 반드시 토픽에 대한 장점과 단점을 모두 논해야 한다. Body 1과 Body 2에 각각 장점과 단점을 논하고 분량은 비슷하게 작성한다. 특히 문제에 advantages and disadvantages, '복수' 인 것을 확인해서 장점과 단점을 두 개 이상씩 적는다. 일반적으로 2~3개 정도 제시하면 270자에서 300자 사이의 에세이를 작성할 수 있다.

　결론은 장점도 있지만 단점도 있다는 식으로 본론에서 언급한 내용을 균형감 있게 간단히 요약한다. 장점을 살리고 단점을 보완해서 더 좋게 발전시켜야 한다라는 식으로 대안을 제시하거나, 장점이 많다 혹은 단점이 많다고 2-1처럼 작성해서는 안 된다.

Brainstorming Note

다음 빈칸에 '관광산업을 발달시키는 것의 장점과 단점'을 영어로 작성해 보자.

Advantages	Disadvantages
관광산업을 발달시키는 것의 장점들	관광산업을 발달시키는 것의 단점들
1.	1.
2.	2.

Translation

다음 우리말을 영작해 보자.

Advantages	Disadvantages
관광산업을 발달시키는 것의 장점들	관광산업을 발달시키는 것의 단점들
1. 국내 총 생산 증가 어떤 나라들은 국가의 국내 총 생산의 상당 부분을 차지하는 관광산업에 의존한다. 국내 총 생산 : gross domestic product(GDP) 의존하다 : rely on	1. 환경(지역) 파괴 이 산업은 그림 같은 지역 혹은 외딴 지역을 파괴할 가능성이 있다. 그림 같은 : picturesque 외딴 지역 : remote areas 가능성이 있다 : be likely to
2. 국가 이미지 향상 심지어 이런 종류의 수입에 의존하지 않는 국가에서도, 관광산업의 개발로 국제 무대에서 국가 이미지를 높인다. 관광산업의 개발 : the development of tourism 국제 무대 : the world stage	2. 대도시 혼잡 가중 대도시에 사는 사람들은 종종 관광객 수의 증가가 혼잡을 가중시킨다고 불평한다. 대도시에 사는 사람들 : people who live in big cities 관광객 수의 증가 : an increase in the number of tourists 혼잡을 가중시키다 : exacerbate congestion

Answer

Advantages	Disadvantages
관광산업을 발달시키는 것의 장점들	관광산업을 발달시키는 것의 단점들
1. Some countries rely on tourism to make up a significant portion of their gross domestic product.	1. This industry is likely to destruct picturesque or remote areas.
2. Even in countries that do not rely on this kind of income, the development of tourism improves their image on the world stage.	2. People who live in big cities often complain that an increase in the number of tourists exacerbates congestion.

※ 완성된 에세이는 Day 7(p.169) 참고!

3) Reason (Problem) and Solution

문제의 토픽에 대한 이유와 해결책(3-1) 혹은 문제점과 해결책(3-2)을 제시하는 유형이다.

(3-1) Reasons and Solutions (이유들과 해결책들)

> Nowadays many species of animals and plants are in danger of becoming extinct. What do you think the reasons are? What can you suggest as a solution?
>
> 요즘 많은 동식물들이 멸종 위기에 처해 있다. 이유는 무엇이라고 생각하는가? 해결책으로 무엇을 제시할 수 있는가?

토픽 (topic) : Nowadays many species of animals and plants are in danger of becoming extinct.
질문 (question) : What do you think the reasons are? What can you suggest as a solution?

이 문제 유형은 다음과 같은 구조로 에세이를 작성할 수 있다.

Introduction	**두 문장 : Paraphrasing + Answering** 1. 요즘 많은 동식물들이 멸종 위기에 처해 있다. 2. 이 에세이에서는 많은 동식물들이 멸종 위기에 처한 이유와 이에 대한 해결책을 제시하겠다.
Body 1	**Reason A + B** 많은 동식물들이 멸종 위기에 처한 이유들 : 분량 Body 1 = Body 2 반드시 2개 이상의 이유 제시 (문제에 reasons라고 복수로 제시)

Body 2	**Solution A' + B'**
	많은 동식물들의 멸종을 막기 위한 해결책들
	: 분량 Body 1 = Body 2
	  반드시 2개 이상의 해결책 제시
	  * 문제에서 a solution의 의미는 하나의 해결책이 아닌, 해결책 전체를 통칭한다.
	  * Body 1에서 제시한 두 개의 이유에 대한 각각의 해결책을 제시하는 것이 좋다.

Conclusion	**Restatement** 많은 동식물들이 멸종 위기에 처한 이유는 A + B이고 이에 대한 해결책은 A' + B'이다. : Body 1 + 2의 내용을 요약하며 다시 한 번 강조

Reason and Solution 유형에서 응시자들은 토픽에 대한 이유와 해결책 모두를 제시해야 한다. Body 1에는 이유를, Body 2에는 해결책을 제시하고 분량은 비슷하게 작성한다. 특히 3-1의 문제에서 reasons의 복수를 확인해서 반드시 이유는 2개 이상, 해결책도 각각의 이유에 대해서 하나씩 제시하는 것이 좋다(이유 2개: 해결책 2개, 이유 3개: 해결책 3개). 이유를 A라고 제시했는데, A를 해결할 수 있는 아이디어가 없다면 혹은 그 해결책을 영어로 작성할 수 없다면, 다른 이유를 제시해야 한다. 이유와 해결책은 세트다! 결론에는 본론에서 작성한 이유와 해결책에 대해 간단히 요약하며 강조한다.

간혹 reason(이유) 대신에 cause(원인)을 물어보는 유형도 있는데, 같은 구조로 작성하면 된다.

Brainstorming Note

다음 빈칸에 '요즘 많은 동식물들이 멸종 위기에 처한 이유와 이에 대한 해결책'을 영어로 작성해 보자.

Reasons	Solutions
많은 동식물들이 멸종 위기에 처한 이유들	많은 동식물들의 멸종을 막기 위한 해결책들
1.	1.
2.	2.

Translation

다음 우리말을 영작해 보자.

Reasons	Solutions
많은 동식물들이 멸종 위기에 처한 이유들	많은 동식물들의 멸종을 막기 위한 해결책들
1. 환경 악화와 오염 가장 심각한 이유는 아마도 환경 악화와 오염일 것이다. 가장 심각한 이유 : the most serious reason (최상급) 환경 악화 : environmental degradation (degradation은 질이 떨어지는 뜻) 오염 : pollution	1. 도시 개발과 자연보호 사이의 균형 도시 개발과 자연보호 사이의 균형을 맞추는 것이 그 첫 번째 조치가 될 것이다. 도시 개발 : urban development 자연보호 : nature conservation 균형을 맞추다 : strike a balance 첫 번째 조치 : the first action
2. 밀렵 성행 아프리카의 코끼리를 포함해 밀렵은 세계 일부 지역에서 특정 종에게 가장 중대한 위협이 되고 있다. 밀렵 : poaching 세계 일부 지역에서 : in some parts of the world 가장 중대한 위협 : a major threat	2. 밀렵과 장기 밀매 금지 밀렵 문제를 처리하는 것은 더 간단해 보이는데, 왜냐하면 우리는 멸종위기에 처한 종들을 사냥하는 것을 멈추고 희귀 동물의 장기를 사는 것을 피하기만 되기 때문이다. 처리하다 : deal with 멸종위기에 처한 종들 : endangered species 사냥하는 것을 멈추다 : stop hunting 희귀 동물의 장기 : rare animal organs 우리는 ~하기만 하면 된다 : all we have to do is

Answer

Reasons	Solutions
많은 동식물들이 멸종 위기에 처한 이유들	많은 동식물들의 멸종을 막기 위한 해결책들
1. The most serious reason is probably environmental degradation and pollution.	1. Striking a balance between urban development and nature conservation would be the first action.
2. Poaching continues to be a major threat to certain species in some parts of the world, including elephants in Africa.	2. Dealing with poaching might seem simpler because all we have to do is stop hunting endangered species and avoid buying rare animal organs.

※ 완성된 에세이는 Day 9(p.205) 참고!

(3-2) Problems and Solutions (문제점들과 해결책들)

> In the 21st century, the average life expectancy is increasing. What problems will this cause for individuals and society? Suggest some solutions that could be taken to reduce the effect of aging populations.
>
> 21세기 평균 기대수명은 증가하고 있다. 이러한 현상이 개인과 사회에 어떤 문제들을 일으킬 수 있는가? 인구 노령화의 영향을 줄이기 위해서 취할 수 있는 해결책들을 제시하라.

토픽 (topic) : In the 21st century, the average life expectancy is increasing.
질문 (question) : What problems will this cause for individuals and society? Suggest some solutions that could be taken to reduce the effect of aging populations.

이 문제 유형은 다음과 같은 구조로 에세이를 작성할 수 있다.

Introduction	**두 문장 : Paraphrasing + Answering** 1. 21세기 평균 기대수명은 증가하고 있다. 2. 이 에세이에서는 인구 노령화가 개인과 사회에 미치는 문제들을 논하고, 이에 대한 영향을 줄일 수 있는 해결책을 제시하겠다.
Body 1	**Problem A (개인) + B (사회)** 인구 노령화가 개인들과 사회에 미치는 문제점들 : 분량 Body 1 = Body 2 반드시 개인들과 사회에 미치는 문제점 각각 1개 이상씩 제시 (총 2개 이상)

Body 2	**Solution A' + B'**
	인구 노령화의 영향을 줄일 수 있는 해결책들
	: 분량 Body 1 = Body 2
	  반드시 2개 이상의 해결책 제시
	  * Body 1에서 제시한 두 개의 문제점에 대한 각각의 해결책을 제시하는 것이 좋다.

Conclusion	**Restatement** 인구 노령화가 개인들과 사회에 미치는 문제점은 A와 B이고, 이에 대한 영향을 줄일 수 있는 해결책들은 각각 A' 와 B' 이다. : Body 1 + 2의 내용을 요약하며 다시 한 번 강조

Problem and Solution 유형에서 응시자들은 토픽에 대한 문제점과 해결책을 모두 제시해야 한다. Body 1에는 문제점을, Body 2에는 해결책을 제시하고 분량은 비슷하게 작성한다. 특히 3-2의 문제에서는 문제점을 제시할 때, 각각 individuals와 society에 미치는 문제점에 대해 제시해야 한다. 여기서 society란 government와 같은 개념으로 볼 수 있다. Body 2에는 solutions의 복수에 주의해서 Body 1에서 언급한 문제점에 대한 각각의 해결책을 제시해야 한다. 일반적으로 2~3개 정도 제시하는 것이 무난하다. 결론에는 본론에서 작성한 문제점과 해결책에 대해 간단히 요약하며 강조한다.

Brainstorming Note

다음 빈칸에 '인구 노령화가 개인과 사회에 일으키는 문제들과 이에 대한 영향을 줄일 수 있는 해결책'을 영어로 작성해 보자.

Problems	Solutions
인구 노령화가 개인과 사회에 미치는 문제들	인구 노령화의 영향을 줄일 수 있는 해결책들
1.	1.
2.	2.

Translation

다음 우리말을 영작해 보자.

Problems	Solutions
인구 노령화가 개인과 사회에 미치는 문제들	인구 노령화의 영향을 줄일 수 있는 해결책들
1. 개인 : 건강 상의 문제 노인들은 질병으로부터 고통 받는 것을 피할 수 있는 가능성이 낮다(피하기 어렵다.). 노인들 : aged people = the elderly 피하다 : avoid 가능성이 낮다 : be less likely to	1. 개인 : 규칙적인 운동과 균형 잡힌 식사 권장 노인들에게 규칙적인 운동을 하고 균형 잡힌 식사를 하도록 권장하는 것이 근본적인 일일 것이고, 그 다음이 의료 부분 개선일 것이다. 규칙적인 운동을 하다 : do regular exercise 균형 잡힌 식사를 하다 : eat a well-balanced diet 권장하다 : encourage 의료 부분을 개선하다 : improve the medical sector 근본적인 : fundamental
2. 사회 : 세제 수입의 안정성 확보 문제 경제 활동 인구 수가 줄어듦에 따라, 정부가 세제 수입의 안정성을 확보하는 데 차질이 예상된다. 경제 활동 인구 수 : the number of economically active people 세제 수입 : tax revenue 차질 : setback	2. 사회 연금과 퇴직 체계 재조정 우리는 또한 국세의 부족을 방지하기 위해 고령사회의 특성을 반영할 수 있도록 연금과 퇴직 체계를 재조정할 수 있을 것이다. 국세 부족 : the shortage of national taxes 방지하다 : prevent 연금 : pension 퇴직 체계 : retirement system 재조정하다 : re-assess

Answer

Problems	Solutions
인구 노령화가 개인과 사회에 미치는 문제들	인구 노령화의 영향을 줄일 수 있는 해결책들
1. Aged people are less likely to avoid suffering from diseases.	1. Encouraging the elderly both doing regular exercise and eating a well-balanced diet would be fundamental followed by improving the medical sector.
2. As the number of economically active people decreases, the government is expecting a setback in securing tax revenue.	2. We could also re-assess our pension and retirement systems to reflect an aging society to prevent in the shortage of national taxes.

※ 완성된 에세이는 Day 2(p.79) 참고!

2-2. Task 2 서론, 본론, 결론 작성 공식

1) 서론 (Introduction)

서론은 두 문장으로 작성한다. (Paraphrasing + Answering)

서론 Introduction	첫 번째 문장	Paraphrasing	문제의 토픽(topic)을 본인의 표현으로 다시 작성
	두 번째 문장	Answering	주어진 질문에 대한 응시자의 간단한 대답

서론의 목적은 에세이의 주제를 제시하고, 주어진 질문에 대한 응시자의 대답을 간단하게 작성하는 것이다. 따라서 많은 시간과 분량을 할애하지 말고, 위와 같이 두 가지 문장으로만 명료하고 빠르게 작성해야 한다. 단, 문제를 paraphrasing 하지 않고 그대로 옮겨 적으면 감점이 된다. 대략 50단어 내외로 작성하는 것이 좋다.

Question	Some people think governments should spend as much money as possible exploring outer space. Others argue they should spend the money for poor people. Discuss both views and give your own opinion. 어떤 사람들은 정부가 가능한 한 많은 돈을 우주 탐험에 써야 한다고 생각한다. 다른 사람들은 정부는 가난한 사람들을 위해 그 돈을 써야 한다고 주장한다. 양쪽의 견해를 논하고 당신의 주장을 제시하라. 1-2) Discuss both views and give your own opinion. 유형

서론 작성

단계	Question		서론 작성
1단계 Paraphrasing	토픽: Some people think governments should spend as much money as possible exploring outer space. Others argue they should spend the money for poor people.		**Paraphrasing:** When it comes to considering billions of US dollars spent on space exploration by countries worldwide, there is a growing debate over whether we should aim to resolve issues like poverty before focusing too much on this space race.
2단계 Answering	질문: Discuss both views and give your own opinion.		**Answering : Disagree일 경우** Although broadening our horizons is important, ultimately the people of our own planet should be our priority.

Introduction
When it comes to considering billions of US dollars spent on space exploration by countries worldwide, there is a growing debate over whether we should aim to resolve issues like poverty before focusing too much on this space race. Although broadening our horizons is important, ultimately the people of our own planet should be our priority.

Template
When it comes to + 키워드(considering billions of US dollars spent on space exploration by countries worldwide), **there is a growing debate over whether + 에세이에서 논란이 되는 주제**(we should aim to resolve issues like poverty before focusing too much on this space race.) **Although + 상대방 의견, 내 의견** (broadening our horizons is important, ultimately the people of our own planet should be our priority.)

※ 이 템플릿은 Task 2 작성이 막막한 학생들을 위한 참고 자료이다. 1-1, 1-2, 2-1 유형에 적용하면 서론을 쉽고 빠르게 작성할 수 있다. 하지만 억지로 이 템플릿에 맞춰 작성할 필요는 없다.

when it comes to + 키워드 (명사 / 명사구)
: ~관해서 (말하자면), in terms of, as for와 동의어, 키워드를 강조하기 위해 키워드 앞에 쓴다. 뒤에 동사나 문장이 아닌 명사나 명사구를 써야 한다.

there is a growing debate over whether + 에세이에서 논란이 되는 주제 (문장=S+V)
: ~인지 아닌지에 대한 논쟁이 커지고 있다. 찬반이나 장단점 등 의견이 양쪽으로 갈리는 주제 앞에 써주면 좋다. whether 다음에는 문장이 온다.

although + 상대방 의견, 내 의견
: although A, B = 비록 A이지만, B이다. 강조하는 의견을 B에다 작성한다. 반드시 A다음에 콤마 (,)를 쓸 것!

우리말 해석
전 세계 국가들에 의해 수십억 미국 달러가 우주 탐사에 쓰여지는 것에 관해서 말하자면, 이 우주 개발 경쟁에 지나치게 집중하기 전에 빈곤과 같은 문제들을 해결하는 것을 목표로 해야 할지 여부에 대한 논쟁이 커지고 있다. 우리의 시야를 넓히는 것도 중요하지만, 궁극적으로 우리(자신의) 행성 사람들이 우선시 되어야 한다.

불법 포인트

서론 작성시에는 문제의 토픽을 paraphrasing하는 것이 중요하다. 이 문제의 키워드인 money, exploring outer space 등의 동의어를 다양하게 사용해 보자.
billions of : 수십억의
US dollars : 미국 달러, money와 동의어
space exploration : 우주 탐사, 문제의 exploring outer space와 동의어
a growing debate : 커지는 논쟁
resolve issues : 문제들을 해결하다, issue라는 단어 앞에는 solve가 아닌 resolve를 쓴다.
poverty : 빈곤
space race : 우주 개발 경쟁, 문제의 exploring outer space와 동의어
broaden one's horizons : 시야를 넓히다
priority : 우선순위

※ 완성된 에세이는 Day 10(p.223) 참고!

2) 본론 (Body)

본론은 3단계로 작성한다. (Topic Sentence + Supporting Sentence + Specific Example)

본론 Body	1단계	Topic Sentence (TS)	본론의 주제문
	2단계	Supporting Sentence (SS)	Topic Sentence를 뒷받침하는 근거 왜냐하면 (because)의 느낌으로 작성
	3단계	Specific Example (SE)	Supporting Sentence를 설명해주는 구체적인 예 주로 예를 들면 (for example)의 느낌으로 작성

본문은 에세이에서 가장 중요한 부분이고, 가장 높은 점수를 차지한다. 따라서 본문에 가장 많은 시간과 분량을 할애해야 한다. 본론은 주제문인 Topic Sentence를 명료하게 제시한 후 Supporting Sentence로 주제문을 뒷받침하는 근거를 들고 Specific Example로 이 근거를 예를 들어 구체적으로 설명한다.

Task 2 Body에는 주제문을 뒷받침하는 근거를 두 가지씩 제시하는 것이 좋다. 한 가지를 제시할 경우에는 글자 수가 부족해서 감점 당할 수도 있고, 세 가지 이상을 제시할 경우에는 너무 많아져서 시간 내에 글을 완성하기 어렵기 때문이다.

Question	Young people are strongly influenced by fashion, such as clothing or hairstyle. Is it a positive or negative development? 젊은 사람들은 옷이나 머리스타일 같은 패션으로부터 영향을 크게 받는다. 이것은 긍정적인 발전인가? 부정적인 발전인가? 2-1) Is it a positive or negative development? 유형

Body 1과 Body 2를 작성하는 공식은 같다. 여기에서는 Body 1 작성을 예로 들어보자. 내 주장이 negative이고 상대방의 의견도 언급하는 B type으로 작성할 경우, Body 1에서는 내 의견과 반대인 positive에 대한 내용(젊은이들이 패션에 매료되는 것은 긍정적이다.)을 작성한다.

Brainstorming Note

브레인스토밍을 할 때는 Topic Sentence에 대한 두 가지 근거(Supporting Sentence) A와 B를 들고 각각의 근거에 대한 예시(Specific Example)까지도 함께 생각해야 한다. Supporting Sentence만 적고 Specific Example를 적지 않는다면, 설득력이 떨어져서 낮은 점수를 받게 된다. 만약 Specific Example이 생각나지 않는다면, 아예 다른 Supporting Sentence로 바꿔야 한다. **Supporting Sentence와 Specific Example은 세트다!**

아이엘츠를 처음 시작하는 단계라면, 먼저 한글로 브레인스토밍을 하고 사전 등을 찾아가면서 영어로 번역하는 것도 좋지만 시험을 2주 앞둔 학생이라면 반드시 **영어로 직접 브레인스토밍** 해야 한다. 시험장에서 영어로 쓸 수 없는 단어를 한글로 브레인스토밍 하는 것은 무의미하다.

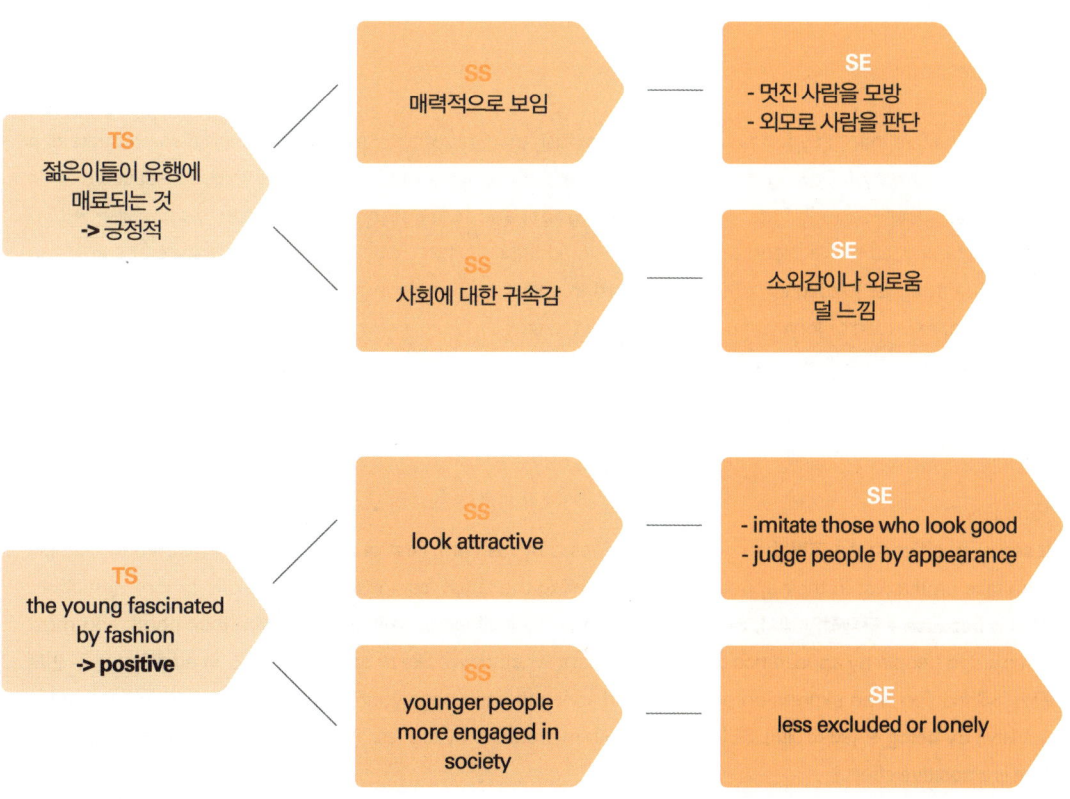

Body 작성

위의 Brainstorming Note를 바탕으로 다음과 같이 본문을 작성한다.

1단계	Topic Sentence	It seems positive that the young are fascinated by fashion.
2단계 (A)	Supporting Sentence (A)	First of all, young people who take an interest in their appearance by following the latest fashions are more likely to look attractive.
3단계 (A)	Specific Example (A)	This is because people are naturally inclined to imitate those who look good, and most of us judge people by appearance to a certain extent whether we like to admit it or not.
2단계 (B)	Supporting Sentence (B)	In addition, fashion is an expression of culture and so it can encourage younger people to be more engaged in society.
3단계 (B)	Specific Example (B)	By being interested in new trends they are less likely to feel excluded or lonely and that is a positive effect.

Body 1

It seems positive that the young are fascinated by fashion. First of all, young people who take an interest in their appearance by following the latest fashions are more likely to look attractive. This is because people are naturally inclined to imitate those who look good, and most of us judge people by appearance to a certain extent whether we like to admit it or not. In addition, fashion is an expression of culture and so it can encourage younger people to be more engaged in society. By being interested in new trends they are less likely to feel excluded or lonely and that is a positive effect.

Template

It seems positive that + 토픽(the young are fascinated by fashion). **First of all,** + 첫 번째 근거, **SS**(young people who take an interest in their appearance by following the latest fashions are more likely to look attractive.) **This is because** + 구체적인 예시, **SE**(people are naturally inclined to imitate those who look good, and most of us judge people by appearance to a certain extent whether we like to admit it or not). **In addition,** + 두 번째 근거, **SS**(fashion is an expression of culture and so it can encourage younger people to be more engaged in society.) **By being** + 구체적 예시, **SE**(interested in new trends they are less likely to feel excluded or lonely and that is a positive effect.)

※ 이 템플릿은 Task 2 작성이 막막한 학생들을 위한 참고 자료이다. 1-1, 1-2, 2-1 유형에서 상대방의 의견을 제시하는 Body 1 에 적용하면 좀 더 쉽고 빠르게 작성할 수 있다. 하지만 억지로 이 템플릿에 맞춰 작성할 필요는 없다.

it seems positive that + 토픽 (문장 = S + V)
: 토픽이 긍정적인 것처럼 보인다. seem이라는 단어는 자기가 말하는 내용의 강도를 약하게 하기 위해 쓰는 동사로 내 주장이 아닌 상대방의 주장을 언급하는 Body 1에 잘 어울린다.

first of all, + 첫 번째 근거, SS (문장 = S + V)
: 첫 번째 근거를 들 때 쓰는 표현

this is because + 구체적인 예시, SE (문장 = S + V)
: this is because = 이것은 ~때문입니다.

in addition, + 두 번째 근거, SS (문장 = S + V)
: 두 번째 근거를 들 때 쓰는 표현 = secondly (second of all이라는 표현은 없다!)

by ~ing + 구체적 예시, SE
: by ~ing = ~함으로써 구체적인 예시를 들 때 사용하면 좋은 표현이다.

우리말 해석

젊은이들이 유행에 매료되는 것은 긍정적으로 보인다. 무엇보다도 최신 유행을 따르며 자신들의 외모에 관심을 갖는 젊은이들은 매력적으로 보일 가능성이 더 많다. 이것은 사람들은 자연히 멋지게 보이는 사람들을 모방하는 경향이 있고 또 우리 대부분이 인정하고 싶어하든 아니든 어느 정도 외모로 판단하기 때문이다. 게다가 유행은 문화의 표현이며, 따라서 이는 젊은이들이 더욱 사회에 귀속감을 가지도록 할 수 있을 것이다. 새로운 유행에 대해 관심을 가짐으로써 그들은 소외감이나 외로움을 덜 느끼게 될 것이고 그것은 긍정적인 면이 될 것이다.

be fascinated by : ~에 매료되다

take[have] an interest in : ~에 흥미를 갖다 = be interested in

the latest fashion : 최신 유행

be more[less] likely to : ~할 가능성이 더 높다[낮다], 최신 유행을 따르는 사람들이 대체적으로 매력적으로 보이지만, 그 중에도 매력적으로 보이지는 않는 사람들도 있기 때문에 단정짓기보다는 ~할 가능성이 더 높다고 표현하는 것이 논리적이다.

incline : ~쪽으로 (마음이) 기울다

imitate : 모방하다 = copy, mimic

to a certain extent : 어느 정도

admit : 인정하다

be engaged in : 참가하다, 속하다, 직업과 관련하여 종사하다의 뜻으로 많이 사용된다.

feel excluded : 소외감을 느끼다 = feel isolated

※ 완성된 에세이는 Day 13(p.277) 참고!

3) 결론 (Conclusion)

결론은 다음에 나오는 Conclusion Template을 문제 유형별로 이용해서 작성한다.

결론은 본론에서 언급한 내용을 요약해서 내 의견을 다시 한 번 강력하게 주장하는 단락이다 (Restatement). 따라서 결론에는 본론에서 언급하지 않은 새로운 아이디어를 제시해서는 안 된다. 또한 분량이 너무 길거나 for example 등 예를 드는 표현이나 문장이 등장하는 것은 적절하지 않다. 결론은 가장 짧은 요약 단락이라는 것을 기억하자. 대략 40단어 내외로 작성하는 것이 좋다.

시험장에서 결론 작성 시, 대부분의 응시자들은 시간적 여유가 없어서 결론을 아예 작성하지 못하거나 혹은 다급한 나머지 서론에는 '동의한다' 라고 주장했지만 결론에는 '동의하지 않는다' 라는 내용을 작성하기도 한다. 이러한 용두사미 식의 에세이는 결코 높은 점수를 받을 수 없다. 그러므로 다음에 나오는 각 문제 유형별 결론 상용어구(template)를 익혀서 빠르고 정확하게 결론을 작성할 수 있도록 하자. 또한 결론을 작성하기 전에 주어진 문제를 다시 한 번 읽어서 논점에서 벗어나는 일을 막도록 하자!

서론과 본론에서는 template을 본인의 판단에 따라 적용 여부를 결정해도 되지만 결론에서는 template을 적용하는 것이 좋다. 서론과 본론에서는 창의력이 중요하지만 결론에서는 일관성과 스피드 그리고 글을 완성하는 것이 더욱 중요하기 때문이다.

다음 template은 처음부터 외울 필요는 없다. 에세이를 작성할때마다 이 부분을 펴놓고 참고해서 쓴다면, 어느새 자연스럽게 외워질 것이다.

* Conclusion Template

1. Agree or Disagree	1-1) Do you agree or disagree?	For the reasons mentioned above, I totally agree(disagree) with the opinion because ... 본론에 제시한 내 주장 간단히 요약 위에서 언급한 이유들 때문에, 나는 이 의견에 완전히 동의한다(동의하지 않는다). 왜냐하면...
	1-2) Discuss both views and give your own opinion.	In conclusion, there are convincing arguments both for and against... (토픽), but I am convinced that... 본론에 제시한 내 주장 간단히 요약 결론적으로 (토픽)에 대해 찬성과 반대를 하는 설득력 있는 주장들이 있지만, 나는 확신한다 that 이하를...
2. Advantages or Disadvantages	2-1) Is it a positive or negative development?	For the reasons mentioned above, I would argue that the benefits(drawbacks) of... (토픽) outweigh its drawbacks(benefits) because... 본론에 제시한 장점(단점) 간략히 요약 위에서 언급한 이유들 때문에, 나는 (토픽)의 장점(단점)들이 단점(장점)들을 능가한다고 주장한다. 왜냐하면...
	2-2) Discuss the advantages and disadvantages of 토픽.	In conclusion, although there are benefits(drawbacks) of ... (토픽), its drawbacks(benefits) also should not be ignored because... 본론에 제시한 장점과 단점 간략히 요약 결론적으로 비록 (토픽)에 대한 장점(단점)들이 있지만, 이것의 단점(장점)들도 무시되어서는 안 된다. 왜냐하면...
3. Reason (Problem) and Solution	3-1) Reasons and Solutions	In conclusion, it is clear that there are various reasons for... (토픽), and steps* are needed to tackle this phenomenon. * steps에 본론에서 제시한 해결책 간단히 요약 결론적으로 (토픽)에 대해 다양한 이유들이 있는 것은 분명하다. 이러한 현상을 방지하기 위해서는 (어떠한)조치들이 요구된다.
	3-2) Problems and Solutions	In conclusion, it is clear that there are various problems for... (토픽), and steps* are needed to tackle this phenomenon. * steps에 본론에서 제시한 해결책 간단히 요약 결론적으로 (토픽)에 대해 다양한 문제점들이 있는 것은 분명하다. 이러한 현상을 방지하기 위해서는 (어떠한)조치들이 요구된다.

Question	Nowadays many species of animals and plants are in danger of becoming extinct. What do you think the reasons are? What can you suggest as a solution? 요즘 많은 동식물들이 멸종 위기에 처해 있다. 이유는 무엇이라고 생각하는가? 해결책으로 무엇을 제시할 수 있는가?

3-1) Reasons and Solutions 유형

결론 작성 시에는 먼저 문제 유형을 파악한 후, 'Conclusion Template'의 표현을 인용한다.

| 결론 Conclusion | 문제 유형 파악 | 3-1) Reasons and Solutions |
| | Conclusion Template 인용 | In conclusion, it is clear that there are various reasons for...(토픽), and steps are needed to tackle this phenomenon. |

Conclusion

In conclusion, it is clear that there are various reasons for the threat of extinction faced by various species of animals and plants, **and** both individual and government efforts **are needed to tackle this phenomenon.**

NB

steps에 해당하는 내용이 both individual and government efforts이다.

이 결론은 Body 1에는 멸종 위기에 처한 동물들이 증가하는 이유를, Body 2에는 멸종 위기에 처한 동물들을 구하기 위한 개인과 정부의 노력이 언급된 경우다. steps에 '개인은 밀렵 행위를 하지 말고, 정부는 도시 개발과 자연보호 사이의 균형을 맞추자.' 라고 좀 더 구체적으로 작성할 수도 있지만 이럴 경우, 자칫 같은 표현이 반복되고 결론이 너무 길어질 수 있다.

점수를 결정짓는 단락은 본론이다. 결론에서는 서론과 본론에서 언급한 내 주장을 일관성 있게 다시 한 번 강조하고 글을 끝맺는 것이 가장 중요하다. 아무리 잘 쓴 글도 결론을 끝맺지 못하면 높은 점수를 기대할 수 없다.

우리말 해석

결론적으로 동물과 식물의 다양한 종들이 직면한 멸종위기에는 다양한 이유가 있으며 개인과 정부 양쪽의 노력이 이런 현상을 해결하기 위해 필요하다는 것은 명백하다.

the threat of extinction : 멸종 위기 (위협)
tackle : (힘든 문제 · 상황을 해결하려고) 씨름하다
phenomenon : 현상

※ 완성된 에세이는 Day 9(p.205) 참고!

Chapter 03

주제별 Writing Task II

Day 1. **Family** 가족		61
Day 2. **Growing Up** 성장		79
Day 3. **Health & Food** 건강과 음식		97
Day 4. **Lifestyles & Leisure Activities** 생활방식과 여가활동		115
Day 5. **Student Life** 학교(학생) 생활		133
Day 6. **Communication** 의사소통		151
Day 7. **Travelling & Transport** 여행과 교통		169
Day 8. **Past & History** 과거와 역사		187
Day 9. **Natural Environment & Wildlife** 자연환경과 야생동식물		205
Day 10. **Earth & Space** 지구와 우주		223
Day 11. **Building & Design** 빌딩과 디자인		241
Day 12. **IT(Information Technology)** 정보기술		259
Day 13. **Shopping & Party** 쇼핑과 파티		277
Day 14. **International Relations & Urbanisation** 국제관계와 도시화		295
Day 15. **Environmental Pollution** 환경오염		313
Day 16. **The Energy Crisis** 에너지 위기		331
Day 17. **Economy & Business** 경제와 산업		349
Day 18. **The Government & Law** 정부와 법		367
Day 19. **Mass Media, Movie & Play** 대중매체, 영화와 연극		385
Day 20. **Art** 예술		403

Day 1 Family 가족

Question

Some people argue that parents have the most important role in their child's development. However, others say that other factors like TV or peer groups have the most significant influence. Discuss both views and give your own opinion.

어떤 사람들은 아이의 발달에 부모가 가장 중요한 역할을 한다고 주장한다. 반면 다른 사람들은 TV 나 또래 집단 같은 다른 요소들이 가장 중요한 영향을 미친다고 말한다. 양쪽의 견해를 논하고 당신의 주장을 제시하라.

 빈출 문제

1. Some people insist that parents should ask their children to help with household chores. To what extent do you agree or disagree with this opinion?

2. Today, parents are not close to their children compared to the past. What do you think the reasons are? Suggest some solutions that they can be closer.

3. Some people say that fathers and mothers should have the same responsibility for bringing their children up. To what extent do you agree or disagree with this opinion?

4. Some people say that parents are the best teachers. To what extent do you agree or disagree with this opinion?

1. 어떤 사람들은 부모들이 자식들에게 집안일을 도와줄 것을 요구해야 한다고 주장한다. 당신은 이 의견에 얼마만큼 동의하는가? 또는 동의하지 않는가?

2. 오늘날 부모들은 과거에 비해 자식들과 가깝지 않다. 이유는 무엇이라고 생각하는가? 그들이 좀 더 가까워질 수 있는 해결책을 제시하라.

3. 어떤 사람들은 자식을 키우는 데 아버지와 어머니가 반드시 똑같이 책임을 져야 한다고 말한다. 당신은 이 의견에 얼마만큼 동의하는가? 또는 동의하지 않는가?

4. 어떤 사람들은 부모가 가장 좋은 교사라고 말한다. 당신은 이 의견에 얼마만큼 동의하는가? 또는 동의하지 않는가?

 브레인스토밍

Family와 관련한 브레인스토밍을 불법 단어와 표현을 넣어서 영작 연습으로 구성하였다. 충분한 브레인스토밍과 영작 연습이야말로 에세이 고득점 비법임을 기억하자! 영작을 할 땐 우리말로는 쉽게 생략되는 소유격이나 단복수에 주의해야 한다. 특히 셀 수 있는 명사는 가급적 복수로 쓰고, 단수일 경우 명사 앞에 관사 등을 반드시 빠뜨리지 않도록 신경 쓸 것! e.g. child (×) → children or a child (○) / parent (×) → parents or a parent (○)

1) 최근, 부모와 자식간의 관계는 과거에 비해 덜 가까워 보인다.
   부모와 자식간의 관계 : the relationship between parents and their children / 덜 가까워 보이다 : seem to be less close

2) 가정에서 친밀함의 부족은 아이들에게 부정적인 영향을 미칠 수 있다.
   친밀함의 부족 : the lack of closeness / ~에 부정적인 영향을 미치다 : have a negative effect on

3) 맞벌이 가정의 수가 증가함에 따라, 부모는 아이들과 시간을 덜 보낸다.
   맞벌이 가정의 수 : the number of double-income families / 시간을 덜 보내다 : spend less time

4) 아이들은 바쁜 부모 때문에 친구나 인터넷을 서핑하는 데 더 많은 시간을 보낸다.
   (그들의) 바쁜 부모 때문에 : due to their busy parents

5) 친구들, 텔레비전 그리고 인터넷은 아이들의 행동에 주된 영향이 되었다.
   ~에 주된 영향이 되었다 (현재 완료) : have become the main influence on

6) 전통적으로 어머니는 요리하고 청소하고 그들의 아이들을 돌보기 위해 집에 머물렀다.
   집에 머무르다 : stay at home / 돌보다 : look after

7) 많은 가족들이 더 이상 식사를 함께하지 않는다.
   더 이상 ~않다 : no longer

8) 많은 나라에서 가족은 그들이 (과거에) 그러했던 것처럼 크지 않다.
   ~만큼 크지 않은 : not as large as / 그들이 (과거에) 그러했던 것처럼 : as they used to be

9) 오늘날 우리는 도시화와 산업화의 영향 때문에 대가족보다는 핵가족으로 사는 경향이 있다.
   도시화와 산업화 : urbanisation and industrialisation / 대가족 : extended families / 핵가족 : nuclear families

10) 대부분의 부모들은 그들의 아이들이 어떻게 시간을 보내는지 모른다.
    모르다 : have no idea

11) 청소년 범죄가 증가하는 것을 막기 위해, 부모는 반드시 아이들의 양육에 좀 더 관여해야 한다.
    청소년 범죄 : juvenile delinquency / ~에 좀 더 관여하다 : be more involved with / 양육 : upbringing

12) 십대들은 또래들의 압박에 강하게 영향을 받는다.
    또래들의 압박 : peer pressure

13) 집안일을 맡은 아이들은 시간을 관리하는 방법을 배울 수 있다.
    (어떠한 일을) 맡다 : be assigned / 집안일 : household chores / 시간을 관리하는 법 : how to organise their time

14) 어린 아이들은 옳고 그름의 차이를 모르고 부모는 이것을 그들에게 가르치는 최고의 교사다.
    옳고 그름의 차이 : the difference between right and wrong

15) 부모는 아이들에게 도덕과 안전에 대한 조언을 해야 한다.
    A에게 B에 대해 조언하다 : give A advice on B / 도덕과 안전 : morals and safety

Answer

1) Recently, the relationship between parents and their children seems to be less close compared to the past.
2) The lack of closeness in families can have a negative effect on children.
3) As the number of double-income families increases, parents spend less time with their children.
4) Children spend more time with friends or surfing the Internet due to their busy parents.
5) Friends, television and the Internet have become the main influence on children's behaviour.
6) Traditionally, mothers stayed at home to cook, clean and look after their children.
7) Many families no longer eat meals together.
8) Families in many countries are not as large as they used to be.
9) Today, we tend to live in nuclear families rather than extended families because of the impact of urbanisation and industrialisation.
10) Most parents have no idea how their children spend their time.
11) To prevent juvenile delinquency from increasing, parents should be more involved with their children's upbringing.
12) Teenagers are strongly influenced by peer pressure.
13) Children who are assigned household chores can learn how to organise their time.
14) Young children do not know the difference between right and wrong, and their parents are the best teachers to teach them this.
15) Parents need to give their children advice on morals and safety.

 실전문제

You should spend about 40 minutes on this task.
Write about the following topic :

> Some people argue that parents have the most important role in their child's development. However, others say that other factors like TV or peer groups have the most significant influence. Discuss both views and give your own opinion.

Give reasons for your answer and include any relevant examples from your own knowledge or experience.

Write at least 250 words.

 **1 단계** 문제 정독, 문제 유형 파악, 브레인스토밍 (0 ~ 5분)

Question	Some people argue that parents have the most important role in their child's development. However, others say that other factors like TV or peer groups have the most significant influence. Discuss both views and give your own opinion.

문제 정독
어떤 사람들은 아이의 발달에 부모가 가장 중요한 역할을 한다고 주장한다. 반면 다른 사람들은 TV나 또래 집단 같은 다른 요소들이 가장 중요한 영향을 미친다고 말한다. 양쪽의 견해를 논하고 당신의 주장을 제시하라.

some people VS others : 주로 두 가지 상반되는 의견을 some people과 others(=other people)로 제시
argue = say : 단어의 중복을 피하기 위해 동의어 사용
child's development : 아이의 발달, 아이가 사회 구성원으로서 성장하는 것을 의미
peer groups : 또래 집단, 친구들을 의미

문제 유형 파악

1-2. Discuss both views and give your own opinion. 유형

Brainstorming

Topic : 아이의 발달에 있어 가장 중요한 요인은 무엇인가?	
Some People : 부모의 역할	Others : TV나 또래 집단 같은 다른 요소
1. 아이들은 기본적인 욕구를 지도하고 지원해 주기를 기대함 children look to their parents for guidance and support for their basic needs → 아이들의 삶의 질과 교육 수준은 부모에게 달려있음 children's quality of life and level of education depend on their parents 2. 건강한 부모 자식간의 관계는 아이들의 법과 규칙을 준수하도록 장려함 a healthy parent-child relationship encourages children to obey laws and regulations → 부모를 존경하면 규칙을 준수하고 다른 사람들을 돌봄 children who respect their parents abide by rules and take care of others → 부모의 지도를 받은 아이는 반사회적 인격 장애자 또는 범죄자가 될 가능성이 낮음 a child guided by parents is less likely to become a sociopath or criminal	1. 맞벌이 가정의 증가로 아이들은 TV를 보거나 인터넷 서핑을 함 as the number of double-income families increases, children watch TV or surf the Internet → 이러한 요소들은 아이들을 외부 영향에 노출시킴 these factors open them up to external influences 2. 부모가 통제를 해도 아이들은 또래의 영향하에 있음 even if parents control, their child comes under peer influence → 이 결과 아이들의 발달은 영향을 받을 수 있음 the result is that a child's development can be affected

* 아이디어의 수는 같지만 some people의 주장에 대해 영어로 쓸 수 있는 말이 더 많으므로 내 대답은 '아이의 발달에 부모의 역할이 가장 중요하다'이다.

2단계 서론 (Introduction) (6~10분) : 두 문장으로 작성

| Question | Some people argue that parents have the most important role in their child's development. However, others say that other factors like TV or peer groups have the most significant influence. Discuss both views and give your own opinion. |

단계	Question	서론 작성
1단계 Paraphrasing	**토픽 :** Some people argue that parents have the most important role in their child's development. However, others say that other factors like TV or peer groups have the most significant influence.	**Paraphrasing :** It is often said that parents hold the key to their child's future, while others claim there are more influential factors such as the media and friends.
2단계 Answering	**질문 :** Discuss both views and give your own opinion.	**Answering : Some people에 동의할 경우** Although other influences are becoming more powerful, I believe that parents still play the most decisive role in shaping a child's skill set.

Introduction
It is often said that parents hold the key to their child's future, while others claim there are more influential factors such as the media and friends. Although other influences are becoming more powerful, I believe that parents still play the most decisive role in shaping a child's skill set.

it is often said that S+V : 흔히들 that 이하라고 말한다
hold the key to : ~에 대한 열쇠를 쥐다, to 다음에는 명사(동명사)가 오는 것에 주의!
the media : 언론, the와 함께 쓴다
play the most decisive role in : ~에 가장 결정적인 역할을 하다 (기본형 play a role in : ~에 역할을 하다)
skill set : 능력 (사회 구성원으로서의 살아가는 데 필요한 기본적인 능력)

우리말 해석
부모가 자녀의 미래에 대한 열쇠를 쥐고 있다고 흔히들 말하지만, 다른 사람들은 각종 매체나 친구 같은 더 많은 영향력이 있는 요인이 있다고 주장한다. 비록 다른 영향들이 더욱 강력해지고 있지만, 나는 아이의 능력을 형성하는 데에는 여전히 부모가 가장 결정적인 역할을 한다고 믿는다.

 **본론 1 (Body 1) (11~20분) : 나와 다른 의견 = Others** (TV나 또래 집단 같은 다른 요소가 아이의 발달에 가장 중요한 요인이다)

> **Question**
>
> Some people argue that parents have the most important role in their child's development. However, others say that other factors like TV or peer groups have the most significant influence. Discuss both views and give your own opinion.

Body 1은 1단계에서 브레인스토밍한 'Others'의 주장을 바탕으로 작성한다.

1단계	Topic Sentence	Nowadays, many children spend a relatively significant amount of time away from their parents.
2단계 (1)	Supporting Sentence (1)	*as the number of double-income families increases, children watch TV or surf the Internet* As the number of double-income families increases, more children are more likely to be allowed to watch TV or surf the Internet.
3단계 (1)	Supporting Sentence or Specific Example (1)	*these factors open them up to external influences* These factors have the power to open them up to both positive and negative external influences.
2단계 (2)	Supporting Sentence (2)	*even if parents control, their child comes under peer influence* Even if parents are able to control what happens at home, their child is still likely to come under peer influence at school or when they are out with friends.
3단계 (2)	Supporting Sentence or Specific Example (2)	*the result is that a child's development can be affected* The result is that a child's development can clearly be affected for better or worse.

Body 1

Nowadays, many children spend a relatively significant amount of time away from their parents. As the number of double-income families increases, more children are more likely to be allowed to watch TV or surf the Internet. These factors have the power to open them up to both positive and negative external influences. Even if parents are able to control what happens at home, their child is still likely to come under peer influence at school or when they are out with friends. The result is that a child's development can clearly be affected for better or worse.

불법포인트

away from : ~에서 떠나서
double-income families : 맞벌이 가정
be more likely to : ~할 가능성이 더 높다
　(기본형 : be likely to : ~할 가능성이 있다)
surf the Internet : 인터넷을 서핑하다
external influences : 외부 영향
come under : ~의 (영향)하에 있다, (영향)을 받다
be out with : ~와 나가다, 나가서 놀다

우리말 해석

오늘날, 많은 아이들은 상대적으로 많은 시간을 부모와 떨어져 지낸다. 맞벌이 가족의 수가 증가함에 따라, 더 많은 아이들이 TV를 보거나 인터넷 서핑을 하도록 허용되는 경우가 더 높아지고 있다. 이러한 요인들은 긍정적인 또는 부정적인 외부 영향 모두에 아이들을 노출하는 힘을 가졌다. 심지어 부모가 가정에서 무슨 일이 일어나는지 통제할 수 있다 하더라도, 아이들은 학교에서건, 친구들과 나가있건 간에 여전히 또래의 영향 하에 있게 될 가능성이 있다. 그 결과 아이들의 발달은 더 좋든 더 나쁘든 분명히 영향을 받게 된다.

4 단계 본론 2 (Body 2) (21~30분) : 내 의견 = Some people (부모가 아이의 발달에 가장 중요한 요인이다)

Question	Some people argue that parents have the most important role in their child's development. However, others say that other factors like TV or peer groups have the most significant influence. Discuss both views and give your own opinion.

Body 2는 1단계에서 브레인스토밍한 'Some people'의 주장을 바탕으로 작성한다.

1단계	Topic Sentence	However, the value of parents in their child's development is obvious.
2단계 (1)	Supporting Sentence (1)	*children look to their parents for guidance and support for their basic needs* Needless to say children look to their parents for guidance and support for their most basic needs from eating to learning.
3단계 (1)	Supporting Sentence or Specific Example (1)	*children's quality of life and level of education depend on their parents* Therefore children's quality of life and level of education would depend on their parents' affection and financial capacity.
2단계 (2)	Supporting Sentence (2)	*a healthy parent-child relationship encourages children to obey laws and regulations* In addition, a healthy parent-child relationship could encourage children to obey laws and regulations in their community because their sense of values is often based on guidance at home.
3단계 (2)	Supporting Sentence or Specific Example (2)	*children who respect their parents abide by rules and take care of others* Children who respect their parents are willing to abide by rules and take care of others. *a child guided by parents is less likely to become a sociopath or criminal* A child guided by parents is less likely to become a sociopath or criminal in later life.

Body 2

However, the value of parents in their child's development is obvious. Needless to say children look to their parents for guidance and support for their most basic needs from eating to learning. Therefore children's quality of life and level of education would depend on their parents' affection and financial capacity. In addition, a healthy parent–child relationship could encourage children to obey laws and regulations in their community because their sense of values is often based on guidance at home. Children who respect their parents are willing to abide by rules and take care of others. A child guided by parents is less likely to become a sociopath or criminal in later life.

look to : 기대하다
basic needs : 기본적 욕구
quality of life : 삶의 질
level of education : 교육 수준
depend on : 달려 있다
affection : 애정
financial capacity : 재정적 능력
a healthy parent–child relationship :
  건강한 부모 자식 간의 관계

encourage A to B : A(사람)로 하여금 B
  (행위를 나타내는 동사)하도록 장려하다
obey laws and regulations : 법과 규칙을 준수하다
  (따르다)
sense of values : 가치관
abide by rules : 규칙을 준수하다(따르다)
sociopath : 소시오패스, 반사회적 인격 장애자
in later life : 나중에 커서

우리말 해석

그러나 아이들의 발달에 부모의 가치는 분명하다. 말할 필요도 없이, 아이들은 먹는 것에서 공부하는 것까지 자신들의 대부분의 기본적 욕구를 지도하고 지원해 주기를 부모에게 기대한다. 따라서 아이들의 생활의 질과 교육수준은 그들 부모의 애정과 재정능력에 달려있다고 할 것이다. 게다가, 건강한 부모 자식 간의 관계는 아이들이 공동체 내의 법과 규칙을 준수하도록 장려할 수 있는데, 왜냐하면 그들의 가치관은 종종 가정에서의 지도를 바탕으로 하기 때문이다. 부모를 존경하는 아이들은 기꺼이 규칙을 준수하며 다른 이들을 돌볼 것이다. 부모의 지도를 받은 아이는 나중에 커서 반사회적 인격 장애자 또는 범죄자가 될 가능성이 낮다.

 **5 단계**   결론 (Conclusion) (31~35분) : 본문에 제시한 내 주장 요약하며 다시 한 번 강조

Question	Some people argue that parents have the most important role in their child's development. However, others say that other factors like TV or peer groups have the most significant influence. Discuss both views and give your own opinion.

결론 작성 시, 먼저 문제 유형을 파악한 후, 'Conclusion Template'의 표현을 인용한다. (See p58)

문제 유형 파악	1-2) Discuss both views and give your own opinion.
Conclusion Template 인용	In conclusion, there are convincing arguments both for and against…(토픽), but I am convinced that… 본론에서 제시한 내 주장 간단히 요약

결론을 작성하기 전, 서론과 본론 2에서 some people의 의견(부모가 아이의 발달에 가장 중요한 요인이다)에 동의했는지 다시 한 번 확인하자!

> **Conclusion**
> **In conclusion, there are convincing arguments both for and against** the importance of parents in a child's development, **but I am convinced that** this debate actually highlights the prominent role parents should be playing as an anchor in their child's life.

* 상황에 따라 템플릿을 살짝 변형해도 좋다.

highlight : 강조하다
prominent : 중요한
anchor : 정신적 지주 (앵커는 뉴스 앵커, 닻 등의 뜻이 있지만 여기서는 정신적 지주라는 뜻으로 해석)

우리말 해석
결론적으로 아이의 발달에 있어 부모의 중요성에 대해 찬성과 반대를 하는 설득력 있는 주장들이 있지만, 나는 이 논쟁은 실질적으로 부모가 아이의 인생에 정신적 지주로서 수행해야 할 중요한 역할을 강조해야 한다고 확신한다.

6 단계   교정 (Self-correction) (36~40분) : 내용의 일관성 및 문법 검토

글을 완성한 후, 반드시 스스로 교정할 수 있는 시간 5분을 남겨두어야 한다. 간신히 시간 안에 Task 1과 2를 모두 완성했더라도 교정하지 않고 답안지를 제출한다면 내용의 일관성과 문법에서 점수를 잃을 수 있다. 최소 0.5~1.0점을 올릴 수 있는 마지막 필살기!

다음 Body 2의 내용을 교정해 보자. 틀린 부분은 총 몇 개일까?

교정 전 (직접 문장 부호를 이용하여 틀린 부분을 교정해 보자.)

However, The value of parent in their child's development is obvious.

Needless on say children look after their parents for guidance and support for their most basic needs from eat to learn. Therefore children's quality for life and level of education would depends at their parents' affection and financial capacity. In addition, A healthy parent-child relationship could encourage children on obey laws and regulations in their community because their sense of values are often based on guidance at home. Children who respects their parents is willing to abide by rules and take care of other. A child guided by parents is more likely to become a sociopath or criminal in later life.

교정

> However, ~~T~~**t**he value of parent**s** in their child's development is obvious.
>
> Needless ~~on~~ **to** say children look ~~after~~ **to** their parents for guidance and support for their most basic needs from ~~eat~~ **eating** to ~~learn~~ **learning**. Therefore children's quality ~~for~~ **of** life and level of education would ~~depends~~ **depend** ~~at~~ **on** their parents' affection and financial capacity. In addition, ~~A~~ **a** healthy parent-child relationship could encourage children ~~on~~ **to** obey laws and regulations in their community because their sense of values ~~are~~ **is** often based on guidance at home. Children who ~~respects~~ **respect** their parents ~~is~~ **are** willing to abide by rules and take care of ~~other~~ **others**. A child guided by parents is ~~more~~ **less** likely to become a sociopath or criminal in later life.

1. T → t : 콤마(,) 다음에는 소문자로 쓴다.
2. parent → parents : 셀 수 있는 명사는 주로 복수로 쓰고, 단수로 쓸 경우 명사 앞에 관사 등을 붙인다.
3. 붙여쓰기 : 위의 글은 Body 2 단락이다. 단락이 바뀌지 않는 한, 줄을 바꿔 쓰지 않는다.
4. on → to : needless to say은 '말할 필요도 없이'라는 뜻
5. after → to : look to는 '~기대하다', look after는 '돌보다'라는 뜻
6 & 7. eat → eating / learn → learning : 전치사 (from / to) 다음에는 명사를 쓰는 것이 원칙. 동사가 나온 경우 동사에 ~ing를 붙여 동명사로 만든다.
8. for → of : quality of life는 '삶의 질'이라는 뜻
9. depends → depend : 조동사 (would) 다음에는 동사 원형을 쓴다.
10. at → on : depend on은 '~에 달려 있다'라는 뜻
11. A → a : 콤마(,) 다음에는 소문자로 쓴다.
12. on → to : encourage A to B는 'A(사람)로 하여금 B(행위를 나타내는 동사)하도록 장려하다'라는 뜻
13. are → is : 주어인 sense가 단수이므로 단수 동사 is를 쓴다.
14. respects → respect : 주어인 children이 복수이므로 복수 동사인 respect를 쓴다.
15. is → are : 주어인 children이 복수이므로 복수 동사인 are를 쓴다.
16. other → others : others는 '다른 사람들'이라는 뜻
17. more → less : 소시오패스나 범죄자가 될 가능성이 적다고 해야 논리에 맞다. 이걸 놓치면 절대 안 된다!

틀린 개수 : 총 17개

Sample Answer

Question: Some people argue that parents have the most important role in their child's development. However, others say that other factors like TV or peer groups have the most significant influence. Discuss both views and give your own opinion.

It is often said that parents hold the key to their child's future, while others claim there are more influential factors such as the media and friends. Although other influences are becoming more powerful, I believe that parents still play the most decisive role in shaping a child's skill set.

Nowadays, many children spend a relatively significant amount of time away from their parents. As the number of double-income families increases, more children are more likely to be allowed to watch TV or surf the Internet. These factors have the power to open them up to both positive and negative external influences. Even if parents are able to control what happens at home, their child is still likely to come under peer influence at school or when they are out with friends. The result is that a child's development can clearly be affected for better or worse.

However, the value of parents in their child's development is obvious. Needless to say children look to their parents for guidance and support for their most basic needs from eating to learning. Therefore children's quality of life and level of education would depend on their parents' affection and financial capacity. In addition, a healthy parent-child relationship could encourage children to obey laws and regulations in their community because their sense of values is often based on guidance at home. Children who respect their parents are willing to abide by rules and take care of others. A child guided by parents is less likely to become a sociopath or criminal in later life.

In conclusion, there are convincing arguments both for and against the importance of parents in a child's development, but I am convinced that this debate actually highlights the prominent role parents should be playing as an anchor in their child's life.

word counts : 300 words

우리말 해석

부모가 자녀의 미래에 대한 열쇠를 쥐고 있다고 흔히들 말하지만, 다른 사람들은 각종 매체나 친구 같은 더 많은 영향력이 있는 요인이 있다고 주장한다. 비록 다른 영향들이 더욱 강력해지고 있지만, 나는 아이의 능력을 형성하는 데에는 여전히 부모가 가장 결정적인 역할을 한다고 믿는다.

오늘날, 많은 아이들은 상대적으로 많은 시간을 부모와 떨어져 지낸다. 맞벌이 가족의 수가 증가함에 따라, 더 많은 아이들이 TV를 보거나 인터넷 서핑을 하도록 허용되는 경우가 더 높아지고 있다. 이러한 요인들은 긍정적인 또 부정적인 외부 영향 모두에 아이들을 노출하는 힘을 가졌다. 심지어 부모가 가정에서 무슨 일이 일어나는지 통제할 수 있다 하더라도, 아이들은 학교에서건, 친구들과 나가있건 간에 여전히 또래의 영향 하에 있게 될 가능성이 있다. 그 결과 아이들의 발달은 더 좋든 더 나쁘든 분명히 영향을 받게 된다.

그러나 아이들의 발달에 부모의 가치는 분명하다. 말할 필요도 없이, 아이들은 먹는 것에서 공부하는 것까지 자신들의 대부분의 기본적 욕구를 지도하고 지원해 주기를 부모에게 기대한다. 따라서 아이들의 생활의 질과 교육수준은 그들 부모의 애정과 재정능력에 달려있다고 할 것이다. 게다가, 건강한 부모 자식 간의 관계는 아이들이 공동체 내의 법과 규칙을 준수하도록 장려할 수 있는데, 왜냐하면 그들의 가치관은 종종 가정에서의 지도를 바탕으로 하기 때문이다. 부모를 존경하는 아이들은 기꺼이 규칙을 준수하며 다른 이들을 돌볼 것이다. 부모의 지도를 받은 아이는 나중에 커서 반사회적 인격 장애자 또는 범죄자가 될 가능성이 낮다.

결론적으로 아이의 발달에 있어 부모의 중요성에 대해 찬성과 반대를 하는 설득력 있는 주장들이 있지만, 나는 이 논쟁은 실질적으로 부모가 아이의 인생에 정신적 지주로서 수행해야 할 중요한 역할을 강조해야 한다고 확신한다.

STEP 4 불법 Review

앞에서 배운 내용을 바탕으로 다음 빈칸을 영어로 작성해 보자.

[_____] (1. 흔히들 말한다) parents [_____] (2. 열쇠를 쥐다) their child's future, while others claim there are [_____] (3. 더 많은 영향력이 있는 요인들) such as the media and friends. Although other influences are becoming more powerful, I believe that parents still [_____] (4. ~에 가장 결정적인 역할을 하다) shaping a child's skill set.

Nowadays, many children spend a relatively significant amount of time [_____] (5. ~에서 떠나서) their parents. [_____] (6. 맞벌이 가정의 수가 증가함에 따라), more children are more likely to be allowed to watch TV or [_____] (7. 인터넷을 서핑하다). These factors have the power to open them up to both positive and negative external influences. Even if parents are able to control what happens at home, their child is still likely to [_____] (8. 또래의 영향 하에 있다) at school or when they are out with friends. The result is that a child's development can clearly be affected for [_____] (9. 더 좋거나 더 나쁘거나).

However, the value of parents in their child's development is obvious. [_____] (10. 말할 필요도 없이) children look to their parents for guidance and support for their most basic needs from eating to learning. Therefore children's quality of life and level of education would depend on their parents' affection and [_____] (11. 재정적 능력). In addition, [_____] (12. 건강한 부모 자식 간의 관계) could encourage children to [_____] (13. 법과 규칙을 준수하다) in their community because their sense of values is often based on guidance at home. Children who respect their parents are willing to abide by rules and [_____] (14. 다른 사람들을 돌보다). A child guided by parents is less likely to become a sociopath or criminal in later life.

In conclusion, there are convincing arguments both for and against the importance of parents in a child's development, but I am convinced that this debate actually highlights the prominent role parents should be playing [_____] (15. 정신적 지주로서) in their child's life.

Answer 1. It is often said that / 2. hold the key to / 3. more influential factors / 4. play the most decisive role in
5. away from / 6. As the number of double-income families increases / 7. surf the Internet
8. come under peer influence / 9. better or worse / 10. Needless to say / 11. financial capacity
12. a healthy parent-child relationship / 13. obey laws and regulations / 14. take care of others
15. as an anchor

Day 1 Family 불법 포인트 정리

부모와 자식 간의 관계	the relationship between parents and their children	흔히들 that이하라고 말한다	it is often said that S+V
덜 가까워 보이다	seem to be less close	~에 대한 열쇠를 쥐다	hold the key to
친밀함의 부족	the lack of closeness	언론	the media
~에 부정적인 영향을 미치다	have a negative effect on	~에 가장 결정적인 역할을 하다	play the most decisive role in
맞벌이 가정의 수	the number of double-income families	능력	skill set
시간을 덜 보내다	spend less time	~에서 떠나서	away from
(그들의) 바쁜 부모 때문에	due to their busy parents	맞벌이 가정	double-income families
~에 주된 영향이 되었다(현재완료)	have become the main influence on	~할 가능성이 더 높다	be more likely to
집에 머무르다	stay at home	인터넷을 서핑하다	surf the Internet
돌보다	care / look after / take care of	외부 영향	external influences
더 이상 ~않다	no longer	~의 (영향)하에 있다	come under
~만큼 크지 않은	not as large as	~와 나가다	be out with
그들이 그러했던 것처럼	as they used to be	기대하다	look to
도시화와 산업화	urbanisation and industrialisation	기본적 욕구	basic needs
대가족	extended families	삶의 질	quality of life
핵가족	nuclear families	교육 수준	level of education
모르다 / 생각이 없다	have no idea	달려 있다	depend on
청소년 범죄	juvenile delinquency	애정	affection
~에 좀 더 관여하다	be more involved with	재정적 능력	financial capacity
양육	upbringing	건강한 부모 자식 간의 관계	a healthy parent-child relationship
또래들의 압박	peer pressure	A로 하여금 B하도록 장려하다	encourage A to B
(어떠한 일을) 맡다	be assigned	법과 규칙을 준수하다	obey laws and regulations
집안일	household chores / housework	가치관	sense of values
시간을 관리하는 법	how to organise their time	규칙을 준수하다	abide by rules
옳고 그름의 차이	the difference between right and wrong	소시오패스	sociopath
A에게 B에 대해 조언하다	give A advice on B	나중에 커서	in later life
도덕과 안전	morals and safety	강조하다	highlight
아이의 발달	child's development	중요한	prominent
또래 집단	peer groups	정신적 지주	anchor

Day 2 Growing Up 성장

Question	In the 21st century, the average life expectancy is increasing. What problems will this cause for individuals and society? Suggest some solutions that could be taken to reduce the effect of aging populations. 21세기 평균 기대수명은 증가하고 있다. 이러한 현상이 개인과 사회에 어떤 문제를 일으킬 수 있는가? 인구 노령화의 영향을 줄이기 위해서 취할 수 있는 해결책들을 제시하라.

 빈출 문제

1. Some people say it is wrong that children have a part-time job. However, others consider it as valuable work experience. Discuss both sides and give your own opinion.

2. Some people insist that society should accept that children mature at a younger age these days and should adjust the legal age of voting and marriage accordingly. To what extent do you agree or disagree with this opinion?

3. Gifts such as a camera and a soccer ball can contribute to a child's development. What gifts would you give to help a child develop? Why do you think the gifts help a child develop?

4. Some people say that children should be made to obey rules while others think children who are controlled too much cannot be well-prepared for their adult life. Discuss both sides and give your own opinion.

1. 어떤 사람들은 아이들이 아르바이트를 하는 것이 잘못되었다고 말한다. 반면 이것을 가치 있는 경험이라고 생각하는 사람들도 있다. 양쪽의 견해를 논하고 당신의 주장을 제시하라.

2. 어떤 사람들은 사회가 요즘 아이들이 더 빨리 성숙해진다는 것을 인정하고 이에 따라 선거와 결혼에 대한 법적인 나이를 조정해야 한다고 주장한다. 당신은 이 의견에 얼마만큼 동의하는가? 또는 동의하지 않는가?

3. 카메라와 축구공 같은 선물들은 아이의 발달에 기여할 수 있다. 당신은 아이의 발달을 돕기 위해 어떤 선물들을 줄 것인가? 왜 이러한 선물들이 아이의 발달에 도움이 된다고 생각하는가?

4. 어떤 사람들은 반드시 아이들이 규칙을 따라야 한다고 말하지만, 과도한 통제를 받은 아이들은 성인으로서의 삶을 잘 준비할 수 없다고 말하는 사람들도 있다. 양쪽의 견해를 논하고 당신의 주장을 제시하라.

 **브레인스토밍**

1) 교육은 아동의 노동을 막는 강력한 수단이다.
   ~의 강력한 수단 : a powerful means of

2) 여자 아이들의 집안일은 가장 보이지 않는 아동 착취의 형태이고, 이것은 아동 노동자들의 대다수가 될지도 모른다.
   보이지 않는 : invisible / 아동 (노동) 착취 : child exploitation / 되다 : constitute

3) 어떤 나라에서는 가난한 집의 아이들은 종종 가정부가 되기 위해 도시로 보내지거나, 다른 지역에서 일자리를 찾기 위해 보내진다.
   가난한 집의 아이들 : children from impoverished families / 가정부 : domestic workers

4) 아이들의 취업은 대부분의 후진국에서는 금지된다.
   아이들의 취업 : the employment of children

5) 어떤 사람들은 아이들이 어린 시절을 즐겁게 보낼 수 있도록 자유로워야 한다고 주장한다.
   어린 시절 : childhood / 자유롭다 : be free

6) 아동학대를 막기 위해, 정부는 교육을 우선으로 삼아야 한다.
  아동학대 : child abuse / 우선순위 : priority(셀 수 있는 명사임에 주의)

7) 아이들에겐 어른으로서의 삶을 위해 필요한 지식과 기술이 주어져야 하고, 그러므로 정부는 그들을 교육하기 위한 자원들을 공급해야 한다.
  어른으로서의 삶 : adult life / 공급하다 : supply

8) 십대들은 극도로 남의 시선을 의식하게 되고 그들의 외모에 대해 지나치게 예민할지도 모른다.
  남의 시선을 의식하는 : self-conscious / 지나치게 : overly

9) 청소년들의 인지발달에 관해서 말하자면, 그들은 더 큰 추리력을 갖고 있고, 논리적으로 그리고 가설에 근거해서 생각하는 능력이 발달되었다.
  청소년 : adolescents / 인지 발달 : cognitive development / 추리력 : reasoning skills / 논리적으로 : logically
  가설에 근거해서 : hypothetically

10) 연금을 받을 은퇴한 사람들의 수가 증가해 왔고 이 상황은 일하는 성인들에게 더 큰 세금 부담이 될 가능성이 높다.
  연금을 받다 : receive a pension / 은퇴한 사람 : retired people / 세금 부담 : tax burden

11) 의학과 과학의 진보는 사람들이 이전보다 더 오래 그리고 더 나은 삶을 살도록 돕고 있다.
  이전보다 더 : than ever before

12) 사람들이 더 오래 삶에 따라, 의료서비스와 시설에 대한 요구 증가가 있을 것이다.
  의료서비스와 시설 : healthcare services and facilities

13) 가까운 미래에 젊은 성인들은 나이든 친척들을 돌봐야 할 필요가 증대될 것이다.
  가까운 미래에 : in the near future / 나이든 친척들 : elderly relatives

14) 의학의 진전과 건강 프로그램은 노인들이 건강을 유지하고 더 오랫동안 일하는 것을 가능하게 할지도 모른다.
    의학의 진전 : medical advances / 건강을 유지하다 : stay healthy / 가능하게 하다 : allow A(사람) to B(동사)

---

15) 정부는 젊은 노동자의 수를 늘리기 위해 이민을 장려해야 한다.
    이민 : immigration

Answer

1) Education is a powerful means of preventing child labour.
2) Girls' domestic work is the most invisible form of child exploitation and it may constitute the majority of child workers.
3) In some countries, children from impoverished families are often sent to urban areas to become domestic workers or to find employment in other areas.
4) The employment of children is prohibited in most underdeveloped countries.
5) Some people insist that children should be free to enjoy their childhood.
6) To prevent child abuse, governments should make education a priority.
7) Children need to be given the knowledge and skills necessary for adult life, therefore governments should supply the resources to educate them.
8) Teenagers become extremely self-conscious and may be overly sensitive about their appearance.
9) In terms of adolescents' cognitive development, they have greater reasoning skills and have developed the ability to think logically and hypothetically.
10) The number of retired people who will receive a pension has increased and this situation is more likely to be a greater tax burden on working adults.
11) Advances in medicine and science are helping people to live longer and better than ever before.
12) As people live longer, there will be a rise in the demand for healthcare services and facilities.
13) In the near future, young adults will increasingly need to take care of their elderly relatives.
14) Medical advances and health programmes may allow elderly people to stay healthy and work for longer.
15) Governments should encourage immigration to increase the number of young workers.

 실전문제

You should spend about 40 minutes on this task.
Write about the following topic :

> In the 21st century, the average life expectancy is increasing. What problems will this cause for individuals and society? Suggest some solutions that could be taken to reduce the effect of aging populations.

Give reasons for your answer and include any relevant examples from your own knowledge or experience.

Write at least 250 words.

 **1 단계** 문제 정독, 문제 유형 파악, 브레인스토밍 (0 ~ 5분)

Question	In the 21st century, the average life expectancy is increasing. What problems will this cause for individuals and society? Suggest some solutions that could be taken to reduce the effect of aging populations.

문제 정독
21세기 평균 기대수명은 증가하고 있다. 이러한 현상이 개인과 사회에 어떤 문제를 일으킬 수 있는가? 인구 노령화의 영향을 줄이기 위해서 취할 수 있는 해결책들을 제시하라.

in the 21st century : 21세기에, 21은 서수로 쓰고 앞에 관사 the를 붙인다.
average life expectancy : 평균 기대수명
aging populations : 인구 노령화
* 반드시 individuals and society, 개인과 사회에 발생하는 문제와 각각에 대한 해결책을 모두 제시해야 한다.

문제 유형 파악
3-2. Problems and Solutions 유형

Brainstorming

Topic : 인구 노령화	
Problems : 인구 노령화가 개인과 사회에 미치는 문제	Solutions : 인구 노령화의 영향을 줄일 수 있는 해결책
1. 개인 : 노인들은 병으로 고통을 겪음 aged people suffer from diseases → 대부분의 나라들은 병원 시설을 충분히 갖추지 못함 most countries do not have enough hospital facilities	1. 개인 : 노인들에게 규칙적인 운동과 균형 잡힌 식사권장 encouraging the elderly both doing regular exercise and eating a well-balanced diet → 예방이 항상 치료보다 더 나음 preventing is always better than cure
2. 사회 : 정부가 세제수입 안정성 확보에 차질 예상 the government expects a setback in securing tax revenue → 한국에서는 대부분의 근로자들이 60세 이전 혹은 좀 더 일찍 퇴직함 in Korea, most workers retire before they are 60 or earlier → 국가에 큰 부담 a big burden to the country	2. 사회 : 연금과 퇴직 체계를 재조정 re-assess our pension and retirement systems → 노인들의 권리와 존엄성을 인식하고 정년 연장 정책 도입 recognizing the rights and dignity of older people and inducing the retirement age extension policy → 노인들 사이의 빈곤에 대한 잠재력 줄임 reducing the potential for poverty among the aged

* 개인에게 미치는 문제점에 대한 해결책, 사회에 미치는 문제점에 대한 해결책을 각각 연관성 있게 작성해야 한다.

2단계   서론 (Introduction) (6~10분) : 두 문장으로 작성

Question	In the 21st century, the average life expectancy is increasing. What problems will this cause for individuals and society? Suggest some solutions that could be taken to reduce the effect of aging populations.

단계	Question	서론 작성
1단계 Paraphrasing	토픽 : In the 21st century, the average life expectancy is increasing.	Paraphrasing : We are living longer than ever before these days, so society as well as individuals are confronted with a range of new challenges.
2단계 Answering	질문 : What problems will this cause for individuals and society? Suggest some solutions that could be taken to reduce the effect of aging populations.	Answering : 문제와 해결책 간단히 언급 Although we face to solve those difficulties in an effective manner, we have the opportunity to make a far more smooth transition into the future.

Introduction
We are living longer than ever before these days, so society as well as individuals are confronted with a range of new challenges. Although we face to solve those difficulties in an effective manner, we have the opportunity to make a far more smooth transition into the future.

be confronted with : = be faced with, ~에 직면하다

a far more smooth transition : 훨씬 더 순조로운 이행, far는 '훨씬'이라는 비교급(more) 강조의 뜻, 관사 a는 transition이 셀 수 있는 명사의 단수이기 때문에 반드시 써야 함

우리말 해석
우리는 요즘 이전보다 더 오래 살고 있고 그래서 개인뿐만 아니라 사회도 새로운 영역의 어려움에 직면하고 있다. 비록 우리는 효과적인 방법으로 이러한 어려움들을 해결해야 하는 것에 직면했지만, 우리는 미래로 훨씬 더 순조로운 이행을 할 기회를 가지고 있다.

3단계 　본론 1 (Body 1) (11~20분) : Problems (인구 노령화가 개인들과 사회에 미치는 문제점들)

Question	In the 21st century, the average life expectancy is increasing. What problems will this cause for individuals and society? Suggest some solutions that could be taken to reduce the effect of aging populations.

Body 1은 1단계에서 브레인스토밍한 'Problems'를 바탕으로 작성한다.

1단계	Topic Sentence	The most obvious problems with the average life span getting longer are the shortfall in tax revenues as well as the health of the elderly.
2단계 (1)	Supporting Sentence (1)	*aged people suffer from diseases* Aged people are less likely to avoid suffering from diseases.
3단계 (1)	Supporting Sentence or Specific Example (1)	*most countries do not have enough hospital facilities* Most countries do not have enough hospital facilities such as hospitals, doctors and other medical personnel to meet the demands of the elderly patients.
2단계 (2)	Supporting Sentence (2)	*the government expect a setback in securing tax revenue* In addition, as the number of economically active people decreases, the government is expecting a setback in securing tax revenue.
3단계 (2)	Supporting Sentence or Specific Example (2)	*in Korea, most workers retire before they are 60 or earlier* In Korea, most workers are forced to be retired before they are 60 or earlier. *a big burden to the country* Therefore it would be a big burden to the country imposing less tax compared to spending more welfare budget.

Body 1

The most obvious problems with the average life span getting longer are the shortfall in tax revenues as well as the health of the elderly. Aged people are less likely to avoid suffering from diseases. Most countries do not have enough hospital facilities such as hospitals, doctors and other medical personnel to meet the demands of the elderly patients. In addition, as the number of economically active people decreases, the government is expecting a setback in securing tax revenue. In Korea, most workers are forced to be retired before they are 60 or earlier. Therefore it would be a big burden to the country imposing less tax compared to spending more welfare budget.

life span : 수명
the shortfall in tax revenues : 세제수입의 부족
the elderly : = aged people, 노인들
be less likely to : ~할 가능성이 낮다
avoid : 피하다, avoid 다음에 동사가 나오면 ing를 붙여 동명사로 만든다.
suffer from diseases : 병으로 고통 받다
medical personnel : 의료인력들, personnel은 복수 명사

meet the demands : 요구를 맞추다, 기본형은 meet a demand
economically active people : 경제 활동 인구
setback : 차질
securing tax revenue : 세제수입의 안정성
be forced to : ~하도록 강요 받다
burden : 부담
impose tax : 세금을 부과하다
welfare budget : 복지 예산

우리말 해석

평균 수명 증가와 함께 가장 명확한 문제점들은 노인들의 건강과 세제수입의 부족이다. 노인들은 질병으로부터 고통 받는 것을 피할 수 있는 가능성이 낮다(피하기 어렵다). 대부분의 나라들은 노인 환자들의 수요를 충족시킬 병원, 의사 및 다른 의료인력과 같은 병원 설비를 충분히 갖추지 못했다, 게다가, 경제 활동 인구 수가 줄어듦에 따라, 정부가 세제수입의 안정성을 확보하는 데 차질이 예상된다. 한국에서는 대부분의 근로자들이 60세 이전 혹은 좀 더 일찍 퇴직을 강요 받는다. 그러므로 이것은(이러한 상황은) 더 많은 복지 예산을 쓰는 것에 비해 세금을 덜 부과하게 되면서 국가에 큰 부담이 될 것이다.

 **본론 2 (Body 2) (21~30분) : Solutions** (인구 노령화의 영향을 줄일 수 있는 해결책들)

> **Question**
> In the 21st century, the average life expectancy is increasing. What problems will this cause for individuals and society? Suggest some solutions that could be taken to reduce the effect of aging populations.

Body 2는 1단계에서 브레인스토밍한 'Solutions'를 바탕으로 작성한다.

1단계	Topic Sentence	However, the good news is that these concerns mentioned above can be tackled if there is a desire to take them on.
2단계 (1)	Supporting Sentence (1)	*encouraging the elderly both doing regular exercise and eating a well-balanced diet* Encouraging the elderly both doing regular exercise and eating a well-balanced diet would be fundamental followed by improving the medical sector.
3단계 (1)	Supporting Sentence or Specific Example (1)	*preventing is always better than cure* This is because preventing is always better than cure.
2단계 (2)	Supporting Sentence (2)	*re-assess our pension and retirement systems* We could also re-assess our pension and retirement systems to reflect an aging society to prevent in the shortage of national taxes.
3단계 (2)	Supporting Sentence or Specific Example (2)	*recognizing the rights and dignity of older people and inducing the retirement age extension policy* By recognizing the rights and dignity of older people and inducing the retirement age extension policy, they could be economically active for longer and consume more goods and services. *reducing the potential for poverty among the aged* This would boost the nation as a whole while reducing the potential for poverty among the aged.

Body 2

However, the good news is that these concerns mentioned above can be tackled if there is a desire to take them on. Encouraging the elderly both doing regular exercise and eating a well-balanced diet would be fundamental followed by improving the medical sector. This is because preventing is always better than cure. We could also re-assess our pension and retirement systems to reflect an aging society to prevent in the shortage of national taxes. By recognizing the rights and dignity of older people and inducing the retirement age extension policy, they could be economically active for longer and consume more goods and services. This would boost the nation as a whole while reducing the potential for poverty among the aged.

- take 목적어 on : 목적어를 떠맡다, 책임지다
- do regular exercise : 규칙적인 운동을 하다
- eat a well-balanced diet : 균형 잡힌 식사를 하다
- followed by : ~에 이은, 잇달아, A followed by B (A가 B보다 앞서다)
- improve the medical sector : 의료 부분을 개선하다
- preventing is always better than cure : 예방이 항상 치료보다 더 낫다
- re-assess : 재평가하다, 재조정하다
- pension : 연금
- retirement systems : 퇴직 체계
- an aging society : 고령사회
- the shortage of national taxes : 국세 부족
- the rights and dignity : 권리와 존엄성
- induce the retirement age extension policy : 정년 연장 정책을 도입하다
- goods and services : 상품과 서비스
- boost : 활력을 불어넣다
- poverty : 가난
- the aged : = aged people, 노인들, the + 형용사 = 복수 명사

우리말 해석

그러나 희소식은 위에서 언급한 이러한 걱정들은, 그것들을 책임지고자 하는 열망이 있다면 막을 수 있다는 것이다. 노인들에게 규칙적인 운동을 하고 균형 잡힌 식사를 하도록 권장하는 것이 근본적인 일일 것이고 그 다음이 의료부분 개선일 것이다. 이것은 예방이 항상 치료보다 더 낫기 때문이다. 우리는 또한 우리 국세의 부족을 방지하기 위해 고령사회의 특성을 반영할 수 있도록 연금과 퇴직 체계를 재조정 할 수 있을 것이다. 노인들의 권리와 존엄성을 인식하고 정년 연장 정책을 도입함으로써, 그들은 좀 더 오래 경제적으로 활동할 수 있고 더 많은 상품과 서비스를 소비할 수 있을 것이다. 이것은 노인들 사이의 빈곤에 대한 잠재력을 줄이는 동시에 국가 전체에 활력을 불어넣을 것이다.

5 단계 결론 (Conclusion) (31~35분) : 본문에 제시한 내 주장 요약하며 다시 한 번 강조

Question	In the 21st century, the average life expectancy is increasing. What problems will this cause for individuals and society? Suggest some solutions that could be taken to reduce the effect of aging populations.

결론 작성 시, 먼저 문제 유형을 파악한 후, 'Conclusion Template'의 표현을 인용한다. (See p58)

문제 유형 파악	3-2) Problems and Solutions
Conclusion Template 인용	In conclusion, it is clear that there are various problems for…(토픽), steps are needed to tackle this phenomenon.

3-2 유형의 결론을 작성할 때 문제와 해결책을 구체적으로 작성하게 되면 자칫 결론이 너무 길어질 수 있기 때문에 포괄적으로 작성한다.

> **Conclusion**
> **In conclusion, it is clear that there are various problems** associated with a longer average life expectancy, and **we need to both take steps** as a nation as well as the elderly themselves **to tackle this phenomenon**.

* 상황에 따라 템플릿을 살짝 변형해도 좋다.

associated with : ~와 관련해서
take steps : 조치를 취하다
phenomenon : 현상

우리말 해석
결론적으로 더 길어진 평균 기대 수명과 관련해서 다양한 문제들이 존재하는 것은 분명하고, 이런 현상을 방지하기 위해서 노인 스스로 뿐만 아니라 국가적 차원의 조치들도 모두 요구된다.

6 단계 교정 (Self-correction) (36~40분) : 내용의 일관성 및 문법 검토

다음 Body 2의 내용을 교정해 보자. 틀린 부분은 총 몇 개일까?

교정 전 (직접 문장 부호를 이용하여 틀린 부분을 교정해 보자.)

however, The good news are that these concerns mentioned below can be tackled if there is a desire to take them at. Encouraging the elderly both doing regular exercise and eating a well-balanced diet would be fundamental followed to improving the medical sector. This is because preventing are always good than cure.

We could also re-assess our pension and retirement systems to reflect a aging society to prevent in the shortage of national taxes. By recognize the rights and dignity of older people and inducing the retirement age extension policy, they could be economically active for longer and consume more good and services. This would boost the nation as a whole while reducing the potential for poverty among an aged.

교정

> ~~however~~, **H** ~~The~~ **t** good news ~~are~~ **is** that these concerns mentioned ~~below~~ **above** can be tackled if there is a desire to take them ~~at~~ **on** Encouraging the elderly both doing regular exercise and eating a well-balanced diet would be fundamental followed ~~to~~ **by** improving the medical sector. This is because preventing ~~are~~ **is** always ~~good~~ **better** than cure.
>
> We could also re-assess our pension and retirement systems to reflect ~~a~~ **an** aging society to prevent in the shortage of national taxes. By ~~recognize~~ **recognizing** the rights and dignity of older people and inducing the retirement age extension policy, they could be economically active for longer and consume more ~~good~~ **goods** and services. This would boost the nation as a whole while reducing the potential for poverty among ~~an~~ **the** aged.

1. h → H : 문장의 첫 글자는 반드시 대문자로 시작한다.
2. T → t : 콤마(,) 다음에는 소문자로 쓴다.
3. are → is : news는 셀 수 없는 명사로 단수이다.
4. below → above : '위에서' 언급했다고 해야 논리에 맞다. 이걸 놓치면 절대 안 된다!
5. at → on : take 목적어 on은 '목적어를 떠맡다, 책임지다'라는 뜻
6. to → by : followed by는 '~에 이은, 잇달아'의 뜻
7. are → is : 주어 preventing은 동명사이고 동명사는 단수이다.
8. good → better : 뒤에 than에 맞춰 good의 비교급 better를 쓴다.
9. 붙여쓰기 : 위의 글은 Body 2 단락이다. 단락이 바뀌지 않는 한, 줄을 바꿔 쓰지 않는다.
10. a → an : 모음(a/i/u/e/o)으로 발음이 시작되는 단어 aging[éidʒiŋ] 앞에는 a가 아닌 an으로 쓰고 말한다.
11. recognize → recognizing : by~ing는 '~함으로써'의 뜻으로 by 다음에 동명사가 와야 한다.
12. good → goods : good은 '좋은'이라는 형용사, goods는 '상품'이라는 명사다.
13. an → the : the+형용사는 복수 명사, the aged라고 해야 '노인들'이라는 뜻이 된다.

틀린 개수 : 총 13개

Sample Answer

> **Question**
>
> In the 21st century, the average life expectancy is increasing. What problems will this cause for individuals and society? Suggest some solutions that could be taken to reduce the effect of aging populations.

We are living longer than ever before these days, so society as well as individuals are confronted with a range of new challenges. Although we face to solve those difficulties in an effective manner, we have the opportunity to make a far more smooth transition into the future.

The most obvious problems with the average life span getting longer are the shortfall in tax revenues as well as the health of the elderly. Aged people are less likely to avoid suffering from diseases. Most countries do not have enough hospital facilities such as hospitals, doctors and other medical personnel to meet the demands of the elderly patients. In addition, as the number of economically active people decreases, the government is expecting a setback in securing tax revenue. In Korea, most workers are forced to be retired before they are 60 or earlier. Therefore it would be a big burden to the country imposing less tax compared to spending more welfare budget.

However, the good news is that these concerns mentioned above can be tackled if there is a desire to take them on. Encouraging the elderly both doing regular exercise and eating a well-balanced diet would be fundamental followed by improving the medical sector. This is because preventing is always better than cure. We could also re-assess our pension and retirement systems to reflect an aging society to prevent in the shortage of national taxes. By recognizing the rights and dignity of older people and inducing the retirement age extension policy, they could be economically active for longer and consume more goods and services. This would boost the nation as a whole while reducing the potential for poverty among the aged.

In conclusion, it is clear that there are various problems associated with a longer average life expectancy, and we need to both take steps as a nation as well as the elderly themselves to tackle this phenomenon.

word counts : 318 words

우리말 해석

우리는 요즘 이전보다 더 오래 살고 있고 그래서 개인뿐만 아니라 사회도 새로운 영역의 어려움에 직면하고 있다. 비록 우리는 효과적인 방법으로 이러한 어려움들을 해결해야 하는 것에 직면했지만, 우리는 미래로 훨씬 더 순조로운 이행을 할 기회를 가지고 있다.

평균 수명 증가와 함께 가장 명확한 문제점들은 노인들의 건강과 세제수입의 부족이다. 노인들은 질병으로부터 고통 받는 것을 피할 수 있는 가능성이 낮다(피하기 어렵다). 대부분의 나라들은 노인 환자들의 수요를 충족시킬 병원, 의사 및 다른 의료인력과 같은 병원 설비를 충분히 갖추지 못했다. 게다가, 경제 활동 인구 수가 줄어듦에 따라, 정부가 세제수입의 안정성을 확보하는 데 차질이 예상된다. 한국에서는 대부분의 근로자들이 60세 이전 혹은 좀 더 일찍 퇴직을 강요 받는다. 그러므로 이것은(이러한 상황은) 더 많은 복지 예산을 쓰는 것에 비해 세금을 덜 부가하게 되면서 국가에 큰 부담이 될 것이다.

그러나 희소식은 위에서 언급한 이러한 걱정들은, 그것들을 책임지고자 하는 열망이 있다면 막을 수 있다는 것이다. 노인들에게 규칙적인 운동을 하고 균형 잡힌 식사를 하도록 권장하는 것이 근본적인 일일 것이고 그 다음이 의료부분 개선일 것이다. 이것은 예방이 항상 치료보다 더 낫기 때문이다. 우리는 또한 우리 국세의 부족을 방지하기 위해 고령사회의 특성을 반영할 수 있도록 연금과 퇴직 체계를 재조정 할 수 있을 것이다. 노인들의 권리와 존엄성을 인식하고 정년 연장 정책을 도입함으로써, 그들은 좀 더 오래 경제적으로 활동할 수 있고 더 많은 상품과 서비스를 소비할 수 있을 것이다. 이것은 노인들 사이의 빈곤에 대한 잠재력을 줄이는 동시에 국가 전체에 활력을 불어넣을 것이다.

결론적으로 더 길어진 평균 기대 수명과 관련해서 다양한 문제들이 존재하는 것은 분명하고, 이런 현상을 방지하기 위해서 노인 스스로 뿐만 아니라 국가적 차원의 조치들도 모두 요구된다.

불법 Review

앞에서 배운 내용을 바탕으로 다음 빈칸을 영어로 작성해 보자.

We _____ (1. 이전보다 더 오래 살고 있다) these days, so society as well as individuals are confronted with a range of new challenges. Although we face to solve those difficulties in an effective manner, we have the opportunity to make _____ (2. 훨씬 더 순조로운 이행) into the future.

The most obvious problems with the average _____ (3. 수명) getting longer are _____ (4. 세제수입의 부족) as well as the health of the elderly. Aged people are less likely to _____ (5. 질병으로부터 고통 받는 것을 피하다). Most countries do not have enough hospital facilities such as hospitals, doctors and other _____ (6. 의료 인력) to meet the demands of the elderly patients. In addition, as the number of _____ (7. 경제 활동 인구) decreases, the government is expecting a setback in _____ (8. 세제수입의 안정성). In Korea, most workers _____ (9. 강요 받다) be retired before they are 60 or earlier. Therefore it would be a big burden to the country imposing less tax compared to spending more _____ (10. 복지 예산).

However, the good news is that these concerns mentioned above can be tackled if there is a desire to take them on. Encouraging the elderly both doing _____ (11. 규칙적인 운동) and eating _____ (12. 균형 잡힌 식사) would be fundamental followed by improving the medical sector. This is because _____ (13. 예방이 항상 치료보다 더 낫다). We could also re-assess our pension and retirement systems to reflect _____ (14. 고령사회) to prevent in the shortage of national taxes. By recognizing the rights and dignity of older people and inducing the retirement age extension policy, they could be economically active for longer and consume more _____ (15. 상품과 서비스). This would boost the nation as a whole while reducing the potential for poverty among the aged.

In conclusion, it is clear that there are various problems associated with a longer _____ (16. 평균 기대 수명), and we need to both take steps as a nation as well as the elderly themselves to tackle this phenomenon.

Answer 1. are living longer than ever before / 2. a far more smooth transition / 3. life span
4. the shortfall in tax revenues / 5. avoid suffering from diseases / 6. medical personnel
7. economically active people / 8. securing tax revenue / 9. are forced to / 10. welfare budget
11. regular exercise / 12. a well-balanced diet / 13. preventing is always better than cure
14. an aging society / 15. goods and services / 16. average life expectancy

Day 2 Growing Up 불법 포인트 정리

~의 강력한 수단	a powerful means of	수명	life span
보이지 않는	invisible	세제수입의 부족	the shortfall in tax revenues
아동 (노동) 착취	child exploitation	노인들	the elderly / aged people
되다	constitute	~할 가능성이 낮다	be less likely to
가난한 집의 아이들	children from impoverished families	피하다	avoid+Ving
가정부	domestic workers	병으로 고통 받다	suffer from diseases
아이들의 취업	the employment of children	의료인력들	medical personnel
어린 시절	childhood	요구를 맞추다	meet a demand
자유롭다	be free	경제 활동 인구	economically active people
아동학대	child abuse	차질	setback
우선순위	priority	세제수입의 안정성	securing tax revenue
어른으로서의 삶	adult life	~하도록 강요 받다	be forced to
공급하다	supply	부담	burden
남의 시선을 의식하는	self-conscious	세금을 부과하다	impose tax
지나치게	overly	복지 예산	welfare budget
청소년	adolescents	목적어를 떠맡다, 책임지다	take 목적어 on
인지 발달	cognitive development	규칙적인 운동을 하다	do regular exercise
추리력	reasoning skills	균형 잡힌 식사를 하다	eat a well-balanced diet
논리적으로	logically	~에 이은, 잇달아	followed by
가설에 근거해서	hypothetically	의료 부분을 개선하다	improve the medical sector
연금을 받다	receive a pension	예방이 항상 치료보다 더 낫다	preventing is always better than cure
은퇴한 사람	retired people	재평가하다, 재조정하다	re-assess
세금 부담	tax burden	연금	pension
이전보다 더	than ever before	퇴직 체계	retirement systems
의료서비스와 시설	healthcare services and facilities	고령사회	an aging society
가까운 미래에	in the near future	국세 부족	the shortage of national taxes
나이든 친척들	elderly relatives	권리와 존엄성	the rights and dignity
의학의 진전	medical advances	정년 연장 정책을 도입하다	induce the retirement age extension policy
건강을 유지하다	stay healthy	상품과 서비스	goods and services
가능하게 하다	allow A(사람) to B(동사)	활력을 불어넣다	boost
이민	immigration	가난	poverty
21세기에	in the 21st century	노인들	the aged / aged people
평균 기대 수명	average life expectancy	~와 관련해서	associated with
인구 노령화	aging populations	조치를 취하다	take steps
~에 직면하다	be confronted with / be faced with	현상	phenomenon
훨씬 더 순조로운 이행	a far more smooth transition		

Day 3 Health & Food 건강과 음식

Question

In modern society traditional food is being replaced by fast food. This trend has a negative impact on both individuals and society. Do you agree or disagree with this statement?

현대 사회에서 전통 음식이 패스트푸드에 의해 대체되고 있다. 이러한 경향은 개인과 사회에 모두 부정적인 영향을 미친다. 당신은 이 말에 동의하는가? 또는 동의하지 않는가?

 빈출 문제

1. Although people's weight is increasing, their level of health is decreasing. What do you think the reasons are? What can you suggest as a solution?

2. A well-balanced diet is the key to a healthy life. Do you agree or disagree with this statement?

3. Childhood obesity is becoming a serious problem in many countries. Explain the main causes and effects of this problem, and suggest some possible solutions.

4. Some people think that to spend public money on preventing illness is more important than to spend it on treating people who are already ill. To what extent do you agree or disagree with this opinion?

1. 사람들의 몸무게는 증가하고 있지만 그들의 건강 상태는 나빠지고 있다. 원인들은 무엇이라고 생각하는가? 해결책으로 무엇을 제시할 수 있는가?

2. 균형이 잘 잡힌 식단은 건강한 삶의 비결이다. 당신은 이 말에 동의하는가? 또는 동의하지 않는가?

3. 많은 나라에서 아동 비만은 심각한 문제가 되고 있다. 이 문제의 주된 원인과 영향을 설명하고 가능한 해결책을 제시하라.

4. 어떤 사람들은 이미 병든 사람들을 치료하는 데 공공 자금을 쓰는 것보다는 질병을 예방하는 데 공공 자금을 쓰는 것이 더 중요하다고 생각한다. 당신은 이 의견에 얼마만큼 동의하는가? 또는 동의하지 않는가?

 브레인스토밍

1) 건강하지 않은 식단은 다양한 건강 문제의 원인이 될 수 있다.
   건강하지 않는 식단 : an unhealthy diet / 원인이 되다 : cause

2) 비만, 당뇨 그리고 심장병 같은 성인병이 증가하고 있다.
   비만 : obesity / 당뇨 : diabetes / 성인병 : adult diseases / 증가하고 있다 : be on the increase

3) 많은 사람들은 오늘날 패스트푸드나 간편식에 의존하는데 이러한 음식에는 종종 너무 많은 지방과 소금 그리고 설탕이 함유되어 있다.
   간편식 : pre-prepared meals (사전에 준비된 음식, 간편식으로 의역함) / 함유되어 있다 : contain

4) 규칙적인 운동은 건강한 몸을 유지하는 데 필수다.
   건강한 몸 : a healthy body / 유지하다 : maintain / 필수인 : essential

5) 운동은 칼로리를 태우고 건강한 뼈와 근육을 만드는 데 도움을 줌으로 의사들은 적어도 일주일에 3번 30분 동안 운동할 것을 조언한다.
   칼로리를 태우다 : burn calories / 뼈와 근육 : bones and muscles / 적어도 : at least

6) 현대 사회에서 대부분의 사람들은 주로 앉아서 생활한다.
주로 앉아서 생활하다 : lead a sedentary life

7) 아이들은 야외 스포츠를 하기 보다는 컴퓨터 게임을 한다.
야외 스포츠 : outdoor sports

8) 과거에 사람들은 직장과 집에서 좀 더 활동적이었다.
직장에서 : in the workplace / 집에서 : at home

9) 점점 더 많은 사람들이 심각하게 과체중이고 이 상황은 병원과 납세자에게 부담을 증가시킬 것이다.
과체중의 : overweight / 납세자 : taxpayers

10) 학교 시간표에 스포츠를 위한 좀 더 많은 시간이 있어야 하고, 건강하지 못한 정크푸드는 학교 메뉴에서 금지되어야 한다.
학교 시간표 : school timetables / 금지하다 : ban

11) 영양학자들은 하루에 과일과 야채를 5인분 먹을 것을 권한다.
영양학자 : nutritionists, dieticians / 5인분 : five portions / 권하다 : recommend

12) 민간 의료는 불공평한데 오직 부자인 사람들만 경제적으로 여유가 있기 때문이다.
민간 의료 : private healthcare / 경제적으로 여유가 있다 : afford

13) 사립 병원은 수술과 진료예약에 대한 대기 명단이 더 짧다.
수술 : operations / 진료예약 : appointments / 대기 명단 : waiting lists

14) 영국의 국민 건강 서비스는 모든 거주자들을 위해 무상 의료를 제공한다.
국민 건강 서비스 : national health service / 거주자 : residents / 무상 의료 : free healthcare

15) 비록 유기농 식품은 화학 비료나 살충제 그리고 유전자 조작 없이 생산되지만, 유기 농업은 더 느리고 더 비쌀지도 모른다.

유기농 식품 : organic foods / 화학 비료 : chemical fertilizers / 살충제 : pesticides / 유전자 조작 : genetic modification

---

Answer

1) An unhealthy diet can cause a variety of health problems.
2) Adult diseases such as obesity, diabetes and heart disease are on the increase.
3) Many people nowadays rely on fast food or pre-prepared meals and these foods often contain too much fat, salt and sugar.
4) Regular exercise is essential in maintaining a healthy body.
5) Exercise burns calories and helps to build healthy bones and muscles, therefore doctors advise exercising at least three times a week for 30 minutes.
6) In modern society, most people lead a sedentary life.
7) Children play computer games rather than doing outdoor sports.
8) In the past, people were more active in the workplace and at home.
9) More and more people are seriously overweight and this situation will increase the burden on hospitals and taxpayers.
10) There should be more time for sports on school timetables and unhealthy junk food should be banned from school menus.
11) Nutritionists recommend eating five portions of fruit and vegetables per day.
12) Private healthcare is unfair because only wealthy people can afford it.
13) Private hospitals have shorter waiting lists for operations and appointments.
14) The National Health Service(NHS) in the UK provides free healthcare for all residents.
15) Although organic foods are produced without chemical fertilizers, pesticides or genetic modification, organic farming may be slower and more expensive.

 실전문제

You should spend about 40 minutes on this task.
Write about the following topic :

> In modern society traditional food is being replaced by fast food. This trend has a negative impact on both individuals and society. Do you agree or disagree with this statement?

Give reasons for your answer and include any relevant examples from your own knowledge or experience.

Write at least 250 words.

1 단계 문제 정독, 문제 유형 파악, 브레인스토밍 (0 ~ 5분)

Question	In modern society traditional food is being replaced by fast food. This trend has a negative impact on both individuals and society. Do you agree or disagree with this statement?

문제 정독
현대 사회에서 전통 음식이 패스트푸드에 의해 대체되고 있다. 이러한 경향은 개인과 사회에 모두 부정적인 영향을 미친다. 당신은 이 말에 동의하는가? 또는 동의하지 않는가?

traditional food 동의어 : food made at home / slow food / traditionally prepared meals / handmade food
fast food의 동의어 : convenience food / pre-prepared meal / ready-to-eat food / processed food
* 문제에 있는 단어를 그대로 여러 번 에세이에 쓰면 감점이다. 키워드의 동의어를 외워서 풍부한 어휘력을 보여줘야 한다. 아이엘츠에서는 동의어의 폭이 넓다. 100% 똑같은 단어가 아니더라도 의미상 비슷하다면 동의어로 사용해도 괜찮다.
have a negative impact on : ~에 부정적인 영향을 미치다. 전치사 on에 주의!

문제 유형 파악

1-1. Do you agree or disagree? 유형

Brainstorming

Topic : 전통 음식이 패스트푸드에 의해 대체되고 있다.	
Agree : 이것은 개인과 사회에 부정적인 영향을 미친다.	**Disagree** : 이것은 개인과 사회에 긍정적인 영향을 미친다.
1. 개인 : 나쁜 건강 상태 poor health → 비만과 질병 발달에 기여 contribute to the development of obesity and diseases	1. 개인 : 현대인들의 성급함을 반영 reflect the impatience of modern people → 취급하기 쉬운 포장으로 훨씬 더 빨리 제공됨 served far more quickly and in a manageable package
2. 사회 : 전통 문화를 위협 threaten traditional culture → 음식은 어떠한 문화의 특성을 표현하는 것이다 food is an expression of a culture's characteristic → 세계적 패스트푸드 브랜드의 성공은 한 나라의 정체성에 위협이 된다 the success of international fast food brands poses a threat to a country's identity	2. 사회 : 상대적으로 저렴한 비용 relatively cheap cost → 전통 음식은 패스트푸드 가격의 2배가 넘는다 traditional food is well over double the price of fast food

* 이 문제에서 Agree는 전통 음식이 패스트푸드에 의해 대체되고 있는 경향에 대한 **부정적인** 영향, Disagree는 **긍정적인** 영향이다. 절대로 혼동해서는 안 된다!
** 개인과 사회에 미치는 영향을 모두 다뤄야 한다.
*** 아이디어의 수는 같지만 Agree에 대해 영어로 쓸 수 있는 말이 더 많으므로 내 대답은 '전통 음식이 패스트푸드에 의해 대체되고 있는 경향은 개인과 사회에 부정적인 영향을 미친다'이다.

2단계 서론 (Introduction) (6~10분) : 두 문장으로 작성

	Question
Question	In modern society traditional food is being replaced by fast food. This trend has a negative impact on both individuals and society. Do you agree or disagree with this statement?

단계	Question	서론 작성
1단계 Paraphrasing	**토픽:** In modern society traditional food is being replaced by fast food. This trend has a negative impact on both individuals and society.	**Paraphrasing:** Nowadays we are surrounded by fast food outlets, suggesting their growing popularity at the expense of nutrient-rich traditional food.
2단계 Answering	**질문:** Do you agree or disagree with this statement?	**Answering : Agree일 경우** Some might find these newer options to be more attractive, but we should all be aware of the health and cultural costs that come with them.

Introduction
Nowadays we are surrounded by fast food outlets, suggesting their growing popularity at the expense of nutrient-rich traditional food. Some might find these newer options to be more attractive, but we should all be aware of the health and cultural costs that come with them.

불법 포인트

nowadays : 오늘날에는, 요즘에는, 쉬운 단어이지만 nowday 혹은 nowaday라고 스펠링 실수를 많이 하는 단어
be surrounded by : ~에 둘러싸여 있다
at the expense of : = at the cost of, at the price of, ~을 희생하고, ~을 비용으로
nutrient-rich : 영양가 풍부한
be aware of : ~을 알다
come with : 동반하다

우리말 해석
오늘날 우리는 영양가 풍부한 전통음식을 희생시키고, 높아져가는 인기를 시사하고 있는 패스트푸드 상점들에 둘러싸여 있다. 어떤 사람들은 이러한 보다 새로운 선택권이 더 매력적이라고 여길지도 모르지만, 우리는 그것들과 동반한 건강과 문화적 비용에 대해 바로 알고 있어야 한다.

3 단계　본론 1 (Body 1) (11~20분) : 나와 다른 의견 = Disagree (개인과 사회에 긍정적인 영향을 미친다)

Question	In modern society traditional food is being replaced by fast food. This trend has a negative impact on both individuals and society. Do you agree or disagree with this statement?

Body 1은 1단계에서 브레인스토밍한 'Disagree'의 주장을 바탕으로 작성한다.

1단계	Topic Sentence	There is no doubt that fast food is more convenient and cheaper.
2단계 (1)	Supporting Sentence (1)	*reflect the impatience of modern people* The desire to eat within a limited period and to avoid waiting too long reflects the impatience of modern people who rush to spend time on work or other pursuits.
3단계 (1)	Supporting Sentence or Specific Example (1)	*served far more quickly and in a manageable package* It is usually served far more quickly than traditional food and in a manageable package.
2단계 (2)	Supporting Sentence (2)	*relatively cheap cost* The relatively cheap cost of fast food also has an appeal for lower-income individuals and so fewer members of society suffer from hunger.
3단계 (2)	Supporting Sentence or Specific Example (2)	*traditional food is well over double the price of fast food* In most cases, a traditional food serving is well over double the price of a meal deal in a fast food chain store.

Body 1

There is no doubt that fast food is more convenient and cheaper. The desire to eat within a limited period and to avoid waiting too long reflects the impatience of modern people who rush to spend time on work or other pursuits. It is usually served far more quickly than traditional food and in a manageable package. The relatively cheap cost of fast food also has an appeal for lower-income individuals and so fewer members of society suffer from hunger. In most cases, a traditional food serving is well over double the price of a meal deal in a fast food chain store.

there is no doubt that S+V : that 이하에 대한 의심의 여지가 없다, that 이하의 말이 사실이라는 뜻
within a limited period : 제한된 시간 내에
reflect : 반영하다
the impatience of modern people : 현대인들의 성급함
pursuits : 취미, pursuit가 복수일 경우, pastime, hobby와 동의어로 캠브리지 아이엘츠에 자주 나온다.

far : 훨씬, 비교급 강조
a manageable package : 간편한 포장
lower-income individuals : 저소득 사람들
fewer : 더 거의 없다, few의 비교급
hunger : 배고픔, 기아
serving : = portion, 1회 제공량
well over : ~넘는

우리말 해석

패스트푸드가 더 편리하고 더 저렴하다는 것에는 의심의 여지가 없다. 제한된 시간 내에 먹고 장시간 기다리는 것을 피하고자 하는 욕구는 일이나 다른 취미에 시간을 쓰는 데 서두르는 현대인들의 성급함을 반영한다. 이것은 보통 간편한 포장으로 전통 음식보다 훨씬 더 빨리 제공된다. 패스트푸드의 상대적으로 저렴한 비용 또한 저소득 사람들에게 호소력이 있어서 배고픔으로 고통 겪는 사람들이 더 거의 없을 것이다. 대부분의 경우, 전통적 음식 한 그릇은 패스트푸드 체인점의 음식 값의 두 배가 넘는다.

4단계　본론 2 (Body 2) (21~30분) : 내 의견 = Agree (개인과 사회에 부정적인 영향을 미친다)

Question	In modern society traditional food is being replaced by fast food. This trend has a negative impact on both individuals and society. Do you agree or disagree with this statement?

Body 2는 1단계에서 브레인스토밍한 'Agree'의 주장을 바탕으로 작성한다.

1단계	Topic Sentence	Nevertheless, we should not overlook its drawbacks.
2단계 (1)	Supporting Sentence (1)	*poor health* The greater cost of fast food in the form of poor health is significant.
3단계 (1)	Supporting Sentence or Specific Example (1)	*contribute to the development of obesity and diseases* Most dieticians and medical professionals would agree that the harmful food additives, trans fats and cooking methods associated with fast food contribute to the development of obesity and diseases in people.
2단계 (2)	Supporting Sentence (2)	*threaten traditional culture* Then there is the globalisation of fast food, which threatens traditional culture.
3단계 (2)	Supporting Sentence or Specific Example (2)	*Food is an expression of a culture's characteristic* Food is often seen as an expression of a culture's characteristic. *the success of international fast food brands poses a threat to a country's identity* Therefore the success of international fast food brands poses a threat to a country's identity when our tastes start to move away from traditional food and towards the easy, quick fix of a fast food meal.

Body 2

Nevertheless, we should not overlook its drawbacks. The greater cost of fast food in the form of poor health is significant. Most dieticians and medical professionals would agree that the harmful food additives, trans fats and cooking methods associated with fast food contribute to the development of obesity and diseases in people. Then there is the globalisation of fast food, which threatens traditional culture. Food is often seen as an expression of a culture's characteristic. Therefore the success of international fast food brands poses a threat to a country's identity when our tastes start to move away from traditional food and towards the easy, quick fix of a fast food meal.

overlook : 간과하다
drawbacks : 단점
in the form of : ~한 형태로
harmful food additives : 해로운 식품 첨가물
trans fats : 트랜스 지방
threaten : 위협하다
traditional culture : 전통 문화

characteristic : 특성
pose a threat : 위협이 되다
a country's identity : 한 나라의 정체성
tastes : 입맛
move away from : ~에서 멀어지다
towards : ~로 향하여
quick fix : 일시적인 해결책, 여기서는 '때우기 식'으로 의역했다.

우리말 해석

그럼에도 불구하고, 우리는 패스트푸드의의 단점을 간과해서는 안 된다. 나쁜 건강상태라는 형태로 지불해야 하는 패스트푸드의 대가는 더 크다. 대부분의 영양사들과 의학 교수들은 패스트푸드에 관계된 해로운 식품 첨가물, 트랜스 지방과 조리방법이 사람들의 비만과 질병 발달에 기여한다는 점에 동의할 것이다. 이 밖에도, 패스트푸드의 세계화가 있는데, 이것은 전통 문화를 위협한다. 음식은 종종 어떠한 문화의 특성을 표현하는 것으로 보여진다. 그러므로 우리의 입맛이 전통 음식을 멀리하기 시작하고 간편하고 때우기 식의 패스트푸드 음식으로 향할 때, 세계적 패스트푸드 브랜드의 성공은 한 나라의 정체성에 위협이 된다.

5 단계 결론 (Conclusion) (31~35분) : 본문에 제시한 내 주장 요약하며 다시 한 번 강조

Question	In modern society traditional food is being replaced by fast food. This trend has a negative impact on both individuals and society. Do you agree or disagree with this statement?

결론 작성 시, 먼저 문제 유형을 파악한 후, 'Conclusion Template'의 표현을 인용한다. (See p58)

문제 유형 파악	1-1) Do you agree or disagree? 유형
Conclusion Template 인용	For the reasons mentioned above, I totally agree(disagree) with the opinion because… 본문에 제시한 내 주장 간단히 요약

결론을 작성하기 전, 서론과 본문 2에서 Agree (전통 음식이 패스트푸드에 의해 대체되고 있는 경향은 개인과 사회에 부정적인 영향을 미친다) 라고 했는지 다시 한 번 확인하자!

> **Conclusion**
> **For the reasons mentioned above, I totally agree that** we do need to be wary about the negative impact of fast food **because of** the threat to both individual health and our cultural heritage.

* 상황에 따라 템플릿을 살짝 변형해도 좋다.

be wary about : ~에 대해 경계하다, 조심하다
cultural heritage : 문화 유산

> **우리말 해석**
> 위에서 언급한 이런 이유들 때문에 나는 개인의 건강과 우리의 문화 유산 모두를 위협하는 패스트푸드의 부정적 영향에 대해 경계해야 할 필요가 있다는 의견에 완전히 동의한다.

6 단계 교정 (Self-correction) (36~40분) : 내용의 일관성 및 문법 검토

다음 Body 2의 내용을 교정해 보자. 틀린 부분은 총 몇 개일까?

교정 전 (직접 문장 부호를 이용하여 틀린 부분을 교정해 보자.)

Nevertheless, We should not overlook its drawbacks.

The greater cost of fast food on the form of poor health are significant. Most dietician and medical professionals would disagree that the harmful food additives, trans fats and cooking methods associated with fast food contribute to the development of obesity and diseases in people. Then There was the globalisation of fast food, which threatens traditional culture.

Food is often seen as a expression of a culture's characteristic. Therefore the success of international fast food brands pose a threat to a country's identity when our tastes start to move away from traditional food and towards the easy, quick fix of a fast food meal.

교정

Nevertheless, We should not overlook its drawbacks.

The greater cost of fast food on the form of poor health are significant. Most dietician and medical professionals would disagree that the harmful food additives, trans fats and cooking methods associated with fast food contribute to the development of obesity and diseases in people. Then There was the globalisation of fast food, which threatens traditional culture. Food is often seen as a expression of a culture's characteristic. Therefore the success of international fast food brands pose a threat to a country's identity when our tastes start to move away from traditional food and towards the easy, quick fix of a fast food meal.

1. W → w : 콤마(,) 다음에는 소문자로 쓴다.
2. 붙여쓰기 : 위의 글은 Body 2 단락이다. 단락이 바뀌지 않는 한, 줄을 바꿔 쓰지 않는다.
3. on → in : in the form of는 '~한 형태로'라는 뜻
4. are → is : 주어인 cost가 단수이므로 단수 동사 is를 쓴다.
5. dietician → dieticians : most 다음에 셀 수 있는 명사가 올 경우, 복수형으로 쓴다.
6. disagree → agree : 동의한다고 해야 논리에 맞다. 이걸 놓치면 절대 안 된다!
7. T → t : 갑자기 대문자를 문장 중간에 쓰지 않는다(고유명사 예외).
8. was → is : 현재 사실은 현재 시제로 쓴다.
9. a → an : 모음(a/i/u/e/o)으로 발음이 시작되는 단어 expression[ɪkspreʃn] 앞에는 a가 아닌 an으로 쓰고 말한다.
10. pose → poses : 주어인 success가 단수이므로 단수 동사 poses를 쓴다.

틀린 개수 : 총 10개

Sample Answer

> **Question**
>
> In modern society traditional food is being replaced by fast food. This trend has a negative impact on both individuals and society. Do you agree or disagree with this statement?

Nowadays we are surrounded by fast food outlets, suggesting their growing popularity at the expense of nutrient-rich traditional food. Some might find these newer options to be more attractive, but we should all be aware of the health and cultural costs that come with them.

There is no doubt that fast food is more convenient and cheaper. The desire to eat within a limited period and to avoid waiting too long reflects the impatience of modern people who rush to spend time on work or other pursuits. It is usually served far more quickly than traditional food and in a manageable package. The relatively cheap cost of fast food also has an appeal for lower-income individuals and so fewer members of society suffer from hunger. In most cases, a traditional food serving is well over double the price of a meal deal in a fast food chain store.

Nevertheless, we should not overlook its drawbacks. The greater cost of fast food in the form of poor health is significant. Most dieticians and medical professionals would agree that the harmful food additives, trans fats and cooking methods associated with fast food contribute to the development of obesity and diseases in people. Then there is the globalisation of fast food, which threatens traditional culture. Food is often seen as an expression of a culture's characteristic. Therefore the success of international fast food brands poses a threat to a country's identity when our tastes start to move away from traditional food and towards the easy, quick fix of a fast food meal.

For the reasons mentioned above, I totally agree that we do need to be wary about the negative impact of fast food because of the threat to both individual health and our cultural heritage.

word counts : 293 words

우리말 해석

오늘날 우리는 영양가 풍부한 전통음식을 희생시키고, 높아져가는 인기를 시사하고 있는 패스트푸드 상점들에 둘러싸여 있다. 어떤 사람들은 이러한 보다 새로운 선택권이 더 매력적이라고 여길지도 모르지만, 우리는 그것들과 동반한 건강과 문화적 비용에 대해 바로 알고 있어야 한다.

패스트푸드가 더 편리하고 더 저렴하다는 것에는 의심의 여지가 없다. 제한된 시간 내에 먹고 장시간 기다리는 것을 피하고자 하는 욕구는 일이나 다른 취미에 시간을 쓰는 데 서두르는 현대인들의 성급함을 반영한다. 이것은 보통 간편한 포장으로 전통 음식보다 훨씬 더 빨리 제공된다. 패스트푸드의 상대적으로 저렴한 비용 또한 저소득 사람들에게 호소력이 있어서 배고픔으로 고통 겪는 사람들이 더 거의 없을 것이다. 대부분의 경우, 전통적 음식 한 그릇은 패스트푸드 체인점의 음식값의 두 배가 넘는다.

그럼에도 불구하고, 우리는 패스트푸드의의 단점을 간과해서는 안 된다. 나쁜 건강상태라는 형태로 지불해야 하는 패스트푸드의 대가는 더 크다. 대부분의 영양사들과 의학 교수들은 패스트푸드에 관계된 해로운 식품 첨가물, 트랜스 지방과 조리방법이 사람들의 비만과 질병 발달에 기여한다는 점에 동의할 것이다. 이 밖에도, 패스트푸드의 세계화가 있는데, 이것은 전통 문화를 위협한다. 음식은 종종 어떠한 문화의 특성을 표현하는 것으로 보여진다. 그러므로 우리의 입맛이 전통 음식을 멀리하기 시작하고 간편하고 때우기 식의 패스트푸드 음식으로 향할 때, 세계적 패스트푸드 브랜드의 성공은 한 나라의 정체성에 위협이 된다.

위에서 언급한 이런 이유들 때문에 나는 개인의 건강과 우리의 문화 유산 모두를 위협하는 패스트푸드의 부정적 영향에 대해 경계해야 할 필요가 있다는 의견에 완전히 동의한다.

불법 Review

앞에서 배운 내용을 바탕으로 다음 빈칸을 영어로 작성해 보자.

Nowadays we _____ (1. 둘러싸여 있다) fast food outlets, suggesting their growing popularity _____ (2. ~을 희생시키고) nutrient-rich traditional food. Some might find these newer options to be _____ (3. 좀 더 매력적인), but we should all be aware of the health and cultural costs that _____ (4. 동반한) them.

_____ (5. 의심의 여지가 없다) fast food is _____ (6. 더 편리하고 더 저렴한). The desire to eat within a limited period and to avoid waiting too long reflects the impatience of modern people who rush to spend time on work or _____ (7. 다른 취미). It is usually served far more quickly than traditional food and in a manageable package. The relatively cheap cost of fast food also has an appeal for _____ (8. 저소득 사람들) and so fewer members of society _____ (9. 배고픔으로 고통 겪다). In most cases, a traditional food serving is well over double the price of a meal deal in a fast food chain store.

Nevertheless, we should not overlook its drawbacks. The greater cost of fast food _____ (10. ~라는 형태로) poor health is significant. Most dieticians and medical professionals would agree that _____ (11. 해로운 식품 첨가물), trans fats and cooking methods associated with fast food contribute to the development of obesity and diseases in people. Then there is the globalisation of fast food, which threatens traditional culture. Food is often seen as an expression of a culture's characteristic. Therefore the success of international fast food brands poses a threat to a country's identity when our tastes start to _____ (12. 멀리하다) traditional food and towards the easy, quick fix of a fast food meal.

For the reasons mentioned above, I totally agree that we do need to _____ (13. 경계하다) the negative impact of fast food because of the threat to both individual health and our cultural heritage.

Answer 1. are surrounded by / 2. at the expense of / 3. more attractive / 4. come with
5. There is no doubt that / 6. more convenient and cheaper / 7. other pursuits
8. lower-income individuals / 9. suffer from hunger / 10. in the form of
11. the harmful food additives / 12. move away from / 13. be wary about

STEP5 Day 3 Health & Food 불법 포인트 정리

건강하지 않는 식단	an unhealthy diet	전통 음식	traditional food / food made at home / slow food / traditionally prepared meals / handmade food
원인이 되다	cause	패스트푸드	fast food / convenience food / pre-prepared meal / ready-to-eat food / processed food
비만	obesity	~에 부정적인 영향을 미치다	have a negative impact on
당뇨	diabetes	오늘날에는	nowadays
성인병	adult diseases	~에 둘러싸여 있다	be surrounded by
증가하고 있다	be on the increase	~을 희생하고, ~을 비용으로	at the expense of / at the cost of / at the price of
간편식	pre-prepared meals	영양가 풍부한	nutrient-rich
함유되어 있다	contain	~을 알다	be aware of
건강한 몸	a healthy body	동반하다	come with
유지하다	maintain	that 이하에 대한 의심의 여지가 없다	there is no doubt that S+V
필수인	essential	제한된 시간 내에	within a limited period
칼로리를 태우다	burn calories	반영하다	reflect
뼈와 근육	bones and muscles	현대인들의 성급함	the impatience of modern people
적어도	at least	취미	pursuits
주로 앉아서 생활하다	lead a sedentary life	훨씬	far
야외 스포츠	outdoor sports	간편한 포장	a manageable package
직장에서	in the workplace	저소득 사람들	lower-income individuals
집에서	at home	더 거의 없다	fewer
과체중의	overweight	배고픔	hunger
납세자	taxpayers	1회 제공량	serving / portion
학교 시간표	school timetables	~넘는	well over
금지하다	ban	간과하다	overlook
영양학자	nutritionists / dieticians	단점	drawbacks
5인분	five portions	~한 형태로	in the form of
권하다	recommend	해로운 식품 첨가물	harmful food additives
민간 의료	private healthcare	트랜스 지방	trans fats
경제적으로 여유가 있다	afford	위협하다	threaten
수술	operations	전통 문화	traditional culture
진료예약	appointments	특성	characteristic
대기 명단	waiting lists	위협이 되다	pose a threat
국민 건강 서비스	national health service	한 나라의 정체성	a country's identity
거주자	residents	입맛	tastes
무상 의료	free healthcare	~에서 멀어지다	move away from
유기농 식품	organic foods	~로 향하여	towards
화학 비료	chemical fertilizers	일시적인 해결책	quick fix
살충제	pesticides	~에 대해 경계하다	be wary about
유전자 조작	genetic modification	문화 유산	cultural heritage

Day 4 Lifestyles & Leisure Activities

생활방식과 여가활동

Question

Some say that the government should make a decision about people's lifestyle. Others argue that individuals should make their own decisions about it. Discuss both views and give your own opinion.

어떤 사람들은 정부가 개인의 생활방식을 결정해야 한다고 말한다. 다른 사람들은 개인 스스로가 그것을 정해야 한다고 주장한다. 양쪽의 견해를 논하고 당신의 주장을 제시하라.

 빈출 문제

1. Some say that children are given too much free time. They argue that this time should be used to do more schoolwork. To what extent do you agree or disagree with this opinion?

2. Some people think that children's leisure activities must be educational, otherwise these activities are a waste of time. To what extent do you agree or disagree with this opinion?

3. Happiness is a very important factor in our lives. Why is it difficult to define? What factors are important in achieving happiness?

4. Some people believe that personal happiness is directly related to money. Others argue that it depends on other factors. Discuss both of the views and give your own opinion.

1. 어떤 사람들은 아이들에게 자유 시간이 너무 많이 주어졌다고 말한다. 그들은 이러한 시간을 학교 공부에 더 많이 할애해야 한다고 주장한다. 당신은 이 의견에 얼마만큼 동의하는가? 또는 동의하지 않는가?

2. 어떤 사람들은 아이들의 여가활동이 반드시 교육적이어야 하고, 그렇지 않으면 이러한 활동이 시간 낭비라고 생각한다. 당신은 이 의견에 얼마만큼 동의하는가? 또는 동의하지 않는가?

3. 행복은 우리의 삶에 매우 중요한 요소이다. 왜 이것은 정의하기 어려운가? 행복해지는 데 어떤 요소들이 필요한가?

4. 어떤 사람들은 개인의 행복이 돈과 직결된다고 믿는다. 반면 이것이 다른 요소에 달려있다고 주장하는 사람들도 있다. 양쪽의 견해를 논하고 당신의 주장을 제시하라.

 브레인스토밍

1) 우리는 부와 물질적 소유를 행복과 성공에 연관시킨다.
   부 : wealth / 물질적 소유 : material possessions / A와 B를 연관시키다 : connect A with B

2) 행복이라는 것은 다른 사람들에게 다른 것을 의미한다. (의역 : 행복이라고 하는 것은 사람에 따라 다르다.)

3) 취미, 스포츠 그리고 게임은 재미와 즐거움의 원천이다.
   ~의 원천 : a source of

4) 바쁜 현대 생활방식은 우리가 쉴 시간이 줄어들었다는 것을 의미한다.
   바쁜 현대 생활방식 : busy modern lifestyles

5) 주요 도시의 사람들은 엄격한 마감일과 함께 오랜 시간 일한다.
   엄격한 마감일 : strict deadlines

6) 스트레스를 완화하고 줄이는 데 가장 좋은 방법은 충분한 잠을 자고 여가시간을 최우선으로 하는 것이다.
   충분한 잠을 자다 : get sufficient sleep / ~을 최우선으로 하다 : make ~ a priority

7) 만약 학교가 심리학자를 고용하기 시작한다면, 그들은 학생들이 시험 스트레스에 대처하는 것을 도울 수 있을 것이다.
   심리학자 : psychologists / 대처하다 : cope with, deal with, handle

8) 근무시간과 여가나 가족을 위한 시간의 균형을 맞추는 것은 중요하다.
   A와 B의 균형을 맞추다 : strike a balance between A and B

9) 너무 많은 업무는 스트레스와 나쁜 건강이라는 결과를 낳을 수 있기 때문에, 어떤 사람들은 파트타임으로 일하거나 탄력적인 근무 시간을 갖는다.
   결과를 낳다 : result in / 탄력적인 근무 시간 : flexible working hours

10) 어떤 심리학자들은 가장 강력한 경쟁심을 제공하는 것은 스포츠가 아니라 컴퓨터 게임이라고 말한다.
    가장 강력한 경쟁심 : the strongest sense of competition / A가 아니라 B다 : not A but B

11) 가장 행복한 사람은 취미로부터 생계를 유지하는 방법을 찾은 사람들일지도 모른다.
    생계를 유지하다 : make a living

12) 일상생활은 오늘날 과거보다 훨씬 더 복잡하다.
    일상 생활 : everyday life / 복잡한 : complicated

13) 현대인은 그들의 성공을 그들이 소유한 물질적인 것들로 측정하므로 이러한 사치품들을 갈망하는 것이 그들이 과거에 비해 훨씬 더 열심히 일하게 동기부여 하는 것이다.
    측정하다 : measure / 사치품 : luxuries / 동기부여 하다 : motivate

14) 명상은 스트레스 증상을 해소하는 좋은 방법인데, 이것은 스트레스 받는 상황에서 사람들이 진정하고 한 걸음 물러설 수 있게 도와줄 수 있기 때문이다.

명상 : meditation / 스트레스 증상을 해소하다 : relieve the symptoms of stress / 진정하다 : calm down

한 걸음 물러서다 : take a step back

---

15) 삶에 대한 긍정적인 시각을 유지하는 것은 행복해지는 방법 중의 하나이다.

삶에 대한 긍정적인 시각을 유지하다 : maintain a positive outlook on life

Answer

1) We connect wealth and material possessions with happiness and success.
2) Happiness means different things to different people.
3) Hobbies, sports and games can be a source of fun and enjoyment.
4) Busy modern lifestyles mean we have less time to relax.
5) People in major cities work long hours with strict deadlines.
6) The best way to relax and reduce stress is to get sufficient sleep and make leisure time a priority.
7) If schools start to employ psychologists, they can help students to cope with exam stress.
8) It is important to strike a balance between work time and leisure or family time.
9) As too much work can result in stress and poor health, some people work part-time or have flexible working hours.
10) Some psychologists say that activities providing the strongest sense of competition are not sports, but computer games.
11) The happiest people might be those who have found a way to make a living from their hobby.
12) Everyday life today is much more complicated than in the past.
13) Modern people measure their success by the material things they own so desiring these luxuries is what motivates them to work much harder than in the past.
14) Meditation is a good way to relieve the symptoms of stress because it can help people calm down and take a step back from a stressful situation.
15) Maintaining a positive outlook on life is one of the ways to be happy.

 실전문제

You should spend about 40 minutes on this task.
Write about the following topic :

> Some say that the government should make a decision about people's lifestyle. Others argue that individuals should make their own decisions about it. Discuss both views and give your own opinion.

Give reasons for your answer and include any relevant examples from your own knowledge or experience.

Write at least 250 words.

| 1 단계 | 문제 정독, 문제 유형 파악, 브레인스토밍 (0 ~ 5분) |

> **Question**
> Some say that the government should make a decision about people's lifestyle. Others argue that individuals should make their own decisions about it. Discuss both views and give your own opinion.

문제 정독
어떤 사람들은 정부가 개인의 생활방식을 결정해야 한다고 말한다. 다른 사람들은 개인 스스로가 그것을 정해야 한다고 주장한다. 양쪽의 견해를 논하고 당신의 주장을 제시하라.

some : = some people, 어떤 사람들
make a decision : 결정하다
lifestyle : 생활방식

문제 유형 파악

1-2. Discuss both views and give your own opinion. 유형

Brainstorming

Topic : 개인의 생활방식을 누가 결정해야 하는가?	
Some People : 정부	Others : 개인 스스로
1. 우리가 정치가들 선출 we elect politicians → 정부는 자원들을 할당 the government allocates resources 2. 정부는 특정 제품의 사용을 금하거나 규제 the government prohibits or restricts the use of certain products → 많은 사람들이 특정 약물 사용 규제법 지지 many people support laws that curb the use of certain drugs	1. 인터넷 스파잉(감시)을 포함해 널리 퍼진 스캔들 widely-publicised scandals involving Internet spying → 기술은 정부가 사생활을 침해하는 것을 가능하게 함 technology allows the state to invade privacy 2. 대중들은 기본적 자유권을 잃음 the public lose a sense of basic freedom → 흡연자는 담배를 피우지 못하게 될 때 자유를 느끼지 못함 smokers cannot feel free when they are prevented from smoking

* 아이디어의 수도 같고 영어로 쓸 수 있는 말도 비슷하다면, 좀 더 설득력 있게 논리적으로 접근할 수 있는 쪽을 내 의견으로 한다. 이 에세이에서는 others의 주장, '개인의 생활방식은 개인 스스로 결정해야 한다'를 내 주장으로 삼았다.

2단계 서론 (Introduction) (6~10분) : 두 문장으로 작성

> **Question**
> Some say that the government should make a decision about people's lifestyle. Others argue that individuals should make their own decisions about it. Discuss both views and give your own opinion.

단계	Question	서론 작성
1단계 Paraphrasing	토픽 : Some say that the government should make a decision about people's lifestyle. Others argue that individuals should make their own decisions about it.	Paraphrasing : The government is faced with the challenge of giving people the chance to lead satisfying lives.
2단계 Answering	질문 : Discuss both views and give your own opinion.	Answering : Others에 동의할 경우 Although some think that the government's intervention in our lifestyles is necessary, I would urge officials not to intrude upon people's privacy.

Introduction
The government is faced with the challenge of giving people the chance to lead satisfying lives. Although some think that the government's intervention in our lifestyles is necessary, I would urge officials not to intrude upon people's privacy.

불법 포인트

the government : government를 단수로 쓸 때는 a가 아닌 the라고 반드시 써야 한다. 정부는 한 나라에 하나만 있기 때문이다. 하지만 governments라고 복수로 쓸 경우에는 특정한 정부들을 의미하지 않으면 the를 붙이지 않고 그냥 쓴다.

intervention : 개입, 간섭
urge A to B : A에게 B할 것을 강력히 권고(충고)하다
officials : 정부관리, 공무원
intrude upon one's privacy :
 = invade one's privacy, 사생활을 침해하다

우리말 해석
정부는 사람들에게 만족해 하는 삶을 사는 기회를 제공하는 도전에 직면해 있다. 비록 어떤 사람들은 우리의 생활 방식에 정부의 개입이 필요하다고 생각하지만, 나는 정부관리들이 사람들의 사생활을 침범해서는 안 된다고 강력히 권고한다.

3 단계 본론 1 (Body 1) (11~20분) : 나와 다른 의견 = Some people (개인의 생활방식은 정부가 결정해야 한다)

Question	Some say that the government should make a decision about people's lifestyle. Others argue that individuals should make their own decisions about it. Discuss both views and give your own opinion.

Body 1은 1단계에서 브레인스토밍한 'Some people'의 주장을 바탕으로 작성한다.

1단계	Topic Sentence	There is an opinion that the government should maintain or create a society in which we can both prosper and live peacefully.
2단계 (1)	Supporting Sentence (1)	*we elect politicians* This is because we elect politicians, and therefore we should not be surprised when they come up with policies that have an effect on our lifestyles.
3단계 (1)	Supporting Sentence or Specific Example (1)	*the government allocates resources* For example, by forcing us to pay taxes, the government can allocate resources where they are needed.
2단계 (2)	Supporting Sentence (2)	*the government prohibits or restricts the use of certain products* They might also prohibit or restrict the use of certain products because they are considered unhealthy for society.
3단계 (2)	Supporting Sentence or Specific Example (2)	*many people support laws that curb the use of certain drugs* It is a controversial issue, but many people do support laws that curb the use of certain drugs.

Body 1

There is an opinion that the government should maintain or create a society in which we can both prosper and live peacefully. This is because we elect politicians, and therefore we should not be surprised when they come up with policies that have an effect on our lifestyles. For example, by forcing us to pay taxes, the government can allocate resources where they are needed. They might also prohibit or restrict the use of certain products because they are considered unhealthy for society. It is a controversial issue, but many people do support laws that curb the use of certain drugs.

there is an opinion that S+V : that 이하라는 주장이 있다. 보통 Body 1(상대방의 의견)을 시작할 때 쓰면 좋다.
prosper : 번영하다
elect politicians : 정치가들을 선출하다
come up with : 제시하다, 제안하다
force A to B : A가 B하도록 강요하다

allocate resources : 자원을 할당하다
prohibit : 금지하다
restrict : 제한하다
a controversial issue : 논란이 되는 주제
curb : 규제하다, 억제하다

우리말 해석

정부는 우리가 번영하고 평화롭게 살 수 있는 사회를 유지하거나 만들어야 한다는 주장이 있다. 이것은 우리가 정치가들을 선출하기 때문이고 그러므로 그들이 우리의 생활 방식에 영향을 미치는 정책들을 제시할 때 우리는 놀라서는 안 된다. 예를 들면, 우리에게 세금을 내도록 강요함으로써 정부는 필요한 곳에 자원들을 할당할 수 있다. 정부는 또한 사회에 불건전하게 간주되는 특정 제품의 사용을 금하거나 규제할지도 모른다. 이것은 논란이 되는 주제이나, 많은 사람들이 특정 약물의 사용을 규제하는 법을 지지한다.

4 단계   본론 2 (Body 2) (21~30분) : 내 의견 = Others (개인의 생활방식은 개인 스스로 결정해야 한다)

Question	Some say that the government should make a decision about people's lifestyle. Others argue that individuals should make their own decisions about it. Discuss both views and give your own opinion.

Body 2는 1단계에서 브레인스토밍한 'Others'의 주장을 바탕으로 작성한다.

1단계	Topic Sentence	But the line needs to be drawn somewhere, as an increasing number of us are growing restless over the thought of government control in our lives.
2단계 (1)	Supporting Sentence (1)	*widely-publicised scandals involving Internet spying* Widely-publicised scandals involving Internet spying have fuelled the idea that we need to be more watchful than ever of the government's role.
3단계 (1)	Supporting Sentence or Specific Example (1)	*technology allows the state to invade privacy* The continued improvement of technology is allowing the state to further invade our privacy.
2단계 (2)	Supporting Sentence (2)	*the public lose a sense of basic freedom* Also, the public could lose a sense of basic freedom if legal habits like smoking come under official control.
3단계 (2)	Supporting Sentence or Specific Example (2)	*smokers cannot feel free when they are prevented from smoking* Although the government deciding who can smoke where may lead to overall public health benefits, smokers might complain that they cannot feel free when they are prevented from smoking even in some outdoor areas.

Body 2

But the line needs to be drawn somewhere, as an increasing number of us are growing restless over the thought of government control in our lives. Widely-publicised scandals involving Internet spying have fuelled the idea that we need to be more watchful than ever of the government's role. The continued improvement of technology is allowing the state to further invade our privacy. Also, the public could lose a sense of basic freedom if legal habits like smoking come under official control. Although the government deciding who can smoke where may lead to overall public health benefits, smokers might complain that they cannot feel free when they are prevented from smoking even in some outdoor areas.

draw the line : 한계를 정하다
come under~ : (~의 통제를)받다
restless : 가만있지 못하는, 뒤숭숭한, 여기서는 '불안한'으로 의역했다.
fuel : 부채질하다, 명사로는 '연료'의 뜻, 동사로는 '부채질하다', '연료를 공급하다'라는 뜻이다.

the public : 일반 대중들, the + 형용사 = 복수 명사
a sense of basic freedom : 기본적 자유권
come under official control : 정부의 통제를 받다
outdoor areas : 야외 공간

우리말 해석

그러나 점점 더 많은 사람들은 우리의 삶에 있어 정부의 통제라는 생각 자체에 대해 커지는 불안감이 있기 때문에, 어딘가에는 한계를 정해야 할 필요가 있다. 인터넷 스파잉(감시)을 포함해 널리 퍼진 스캔들은 정부의 역할에 대해 전보다 더 눈여겨 보아야 한다는 생각을 부채질 해 왔다. 지속적인 기술 향상은 정부가 우리의 사생활을 더욱더 침해하는 것을 가능하게 하고 있다. 또한 만약 흡연과 같은 합법적인 습관들이 정부의 통제를 받는다면, 대중들은 기본적 자유권을 잃을 수 있다. 비록 정부가 누가 어디에서 흡연할 수 있는지 결정하는 것은 전반적으로 국민건강에 이점을 가져올 수 있지만, 흡연자들은 일부 야외 공간에서조차 담배를 피우지 못하게 될 때 자유를 느끼지 못하는 것을 불평할지도 모른다.

5 단계 결론 (Conclusion) (31~35분) : 본문에 제시한 내 주장 요약하며 다시 한 번 강조

> **Question**
> Some say that the government should make a decision about people's lifestyle. Others argue that individuals should make their own decisions about it. Discuss both views and give your own opinion.

결론 작성 시, 먼저 문제 유형을 파악한 후, 'Conclusion Template'의 표현을 인용한다. (See p58)

문제 유형 파악	1-2) Discuss both views and give your own opinion.
Conclusion Template 인용	In conclusion, there are convincing arguments both for and against…(토픽), but I am convinced that… 본론에서 제시한 내 주장 간단히 요약

결론을 작성하기 전, 서론과 본론 2에서 others의 의견(개인의 생활방식은 개인 스스로 결정해야 한다)에 동의했는지 다시 한 번 확인하자!

> **Conclusion**
> **In conclusion, there are convincing arguments both for and against** intervention by the government in our lives, **but I am convinced that** we should be able to make our own choices about how we live as long as others are not directly harmed.

make a choice : 선택하다
as long as : ~하는 한

> **우리말 해석**
> 결론적으로, 우리의 삶에 정부가 개입하는 것에 대해 찬성과 반대를 하는 설득력 있는 주장들이 있지만, 나는 다른 사람들이 직접적으로 피해를 받지 않는 한, 우리가 어떻게 살아갈지에 대해 우리 스스로 선택할 수 있어야 한다고 확신한다.

6 단계 교정 (Self-correction) (36~40분) : 내용의 일관성 및 문법 검토

다음 Body 2의 내용을 교정해 보자. 틀린 부분은 총 몇 개일까?

교정 전 (직접 문장 부호를 이용하여 틀린 부분을 교정해 보자.)

But the line needs to be drawn somewhere, as an increasing number of us are growing restless over the thought of goverment control in our live. Widely-publicised scandals involving Internet spying has fuelled the idea that we need to be more watchful then ever of the government's role. The continued improvement of technology are allowing the state for further invade our privacy.

Also, The public could lose a sense of basic freedom if legal habits like smoking comes under official control. Although the government deciding who can smoke where may lead to overall public health benefits, smokers might complain that they can feel free when they are prevented from smoke even in some outdoor areas.

교정

But the line needs to be drawn somewhere, as an increasing number of us are growing restless over the thought of ~~goverment~~ (government) control in our ~~live~~ (lives). Widely-publicised scandals involving Internet spying ~~has~~ (have) fuelled the idea that we need to be more watchful ~~then~~ (than) ever of the government's role. The continued improvement of technology ~~are~~ (is) allowing the state ~~for~~ (to) further invade our privacy. Also, ~~T~~(t)he public could lose a sense of basic freedom if legal habits like smoking ~~comes~~ (come) under official control. Although the government deciding who can smoke where may lead to overall public health benefits, smokers might complain that they ~~can~~ (cannot) feel free when they are prevented from ~~smoke~~ (smoking) even in some outdoor areas.

1. goverment → government : 상당히 많은 학생들이 실수하는 스펠링! n을 빠뜨리지 말자!
2. live → lives : live는 형용사, lives는 명사 life의 복수형. 소유격 our 다음에는 명사를 써야 한다.
3. has → have : 주어는 scandals이므로 복수 조동사인 have를 쓴다.
4. then → than : then은 '그리고 나서', than은 비교급과 함께 사용하는 '~보다'라는 뜻
5. are → is : 주어는 improvement이므로 단수 동사인 is를 쓴다.
6. for → to : allow A to B는 'A가 B하는 것을 허락하다'라는 뜻
7. 붙여쓰기 : 위의 글은 Body 2 단락이다. 단락이 바뀌지 않는 한, 줄을 바꿔 쓰지 않는다.
8. T → t : 콤마(,) 다음에는 소문자로 쓴다.
9. comes → come : 주어는 habits이므로 복수 동사인 come을 쓴다.
10. can → cannot : 흡연자들이 자유를 느낄 수 없다라고 해야 논리에 맞다. 이걸 놓치면 절대 안 된다!
11. smoke → smoking : 전치사 from 다음에는 명사를 쓰는 것이 원칙. 동사가 나온 경우 동사에 ~ing를 붙여 동명사로 만든다.

틀린 개수 : 총 11개

Sample Answer

Question	Some say that the government should make a decision about people's lifestyle. Others argue that individuals should make their own decisions about it. Discuss both views and give your own opinion.

The government is faced with the challenge of giving people the chance to lead satisfying lives. Although some think that the government's intervention in our lifestyles is necessary, I would urge officials not to intrude upon people's privacy.

There is an opinion that the government should maintain or create a society in which we can both prosper and live peacefully. This is because we elect politicians, and therefore we should not be surprised when they come up with policies that have an effect on our lifestyles. For example, by forcing us to pay taxes, the government can allocate resources where they are needed. They might also prohibit or restrict the use of certain products because they are considered unhealthy for society. It is a controversial issue, but many people do support laws that curb the use of certain drugs.

But the line needs to be drawn somewhere, as an increasing number of us are growing restless over the thought of government control in our lives. Widely-publicised scandals involving Internet spying have fuelled the idea that we need to be more watchful than ever of the government's role. The continued improvement of technology is allowing the state to further invade our privacy. Also, the public could lose a sense of basic freedom if legal habits like smoking come under official control. Although the government deciding who can smoke where may lead to overall public health benefits, smokers might complain that they cannot feel free when they are prevented from smoking even in some outdoor areas.

In conclusion, there are convincing arguments both for and against intervention by the government in our lives, but I am convinced that we should be able to make our own choices about how we live as long as others are not directly harmed.

word counts : 297 words

우리말 해석

정부는 사람들에게 만족해 하는 삶을 사는 기회를 제공하는 도전에 직면해 있다. 비록 어떤 사람들은 우리의 생활 방식에 정부의 개입이 필요하다고 생각하지만, 나는 정부관리들이 사람들의 사생활을 침범해서는 안 된다고 강력히 권고한다.

정부는 우리가 번영하고 평화롭게 살 수 있는 사회를 유지하거나 만들어야 한다는 주장이 있다. 이것은 우리가 정치가들을 선출하기 때문이고 그러므로 그들이 우리의 생활 방식에 영향을 미치는 정책들을 제시할 때 우리는 놀라서는 안 된다. 예를 들면, 우리에게 세금을 내도록 강요함으로써 정부는 필요한 곳에 자원들을 할당할 수 있다. 정부는 또한 사회에 불건전하게 간주되는 특정 제품의 사용을 금하거나 규제할지도 모른다. 이것은 논란이 되는 주제이나, 많은 사람들이 특정 약물의 사용을 규제하는 법을 지지한다.

그러나 점점 더 많은 사람들은 우리의 삶에 있어 정부의 통제라는 생각 자체에 대해 커지는 불안감이 있기 때문에, 어딘가에는 한계를 정해야 할 필요가 있다. 인터넷 스파잉(감시)을 포함해 널리 퍼진 스캔들은 정부의 역할에 대해 전보다 더 눈여겨 보아야 한다는 생각을 부채질 해 왔다. 지속적인 기술 향상은 정부가 우리의 사생활을 더욱더 침해하는 것을 가능하게 하고 있다. 또한 만약 흡연과 같은 합법적인 습관들이 정부의 통제를 받는다면, 대중들은 기본적 자유권을 잃을 수 있다. 비록 정부가 누가 어디에서 흡연할 수 있는지 결정하는 것은 전반적으로 국민건강에 이점을 가져올 수 있지만, 흡연자들은 일부 야외 공간에서조차 담배를 피우지 못하게 될 때 자유를 느끼지 못하는 것을 불평할지도 모른다.

결론적으로, 우리의 삶에 정부가 개입하는 것에 대해 찬성과 반대를 하는 설득력 있는 주장들이 있지만, 나는 다른 사람들이 직접적으로 피해를 받지 않는 한, 우리가 어떻게 살아갈지에 대해 우리 스스로 선택할 수 있어야 한다고 확신한다.

불법 Review

앞에서 배운 내용을 바탕으로 다음 빈칸을 영어로 작성해 보자.

The government is faced with the challenge of giving people the chance to _____ (1. 만족스러운 삶을 살다). Although some think that the government's intervention in our lifestyles is necessary, I would urge officials not to _____ (2. 사람들의 사생활을 침범하다).

_____ (3. that 이하라는 주장이 있다) the government should maintain or create a society in which we can both prosper and live peacefully. This is because we elect politicians, and therefore we should not be surprised when they _____ (4. 정책을 제시하다) that have an effect on our lifestyles. For example, by forcing us to pay taxes, the government can allocate resources where they are needed. They might also prohibit or restrict the use of certain products because they are considered unhealthy for society. _____ (5. 이것은 논란이 되는 주제이다), but many people do support laws that curb the use of certain drugs.

But the line needs to be drawn somewhere, as an increasing number of us are growing restless over the thought of government control in our lives. Widely-publicised scandals involving Internet spying have fuelled the idea that we need to be more watchful than ever of _____ (6. 정부의 역할). _____ (7. 지속적인 기술 향상) is allowing the state to further invade our privacy. Also, _____ (8. 대중들) could lose a sense of basic freedom if legal habits like smoking _____ (9. 정부의 통제를 받다). Although the government deciding who can smoke where may lead to overall public health benefits, smokers might complain that they cannot feel free when they are prevented from smoking even _____ (10. 일부 야외 공간에서).

In conclusion, there are convincing arguments both for and against intervention by the government in our lives, but I am convinced that we should be able to make our own choices about how we live _____ (11. ~하는 한) others are not directly harmed.

Answer 1. lead satisfying lives / 2. intrude upon people's privacy / 3. There is an opinion that
4. come up with policies / 5. It is a controversial issue / 6. the government's role
7. The continued improvement of technology / 8. the public / 9. come under official control
10. in some outdoor areas / 11. as long as

Day 4 Lifestyles & Leisure Activities 불법 포인트 정리

부	wealth	결정하다	make a decision
물질적 소유	material possessions	생활방식	lifestyle
A와 B를 연관시키다	connect A with B	개입, 간섭	intervention
~의 원천	a source of	A에게 B할 것을 강력히 권고(충고)하다	urge A to B
바쁜 현대 생활방식	busy modern lifestyles	정부관리, 공무원	officials
엄격한 마감일	strict deadlines	사생활을 침해하다	intrude upon one's privacy / invade one's privacy
충분한 잠을 자다	get sufficient sleep	that 이하라는 주장이 있다	there is an opinion that S+V
~을 최우선으로 하다	make ~ a priority	번영하다	prosper
심리학자	psychologists	정치가들을 선출하다	elect politicians
대처하다	cope with, deal with, handle	제시하다, 제안하다	come up with
A와 B의 균형을 맞추다	strike a balance between A and B	A가 B하도록 강요하다	force A to B
결과를 낳다	result in	자원을 할당하다	allocate resources
탄력적인 근무 시간	flexible working hours	금지하다	prohibit
가장 강력한 경쟁심	the strongest sense of competition	제한하다	restrict
A가 아니라 B다	not A but B	논란이 되는 주제	a controversial issue
생계를 유지하다	make a living	규제하다, 억제하다	curb
일상 생활	everyday life	한계를 정하다	draw the line
복잡한	complicated	(~의 통제를)받다	come under~
측정하다	measure	가만있지 못하는, 뒤숭숭한	restless
사치품	luxuries	부채질하다	fuel
동기부여 하다	motivate	일반 대중들	the public
명상	meditation	기본적 자유권	a sense of basic freedom
스트레스 증상을 해소하다	relieve the symptoms of stress	정부의 통제를 받다	come under official control
진정하다	calm down	야외 공간	outdoor areas
한 걸음 물러서다	take a step back	선택하다	make a choice
삶에 대한 긍정적인 시각을 유지하다	maintain a positive outlook on life	~하는 한	as long as

Day 5 Student Life

Question	University graduates should be paid more money than less educated people. This is because they should pay the full cost of their education. Do you agree or disagree with this statement? 대학 졸업생들은 교육을 덜 받은 사람들보다 더 많은 돈을 받아야 한다. 왜냐하면 그들은 교육비 전액을 지불해야 하기 때문이다. 당신은 이 말에 동의하는가? 또는 동의하지 않는가?

 빈출 문제

1. In modern society, secondary schools should teach science and technology rather than history and art which are useless and boring. Do you agree or disagree with this statement?

2. Some people say that studying at university is the best route to a successful career, while others believe that it is better to get a job straight after finishing high school. Discuss both views and give your opinion.

3. Today schools are facing severe problems with student behaviour. What do you think the reasons are? What can you suggest as a solution?

4. More and more students are choosing to study at universities in English speaking countries. Do the benefits of studying abroad outweigh its drawbacks?

1. 현대 사회에서 중고등학교는 쓸모 없고 지루한 역사와 예술보다는 과학과 기술을 가르쳐야 한다. 당신은 이 말에 동의하는가? 또는 동의하지 않는가?

2. 어떤 사람들은 대학에서 공부하는 것이 성공적인 경력을 위한 가장 좋은 길이라고 말하는 반면, 고등학교를 마친 후에 바로 일자리를 얻는 것이 더 낫다고 생각하는 사람들도 있다. 양쪽의 견해를 논하고 당신의 주장을 제시하라.

3. 오늘날 학교들은 학생의 행동과 관련하여 심각한 문제에 직면해 있다. 원인들은 무엇이라고 생각하는가? 해결책으로 무엇을 제시할 수 있는가?

4. 점점 더 많은 학생들이 영어권 나라의 대학에서 공부하는 것을 선택하고 있다. 해외 유학의 장점이 단점보다 더 많은가?

 브레인스토밍

1) 학교는 젊은 사람들에게 관용과 나눔같은 도덕적 가치를 가르치는 것을 목표로 해야 한다.
   관용과 나눔 : tolerance and sharing / 도덕적 가치 : moral values

2) 점점 더 많은 학생들이 선진국에 있는 일류 대학에 입학하기를 원한다.
   선진국 : developed countries / 일류 대학 : a prestigious university

3) 세계화 시대에 해외에서 얻은 자격증들은 더 좋은 취업 기회로의 문을 열어줄 수 있다.
   세계화 시대에 : in the era of globalisation / 자격증 : qualifications / 취업 기회 : job opportunities

4) 해외에서 사는 것은 학생들의 시야를 넓히고 그들을 좀 더 독립적으로 만든다.
   시야를 넓히다 : broaden one's horizons / 독립적인 : independent

5) 해외에서 살고 공부하는 것은 어려울 수 있는데 학생들이 비자 신청과 같은 서류 작업에 어려움을 갖기 때문이다.
   비자 신청 : visa applications / 서류 작업 : paperwork

6) 언어 장벽은 외국인 학생들이 직면한 가장 심각한 문제 중의 하나이다.
　　언어 장벽 : the language barrier / 외국인 학생들 : foreign students

7) 낯선 문화에서 혼자 사는 것은 향수병을 일으킬 수 있다.
　　낯선 : unfamiliar / 혼자 사는 것 : living alone / 향수병 : homesickness

8) 기술은 수업을 훨씬 더 흥미롭게 만드는 강력한 도구이다.
　　강력한 도구 : a powerful tool

9) 학생들은 인터넷의 출현 덕택에 언제 어디서든 그들이 원할 때 공부할 수 있다.
　　인터넷의 출현 : the emergence of the Internet / 덕택에 : thanks to

10) 젊은 학습자들은 컴퓨터에 너무 많이 의존하므로 그들 중의 일부는 기본적인 읽고 쓰는 능력이 능숙하지 않다.
　　기본적인 읽고 쓰는 능력 : basic literacy skills / 능숙한 : proficient

11) 학교는 전통적인 교수법에 최신 컴퓨터 기술 사용을 보충해야 한다.
　　전통적인 교수법 : traditional teaching methods / 최신 컴퓨터 기술 : the latest computer technology
　　보충하다 : supplement

12) 후진국에서는 문맹률이 종종 높은데 대부분의 아이들이 어린 나이부터 일을 해야 하기 때문이다.
　　후진국 : in underdeveloped countries / 문맹률 : illiteracy rates / 어린 나이부터 : from an early age

13) 인터넷은 학생들이 지식과 정보의 세계를 경험하게 할 수 있다.
　　지식과 정보의 세계 : a world of knowledge and information / A에게 B를 경험하게 하다 : expose A to B

14) 학생들이 성취하는 교육 수준과 그들의 경제적 미래 사이에는 직접적인 상관관계가 있다.
   교육 수준 : the level of education / 직접적인 상관관계 : a direct correlation

15) 학생들을 억지로 교실에 앉아있게 하는 것 대신에, 적절하고 흥미로운 수업 활동을 하는 학교를 만드는 데 힘과 자원이 사용되어야 한다.
   A에게 억지로 B하게 하다 : force A to B / 수업 활동 : coursework

Answer

1) Schools should aim to teach young people moral values such as tolerance and sharing.
2) More and more students want to attend a prestigious university in developed countries.
3) In the era of globalisation, qualifications gained abroad can open the door to better job opportunities.
4) Living abroad broadens students' horizons and makes them more independent.
5) Living and studying abroad can be difficult because students have problems with paperwork such as visa applications.
6) The language barrier is one of the most significant problems faced by foreign students.
7) Living alone in an unfamiliar culture can cause homesickness.
8) Technology is a powerful tool to make lessons much more interesting.
9) Students can study whenever and wherever they want thanks to the emergence of the Internet.
10) Young learners rely too much on computers, therefore some of them are not proficient in basic literacy skills.
11) Schools should supplement traditional teaching methods with the use of the latest computer technology.
12) In underdeveloped countries, illiteracy rates are often high because most children have to work from an early age.
13) The Internet can expose students to a world of knowledge and information.
14) There is a direct correlation between the level of education students achieve and their economic future.
15) Instead of forcing students to sit in a classroom, energy and resources should be used to create schools with relevant and interesting coursework.

 실전문제

You should spend about 40 minutes on this task.
Write about the following topic :

> University graduates should be paid more money than less educated people. This is because they should pay the full cost of their education. Do you agree or disagree with this statement?

Give reasons for your answer and include any relevant examples from your own knowledge or experience.

Write at least 250 words.

 **1 단계** 문제 정독, 문제 유형 파악, 브레인스토밍 (0 ~ 5분)

Question	University graduates should be paid more money than less educated people. This is because they should pay the full cost of their education. Do you agree or disagree with this statement?

문제 정독
대학 졸업생들은 교육을 덜 받은 사람들보다 더 많은 돈을 받아야 한다. 왜냐하면 그들은 교육비 전액을 지불해야 하기 때문이다. 당신은 이 말에 동의하는가? 또는 동의하지 않는가?

university graduates : 대학 졸업생들
be paid : (돈을) 받다

* opinion VS statement
Do you agree or disagree with this opinion?은 **어떤 사람의 주장**(주로 some people로 시작)에 동의하는지 여부를 묻는 문제이고, Do you agree or disagree with this statement?는 **어떤 말**에 동의하는지 여부를 묻는 문제이다. 다시 말해 문제가 some people로 시작하면 opinion, 사람 없이 말이 나오면 statement이다.

문제 유형 파악
1-1. Do you agree or disagree? 유형

Brainstorming

Topic : 대학 졸업생들은 교육을 덜 받은 사람들보다 더 많은 돈을 받아야 한다.	
Agree : 대학 졸업생이 더 많은 돈을 받아야 한다.	**Disagree** : 반드시 대학 졸업생이 더 많은 돈을 받아야 하는 것은 아니다.
1. 대학교육을 대체할 수 없는 특정 분야 special fields in which there is no substitute for a university education → 의사들은 비용이 많이 들어가는 공부를 수년간 해야 함 medical doctors need to undergo years of costly study	1. 수년간의 근무 경력은 훨씬 더 가치 있을 수 있음 years of work experience can be even more valuable → 고용주들은 고도로 숙련되고 특별히 훈련된 사람들을 선호함 employers prefer highly skilled and specially trained people 2. 고등 교육을 받은 전문가들은 노동 시장의 단지 일부만을 구성함 highly educated professionals make up only a fraction of the labour market → 숙련된 직원들이 가장 수요가 많음 skilled workforces are most in demand

* Disagree에 대한 아이디어가 더 많으므로, 이 에세이에서는 Disagree, '반드시 대학 졸업생이 더 많은 돈을 받아야 하는 것은 아니다.'를 내 주장으로 삼았다.
** 여기서 잠깐! Disagree의 주장은 '대학을 가지 못한 사람들이 대학 졸업생보다 더 많은 돈을 받아야 한다'가 아니라, '반드시 대학 졸업생이 대학을 가지 못한 사람들 보다 더 많이 받아야 하는 것은 아니다.'라는 것에 주의하자! 다시 말해 '월급의 기준은 대학 졸업장이 아니라 실력이다'가 Disagree의 주된 논지이다.

2단계 서론 (Introduction) (6~10분) : 두 문장으로 작성

Question	University graduates should be paid more money than less educated people. This is because they should pay the full cost of their education. Do you agree or disagree with this statement?

단계	Question	서론 작성
1단계 Paraphrasing	**토픽 :** University graduates should be paid more money than less educated people. This is because they should pay the full cost of their education.	**Paraphrasing :** It might seem obvious that a university graduate commands a bigger salary than someone who starts working earlier because of the expense of a higher education.
2단계 Answering	**질문 :** Do you agree or disagree with this statement?	**Answering : Disagree일 경우** Although rewards for expertise in certain fields can be justified, we should not overlook the skills acquired outside of universities.

Introduction

It might seem obvious that a university graduate commands a bigger salary than someone who starts working earlier because of the expense of a higher education. Although rewards for expertise in certain fields can be justified, we should not overlook the skills acquired outside of universities.

command : 받다
a higher education : 고등 교육
expertise : 전문 지식

overlook : 간과하다
acquire : 습득하다

우리말 해석

대학 졸업생들이 고등 교육 비용 때문에 더 일찍 일을 시작하는 사람보다 더 많은 월급을 받는 것은 당연하게 보일지도 모른다. 비록 특정 분야에서 전문 지식에 대한 보상은 정당화 될 수 있지만, 우리는 대학교 이외의 곳에서 습득한 기술을 간과해서는 안 된다.

3 단계   본론 1 (Body 1) (11~20분) : 나와 다른 의견 = Agree (대학 졸업생이 더 많은 돈을 받아야 한다)

Question	University graduates should be paid more money than less educated people. This is because they should pay the full cost of their education. Do you agree or disagree with this statement?

Body 1은 1단계에서 브레인스토밍한 'Agree'의 주장을 바탕으로 작성한다.

1단계	Topic Sentence	Some people say that the salaries of well-educated people should be much higher than their counterparts.
2단계 (1)	Supporting Sentence (1)	*special fields in which there is no substitute for a university education* This is because there are special fields in which there is no substitute for a university education.
3단계 (1)	Supporting Sentence or Specific Example (1)	*medical doctors need to undergo years of costly study* Medical doctors, for example, need to undergo years of costly study, and therefore they deserve the financial gains of qualifying for their profession both because of their efforts and the service they can then provide to society.

Body 1

Some people say that the salaries of well-educated people should be much higher than their counterparts. This is because there are special fields in which there is no substitute for a university education. Medical doctors, for example, need to undergo years of costly study, and therefore they deserve the financial gains of qualifying for their profession both because of their efforts and the service they can then provide to society.

well-educated people : 교육을 잘 받은 사람들
counterparts : 상대방들
substitute : 대체, 대리
undergo : 겪다
costly : 비용이 많이 드는
deserve : 받을 만하다
financial gains : 경제적 이득
profession : 직업

우리말 해석
어떤 사람들은 교육을 잘 받은 사람들의 월급이 상대방(대학을 가지 않고 더 일찍 일을 시작하는 사람)보다 훨씬 더 높아야 한다고 말한다. 이는 대학교육을 대체할 수 없는 특정 분야가 있기 때문이다. 예를 들어, 의사들은 비용이 많이 들어가는 공부를 수년간 해야 하고, 그러므로 그들의 노력과 그들이 사회에 제공하는 서비스 이 두 가지 때문에 그들은 직업을 위해 자격을 갖추는 것에 대한 경제적 이득을 받는다.

4단계 본론 2 (Body 2) (21~30분) : 내 의견 = Disagree (대학 졸업생이 더 많은 돈을 받아야 하는 것은 아니다)

Question	University graduates should be paid more money than less educated people. This is because they should pay the full cost of their education. Do you agree or disagree with this statement?

Body 2는 1단계에서 브레인스토밍한 'Disagree'의 주장을 바탕으로 작성한다.

1단계	Topic Sentence	However, income is more likely to be dependent on the contributions employees make to the companies in which they are employed.
2단계 (1)	Supporting Sentence (1)	*years of work experience can be even more valuable* Years of work experience can be even more valuable than academic expertise in many industries.
3단계 (1)	Supporting Sentence or Specific Example (1)	*employers prefer highly skilled and specially trained people* Employers often prefer to hire and pay more to highly skilled and specially trained people rather than fresh university graduates.
2단계 (2)	Supporting Sentence (2)	*highly educated professionals make up only a fraction of the labour market* In addition, while it is true that the labour force in knowledge-intensive fields such as research, education and law primarily consists of highly educated professionals, such people make up only a fraction of the labour market as a whole.
3단계 (2)	Supporting Sentence or Specific Example (2)	*skilled workforces are most in demand* Therefore, skilled workforces are most in demand in the workplace and specific skills are more valuable than an academic degree.

Body 2

However, income is more likely to be dependent on the contributions employees make to the companies in which they are employed. Years of work experience can be even more valuable than academic expertise in many industries. Employers often prefer to hire and pay more to highly skilled and specially trained people rather than fresh university graduates. In addition, while it is true that the labour force in knowledge-intensive fields such as research, education and law primarily consists of highly educated professionals, such people make up only a fraction of the labour market as a whole. Therefore, skilled workforces are most in demand in the workplace and specific skills are more valuable than an academic degree.

be dependent on : ~에 의존하다
years of : 수년간의
work experience : 경력
academic expertise : 학문적 전문 지식
labour force : 인력

knowledge-intensive fields : 지식 집약 분야들
consists of : 구성하다
fraction : 일부, 부분
most in demand : 가장 수요가 많은
in the workplace : 직장에서

우리말 해석

하지만 소득은 고용된 회사에서 근로자가 이뤄낸 기여도에 따라 결정될 가능성이 더 크다. 수년간의 경력은 많은 산업분야에서 학문적 전문 지식보다 훨씬 더 가치 있을 수 있다. 고용주들은 종종 대졸 초년생들보다 고도로 숙련되고 특별히 훈련된 사람들을 고용해 급여를 더 많이 주는 것을 선호한다. 게다가 연구, 교육 그리고 법 같은 지식 집약 분야에 있는 인력들은 주로 고등 교육을 받은 전문가들로 구성되어 있는 것이 사실이지만, 이런 사람들은 전체적으로 볼 때, 노동 시장의 단지 일부만을 구성할 뿐이다. 그러므로 숙련된 직원들이 직장에서 가장 수요가 많고, 구체적인 기술들은 학위보다 더 가치가 있다.

5 단계 결론 (Conclusion) (31~35분) : 본문에 제시한 내 주장 요약하며 다시 한 번 강조

Question	University graduates should be paid more money than less educated people. This is because they should pay the full cost of their education. Do you agree or disagree with this statement?

결론 작성 시, 먼저 문제 유형을 파악한 후, 'Conclusion Template'의 표현을 인용한다. (See p58)

문제 유형 파악	1-1) Do you agree or disagree? 유형
Conclusion Template 인용	For the reasons mentioned above, I totally agree(disagree) with the opinion because… 본문에 제시한 내 주장 간단히 요약

결론을 작성하기 전, 서론과 본론 2에서 Disagree, '대학 졸업생이 더 많은 돈을 받아야 하는 것은 아니다.' 라고 했는지 다시 한 번 확인하자!

> **Conclusion**
> **For the reasons mentioned above, I absolutely do not agree with the opinion** that college graduates should automatically be paid higher salaries, **because** we should place more value on what employees actually offer society than how much they have paid in tuition fees.

* 상황에 따라 템플릿을 살짝 변형해도 좋다.

absolutely : 전적으로
automatically : 자동적으로
tuition fees : 학비

> **우리말 해석**
> 위에서 언급한 이유들 때문에 나는 대학 졸업생들이 자동적으로 더 높은 월급을 받아야 하는 한다는 의견에 전적으로 동의할 수 없는데, 왜냐하면 우리는 직원들이 얼마나 많이 학비를 지불했는지보다 그들이 실질적으로 사회에 제공한 것에 가치를 더 두어야 하기 때문이다.

6 단계   교정 (Self-correction) (36~40분) : 내용의 일관성 및 문법 검토

다음 Body 2의 내용을 교정해 보자. 틀린 부분은 총 몇 개일까?

교정 전 (직접 문장 부호를 이용하여 틀린 부분을 교정해 보자.)

However, income is more likely to being dependent for the contributions employees make to the companies in which they are employed. Years of work experience can be even more valuable than academic expertise in many industry. Employees often prefer to hire and pay more to highly skilled and specially trained people rather than fresh university graduate.

in addition, while it is true that the labour force in knowledge-intensive fields such as research, education and law primarily consist of highly educated professionals, such people make up only an fraction of the labour market as a whole. Therefore, Skilled workforces are most in demand in the workplace and specific skills are more valuable than a academic degree.

교정

> However, income is more likely to ~~being~~ **be** dependent ~~for~~ **on** the contributions employees make to the companies in which they are employed. Years of work experience can be even more valuable than academic expertise in many ~~industry~~ **industries**. ~~Employees~~ **Employers** often prefer to hire and pay more to highly skilled and specially trained people rather than fresh university ~~graduate~~ **graduates**. ~~in~~ **In** addition, while it is true that the labour force in knowledge-intensive fields such as research, education and law primarily ~~consist~~ **consists** of highly educated professionals, such people make up only ~~an~~ **a** fraction of the labour market as a whole. Therefore, ~~Skilled~~ **skilled** workforces are most in demand in the workplace and specific skills are more valuable than ~~a~~ **an** academic degree.

1. being → be : be more likely to + 동사 원형
2. for → on : be dependent on : ~에 의존하다
3. industry → industries : many 다음에는 셀 수 있는 명사의 복수형을 쓴다.
4. Employees → Employers : 고용인이 아니라 고용주라고 해야 논리에 맞다. 이걸 놓치면 절대 안 된다!
5. graduate → graduates : 셀 수 있는 명사이므로 복수형으로 쓴다.
6. 붙여쓰기 : 위의 글은 Body 2 단락이다. 단락이 바뀌지 않는 한, 줄을 바꿔 쓰지 않는다.
7. in → In : 문장의 첫 글자는 반드시 대문자로 시작한다.
8. consist → consists : 주어인 the labour force가 단수이므로 단수 동사인 consists를 쓴다.
9. an → a : fraction[frækʃn]은 모음(a/i/u/e/o)으로 발음이 시작되지 않기 때문에 a라고 쓰고 말한다.
10. Skilled → skilled : 콤마(,) 다음에는 소문자로 쓴다.
11. a → an : 모음(a/i/u/e/o)으로 발음이 시작되는 단어 academic [ækədemɪk] 앞에는 a가 아닌 an으로 쓰고 말한다.

틀린 개수 : 총 11개

Sample Answer

Question: University graduates should be paid more money than less educated people. This is because they should pay the full cost of their education. Do you agree or disagree with this statement?

It might seem obvious that a university graduate commands a bigger salary than someone who starts working earlier because of the expense of a higher education. Although rewards for expertise in certain fields can be justified, we should not overlook the skills acquired outside of universities.

Some people say that the salaries of well-educated people should be much higher than their counterparts. This is because there are special fields in which there is no substitute for a university education. Medical doctors, for example, need to undergo years of costly study, and therefore they deserve the financial gains of qualifying for their profession both because of their efforts and the service they can then provide to society.

However, income is more likely to be dependent on the contributions employees make to the companies in which they are employed. Years of work experience can be even more valuable than academic expertise in many industries. Employers often prefer to hire and pay more to highly skilled and specially trained people rather than fresh university graduates. In addition, while it is true that the labour force in knowledge-intensive fields such as research, education and law primarily consists of highly educated professionals, such people make up only a fraction of the labor market as a whole. Therefore, skilled workforces are most in demand in the workplace and specific skills are more valuable than an academic degree.

For the reasons mentioned above, I absolutely do not agree with the opinion that college graduates should automatically be paid higher salaries, because we should place more value on what employees actually offer society than how much they have paid in tuition fees.

word counts : 274 words

우리말 해석

대학 졸업생들이 고등 교육 비용 때문에 더 일찍 일을 시작하는 사람보다 더 많은 월급을 받는 것은 당연하게 보일지도 모른다. 비록 특정 분야에서 전문 지식에 대한 보상은 정당화될 수 있지만, 우리는 대학교 이외의 곳에서 습득한 기술을 간과해서는 안 된다.

어떤 사람들은 교육을 잘 받은 사람들의 월급이 상대방(대학을 가지 않고 더 일찍 일을 시작하는 사람) 보다 훨씬 더 높아야 한다고 말한다. 이는 대학교육을 대체할 수 없는 특정 분야가 있기 때문이다. 예를 들어, 의사들은 비용이 많이 들어가는 공부를 수년간 해야 하고, 그러므로 그들의 노력과 그들이 사회에 제공하는 서비스 이 두 가지 때문에 그들은 직업을 위해 자격을 갖추는 것에 대한 경제적 이득을 받는다.

하지만 소득은 고용된 회사에서 근로자가 이뤄낸 기여도에 따라 결정될 가능성이 더 크다. 수년간의 경력은 많은 산업분야에서 학문적 전문 지식보다 훨씬 더 가치 있을 수 있다. 고용주들은 종종 대졸 초년생들보다 고도로 숙련되고 특별히 훈련된 사람들을 고용해 급여를 더 많이 주는 것을 선호한다. 게다가 연구, 교육 그리고 법 같은 지식 집약 분야에 있는 인력들은 주로 고등 교육을 받은 전문가들로 구성되어 있는 것이 사실이지만, 이런 사람들은 전체적으로 볼 때, 노동 시장의 단지 일부만을 구성할 뿐이다. 그러므로 숙련된 직원들이 직장에서 가장 수요가 많고, 구체적인 기술들은 학위보다 더 가치가 있다.

위에서 언급한 이유들 때문에 나는 대학 졸업생들이 자동적으로 더 높은 월급을 받아야 하는 한다는 의견에 전적으로 동의할 수 없는데, 왜냐하면 우리는 직원들이 얼마나 많이 학비를 지불했는지보다 그들이 실질적으로 사회에 제공한 것에 가치를 더 두어야 하기 때문이다.

불법 Review

앞에서 배운 내용을 바탕으로 다음 빈칸을 영어로 작성해 보자.

It might seem obvious that _____ (1. 대학 졸업생) commands a bigger salary than someone who starts working earlier because of the expense of _____ (2. 고등 교육). Although rewards for expertise in certain fields can be justified, we should not overlook the skills acquired outside of universities.

Some people say that the salaries of _____ (3. 교육을 잘 받은 사람들) should be much higher than _____ (4. 그들의 상대방들). This is because there are special fields in which there is no substitute for a university education. Medical doctors, for example, need to undergo years of costly study, and therefore they deserve _____ (5. 경제적 이득) of qualifying for their profession both because of their efforts and the service they can then provide to society.

However, income is more likely to be dependent on the contributions employees make to the companies in which they are employed. _____ (6. 수년간의 경력) can be even more valuable than academic expertise in many industries. Employers often prefer to hire and pay more to highly skilled and specially trained people rather than fresh university graduates. In addition, while it is true that the labour force in _____ (7. 지식 집약 분야) such as research, education and law primarily consists of highly educated professionals, such people make up only a fraction of the labor market as a whole. Therefore, skilled workforces are _____ (8. 가장 수요가 많은) in the workplace and specific skills are more valuable than an academic degree.

For the reasons mentioned above, I absolutely do not agree with the opinion that college graduates should automatically be paid higher salaries, because we should place more value on what employees actually offer society than how much they have paid in _____ (9. 학비).

Answer 1. a university graduate / 2. a higher education / 3. well-educated people / 4. their counterparts
5. the financial gains / 6. Years of work experience / 7. knowledge-intensive fields / 8. most in demand
9. tuition fees

Day 5 Student Life 불법 포인트 정리

관용과 나눔	tolerance and sharing	A에게 억지로 B하게 하다	force A to B
도덕적 가치	moral values	수업 활동	coursework
선진국	developed countries	대학 졸업생들	university graduates
일류 대학	a prestigious university	(돈을) 받다	be paid
세계화 시대에	in the era of globalisation	받다	command
자격증	qualifications	고등 교육	a higher education
취업 기회	job opportunities	전문 지식	expertise
시야를 넓히다	broaden one's horizons	간과하다	overlook
독립적인	independent	습득하다	acquire
비자 신청	visa applications	교육을 잘 받은 사람들	well-educated people
서류 작업	paperwork	상대방들	counterparts
언어 장벽	the language barrier	대체, 대리	substitute
외국인 학생들	foreign students	겪다	undergo
낯선	unfamiliar	비용이 많이 드는	costly
혼자 사는 것	living alone	받을 만하다	deserve
향수병	homesickness	경제적 이득	financial gains
강력한 도구	a powerful tool	직업	profession
인터넷의 출현	the emergence of the Internet	~에 의존하다	be dependent on
덕택에	thanks to	수년간의	years of
기본적인 읽고 쓰는 능력	basic literacy skills	경력	work experience
능숙한	proficient	학문적 전문 지식	academic expertise
전통적인 교수법	traditional teaching methods	인력	labour force
최신 컴퓨터 기술	the latest computer technology	지식 집약 분야들	knowledge-intensive fields
보충하다	supplement	구성되다	consists of
후진국	in underdeveloped countries	일부, 부분	fraction
문맹률	illiteracy rates	가장 수요가 많은	most in demand
어린 나이부터	from an early age	직장에서	in the workplace
지식과 정보의 세계	a world of knowledge and information	전적으로	absolutely
A에게 B를 경험하게 하다	expose A to B	자동적으로	automatically
교육 수준	the level of education	학비	tuition fees
직접적인 상관관계	a direct correlation		

Day 6 Communication 의사소통

Question

Some people insist that the world would be a better place if everyone spoke the same language. To what extent do you agree or disagree with this opinion?

어떤 사람들은 모든 사람들이 같은 언어를 사용했다면 더 좋은 세상이 되었을 것이라고 주장한다. 당신은 이 의견에 얼마만큼 동의하는가? 또는 동의하지 않는가?

 빈출 문제

1. As more and more people are communicating via computers and mobile telephones, we are losing the ability to communicate with others face to face. Do you agree or disagree with this statement?

2. The Internet is making it easier for people to communicate with one another. Do you agree or disagree with this statement?

3. The Internet has destroyed communication among friends and family members. Do you agree or disagree with this statement?

4. Compare the advantages and disadvantages of the three following methods for communicating information; audio systems, televisions, the Internet and state which you consider to be the most effective.

1. 점점 더 많은 사람들이 컴퓨터와 휴대 전화로 의사소통함에 따라, 얼굴을 직접 보며 대화하는 능력을 잃어가고 있다. 당신은 이 말에 동의하는가? 또는 동의하지 않는가?

2. 인터넷은 사람들이 서로 대화하는 것을 더욱 쉽게 해 주고 있다. 당신은 이 말에 동의하는가? 또는 동의하지 않는가?

3. 인터넷은 친구 및 가족 구성원 간의 대화를 단절시키고 있다. 당신은 이 말에 동의하는가? 또는 동의하지 않는가?

4. 정보를 전달하는 다음 세 가지 방법인 오디오, TV 그리고 인터넷의 장단점을 비교하고 어떤 것이 가장 효과적인지 말하시오.

 **브레인스토밍**

1) 직장인들은 서로 얼굴을 마주보고 하는 미팅을 갖는 것 대신에 이메일, 온라인 네트워크 그리고 화상회의를 통해 의사소통할 수 있다.
   서로 얼굴을 마주보고 하는 미팅 : a face-to-face meeting / 화상회의 : video conferencing

2) 우리는 언제 어디서든 우리가 원할 때, 이메일이나 인스턴트 메신저 서비스로 가족과 친구 그리고 동료들과 연락할 수 있다.
   언제 어디서든 우리가 원할 때 : whenever and wherever we want / 동료 : colleagues / 연락하다 : keep in touch with

3) 인터넷은 우리가 의사소통하는 방법에 혁신을 일으켰다.
   혁신을 일으키다 : revolutionise

4) 스마트폰은 오늘날의 세상에서 가장 인기 있는 소형 전자제품이다.
   오늘날의 세상에서 : in today's world / 소형 전자제품 : gadget

5) 영어는 국제어로서 전 세계에서 널리 사용된다.
   국제어 : an international language

6) 영어라는 언어는 전세계 제 2의 언어가 되고 있다.
   전세계 제 2의 언어 : a global second language

7) 영어는 지금 전 세계에서 기술, 과학 그리고 해외 사업의 우세하거나 공식적인 언어이다.
   우세한 : dominant / 공식적인 : official

8) 만약 한 언어가 우세하면, 다른 언어들뿐만 아니라 문화들도 사라질지도 모르는데, 언어가 자신의 문화를 가지고 오기 때문이다.
   뿐만 아니라 : as well as / 사라지다 : disappear = diminish

9) 영어에 대한 대안으로써 새로운 글로벌 언어, 에스페란토가 1887년도에 창안되었다.
   대안 : alternative / 에스페란토 : Esperanto (배우기 쉬운 국제 공용어의 명칭) / 창안하다, 발명하다 : invent

10) 에스페란토는 세계 평화와 이해를 촉진하는 데 도움을 줄 수 있다.
    세계 평화 : international peace / 촉진하다 : promote

11) 얼굴을 마주보고 하는 의사소통은 새로운 소셜 미디어 때문에 궁극적으로 사라질 것이다.
    궁극적으로 : ultimately

12) 소셜 미디어는 사실상 오프라인 환경에서 유능하게 상호작용할 수 있는 인간의 능력을 해치고 있다.
    유능하게 : competently / 상호작용하다 : interact

13) 젊은이들은 소셜 미디어를 그들의 또래와 상호 작용하는 부가적인 공간으로써 사용한다.
    젊은이들 : youths / 부가적인 공간으로써 : as an additional space

14) 페이스북과 같은 소셜 네트워킹 웹사이트들은 내성적인 사람들이 상호작용하기 위한 편안한 환경을 찾는 데 좋은 방안이 될 수 있다.
    내성적인 사람들 : introverted people / 방안 : avenue

15) 의사소통의 오직 7퍼센트만이 언어에 기초하는데, 이것은 의사소통의 90퍼센트 이상이 몸짓 언어, 시선의 마주침 그리고 목소리 톤과 같은 비언어적 신호에 기초한다는 것을 의미한다.

언어 : the verbal word / ~에 기초하다 : be based on / 몸짓 언어 : body language / 시선의 마주침 : eye contact
목소리 톤 : tone of voice

Answer

1) Workers can communicate via email, online networks and video conferencing instead of having a face-to-face meeting.
2) We can keep in touch with family, friends and colleagues by email or instant messenger services whenever and wherever we want.
3) The Internet has revolutionised the way we communicate.
4) The smartphone is the most popular gadget in today's world.
5) English is widely used around the world as an international language.
6) The English language is becoming a global second language.
7) English is now the dominant or official language of technology, science and international business in the world.
8) If one language is dominant, other cultures as well as languages may disappear because the language brings its own culture.
9) As an alternative to English, a new global language, Esperanto, was invented in 1887.
10) Esperanto could help to promote international peace and understanding.
11) Face-to-face communication will ultimately diminish because of new social media.
12) Social media is actually harming people's ability to interact competently in an offline environment.
13) Youths use social media as an additional space to interact with their peers.
14) Social networking websites like Facebook can be an excellent avenue for introverted people to find a comfortable setting to interact.
15) Only 7% of communication is based on the verbal word and that means that over 90% of communication is based on nonverbal cues such as body language, eye contact, and tone of voice.

 실전문제

You should spend about 40 minutes on this task.
Write about the following topic :

> *Some people insist that the world would be a better place if everyone spoke the same language. To what extent do you agree or disagree with this opinion?*

Give reasons for your answer and include any relevant examples from your own knowledge or experience.

Write at least 250 words.

 **1단계** 문제 정독, 문제 유형 파악, 브레인스토밍 (0 ~ 5분)

> **Question** Some people insist that the world would be a better place if everyone spoke the same language. To what extent do you agree or disagree with this opinion?

문제 정독
어떤 사람들은 모든 사람들이 같은 언어를 사용했다면 더 좋은 세상이 되었을 것이라고 주장한다. 당신은 이 의견에 얼마만큼 동의하는가? 또는 동의하지 않는가?

 would : ~했다면, 실제로 발생하는 일이 아니기 때문에 가정법을 썼다.

문제 유형 파악

1-1. Do you agree or disagree? 유형

* 간혹 to what extent 때문에 난감해 하는 학생들이 있다. to what extent는 '어느 정도로'라는 뜻이고, 그냥 생략하고 에세이를 작성하는 것이 좋다.

Brainstorming

Topic : 모든 사람들이 같은 언어를 사용했다면?	
Agree : 더 좋은 세상이 되었을 것이다.	Disagree : 더 좋은 세상이 되지 않았을 것이다.
1. 언쟁을 해결하고 논쟁거리를 의논하는 것이 좀 더 효과적으로 가능 resolving arguments and discussing contentious issues would be possible more effectively → 정치적 오해들에 대한 여지가 적음 less room for political misunderstandings	1. 의사소통에는 단지 언어 이해 이상의 것이 있음 there is more to communication than just the comprehension of language → 의사소통이 언어를 뛰어넘고 비언어적 요소들을 포함 communication is beyond language and contains non-verbal factors
2. 우리의 삶 또한 혜택을 받음 our lives might also benefit → 우리의 사교적 사업적 기회가 증가함 our social and business opportunities would increase	2. 언어는 국민적 자존심의 원천 language is a source of national pride → 우리는 풍부한 전통과 문화를 잃었을 것임 we would lose many rich traditions and cultures

* 아이디어의 수도 같고 영어로 쓸 수 있는 말도 비슷하다면, 좀 더 설득력 있게 논리적으로 접근할 수 있는 쪽을 내 의견으로 한다. 이 에세이에서는 disagree, '모든 사람들이 같은 언어를 사용했다면 더 좋은 세상이 되지 않았을 것이다.'를 내 주장으로 삼았다.

2단계 서론 (Introduction) (6~10분) : 두 문장으로 작성

Question	Some people insist that the world would be a better place if everyone spoke the same language. To what extent do you agree or disagree with this opinion?

단계	Question	서론 작성
1단계 Paraphrasing	**토픽** : Some people insist that the world would be a better place if everyone spoke the same language.	**Paraphrasing** : There is an opinion that the world's problems could be solved more easily if we all spoke the same language.
2단계 Answering	**질문** : To what extent do you agree or disagree with this opinion?	**Answering : Disagree일 경우** While I can see how communication might be improved if we all used Globish, it is unrealistic to expect us to abandon our individual cultures.

Introduction

There is an opinion that the world's problems could be solved more easily if we all spoke the same language. While I can see how communication might be improved if we all used Globish, it is unrealistic to expect us to abandon our individual cultures.

Globish : 글로비시
  Globish는 global과 English의 합성어. 영어가 모국어가 아닌 사람들이 쓰는 단순화된 형태의 영어. 가장 일반적인 단어와 구들로 이뤄지고 문법에 크게 구애받지 않고 사용한다.
unrealistic : 비현실적인
abandon : 포기하다

우리말 해석

우리 모두가 같은 언어를 사용했다면 세상의 문제들은 더욱 쉽게 해결되었을 거라는 의견이 있다. 만약 우리 모두가 글로비시를 사용했다면 의사소통이 어느 정도는 향상되었을지도 모르지만, 우리의 개별 문화를 포기하기를 바라는 것은 비현실적이다.

3 단계   본론 1 (Body 1) (11~20분) : 나와 다른 의견 = Agree (더 좋은 세상이 되었을 것이다)

> **Question**   Some people insist that the world would be a better place if everyone spoke the same language. To what extent do you agree or disagree with this opinion?

Body 1은 1단계에서 브레인스토밍한 'Agree'의 주장을 바탕으로 작성한다.

1단계	Topic Sentence	A case could be put forward that if we could communicate freely with one another, we could live in a better world.
2단계 (1)	Supporting Sentence (1)	*resolving arguments and discussing contentious issues would be possible more effectively* Resolving arguments and discussing contentious issues throughout the world would be possible more effectively.
3단계 (1)	Supporting Sentence or Specific Example (1)	*less room for political misunderstandings* There would be less room for political misunderstandings and we could save the time spent translating diplomatic documents in an effort to make a more peaceful world.
2단계 (2)	Supporting Sentence (2)	*our lives might also benefit* When it comes to individuals, many aspects of our lives might also benefit from a common language.
3단계 (2)	Supporting Sentence or Specific Example (2)	*our social and business opportunities would increase* Our social and business opportunities would no doubt increase thanks to being able to interact with more people.

Body 1

A case could be put forward that if we could communicate freely with one another, we could live in a better world. Resolving arguments and discussing contentious issues throughout the world would be possible more effectively. There would be less room for political misunderstandings and we could save the time spent translating diplomatic documents in an effort to make a more peaceful world. When it comes to individuals, many aspects of our lives might also benefit from a common language. Our social and business opportunities would no doubt increase thanks to being able to interact with more people.

put forward : 제안하다
one another : 서로(서로)
resolve : 해결하다
contentious issues : 논쟁거리들, 논란의 여지가 있는 사안들
room : 여지
diplomatic documents : 외교문서들

in an effort to : ~해보려는 노력으로
when it comes to + N : = as for, in terms of, ~에 관해서 말하자면, 반드시 뒤에 명사(구)가 나와야 한다.
no doubt : 의심의 여지가 없다
thanks to : 덕택으로
interact with : 상호작용하다, 교류하다

우리말 해석

만약에 우리가 서로서로 자유롭게 의사소통을 할 수 있었다면, 우리는 더 좋은 세상에서 살 수 있었을 것이라는 주장이 제시될 수 있다. 전세계에 만연한 언쟁을 해결하고 논쟁거리를 의논하는 것이 좀 더 효과적으로 가능했을 것이다. 정치적인 오해들에 대한 여지가 적었을 것이고 우리는 좀 더 평화로운 세상을 만들려는 노력으로 외교문서들을 번역하는 데 드는 시간을 줄일 수 있었을 것이다. 개인적인 측면에서는, 우리 삶의 많은 부분도 공용어의 혜택을 받았을지도 모른다. 더 많은 사람들과 교류할 수 있는 덕택에 우리의 사교적 사업적 기회들도 의심의 여지없이 증가했을 것이다.

 **본론 2 (Body 2) (21~30분) : 내 의견 = Disagree** (더 좋은 세상이 되지 않았을 것이다)

Question Some people insist that the world would be a better place if everyone spoke the same language. To what extent do you agree or disagree with this opinion?

Body 2는 1단계에서 브레인스토밍한 'Disagree'의 주장을 바탕으로 작성한다.

1단계	Topic Sentence	But these arguments can only be made to a certain point.
2단계 (1)	Supporting Sentence (1)	*there is more to communication than just the comprehension of language* This is because there is obviously far more to communication than just the comprehension of language.
3단계 (1)	Supporting Sentence or Specific Example (1)	*communication is beyond language and contains non-verbal factors* We see many misunderstandings between people even when there is no language barrier because communication is beyond language and contains non-verbal factors such as sympathy, intimacy and understanding.
2단계 (2)	Supporting Sentence (2)	*language is a source of national pride* Language is also a source of national pride, having evolved in different climates and within various groups of people over thousands of years.
3단계 (2)	Supporting Sentence or Specific Example (2)	*we would lose many rich traditions and cultures* If we lost the majority of them then we would also lose many rich traditions and cultures, and some of us might actually find the world a more boring rather than better place in such a scenario.

Body 2

But these arguments can only be made to a certain point. This is because there is obviously far more to communication than just the comprehension of language. We see many misunderstandings between people even when there is no language barrier because communication is beyond language and contains non-verbal factors such as sympathy, intimacy and understanding. Language is also a source of national pride, having evolved in different climates and within various groups of people over thousands of years. If we lost the majority of them then we would also lose many rich traditions and cultures, and some of us might actually find the world a more boring rather than better place in such a scenario.

a certain point : 일정 부분, 어느 정도
comprehension : 이해
misunderstandings : 오해
language barrier : 언어 장벽
non-verbal factors : 비언어적인 요소들
sympathy : 공감
intimacy : 친밀감
national pride : 국민적 자존심
evolve : 발달하다, 진화하다
over thousands of years : 수천 년 동안
the majority of : 대다수, 대부분

우리말 해석

하지만 이러한 주장들은 일부에만 국한될 수 있다. 의사소통에는 단지 언어 이해 이상의 것이 있기 때문이다. 우리는 언어 장벽이 없을 때도 사람들 사이에서 많은 오해가 발생하는 것을 볼 수 있는데, 이것은 의사소통이 언어를 뛰어넘고 공감, 친밀감 그리고 이해와 같은 비언어적 요소들을 포함하고 있기 때문이다. 언어는 또한 수천 년 동안 다른 분위기와 다양한 사람들 안에서 발전해 온 국민적 자존심의 원천이다. 만약 우리가 언어의 대부분을 잃었다면, 우리는 또한 많은 풍부한 전통과 문화를 잃었을 것이고, 이러한 시나리오에서 우리 중의 일부는 사실상 세상이 더 좋은 장소라기 보다는 더 지루한 곳이라고 느꼈었을지도 모른다.

 **5 단계** 결론 (Conclusion) (31~35분) : 본문에 제시한 내 주장 요약하며 다시 한 번 강조

Question	Some people insist that the world would be a better place if everyone spoke the same language. To what extent do you agree or disagree with this opinion?

결론 작성 시, 먼저 문제 유형을 파악한 후, 'Conclusion Template'의 표현을 인용한다. (See p58)

문제 유형 파악	1-1) Do you agree or disagree? 유형
Conclusion Template 인용	For the reasons mentioned above, I totally agree(disagree) with the opinion because… 본문에 제시한 내 주장 간단히 요약

결론을 작성하기 전, 서론과 본론 2에서 Disagree, '모든 사람들이 같은 언어를 사용했다면 더 좋은 세상이 되지 않았을 것이다.' 라고 했는지 다시 한 번 확인하자!

Conclusion
For the reasons mentioned above, I disagree that we would all be better off if we spoke the same language **because** cultural diversity is far more important than the efficiency of language.

* 상황에 따라 템플릿을 살짝 변형해도 좋다.

be better off : (형편이나 처지가) 더 좋은
cultural diversity : 문화의 다양성
the efficiency of language : 언어의 효율성

우리말 해석
위에서 언급한 이유들 때문에 나는 우리가 같은 언어를 사용했다면 세상은 더 좋았을 거라는 의견에 동의하지 않는데, 왜냐하면 문화의 다양성이 언어의 효율성보다 훨씬 더 중요하기 때문이다.

6 단계 교정 (Self-correction) (36~40분) : 내용의 일관성 및 문법 검토

다음 Body 2의 내용을 교정해 보자. 틀린 부분은 총 몇 개일까?

교정 전 (직접 문장 부호를 이용하여 틀린 부분을 교정해 보자.)

but these arguments can only be made to a certain point. This is because there is obviously far more to communication than just the comprehension of language. We see many misunderstandings between people even when there are no language barrier because communication is beyond language and contain non-verbal factors such as sympathy and intimacy and understanding.

Language is also a source for national pride, having evolved in different climates and within various group of people over thousand of years. If we lost the majority of them then we would also lose much rich traditions and cultures, and some of us might actually find a world a more boring rather than better place in such a scenario.

교정

~~b~~**B**ut these arguments can only be made to a certain point. This is because there is obviously far more to communication than just the comprehension of language. We see many misunderstandings between people even when there ~~are~~ **is** no language barrier because communication is beyond language and ~~contain~~ **contains** non-verbal factors such as sympathy ~~and~~**,** intimacy and understanding. Language is also a source ~~for~~ **of** national pride, having evolved in different climates and within various ~~group~~ **groups** of people over ~~thousand~~ **thousands** of years. If we lost the majority of them then we would also lose ~~much~~ **many** rich traditions and cultures, and some of us might actually find ~~a~~ **the** world a more boring rather than better place in such a scenario.

1. b → B : 문장의 첫 글자는 반드시 대문자로 시작한다.
2. are → is : barrier가 단수이므로 단수 동사인 is를 쓴다.
3. contain → contains : 주어인 communication이 단수이므로 단수 동사 contains를 쓴다.
4. and → ,(콤마) : 3가지를 나열할 때는 A, B and C라고 쓴다. 맨 마지막 단어 앞에만 and를 쓴다.
5. 붙여쓰기 : 위의 글은 Body 2 단락이다. 단락이 바뀌지 않는 한, 줄을 바꿔 쓰지 않는다.
6. for → of : a source of는 '~의 원천'이라는 뜻
7. group → groups : various(다양한) 다음에 셀 수 있는 명사가 올 때는 복수로 쓴다.
8. thousand → thousands : thousands of years는 '수천 년'이라는 뜻
9. much → many : traditions and cultures 모두 셀 수 있는 복수 명사다. much는 셀 수 없는 명사 앞에 쓴다.
10. a → the : '세상'은 하나밖에 없기 때문에 정관사 the를 앞에 붙인다.

틀린 개수 : 총 10개

Sample Answer

Question: Some people insist that the world would be a better place if everyone spoke the same language. To what extent do you agree or disagree with this opinion?

There is an opinion that the world's problems could be solved more easily if we all spoke the same language. While I can see how communication might be improved if we all used Globish, it is unrealistic to expect us to abandon our individual cultures.

A case could be put forward that if we could communicate freely with one another, we could live in a better world. Resolving arguments and discussing contentious issues throughout the world would be possible more effectively. There would be less room for political misunderstandings and we could save the time spent translating diplomatic documents in an effort to make a more peaceful world. When it comes to individuals, many aspects of our lives might also benefit from a common language. Our social and business opportunities would no doubt increase thanks to being able to interact with more people.

But these arguments can only be made to a certain point. This is because there is obviously far more to communication than just the comprehension of language. We see many misunderstandings between people even when there is no language barrier because communication is beyond language and contains non-verbal factors such as sympathy, intimacy and understanding. Language is also a source of national pride, having evolved in different climates and within various groups of people over thousands of years. If we lost the majority of them then we would also lose many rich traditions and cultures, and some of us might actually find the world a more boring rather than better place in such a scenario.

For the reasons mentioned above, I disagree that we would all be better off if we spoke the same language because cultural diversity is far more important than the efficiency of language.

word counts : 290 words

우리말 해석

우리 모두가 같은 언어를 사용했다면 세상의 문제들은 더욱 쉽게 해결되었을 거라는 의견이 있다. 만약 우리 모두가 글로비시를 사용했다면 의사소통이 어느 정도는 향상되었을지도 모르지만, 우리의 개별 문화를 포기하기를 바라는 것은 비현실적이다.

만약에 우리가 서로서로 자유롭게 의사소통을 할 수 있었다면, 우리는 더 좋은 세상에서 살 수 있었을 것이라는 주장이 제시될 수 있다. 전 세계에 만연한 언쟁을 해결하고 논쟁거리를 의논하는 것이 좀 더 효과적으로 가능했을 것이다. 정치적인 오해들에 대한 여지가 적었을 것이고 우리는 좀 더 평화로운 세상을 만들려는 노력으로 외교문서들을 번역하는 데 드는 시간을 줄일 수 있었을 것이다. 개인적인 측면에서는, 우리 삶의 많은 부분도 공용어의 혜택을 받았을지도 모른다. 더 많은 사람들과 교류할 수 있는 덕택에 우리의 사교적 사업적 기회들도 의심의 여지없이 증가했을 것이다.

하지만 이러한 주장들은 일부에만 국한될 수 있다. 의사소통에는 단지 언어 이해 이상의 것이 있기 때문이다. 우리는 언어장벽이 없을 때도 사람들 사이에서 많은 오해가 발생하는 것을 볼 수 있는데, 이것은 의사소통이 언어를 뛰어넘고 공감, 친밀감 그리고 이해와 같은 비언어적 요소들을 포함하고 있기 때문이다. 언어는 또한 수천 년 동안 다른 분위기와 다양한 사람들 안에서 발전해 온 국민적 자존심의 원천이다. 만약 우리가 언어의 대부분을 잃었다면, 우리는 또한 많은 풍부한 전통과 문화를 잃었을 것이고, 이러한 시나리오에서 우리 중의 일부는 사실상 세상이 더 좋은 장소라기 보다는 더 지루한 곳이라고 느꼈었을지도 모른다.

위에서 언급한 이유들 때문에 나는 우리가 같은 언어를 사용했다면 세상은 더 좋았을 거라는 의견에 동의하지 않는데, 왜냐하면 문화의 다양성이 언어의 효율성보다 훨씬 더 중요하기 때문이다.

불법 Review

앞에서 배운 내용을 바탕으로 다음 빈칸을 영어로 작성해 보자.

There is an opinion that the world's problems could be solved more easily if we all spoke the same language. While I can see how communication might be improved if we all used Globish, _____ (1. 이것은 비현실적이다) to expect us to abandon our individual cultures.

A case could be put forward that if we could communicate freely with one another, we could live _____ (2. 더 좋은 세상에). Resolving arguments and _____ (3. 논쟁거리를 의논하는 것) throughout the world would be possible _____ (4. 좀 더 효과적으로). There would be less room for _____ (5. 정치적인 오해들) and we could save _____ (6. 외교문서들을 번역하는 데 드는 시간) in an effort to make a more peaceful world. When it comes to individuals, many aspects of our lives might also benefit from a common language. Our social and business opportunities would no doubt increase _____ (7. 덕택에) being able to interact with more people.

But these arguments can only be made to a certain point. This is because there is obviously far more to communication than just the comprehension of language. We see many misunderstandings between people even when there is no _____ (8. 언어장벽) because communication is beyond language and contains non-verbal factors such as _____ (9. 공감, 친밀감 그리고 이해). Language is also a source of national pride, having evolved in different climates and within various groups of people _____ (10. 수천 년 동안). If we lost the majority of them then we would also lose many rich traditions and cultures, and some of us might actually find the world a more boring rather than better place in such a scenario.

For the reasons mentioned above, I disagree that we would all be better off if we spoke the same language because _____ (11. 문화의 다양성) is far more important than _____ (12. 언어의 효율성).

Answer
1. it is unrealistic / 2. in a better world / 3. discussing contentious issues / 4. more effectively
5. political misunderstandings / 6. the time spent translating diplomatic documents / 7. thanks to
8. language barrier / 9. sympathy, intimacy and understanding / 10. over thousands of years
11. cultural diversity / 12. the efficiency of language

Day 6 Communication 불법 포인트 정리

서로 얼굴을 마주보고 하는 미팅	a face-to-face meeting	목소리 톤	tone of voice
화상회의	video conferencing	글로비시	Globish
언제 어디서든 우리가 원할 때	whenever and wherever we want	비현실적인	unrealistic
동료	colleagues	포기하다	abandon
연락하다	keep in touch with	제안하다	put forward
혁신을 일으키다	revolutionise	해결하다	resolve
오늘날의 세상에서	in today's world	논쟁거리들	contentious issues
소형 전자제품	gadget	여지	room
국제어	an international language	외교문서들	diplomatic documents
전세계 제 2의 언어	a global second language	~해보려는 노력으로	in an effort to
우세한	dominant	~에 관해서 말하자면	when it comes to + N as for / in terms of
공식적인	official	기본적 욕구	basic needs
뿐만 아니라	as well as	의심할 바 없이	no doubt
사라지다	disappear / diminish	덕택으로	thanks to
대안	alternative	상호작용하다	interact with
에스페란토	Esperanto	일정 부분	a certain point
창안하다, 발명하다	invent	이해	comprehension
세계 평화	international peace	오해	misunderstandings
촉진하다	promote	언어 장벽	language barrier
궁극적으로	ultimately	비언어적인 요소들	non-verbal factors
유능하게	competently	공감	sympathy
상호작용하다	interact	친밀감	intimacy
젊은이들	youths	국민적 자존심	national pride
부가적인 공간으로써	as an additional space	발달하다, 진화하다	evolve
내성적인 사람들	introverted people	수천 년 동안	over thousands of years
방안	avenue	대다수	the majority of
언어	the verbal word	(형편이나 처지가) 더 좋다	be better off
~에 기초하다	be based on	문화의 다양성	cultural diversity
몸짓 언어	body language	언어의 효율성	the efficiency of language
시선의 마주침	eye contact		

Day 7 Travelling & Transport

여행과 교통

| Question | Tourism is becoming a good source of revenue for many countries. Discuss the advantages and the disadvantages of developing this industry.

관광산업은 많은 나라들의 좋은 수입원이 되고 있다. 이러한 산업 발달의 장단점을 논하라. |

 빈출 문제

1. Some people argue that travellers visiting other countries should follow the local customs and behaviour. Others think that the host countries should accept cultural differences. Discuss both these views and give your own opinion.

2. Today more people are travelling than ever before. What is the reason? What are the benefits of travelling?

3. In order to solve traffic problems, the government should impose a heavy tax on private car owners and use the money to improve public transport systems. What are the advantages and disadvantages of such a solution?

4. Traffic congestion is becoming a severe problem for large cities. Suggest some measures that could be taken to reduce traffic in big cities.

1. 어떤 사람들은 다른 나라를 방문하는 관광객들이 그 지역의 관습과 행동을 따라야 한다고 주장한다. 반면 그 관광국들이 문화적 차이를 받아들여야 한다고 생각하는 사람들도 있다. 양쪽의 견해를 논하고 당신의 주장을 제시하라.

2. 오늘날에는 전보다 더 많은 사람들이 여행을 한다. 이유는 무엇인가? 여행이 여행객들에게 주는 이점은 무엇인가?

3. 교통 문제를 해결하기 위해서 정부는 차량 소유자들에게 무거운 세금을 부과하고 이 돈을 대중교통 시스템을 개선하는 데 사용해야 한다. 이러한 해결책의 장단점을 논하라.

4. 교통 체증은 대도시의 심각한 문제가 되고 있다. 대도시 교통량을 줄일 수 있는 방법들을 제시하라.

 **STEP2 브레인스토밍**

1) 관광산업은 숙박, 교통, 오락과 같은 서비스(사업)에서 고용을 창출한다.
   숙박 : accommodation / 교통 : transport / 오락 : entertainment / 고용을 창출하다 : create employment

2) 저가 항공사들은 해외 여행을 훨씬 더 싸게 만들고 있다.
   저가 항공사 : low-cost airlines / 해외로 여행하다 : travel abroad

3) 관광산업은 다국적 회사들의 투자를 이끈다.
   다국적 회사 : multi-national companies / 투자 : investment

4) 어떤 지역은 그들의 소득을 관광 산업에 의존한다.
   소득 : income

5) 관광산업은 자연 환경에 부정적인 영향을 끼칠 수 있다.
   자연 환경 : the natural environment / ~에 부정적인 영향을 끼치다 : have a negative effect on

6) 과도한 개발은 야생 동물의 서식지를 파괴할 수 있다.
   과도한 개발 : excessive development / 야생 동물의 서식지 : the habitat of wild animals

7) 외딴 지역에 있는 아름다운 해변들이 호텔 건설로 인해 훼손된다.
   훼손하다, 망치다 : spoil

8) 생활비의 상승은 지역 사람들에게 영향을 미친다.
   생활비 : the cost of living / 지역 사람들 : local people

9) 교통량을 줄이기 위해서 우리는 좀 더 탄력적인 시간으로 일해야한다.
   교통량 : traffic / 탄력적인 시간 : flexible hours

10) 대도시에서 차를 주차하는 것은 극도로 어려울 수 있다.
    극도로 : extremely

11) 잘 설계된 교통 시스템은 편안하고 편리하다.
    잘 설계된 교통 시스템 : well-designed transport systems

12) 버스와 기차 같은 대중 교통은 도시의 오염을 줄이는 데 도움을 줄 수 있다.
    대중 교통 : public transport

13) 휴대전화들은 운전자에게 위험한 방해물이 될 수 있는데, 이 기기들이 운전자의 관심을 다른 데로 돌리게 하기 때문이다.
    위험한 방해물 : a dangerous distraction / 다른 데로 돌리다 : divert

14) 많은 나라에서 운전 중 휴대전화 사용은 금지된다.
    운전 중 : while driving / 금지하다 : ban

15) 런던에는 도로 교통량을 줄이기 위한 혼잡통행료 구간이 있다.

    도로 교통량 : the amount of road traffic / 혼잡통행료 구간 : a congestion charge zone

---

Answer

1) Tourism creates employment in services like accommodation, transport and entertainment.
2) Low-cost airlines are making it much cheaper to travel abroad.
3) Tourism attracts investment from multi-national companies.
4) Some areas rely on tourism for their income.
5) Tourism can have a negative effect on the natural environment.
6) Excessive development can destroy the habitat of wild animals.
7) Beautiful beaches in remote areas are spoiled by the building of hotels.
8) A rise in the cost of living affects local people.
9) In order to reduce traffic we should work more flexible hours.
10) Parking a car can be extremely difficult in big cities.
11) Well-designed transport systems are comfortable and convenient.
12) Public transport such as buses and trains can help to reduce pollution in cities.
13) Mobile phones can be a dangerous distraction for drivers because the gadgets divert the driver's attention.
14) The use of mobile phones while driving has been banned in many countries.
15) In London, there is a congestion charge zone to reduce the amount of road traffic.

 실전문제

You should spend about 40 minutes on this task.
Write about the following topic :

> Tourism is becoming a good source of revenue for many countries. Discuss the advantages and the disadvantages of developing this industry.

Give reasons for your answer and include any relevant examples from your own knowledge or experience.

Write at least 250 words.

 **1 단계** 문제 정독, 문제 유형 파악, 브레인스토밍 (0 ~ 5분)

Question	Tourism is becoming a good source of revenue for many countries. Discuss the advantages and the disadvantages of developing this industry.

문제 정독
관광 산업은 많은 나라들의 좋은 수입원이 되고 있다. 이러한 산업 발달의 장단점을 논하라.

 revenue : (정부나 기관의) 수입

문제 유형 파악

2-2. Discuss the advantages and the disadvantages of 토픽. 유형

* 장단점을 논하라고 했기 때문에, 어느 쪽이 더 많다고 결론을 내려서는 안 된다. Body 1에는 장점을, Body 2에는 단점을 비슷한 분량으로 적고, 결론에는 '장점도 있지만 단점도 있다'라고 쓴다.

Brainstorming

Topic : 관광 산업은 많은 나라들의 좋은 수입원이 되고 있다.	
Advantages : 관광 산업의 장점	Disadvantages : 관광 산업의 단점
1. 국내 총 생산의 상당 부분을 차지 a significant portion of gross domestic product → 주민들은 그들의 삶을 전환하고 빈곤에서 벗어나 그들 스스로 (삶을) 향상시킬 기회를 얻음 inhabitants have the chance to transform their lives and lift themselves out of poverty 2. 관광은 국제 무대에서 국가 이미지를 높임 tourism improves their image on the world stage → 국제적인 문제에 더 큰 영향력을 확보하고 권위 있는 행사를 주관 gain a greater influence over international affairs and have the honour of hosting prestigious events	1. 그림 같은 혹은 외딴 지역을 파괴 destruct picturesque or remote areas → 해안 경치를 파괴할 뿐만 아니라 적절하지 못한 분위기를 조성 not only ruin coastal scenery, but also encourage an inappropriate atmosphere 2. 관광객 수의 증가가 교통혼잡을 가중시킴 an increase in the number of tourists exacerbates congestion → 교통 시스템은 더 많은 해외 관광객의 유입 없이도 부담을 받는 상태 transport systems are under strain without the influx of more international travellers

* 장점과 단점의 아이디어 수는 같아야 한다.

| 2단계 | 서론 (Introduction) (6~10분) : 두 문장으로 작성 |

> **Question** Tourism is becoming a good source of revenue for many countries. Discuss the advantages and the disadvantages of developing this industry.

단계	Question	서론 작성
1단계 Paraphrasing	토픽 : Tourism is becoming a good source of revenue for many countries.	Paraphrasing : As governments around the world seek to generate economic growth opportunities, an increasing number of countries are trying to develop their tourism industries.
2단계 Answering	질문 : Discuss the advantages and the disadvantages of developing this industry.	Answering : 장단점 간단히 언급 While there are undoubted financial benefits associated with attracting visitors from abroad, it can be a double-edged sword because of the problems linked to an increase in tourists.

Introduction
As governments around the world seek to generate economic growth opportunities, an increasing number of countries are trying to develop their tourism industries. While there are undoubted financial benefits associated with attracting visitors from abroad, it can be a double-edged sword because of the problems linked to an increase in tourists.

generate : 발생시키다, 만들어내다
economic growth : 경제 성장
undoubted : 확실한, 의심할 여지가 없는
a double-edged sword : 양날의 칼(장점과 단점 모두 있는 상태, 2-2 유형에 좋은 표현)

우리말 해석
세계 각국의 정부들이 경제 성장의 기회를 창출해 내려고 하듯이, 점점 더 많은 국가들이 관광산업을 개발하고자 노력하고 있다. 해외에서 방문객을 유치하는 것과 연관해서 확실한 재정적 이득이 있는 반면에, 이것은 관광객의 증가와 연계된 문제들 때문에 양날의 칼이 될 수 있다.

 **3단계** 본론 1 (Body 1) (11~20분) : **Advantages** (관광산업의 장점)

> **Question**
> Tourism is becoming a good source of revenue for many countries. Discuss the advantages and the disadvantages of developing this industry.

Body 1은 1단계에서 브레인스토밍한 'Advantages'를 바탕으로 작성한다.

1단계	Topic Sentence	There are at least a couple of positives that the tourism industry generates.
2단계 (1)	Supporting Sentence (1)	*a significant portion of gross domestic product* Some countries rely on tourism to make up a significant portion of their gross domestic product.
3단계 (1)	Supporting Sentence or Specific Example (1)	*inhabitants have the chance to transform their lives and lift themselves out of poverty* The inhabitants of such nations have the chance to transform their lives and lift themselves out of poverty by welcoming holidaymakers and selling them local services and goods.
2단계 (2)	Supporting Sentence (2)	*tourism improves their image on the world stage* Even in countries that do not rely on this kind of income, the development of tourism improves their image on the world stage.
3단계 (2)	Supporting Sentence or Specific Example (2)	*gain a greater influence over international affairs and have the honour of hosting prestigious events* This explains why we see nations, regions and cities competing with each other to build new hotels and facilities so that they might gain a greater influence over international affairs and have the honour of hosting prestigious events.

Body 1

There are at least a couple of positives that the tourism industry generates. Some countries rely on tourism to make up a significant portion of their gross domestic product. The inhabitants of such nations have the chance to transform their lives and lift themselves out of poverty by welcoming holidaymakers and selling them local services and goods. Even in countries that do not rely on this kind of income, the development of tourism improves their image on the world stage. This explains why we see nations, regions and cities competing with each other to build new hotels and facilities so that they might gain a greater influence over international affairs and have the honour of hosting prestigious events.

at least : 적어도
a couple of : 두(세) 가지의
positives : 장점들, 긍정적인 것들,
　positive는 형용사로도 명사로도 많이 사용된다.
gross domestic product : = GDP, 국내 총생산
inhabitants : 주민들

holidaymakers : = weekenders,
　vacationers, tourists, travellers, visitors 행락객
on the world stage : 국제 무대에서
honour : 영광
prestigious : 일류의, 권위 있는

우리말 해석
관광산업이 창출하는 적어도 두(세)가지 장점들이 있다. 어떤 나라들은 국가의 국내 총생산의 상당 부분을 차지하는 관광산업에 의존한다. 그러한 국가의 주민들은 행락객을 맞이하고 지역 서비스와 상품을 그들에게 판매함으로써 그들의 삶을 전환하고 빈곤에서 벗어나 그들 스스로 (삶을) 향상시킬 기회를 얻는다. 심지어 이런 종류의 수입에 의존하지 않는 국가에서도, 관광산업의 개발은 국제 무대에서 국가 이미지를 높인다. 이것은 왜 우리가 국가와 지역 그리고 도시들이 새로운 호텔과 시설을 건설하는 데 서로 경쟁하는 것을 지켜봐야 하는지를 설명해주고 있는데, 그 결과 그들은 국제적인 문제에 더 큰 영향력을 확보하고 권위 있는 행사를 주관하는 영광을 가질 수 있을지도 모른다.

 **본론 2 (Body 2) (21~30분) : Disadvantages** (관광산업의 단점)

> **Question** Tourism is becoming a good source of revenue for many countries. Discuss the advantages and the disadvantages of developing this industry.

Body 2는 1단계에서 브레인스토밍한 'Disadvantages'를 바탕으로 작성한다.

1단계	Topic Sentence	However, tourism can have several unwanted effects.
2단계 (1)	Supporting Sentence (1)	destruct picturesque or remote areas This industry is likely to destruct picturesque or remote areas.
3단계 (1)	Supporting Sentence or Specific Example (1)	not only ruin coastal scenery, but also encourage an inappropriate atmosphere For example, the construction of seaside resorts along with bars and night-clubs can not only ruin coastal scenery, but also encourage an inappropriate atmosphere for local children and families.
2단계 (2)	Supporting Sentence (2)	an increase in the number of tourists exacerbates congestion Aside from such a scenario in underdeveloped countries, people who live in big cities often complain that an increase in the number of tourists exacerbates congestion.
3단계 (2)	Supporting Sentence or Specific Example (2)	transport systems are under strain without the influx of more international travellers Places like Seoul, Tokyo and New York are already overcrowded and their transport systems are under strain without the influx of more international travellers.

Body 2

However, tourism can have several unwanted effects. This industry is likely to destruct picturesque or remote areas. For example, the construction of seaside resorts along with bars and night-clubs can not only ruin coastal scenery, but also encourage an inappropriate atmosphere for local children and families. Aside from such a scenario in underdeveloped countries, people who live in big cities often complain that an increase in the number of tourists exacerbates congestion. Places like Seoul, Tokyo and New York are already overcrowded and their transport systems are under strain without the influx of more international travellers.

unwanted effects : 원치 않는 효과
destruct picturesque or remote areas :
  그림 같은 혹은 외딴 지역을 파괴하다
seaside resorts : 해변 휴양지
not only A but also B : A뿐만 아니라 B도
ruin coastal scenery : 해안 경치를 망치다
an inappropriate atmosphere : 적절하지 못한
  분위기

aside from : ~ 외에도
underdeveloped countries : = less advanced
  countries, poor countries, 후진국
exacerbate congestion : 교통혼잡을 가중시키다
overcrowded : 초만원인, 너무 붐비는
strain : 부담, 압박
influx : 유입

우리말 해석

그러나, 관광산업은 몇 가지 원치 않는 효과가 발생할 수 있다. 이 산업은 그림 같은 혹은 외딴 지역을 파괴할 가능성이 있다. 예를 들면, 술집이나 나이트 클럽들과 함께 해변 휴양지가 건설되는 것은 해안 경치를 망칠 뿐만 아니라, 현지 어린이들과 가족들에게 적절하지 못한 분위기를 조성할 수 있다. 후진국에서의 이러한 시나리오 외에도, 대도시에 사는 사람들은 종종 관광객 수의 증가가 교통혼잡을 가중시킨다고 불평한다. 서울과 도쿄 그리고 뉴욕 같은 지역들은 이미 초만원 상태이며 그들의 교통 시스템은 더 많은 해외 관광객의 유입 없이도 부담을 받는 상태에 있다.

 **5 단계** 결론 (Conclusion) (31~35분) : 본문에 제시한 장단점을 요약하며 다시 한 번 강조

| Question | Tourism is becoming a good source of revenue for many countries. Discuss the advantages and the disadvantages of developing this industry. |

결론 작성 시, 먼저 문제 유형을 파악한 후, 'Conclusion Template'의 표현을 인용한다. (See p58)

문제 유형 파악	2-2) Discuss the advantages and the disadvantages of 토픽. 유형
Conclusion Template 인용	In conclusion, although there are benefits(drawbacks) of … (토픽), its drawbacks(benefits) also should not be ignored because … 본문에 제시한 장점과 단점 간단히 요약

결론에서 절대로 해결책을 제시해서는 안 된다.

Conclusion

In conclusion, although there are clear motivations for a country to develop its tourism industry, **the drawbacks** of such a policy **should not be ignored because of** general infrastructure concerns and the potential damage to the environment and local communities.

* 상황에 따라 템플릿을 살짝 변형해도 좋다.

clear motivations : 분명한 동기
ignore : 무시하다
infrastructure : 사회기반시설
local communities : 지역사회

우리말 해석

결론적으로, 비록 한 국가가 관광산업을 개발하고자 하는 분명한 동기가 있더라도, 그러한 정책의 결점은 전반적인 사회기반시설에 대한 염려와 자연환경과 지역사회에 입힐 잠재적 피해 때문에 무시되어서는 안 된다.

6 단계　교정 (Self-correction) (36~40분) : 내용의 일관성 및 문법 검토

다음 Body 2의 내용을 교정해 보자. 틀린 부분은 총 몇 개일까?

교정 전 (직접 문장 부호를 이용하여 틀린 부분을 교정해 보자.)

However, Tourism can have several unwanted effect. This industry are likely to destruct picturesque or remote areas. For example, the construction of seaside resorts along with bars and night-clubs can not only ruin coastal scenery, but also encourage a inappropriate atmosphere for local child and families.

Aside from such a scenario in underdeveloped countries, people who lives in big cities often complains that an increase in the number of tourists exacerbate congestions. Places like the Seoul, Tokyo and New York are already overcrowded and their transport systems are under strain without the influx of more international traveller.

교정

> However, ~~T~~(t) ourism can have several unwanted effect(+s→effects). This industry ~~are~~(is) likely to destruct picturesque or remote areas. For example, the construction of seaside resorts along with bars and night-clubs can not only ruin coastal scenery, but also encourage ~~a~~(an) inappropriate atmosphere for local ~~child~~(children) and families. Aside from such a scenario in underdeveloped countries, people who ~~lives~~(live) in big cities often ~~complains~~(complain) that an increase in the number of tourists ~~exacerbate~~(exacerbates) ~~congestions~~(congestion). Places like ~~the~~ Seoul, Tokyo and New York are already overcrowded and their transport systems are under strain without the influx of more international ~~traveller~~(travellers).

1. T → t : 갑자기 대문자를 문장 중간에 쓰지 않는다(고유명사 예외).
2. effect → effects : 셀 수 있는 명사이므로 복수형으로 쓴다.
3. are → is : 주어인 industry가 단수이므로 단수 동사인 is를 쓴다.
4. a → an : 모음(a/i/u/e/o)으로 발음이 시작되는 단어 inappropriate[ɪnəproʊpriət] 앞에는 a가 아닌 an으로 쓰고 말한다.
5. child → children : 셀 수 있는 명사이므로 복수형으로 쓴다.
6. 붙여쓰기 : 위의 글은 Body 2 단락이다. 단락이 바뀌지 않는 한, 줄을 바꿔 쓰지 않는다.
7. lives → live : 주어인 people이 복수이므로 복수 동사인 live를 쓴다.
8. complains → complain : 주어인 people이 복수이므로 복수 동사인 complain을 쓴다.
9. exacerbate → exacerbates : 주어인 an increase가 단수이므로 단수 동사인 exacerbates를 쓴다.
10. congestions → congestion : congestion은 셀 수 없는 명사이기 때문에 ~s를 붙일 수 없다.
11. the → 삭제 : 도시 이름 'Seoul' 앞에는 관사 the를 붙일 수 없다.
12. traveller → travellers : 셀 수 있는 명사이므로 복수형으로 쓴다.

틀린 개수 : 총 12개

Sample Answer

> **Question** Tourism is becoming a good source of revenue for many countries. Discuss the advantages and the disadvantages of developing this industry.

As governments around the world seek to generate economic growth opportunities, an increasing number of countries are trying to develop their tourism industries. While there are undoubted financial benefits associated with attracting visitors from abroad, it can be a double-edged sword because of the problems linked to an increase in tourists.

There are at least a couple of positives that the tourism industry generates. Some countries rely on tourism to make up a significant portion of their gross domestic product. The inhabitants of such nations have the chance to transform their lives and lift themselves out of poverty by welcoming holidaymakers and selling them local services and goods. Even in countries that do not rely on this kind of income, the development of tourism improves their image on the world stage. This explains why we see nations, regions and cities competing with each other to build new hotels and facilities so that they might gain a greater influence over international affairs and have the honour of hosting prestigious events.

However, tourism can have several unwanted effects. This industry is likely to destruct picturesque or remote areas. For example, the construction of seaside resorts along with bars and night-clubs can not only ruin coastal scenery, but also encourage an inappropriate atmosphere for local children and families. Aside from such a scenario in underdeveloped countries, people who live in big cities often complain that an increase in the number of tourists exacerbates congestion. Places like Seoul, Tokyo and New York are already overcrowded and their transport systems are under strain without the influx of more international travellers.

In conclusion, although there are clear motivations for a country to develop its tourism industry, the drawbacks of such a policy should not be ignored because of general infrastructure concerns and the potential damage to the environment and local communities.

word counts : 305 words

우리말 해석

세계 각국의 정부들이 경제 성장의 기회를 창출해 내려고 하듯이, 점점 더 많은 국가들이 관광산업을 개발하고자 노력하고 있다. 해외에서 방문객을 유치하는 것과 연관해서 확실한 재정적 이득이 있는 반면에, 이것은 관광객의 증가와 연계된 문제들 때문에 양날의 칼이 될 수 있다.

관광산업이 창출하는 적어도 두(세)가지 장점들이 있다. 어떤 나라들은 국가의 국내 총생산의 상당 부분을 차지하는 관광산업에 의존한다. 그러한 국가의 주민들은 행락객을 맞이하고 지역 서비스와 상품을 그들에게 판매함으로써 그들의 삶을 전환하고 빈곤에서 벗어나 그들 스스로 (삶을) 향상시킬 기회를 얻는다. 심지어 이런 종류의 수입에 의존하지 않는 국가에서도, 관광산업의 개발은 국제 무대에서 국가 이미지를 높인다. 이것은 왜 우리가 국가와 지역 그리고 도시들이 새로운 호텔과 시설을 건설하는 데 서로 경쟁하는 것을 지켜봐야 하는지를 설명해주고 있는데, 그 결과 그들은 국제적인 문제에 더 큰 영향력을 확보하고 권위 있는 행사를 주관하는 영광을 가질 수 있을지도 모른다.

그러나, 관광산업은 몇 가지 원치 않는 효과가 발생할 수 있다. 이 산업은 그림 같은 혹은 외딴 지역을 파괴할 가능성이 있다. 예를 들면, 술집이나 나이트 클럽들과 함께 해변 휴양지가 건설되는 것은 해안 경치를 망칠 뿐만 아니라, 현지 어린이들과 가족들에게 적절하지 못한 분위기를 조성할 수 있다. 후진국에서의 이러한 시나리오 외에도, 대도시에 사는 사람들은 종종 관광객 수의 증가가 교통혼잡을 가중시킨다고 불평한다. 서울과 도쿄 그리고 뉴욕 같은 지역들은 이미 초만원 상태이며 그들의 교통 시스템은 더 많은 해외 관광객의 유입 없이도 부담을 받는 상태에 있다.

결론적으로, 비록 한 국가가 관광 산업을 개발하고자 하는 분명한 동기가 있더라도, 그러한 정책의 결점은 전반적인 사회 기반시설에 대한 염려와 자연환경과 지역사회에 입힐 잠재적 피해 때문에 무시되어서는 안 된다.

문법 Review

앞에서 배운 내용을 바탕으로 다음 빈칸을 영어로 작성해 보자.

As governments around the world seek to _____ (1. 경제 성장의 기회를 창출해 내다), an increasing number of countries are trying to develop their tourism industries. While there are _____ (2. 확실한 재정적 이득) associated with attracting visitors from abroad, it can be _____ (3. 양날의 칼) because of the problems linked to an increase in tourists.

There are _____ (4. 적어도) a couple of positives that the tourism industry generates. Some countries rely on tourism to make up a significant portion of their _____ (5. 국내 총생산). The inhabitants of such nations have the chance to transform their lives and lift themselves out of poverty _____ (6. 행락객들을 맞이함으로써) and selling them local services and goods. Even in countries that do not rely on this kind of income, the development of tourism improves their image _____ (7. 국제 무대에서). This explains why we see nations, regions and cities competing with each other to build new hotels and facilities so that they might gain a greater influence over international affairs and have the honour of _____ (8. 권위 있는 행사를 주관하는).

However, tourism can have _____ (9. 몇 가지 원치 않는 효과). This industry is likely to destruct picturesque or remote areas. For example, the construction of _____ (10. 해변 휴양지) along with bars and night-clubs can not only ruin coastal scenery, but also encourage an inappropriate atmosphere for local children and families. Aside from such a scenario _____ (11. 후진국에서), people who live in big cities often complain that an increase in the number of tourists _____ (12. 교통혼잡을 가중시키다). Places like Seoul, Tokyo and New York are already overcrowded and their transport systems are under strain without the influx of more international travellers.

In conclusion, although there are clear motivations for a country to develop its tourism industry, the drawbacks of such a policy should not be ignored because of general infrastructure concerns and the potential damage to the environment and _____ (13. 지역사회).

Answer 1. generate economic growth opportunities / 2. undoubted financial benefits / 3. a double-edged sword
4. at least / 5. gross domestic product / 6. by welcoming holidaymakers / 7. on the world stage
8. hosting prestigious events / 9. several unwanted effects / 10. seaside resorts
11. in underdeveloped countries / 12. exacerbates congestion / 13. local communities

Day 7 Travelling & Transport 불법 포인트 정리

숙박	accommodation	경제 성장	economic growth
교통	transport	확실한, 의심할 여지가 없는	undoubted
오락	entertainment	양날의 칼	a double-edged sword
고용을 창출하다	create employment	적어도	at least
저가 항공사	low-cost airlines	두(세) 가지의	a couple of
해외로 여행하다	travel abroad	장점들, 긍정적인 것들	positives
다국적 회사	multi-national companies	국내 총생산	gross domestic product / GDP
투자	investment	주민들	inhabitants
소득	income	행락객, 관광객	holidaymakers / weekenders vacationers / tourists / travellers visitors
자연 환경	the natural environment	국제 무대에서	on the world stage
~에 부정적인 영향을 끼치다	have a negative effect on	영광	honour
과도한 개발	excessive development	일류의, 권위 있는	prestigious
야생 동물의 서식지	the habitat of wild animals	원치않는 효과	unwanted effects
훼손하다, 망치다	spoil	그림 같은 혹은 외딴 지역을 파괴하다	destruct picturesque or remote areas
생활비	the cost of living	해변 휴양지	seaside resorts
지역 사람들	local people	A뿐만 아니라 B도	not only A but also B
교통량	traffic	해안 경치를 망치다	ruin coastal scenery
탄력적인 시간	flexible hours	적절하지 못한 분위기	an inappropriate atmosphere
극도로	extremely	~ 외에도	aside from
잘 설계된 교통 시스템	well-designed transport systems	후진국	underdeveloped countries less advanced countries poor countries
대중 교통	public transport	교통혼잡을 가중시키다	exacerbate congestion
위험한 방해물	a dangerous distraction	초만원인, 너무 붐비는	overcrowded
다른 데로 돌리다	divert	부담, 압박	strain
운전 중	while driving	유입	influx
금지하다	ban	분명한 동기	clear motivations
도로 교통량	the amount of road traffic	무시하다	ignore
혼잡통행료 구간	a congestion charge zone	사회기반시설	infrastructure
(정부나 기관의) 수입	revenue	지역사회	local communities
발생시키다, 만들어내다	generate		

Day 8 Past & History 과거와 역사

Question

Some people think studying history has little value in modern society. Do you agree or disagree with this opinion?

어떤 사람들은 현대 사회에서 역사를 연구하는 것이 거의 가치가 없다고 생각한다. 당신은 이 의견에 동의하는가? 동의하지 않는가?

 빈출 문제

1. Some people feel admission should be free to national museums, galleries, and major historical sites, while others argue that admission fees are necessary. Discuss both views and give your own opinion.

2. Some people say cities should preserve their historic buildings. Others insist that these buildings should be replaced by modern buildings. Discuss both views and give your own opinion.

3. It is more important for students to study history than it is for them to study science. Do you agree or disagree with this statement?

4. Tradition plays a key role in our lives. Therefore it is very essential that we hand down our tradition to our children. Do you agree or disagree with this statement?

1. 어떤 사람들은 국립 박물관, 미술관 그리고 주요 역사 유적지의 입장료를 무료로 해야 한다고 생각하는 반면, 입장료가 필요하다고 주장하는 사람들도 있다. 양쪽의 견해를 논하고 당신의 주장을 제시하라.

2. 어떤 사람들은 도시가 역사적 건물들을 보존해야 한다고 말한다. 반면 이러한 건물들을 현대식 건물로 대체해야 한다고 주장하는 사람들도 있다. 양쪽의 견해를 논하고 당신의 주장을 제시하라.

3. 학생들이 역사를 배우는 것은 과학을 배우는 것보다 더 중요하다. 당신은 이 말에 동의하는가? 또는 동의하지 않는가?

4. 전통은 우리의 삶에 중요한 역할을 한다. 따라서 아이들에게 전통을 물려주는 것은 매우 중요하다. 당신은 이 말에 동의하는가? 또는 동의하지 않는가?

 **STEP2 브레인스토밍**

1) 역사에 대한 우리의 무지는 정보의 부족이 아니라 무관심의 결과이다.
   무지 : ignorance / 무관심 : indifference

2) 과거를 지배하는 사람이 미래를 지배한다.
   지배하다 : control

3) 만약 과거가 악몽 같았다면, 사람들은 이러한 상황이 재발하는 것을 막으려고 행동했을 것이다.
   악몽 같은 : nightmarish / 재발(생)하다 : reoccur

4) 아무도 과거의 사건에 대한 사실 모두를 기록할 수 없다.
   기록하다 : record

5) 역사의 목적은 불필요한 사항들은 누락시키는 반면, 사건의 본질은 포착하는 과거에 대한 이야기를 보여주는 것이다.
   불필요한 사항 : superfluous details / 누락시키다 : omit / 사건의 본질 : the essence of an event

6) 역사의 중요성은 역사학자에 의해서 결정된다.
   역사학자 : historian / 결정되다 : be determined by

7) 역사학자들은 그들이 사는 사회의 지배적인 가치들을 반영하는 이야기를 말하는 경향이 있다.
   지배적인 가치 : dominant values / ~하는 경향이 있다 : tend to

8) 과거는 아무도 일어난 일을 바꿀 수 없기 때문에 고정되어 있지만, 사회의 가치가 변화함에 따라 역사학자들의 과거에 대한 묘사는 변화한다.
   사회의 가치 : the values of society / 묘사 : depiction

9) 대부분의 역사학자들은 그들의 목적으로 사용하기 위해서 역사를 고의적으로 왜곡하지 않는다.
   목적으로 사용하다 : serve a purpose / 고의적으로 : intentionally / 왜곡하다 : distort

10) 사람들은 역사의 힘을 과소평가하는 경향이 있다.
    과소평가하다 : underestimate

11) 역사는 우리가 현재를 이해하도록 돕기 때문에 중요하다.

12) 우리 아이들에게 가르치는 (우리 아이들이 배우는) 역사는 그들의 가치와 믿음을 형성하는 데 중요한 역할을 하고 있다.
    가치와 믿음 : values and beliefs / ~데 중요한 역할을 하다 : play an important role in

13) 고고학은 물질적인 유물들을 통한 고대와 근대 인간 과거에 대한 연구이다.
    고고학 : archaeology / 고대의 : ancient / 물질적인 유물 : material remains / 근대의 : recent

14) 고고학은 우리가 사람들이 어디에서 언제 살았는지 뿐만 아니라 왜 어떻게 살았는지 또한 이해하는 데 도움을 준다.

15) 오늘날 고고학은 정밀한 과학인데, 고고학자들의 방법이 방사선 탄소 연대 측정법과 물리 탐사를 포함하고 있기 때문이다.

정밀한 : precise / 고고학자 : archaeologists / 방사선 탄소 연대 측정법 : radioactive carbon dating

물리 탐사 : geophysical prospecting

Answer

1) Our ignorance of the past is not the result of a lack of information, but of indifference.
2) Whoever controls the past controls the future.
3) If the past were nightmarish, then people would act to prevent such circumstances from reoccurring.
4) No one can record everything that is true about an event in the past.
5) The goal of history is to present a story about the past which captures the essence of an event while omitting superfluous details.
6) The significance of history is determined by the historian.
7) Historians tend to tell stories which reflect the dominant values of the society in which they live.
8) The past is fixed because no one can change what happened but as the values of society change, the historians' depiction of the past changes.
9) Most historians do not intentionally distort history to serve their purposes.
10) People tend to underestimate the power of history.
11) History is important because it helps us to understand the present.
12) The history taught to our children is playing an important role in shaping their values and beliefs.
13) Archaeology is the study of the ancient and recent human past through material remains.
14) Archaeology helps us understand not only where and when people lived, but also why and how they lived.
15) Today archaeology is a precise science because archaeologists' methods include radioactive carbon dating and geophysical prospecting.

 실전문제

You should spend about 40 minutes on this task.
Write about the following topic :

> Some people think studying history has little value in modern society. Do you agree or disagree with this opinion?

Give reasons for your answer and include any relevant examples from your own knowledge or experience.

Write at least 250 words.

 **1 단계** 문제 정독, 문제 유형 파악, 브레인스토밍 (0 ~ 5분)

Question	Some people think studying history has little value in modern society. Do you agree or disagree with this opinion?

문제 정독
어떤 사람들은 현대 사회에서 역사를 연구하는 것이 거의 가치가 없다고 생각한다. 당신은 이 의견에 동의하는가? 동의하지 않는가?

 little : 거의 없는(부정)

문제 유형 파악

1-1. Do you agree or disagree? 유형

Brainstorming

Topic : 현대 사회에서 역사를 연구하는 것	
Agree : 거의 가치가 없다.	Disagree : 가치가 있다.
1. 역사책에 적힌 일부 잘못된 정보들 some wrong information written in the history books → 역사는 늘 승자의 편에서 작성됨 history always written by winners	1. 우리 선조들이 세운 좋은 선례들의 가치 the value of the examples set by our ancestors → 세계대전 같은 이전세대의 공포들 the horrors of previous ages like the World War 2. 이전 문명의 발전 지속 continue the progress of previous civilisations → 우리가 즐기는 모든 것이 과거의 산물 enjoy today is the product of the past

* Disagree에 대한 아이디어가 더 많으므로, 이 에세이에서는 Disagree, '현대 사회에서 역사를 연구하는 것은 가치가 있다.'를 내 주장으로 삼았다

 **2 단계** 서론 (Introduction) (6~10분) : 두 문장으로 작성

| Question | Some people think studying history has little value in modern society. Do you agree or disagree with this opinion? |

단계	Question	서론 작성
1단계 Paraphrasing	토픽 : Some people think studying history has little value in modern society.	**Paraphrasing :** When it comes to studying history, there is a growing debate over whether we are wasting our time and resources examining the past when we could focus on the present and future.
2단계 Answering	질문 : Do you agree or disagree with this opinion?	**Answering : Disagree일 경우** Although current events deserve our attention, I believe we should place a strong emphasis on history if we do not want to repeat past tragedies.

Introduction

When it comes to studying history, there is a growing debate over whether we are wasting our time and resources examining the past when we could focus on the present and future. Although current events deserve our attention, I believe we should place a strong emphasis on history if we do not want to repeat past tragedies.

examine : = study, 조사 검토하다
deserve one's attention : 누구의 관심을 받을 가치가 있다
place a strong emphasis on : ~에 중점을 두다
tragedies : tragedy 비극들

우리말 해석

역사 연구에 관해서 말하자면, 우리가 현재와 미래에 집중할 수 있을 때 과거를 연구하느라 시간과 자원을 낭비하고 있는 것인지 아닌지에 대한 논쟁이 커지고 있다. 비록 현재의 사건들이 우리의 관심을 받아야 하지만 나는 우리가 과거의 비극을 되풀이하기 원치 않는다면 역사에 중점을 두어야 한다고 믿는다.

3 단계 본론 1 (Body 1) (11~20분) : 나와 다른 의견 = **Agree** (현대 사회에서 역사를 연구하는 것은 거의 가치가 없다)

> **Question** Some people think studying history has little value in modern society. Do you agree or disagree with this opinion?

Body 1은 1단계에서 브레인스토밍한 'Agree'의 주장을 바탕으로 작성한다.

1단계	Topic Sentence	There is an opinion that being knowledgeable in a history of a certain country or the world does not have a significant impact on today's life.
2단계 (1)	Supporting Sentence (1)	*some wrong information, written in the history books* Some amount of information written in the history books can be wrong, because no one throughout the world knows exactly when some special events have happened.
3단계 (1)	Supporting Sentence or Specific Example (1)	*history always written by winners* History is always written by winners, therefore, those people could write invalid information in order to leave their own names in history forever.

Body 1
There is an opinion that being knowledgeable in a history of a certain country or the world does not have a significant impact on today's life. Some amount of information written in the history books can be wrong, because no one throughout the world knows exactly when some special events have happened. History is always written by winners, therefore, those people could write invalid information in order to leave their own names in history forever.

knowledgeable : 아는 것이 많은, 정통한
have a significant impact on :
　～ 에 중대한 영향력을 미치다
no one : 아무도, 부정어로 시작되는 문장을
　반드시 써볼 것!

invalid information : 근거 없는 정보,
　information은 셀 수 없는 명사인 것을
　다시 한 번 기억하자!
leave one's own name in history :
　역사에 이름을 남기다

> **우리말 해석**
> 어떤 한 나라나 혹은 세계의 역사에 정통하다는 것이 오늘날의 생활에 중요한 영향력을 행사하지 못한다는 의견이 있다. 역사 책에 적힌 어떤 정보들은 잘못된 것일 수 있는데, 왜냐하면 전세계의 어느 누구도 어떤 특별한 사건들이 일어났을 때를 정확히 알지 못하기 때문이다. 역사는 항상 승자의 편에서 쓰여졌고 따라서 그런 사람들은 영원히 자신들의 이름을 남기고자 근거가 없는 정보를 썼을 가능성이 있다.

 **4단계** 본론 2 (Body 2) (21~30분) : 내 의견 = Disagree (현대 사회에서 역사를 연구하는 것은 가치가 있다)

| Question | Some people think studying history has little value in modern society. Do you agree or disagree with this opinion? |

Body 2는 1단계에서 브레인스토밍한 'Disagree'의 주장을 바탕으로 작성한다.

1단계	Topic Sentence	Although some peripheral records can be fabricated, studying our past is still valuable in contemporary society. An accurate understanding of history not only helps save us from further tragic events but also allows us to prosper in our lives.
2단계 (1)	Supporting Sentence (1)	*the value of the examples set by our ancestors* Those who claim it is irrelevant to concentrate on events of the past ignore the value of the examples set for us by our ancestors.
3단계 (1)	Supporting Sentence or Specific Example (1)	*the horrors of previous ages like the World War* If we do not study those lessons then we risk going through some of the horrors of previous ages like the World War all over again.
2단계 (2)	Supporting Sentence (2)	*continue the progress of previous civilisations* Equally, we can continue the progress of previous civilisations if we find out how they advanced themselves.
3단계 (2)	Supporting Sentence or Specific Example (2)	*enjoy today is the product of the past* Everything we enjoy today is the product of the past, and we should maintain that trend in as positive a way as possible.

Body 2

Although some peripheral records can be fabricated, studying our past is still valuable in contemporary society. An accurate understanding of history not only helps save us from further tragic events but also allows us to prosper in our lives. Those who claim it is irrelevant to concentrate on events of the past ignore the value of the examples set for us by our ancestors. If we do not study those lessons then we risk going through some of the horrors of previous ages like the World War all over again. Equally, we can continue the progress of previous civilisations if we find out how they advanced themselves. Everything we enjoy today is the product of the past, and we should maintain that trend in as positive a way as possible.

peripheral : 지엽적인(부수적이고 중요하지 않은)
fabricated : 조작된, 날조의
contemporary society : 동시대 사회, 현재 사회
prosper : 번영하다
irrelevant : 중요하지 않은, 상관없는
ancestor : 조상, 선조
previous civilisations : 이전 문명들

> **우리말 해석**
> 어떤 지엽적 기록은 조작된 것일 수 있지만, 우리의 과거를 연구하는 것은 현대 사회에서 여전히 가치 있는 일이다. 역사에 대한 정확한 이해는 추가적인 비극적 사건들로부터 우리를 구원하는 데 도움을 주는 것뿐만 아니라 우리의 번영된 삶을 가능하게 해준다. 과거의 사건에 집중하는 것이 중요하지 않다고 주장하는 사람들은 우리 선조들이 세운 좋은 선례들의 가치를 무시하는 것이다. 만일 우리가 그러한 교훈들을 연구하지 않는다면 우리는 세계대전처럼 이전 세대의 공포들을 다시 반복해서 겪을 위험이 있다. 동시에 우리가 선조들이 그들 스스로를 진보시킨 방법을 알아낼 수 있다면 이전 문명의 발전을 지속할 수 있을 것이다. 오늘날 우리가 즐기는 모든 것이 과거의 산물이며 또한 우리는 최대한 긍정적인 방법으로 그러한 추세를 보존해야 한다.

| 5 단계 | 결론 (Conclusion) (31~35분) : 본문에 제시한 내 주장 요약하며 다시 한 번 강조 |

> **Question** Some people think studying history has little value in modern society. Do you agree or disagree with this opinion?

결론 작성 시, 먼저 문제 유형을 파악한 후, 'Conclusion Template'의 표현을 인용한다. (See p58)

문제 유형 파악	1-1) Do you agree or disagree? 유형
Conclusion Template 인용	For the reasons mentioned above, I totally agree(disagree) with the opinion because… 본문에 제시한 내 주장 간단히 요약

결론을 작성하기 전, 서론과 본론 2에서 Disagree, '현대 사회에서 역사를 연구하는 것은 가치가 있다.' 라고 했는지 다시 한 번 확인하자!

Conclusion

For the reasons mentioned above, I totally disagree with the opinion that studying history is worthless **because** through reflecting our past we could prevent horrific conflicts and boost our civilisation.

* 상황에 따라 템플릿을 살짝 변형해도 좋다.

horrific conflicts : 끔찍한 갈등
civilisation : 문명
worthless : = valueless, useless, unimportant 가치 없는

우리말 해석

위에서 언급한 이유들 때문에 나는 역사 연구가 가치 없다는 주장에 전적으로 동의하지 않는다. 왜냐하면 우리의 과거를 반성함으로써 끔찍한 갈등을 막을 수 있고 문명을 번영시킬 수 있기 때문이다.

6 단계 교정 (Self-correction) (36~40분) : 내용의 일관성 및 문법 검토

다음 Body 2의 내용을 교정해 보자. 틀린 부분은 총 몇 개일까?

교정 전 (직접 문장 부호를 이용하여 틀린 부분을 교정해 보자.)

Although some peripheral records can be fabricated, but studying our past are still valuable in contemporary society. A accurate understanding of history not only helps save us from further tragic event but also allows us to prosper in our lives. Those who claim it is irrelevant to concentrate for events of the past ignore the value of the examples set for us by our ancestors.

if we do not study those lessons then we risks going through some of the horrors of previous ages like the World War all over again. Equally, we cannot continue the progress of previous civilisations if we find out how they advanced themselves. Everything we enjoyed today is the product of the past, and we should maintain that trend in as positive a way as possible.

교정

Although some peripheral records can be fabricated, but studying our past are still valuable in contemporary society. A accurate understanding of history not only helps save us from further tragic event but also allows us to prosper in our lives. Those who claim it is irrelevant to concentrate for events of the past ignore the value of the examples set for us by our ancestors. if we do not study those lessons then we risks going through some of the horrors of previous ages like the World War all over again. Equally, we cannot continue the progress of previous civilisations if we find out how they advanced themselves. Everything we enjoyed today is the product of the past, and we should maintain that trend in as positive a way as possible.

1. but → 삭제 : although 자체에 but의 뜻을 포함하고 있기 때문에 절대로 but을 써서는 안 된다.
2. are → is : 주어인 studying은 동명사이고 동명사는 단수이므로 단수 동사인 is를 쓴다.
3. A → An : 모음(a/i/u/e/o)으로 발음이 시작되는 단어 accurate[ækjərət] 앞에는 a가 아닌 an으로 쓰고 말한다.
4. event → events : 셀 수 있는 명사이므로 복수형으로 쓴다.
5. for → on : concentrate on은 '~에 집중하다'라는 뜻
6. 붙여쓰기 : 위의 글은 Body 2 단락이다. 단락이 바뀌지 않는 한, 줄을 바꿔 쓰지 않는다.
7. if → If : 문장의 첫 글자는 반드시 대문자로 시작한다.
8. risks → risk : 주어인 we가 복수이므로 복수 동사인 risk를 쓴다.
9. cannot → can : 이전 문명의 발전을 지속할 수 있을 것이다라고 해야 논리에 맞다. 이걸 놓치면 절대 안 된다!
10. enjoyed → enjoy : today와 is 모두 현재를 나타내는 단어들이고, 내용상 현재형이 맞다.

틀린 개수 : 총 10개

Sample Answer

> **Question** Some people think studying history has little value in modern society. Do you agree or disagree with this opinion?

When it comes to studying history, there is a growing debate over whether we are wasting our time and resources examining the past when we could focus on the present and future. Although current events deserve our attention, I believe we should place a strong emphasis on history if we do not want to repeat past tragedies.

There is an opinion that being knowledgeable in a history of a certain country or the world does not have a significant impact on today's life. Some amount of information written in the history books can be wrong, because no one throughout the world knows exactly when some special events have happened. History is always written by winners, therefore, those people could write invalid information in order to leave their own names in history forever.

Although some peripheral records can be fabricated, studying our past is still valuable in contemporary society. An accurate understanding of history not only helps save us from further tragic events but also allows us to prosper in our lives. Those who claim it is irrelevant to concentrate on events of the past ignore the value of the examples set for us by our ancestors. If we do not study those lessons then we risk going through some of the horrors of previous ages like the World War all over again. Equally, we can continue the progress of previous civilisations if we find out how they advanced themselves. Everything we enjoy today is the product of the past, and we should maintain that trend in as positive a way as possible.

For the reasons mentioned above, I totally disagree with the opinion that studying history is worthless because through reflecting our past we could prevent horrific conflicts and boost our civilisation.

word counts : 292 words

우리말 해석

역사 연구에 관해서 말하자면, 우리가 현재와 미래에 집중할 수 있을 때 과거를 연구하느라 시간과 자원을 낭비하고 있는 것인지 아닌지에 대한 논쟁이 커지고 있다. 비록 현재의 사건들이 우리의 관심을 받아야 하지만 나는 우리가 과거의 비극을 되풀이하기 원치 않는다면 역사에 중점을 두어야 한다고 믿는다.

어떤 한 나라나 혹은 세계의 역사에 정통하다는 것이 오늘날의 생활에 중요한 영향력을 행사하지 못한다는 의견이 있다. 역사 책에 적힌 어떤 정보들은 잘못된 것일 수 있는데, 왜냐하면 전세계의 어느 누구도 어떤 특별한 사건들이 일어났을 때를 정확히 알지 못하기 때문이다. 역사는 항상 승자의 편에서 쓰여졌고 따라서 그런 사람들은 영원히 자신들의 이름을 남기고자 근거가 없는 정보를 썼을 가능성이 있다.

어떤 지엽적 기록은 조작된 것일 수 있지만, 우리의 과거를 연구하는 것은 현대 사회에서 여전히 가치 있는 일이다. 역사에 대한 정확한 이해는 추가적인 비극적 사건들로부터 우리를 구원하는 데 도움을 주는 것뿐만 아니라 우리의 번영된 삶을 가능하게 해준다. 과거의 사건에 집중하는 것이 중요하지 않다고 주장하는 사람들은 우리 선조들이 세운 좋은 선례들의 가치를 무시하는 것이다. 만일 우리가 그러한 교훈들을 연구하지 않는다면 우리는 세계대전처럼 이전 세대의 공포들을 다시 반복해서 겪을 위험이 있다. 동시에 우리가 선조들이 그들 스스로를 진보시킨 방법을 알아낼 수 있다면 이전 문명의 발전을 지속할 수 있을 것이다. 오늘날 우리가 즐기는 모든 것이 과거의 산물이며 또한 우리는 최대한 긍정적인 방법으로 그러한 추세를 보존해야 한다.

위에서 언급한 이유들 때문에 나는 역사 연구가 가치 없다는 주장에 전적으로 동의하지 않는다. 왜냐하면 우리의 과거를 반성함으로써 끔찍한 갈등을 막을 수 있고 문명을 번영시킬 수 있기 때문이다.

불법 Review

앞에서 배운 내용을 바탕으로 다음 빈칸을 영어로 작성해 보자.

_____ (1. 역사 연구에 관해서 말하자면), there is a growing debate over whether we are wasting our time and resources examining the past when we could focus on the present and future. Although current events _____ (2. 우리의 관심을 받다), I believe we should place a strong emphasis on history if we do not want to _____ (3. 과거의 비극을 되풀이하다).

There is an opinion that being knowledgeable in a history of a certain country or the world does not have a significant impact on today's life. Some amount of information written in the history books can be wrong, because no one throughout the world knows exactly when some special events have happened. History is always written by winners, therefore, those people could write _____ (4. 근거가 없는 정보) in order to leave their own names in history forever.

Although _____ (5. 어떤 지엽적 기록은 조작된 것일 수 있다), studying our past is still valuable in contemporary society. An accurate understanding of history not only helps save us from _____ (6. 추가적인 비극적 사건들) but also allows us to prosper in our lives. Those who claim it is irrelevant to concentrate on events of the past ignore the value of the examples set for us by our ancestors. If we do not study those lessons then we risk going through some of the horrors of previous ages like the World War all over again. Equally, we can continue _____ (7. 이전 문명의 발전) if we find out how they advanced themselves. Everything we enjoy today is the product of the past, and we should maintain that trend in as positive a way as possible.

For the reasons mentioned above, I totally disagree with the opinion that studying history is worthless because through reflecting our past we could _____ (8. 끔찍한 갈등을 막다) and boost our civilisation.

Answer
1. When it comes to studying history / 2. deserve our attention / 3. repeat past tragedies
4. invalid information / 5. some peripheral records can be fabricated / 6. further tragic events
7. the progress of previous civilisations / 8. prevent horrific conflicts

Day 8 Past & History 불법 포인트 정리

무지	ignorance	정밀한	precise
무관심	indifference	고고학자	archaeologists
지배하다	control	방사선 탄소 연대 측정법	radioactive carbon dating
악몽 같은	nightmarish	물리 탐사	geophysical prospecting
재발(생)하다	reoccur	거의 없는(부정)	little
기록하다	record	조사, 검토하다	examine / study
불필요한 사항	superfluous details	누구의 관심을 받을 가치가 있다	deserve one's attention
누락시키다 생략하다	omit	~에 중점을 두다	place a strong emphasis on
사건의 본질	the essence of an event	비극	tragedy
역사학자	historian	아는 것이 많은, 정통한	knowledgeable
결정되다	be determined by	~에 중대한 영향력을 미치다	have a significant impact on
지배적인 가치	dominant values	아무도(부정)	no one
~하는 경향이 있다	tend to	근거 없는 정보	invalid information
사회의 가치	the values of society	역사에 이름을 남기다	leave one's own name in history
묘사	depiction	지엽적인	peripheral
목적으로 사용하다	serve a purpose	조작된, 날조의	fabricated
고의적으로	intentionally	동시대 사회, 현재 사회	contemporary society
왜곡하다	distort	번영하다	prosper
과소평가 하다	underestimate	중요하지 않은, 상관없는	irrelevant
가치와 믿음	values and beliefs	조상, 선조	ancestor
~에 중요한 역할을 하다	play an important role in	이전 문명들	previous civilisations
고고학	archaeology	끔찍한 갈등	horrific conflicts
물질적인 유물	material remains	문명	civilisation
고대의	ancient	가치 없는	worthless / valueless useless / unimportant
근대의, 최근의	recent		

Day 9 Natural Environment & Wildlife

자연환경과 야생동식물

Question

Nowadays many species of animals and plants are in danger of becoming extinct. What do you think the reasons are? What can you suggest as a solution?

요즘 많은 동식물들이 멸종 위기에 처해 있다. 이유가 무엇이라고 생각하는가? 해결책으로 무엇을 제시할 수 있는가?

 빈출 문제

1. In the 21st century, environmental problems are too serious to be solved by individuals or one country. In other words, they are international problems. Do you agree or disagree with this statement?

2. International animal rights groups argue it is wrong to use and kill animals for the benefit of human beings. Do you agree or disagree with this statement?

3. Some people insist that keeping animals in a zoo is wrong, while others think that zoos are both educationally and ecologically important. Discuss both views and give your own opinion.

4. Zoos that keep wild animals in an artificial environment should soon disappear. Do you agree or disagree with this statement?

1. 21세기 환경 문제는 개인이나 한 국가에 의해 해결될 수 없을 정도로 심각하다. 다시 말해 이것은 국제적인 문제이다. 당신은 이 말에 동의하는가? 또는 동의하지 않는가?

2. 국제 동물 보호 단체들은 인간의 이익을 위해 동물을 사용하고 죽이는 것이 잘못되었다고 주장한다. 당신은 이 말에 동의하는가? 또는 동의하지 않는가?

3. 어떤 사람들은 동물을 동물원에 가두는 것이 잘못되었다고 주장하는 반면, 동물원이 교육적으로나 생태학적으로 중요하다고 생각하는 사람들도 있다. 양쪽의 견해를 논하고 당신의 주장을 제시하라.

4. 야생동물을 인공적인 환경에 가두는 동물원은 곧 사라져야 한다. 당신은 이 말에 동의하는가? 또는 동의하지 않는가?

 **STEP2 브레인스토밍**

1) 동물은 중요한 과학적 연구에 사용이 되는데, 이것은 신약에 대한 임상실험을 하는 데 필요하기 때문이다.
   임상실험 : clinical trials

2) 동물 실험은 의학적, 과학적 지식을 진보시키는 데 도움을 준다.
   동물 실험 : animal testing

3) 연구자들은 동물들이 겪는 고통을 최소화하는 것을 목표로 한다.
   최소화하다 : minimize / 목표로 하다 : aim

4) 화장용 제품과 성분을 테스트하기 위한 동물 사용은 영국과 다른 모든 유럽 연합 회원국에서 금지된다.
   화장용 제품 : cosmetic products / 성분 : ingredients / 유럽 연합 : the European Union

5) 동물 애호가들은 인간은 동물을 대상으로 실험하는 권리가 없다고 주장한다.
   동물 애호가들 : animal lovers / 실험 : experiments / 권리 : right

6) 교육에 관해서 말하자면, 동물원은 아이의 발달에 매우 중요한 역할을 하고 있다.

_____

7) 동물원은 과학자들에게 연구하는 기회를 제공하고 그들이 모은 정보는 동물의 건강을 증진시키는 새로운 약과 기술을 개발하는 데 도움을 준다.
   연구하다 : conduct research

_____

8) 동물원은 사람에게 동물의 필요와 보호의 중요성에 대해 가르친다.

_____

9) 동물원의 동물들은 인공적인 환경에 가둬진다.
   인공적인 : artificial

_____

10) 동물원에 있는 동물들은 음식을 사냥할 자유를 잃는다.
    자유 : freedom

_____

11) 어떤 사람들은 동물원은 보호와 연구에 중요한 역할을 한다고 말하는 반면 다른 사람들은 동물원은 좋은 점보다 해로운 점이 더 많다고 반박한다.
    반박하다 : counter

_____

12) 서식지 감소는 야생동식물의 생존에 가장 중요한 위협이다.
    서식지 감소 : habitat loss / 생존 : survival

_____

13) 나무를 쓰러뜨리는 불도저는 서식지 파괴의 상징적 이미지이다.
    나무를 쓰러뜨리다 : push down trees / 서식지 파괴 : habitat destruction

_____

14) 우리의 인구와 필요가 증가함에 따라 우리는 야생동식물을 위한 공간을 점점 더 적게 남기고 있다.

_____

15) 야생동식물은 많은 다른 종류의 인간 활동으로부터 위협을 받고 있다.

인간의 활동 : human activities / ~로부터 위협을 받는 : under threat from ~

Answer

1) Animals are used in important scientific research because it is necessary to do clinical trials on new drugs.
2) Animal testing helps to advance medical and scientific knowledge.
3) Researchers aim to minimize the suffering that animals experience.
4) The use of animals to test cosmetic products or their ingredients is banned in the UK and all other member states of the European Union.
5) Animal lovers insist that humans have no right to do experiments on animals.
6) When it comes to education, zoos are playing a very important role in a child's development.
7) Zoos give scientists a chance to conduct research and the information they gather helps them to develop new medicines and techniques to improve animal health.
8) Zoos teach people about the needs of animals and the importance of conservation.
9) Zoo animals are kept in artificial environments.
10) Animals in a zoo lose their freedom to hunt for food.
11) While some people argue that zoos play an important role in conservation and research, others counter that they do more harm than good.
12) Habitat loss is the primary threat to the survival of wildlife.
13) A bulldozer pushing down trees is the iconic image of habitat destruction.
14) As our population and needs grow, we are leaving less and less room for wildlife.
15) Wildlife is under threat from many different kinds of human activities.

You should spend about 40 minutes on this task.
Write about the following topic :

> Nowadays many species of animals and plants are in danger of becoming extinct. What do you think the reasons are? What can you suggest as a solution?

Give reasons for your answer and include any relevant examples from your own knowledge or experience.

Write at least 250 words.

1 단계   문제 정독, 문제 유형 파악, 브레인스토밍 (0~5분)

Question Nowadays many species of animals and plants are in danger of becoming extinct. What do you think the reasons are? What can you suggest as a solution?

문제 정독
요즘 많은 동식물들이 멸종 위기에 처해 있다. 이유가 무엇이라고 생각하는가? 해결책으로 무엇을 제시할 수 있는가?

specie : (동식물의) 종
in danger of becoming extinct : 멸종 위기에 처해 있는

문제 유형 파악

3-1. Reasons and Solutions 유형

Brainstorming

Topic : 요즘 많은 동식물들이 멸종 위기에 처해 있다.	
Reasons : 많은 동식물들이 멸종 위기에 처한 이유들	Solutions : 많은 동식물의 멸종을 막기 위한 해결책들
1. 환경 악화와 오염 environmental degradation and pollution → 도시화와 농업개발 그리고 산림벌채 urbanisation, agricultural development and deforestation 2. 밀렵이 지속됨 poaching continues → 거대한 동물들이 밀렵꾼들의 먹이로 전락함 magnificent animals have fallen prey to poachers	1. 도시 개발과 자연보호 사이의 균형을 맞추는 것 striking a balance between urban development and nature conservation → 환경론자들의 조언을 듣고 좀 더 친환경적인 태도를 채택함 listening to the advice of environmentalists and adopting a more eco-friendly attitude 2. 멸종위기에 처한 종들을 사냥하는 것을 멈추고, 희귀 동물의 장기를 사는 것을 피하기 stop hunting endangered species and avoid buying rare animal organs → 불법거래를 금지하고 밀렵꾼들의 생활환경을 개선하는 정책을 이행 implementing a policy of prohibiting the illegal trade and improving the living conditions of poachers

* 이유와 해결책을 각각 연관성 있게 작성해야 한다.

2단계 서론 (Introduction) (6~10분) : 두 문장으로 작성

Question	Nowadays many species of animals and plants are in danger of becoming extinct. What do you think the reasons are? What can you suggest as a solution?

단계	Question	서론 작성
1단계 Paraphrasing	토픽 : Nowadays many species of animals and plants are in danger of becoming extinct.	Paraphrasing : Animal and plant species throughout the world are being threatened by extinction at an alarming rate.
2단계 Answering	질문 : What do you think the reasons are? What can you suggest as a solution?	Answering : 이유와 해결책 간단히 언급 All of us should bear some responsibility for this worrying trend, and that also means everyone has a role to play in confronting the crisis facing these species.

Introduction
Animal and plant species throughout the world are being threatened by extinction at an alarming rate. All of us should bear some responsibility for this worrying trend, and that also means everyone has a role to play in confronting the crisis facing these species.

extinction : 멸종
at an alarming rate : 놀랄만한 속도로
bear responsibility for : ~에 대해 책임을 지다
crisis : 위기

우리말 해석
전세계의 동식물 종들은 놀랄만한 속도로 멸종의 위협을 받고 있다. 우리 모두는 이러한 걱정스런 추세에 어느 정도 책임져야 하며 그것은 또한 모두가 이러한 종들이 직면한 위기에 맞설 수 있도록 역할을 해야 한다는 의미이다.

 **본론 1 (Body 1) (11~20분) : Reasons** (많은 동식물이 멸종 위기에 처한 이유들)

> **Question** Nowadays many species of animals and plants are in danger of becoming extinct. What do you think the reasons are? What can you suggest as a solution?

Body 1은 1단계에서 브레인스토밍한 'Reasons'를 바탕으로 작성한다.

1단계	Topic Sentence	There are two main reasons why so many species are in danger of extinction these days.
2단계 (1)	Supporting Sentence (1)	*environmental degradation and pollution* The most serious one is probably environmental degradation and pollution.
3단계 (1)	Supporting Sentence or Specific Example (1)	*urbanisation, agricultural development and deforestation* Humans have spread across the globe and disturbed the ecological balance through processes such as urbanisation, agricultural development and deforestation, leaving fewer natural habitats for animals and plants to flourish in.
2단계 (2)	Supporting Sentence (2)	*poaching continues* In addition, poaching continues to be a major threat to certain species in some parts of the world, including elephants in Africa.
3단계 (2)	Supporting Sentence or Specific Example (2)	*magnificent animals have fallen prey to poachers* We often hear in the news how these magnificent animals have fallen prey to poachers who are able to raise considerable funds by selling ivory from their tusks.

Body 1

There are two main reasons why so many species are in danger of extinction these days. The most serious one is probably environmental degradation and pollution. Humans have spread across the globe and disturbed the ecological balance through processes such as urbanisation, agricultural development and deforestation, leaving fewer natural habitats for animals and plants to flourish in. In addition, poaching continues to be a major threat to certain species in some parts of the world, including elephants in Africa. We often hear in the news how these magnificent animals have fallen prey to poachers who are able to raise considerable funds by selling ivory from their tusks.

environmental degradation and pollution
 : 환경 악화와 오염
spread : (여러 장소로) 퍼뜨리다
across the globe : 전세계에서
disturb : 방해하다, 훼방 놓다
the ecological balance : 생태학적 균형
urbanisation : 도시화
agricultural development : 농업개발
deforestation : 산림벌채
natural habitats : 자연 서식지
poaching : 밀렵
magnificent : 거대한
prey : 먹이
poachers : 밀렵꾼
tusks : 어금니
ivory : 상아

우리말 해석

왜 너무나 많은 종들이 요즘 멸종의 위험에 처했는지에 대한 두 가지 주된 이유가 있다. 가장 심각한 이유는 아마도 환경 악화와 오염일 것이다. 인류는 지구상에 널리 분포하여 살아왔고, 동식물이 번성할 수 있는 자연 서식지를 거의 남겨두지 않고, 도시화와 농업개발 그리고 산림벌채와 같은 과정을 통해 생태학적 균형을 무너뜨렸다. 게다가, 아프리카의 코끼리를 포함해 밀렵은 세계 일부 지역에서 특정 종에게 가장 중대한 위협으로 지속되고 있다. 우리는 어떻게 이 거대한 동물들이 그것들의 어금니에서 얻어낸 상아를 팔아서 엄청난 자금을 거둬들일 수 있는 밀렵꾼들의 먹이로 전락했는지에 대해 종종 뉴스에서 듣는다.

4단계 본론 2 (Body 2) (21~30분) : Solutions (많은 동식물의 멸종을 막기 위한 해결책들)

> **Question** Nowadays many species of animals and plants are in danger of becoming extinct. What do you think the reasons are? What can you suggest as a solution?

Body 2는 1단계에서 브레인스토밍한 'Solutions'를 바탕으로 작성한다.

1단계	Topic Sentence	Although solving these problems is not easy, there are feasible steps which we can take.
2단계 (1)	Supporting Sentence (1)	*striking a balance between urban development and nature conservation* Striking a balance between urban development and nature conservation would be the first action.
3단계 (1)	Supporting Sentence or Specific Example (1)	*listening to the advice of environmentalists and adopting a more eco-friendly attitude* Listening to the advice of environmentalists and adopting a more eco-friendly attitude when we set up an urban plan project could be far less likely to exploit animals and plants whether directly or indirectly.
2단계 (2)	Supporting Sentence (2)	*stop hunting endangered species and avoid buying rare animal organs* Dealing with poaching might seem simpler because all we have to do is stop hunting endangered species and avoid buying rare animal organs.
3단계 (2)	Supporting Sentence or Specific Example (2)	*implementing a policy of prohibiting the illegal trade and improving the living conditions of poachers* By implementing a policy of prohibiting the illegal trade and improving the living conditions of poachers who hunt for a living we could conserve the numbers.

Body 2

Although solving these problems is not easy, there are feasible steps which we can take. Striking a balance between urban development and nature conservation would be the first action. Listening to the advice of environmentalists and adopting a more eco-friendly attitude when we set up an urban plan project could be far less likely to exploit animals and plants whether directly or indirectly. Dealing with poaching might seem simpler because all we have to do is stop hunting endangered species and avoid buying rare animal organs. By implementing a policy of prohibiting the illegal trade and improving the living conditions of poachers who hunt for a living we could conserve the numbers.

feasible : 실행 가능한
strike a balance between A and B : A와 B의 균형을 맞추다
urban development : 도시 개발
nature conservation : 자연보호
environmentalists : 환경론자들
eco-friendly : 친환경적인
exploit : 착취하다
rare animal organs : 희귀 동물의 장기
implement : 이행하다, 시행하다

우리말 해석

비록 이러한 문제들을 해결하는 게 쉽진 않지만 우리가 취할 수 있는 실행 가능한 방법들이 있다. 도시 개발과 자연보호 사이의 균형을 맞추는 것이 그 첫 번째 조치가 될 것이다. 우리가 도시 계획 프로젝트를 세울 때 환경론자들의 조언을 듣고 좀 더 친환경적인 태도를 채택한다면 직접적이든 간접적이든 동식물을 착취할 가능성이 훨씬 더 낮다. 밀렵을 다루는 것은 더 간단해 보일지 모르는데, 왜냐하면 우리 모두가 해야 할 일은 멸종위기에 처한 종들을 사냥하는 것을 멈추고, 희귀 동물의 장기를 사는 것을 피하면 되기 때문이다. 불법거래를 금지하고 사냥으로 생계를 이어가는 밀렵꾼들의 생활환경을 개선하는 정책을 이행함으로써, 우리는 이 개체 수를 지킬 수 있을 것이다.

5 단계   결론 (Conclusion) (31~35분) : 본문에 제시한 내 주장 요약하며 다시 한 번 강조

| Question | Nowadays many species of animals and plants are in danger of becoming extinct. What do you think the reasons are? What can you suggest as a solution? |

결론 작성 시, 먼저 문제 유형을 파악한 후, 'Conclusion Template'의 표현을 인용한다. (See p58)

문제 유형 파악	3-1) Reasons and Solutions
Conclusion Template 인용	In conclusion, it is clear that there are various reasons for…(토픽), steps are needed to tackle this phenomenon.

3-1 유형의 결론을 작성할 때 문제와 해결책을 구체적으로 작성하게 되면 자칫 결론이 너무 길어질 수 있기 때문에 포괄적으로 작성한다.

> **Conclusion**
>
> **In conclusion, it is clear that there are various reasons for** the threat of extinction faced by various species of animals and plants, and both individual and government efforts **are needed to tackle this phenomenon**.

* 상황에 따라 템플릿을 살짝 변형해도 좋다.

the threat of extinction : 멸종 위기

우리말 해석

결론적으로, 다양한 동식물의 종들이 직면한 멸종 위기에 대해 여러 가지 이유가 있는 것은 분명하고 이런 현상을 방지하기 위해 개인과 정부 모두의 노력이 요구된다.

6 단계 교정 (Self-correction) (36~40분) : 내용의 일관성 및 문법 검토

다음 Body 2의 내용을 교정해 보자. 틀린 부분은 총 몇 개일까?

교정 전 (직접 문장 부호를 이용하여 틀린 부분을 교정해 보자.)

Although solving these problems are not easy, there are feasible steps which we can take.

Striking a balance between urban development or nature conservation would be a first action. Listening to the advice of environmentalists and adopting a more eco-friendly attitude when we set up an urban plan project could be far less likely to exploit animals and plant whether directly or indirectly. Dealing of poaching might seem more simpler because of all we have to do is stop hunt endangered specie and avoid buying rare animal organs. By implement a policy of prohibiting the legal trade and improving the living conditions of poachers who hunts for a living we could conserve the numbers.

교정

Although solving these problems are[is] not easy, there are feasible steps which we can take. Striking a balance between urban development or[and] nature conservation would be a[the] first action. Listening to the advice of environmentalists and adopting a more eco-friendly attitude when we set up an urban plan project could be far less likely to exploit animals and plant[plants] whether directly or indirectly. Dealing of[with] poaching might seem more simpler because of all we have to do is stop hunt[hunting] endangered specie[species] and avoid buying rare animal organs. By implement[implementing] a policy of prohibiting the legal[illegal] trade and improving the living conditions of poachers who hunts[hunt] for a living we could conserve the numbers.

1. are → is : 주어 solving은 동명사이고 동명사는 단수이다.
2. 붙여쓰기 : 위의 글은 Body 2 단락이다. 단락이 바뀌지 않는 한, 줄을 바꿔 쓰지 않는다.
3. or → and : between A and B는 'A와 B 사이에'라는 뜻
4. a → the : 서수(first) 앞에는 정관사 the를 쓴다.
5. plant → plants : plant는 셀 수 있는 명사로 앞의 animals처럼 복수 명사로 쓴다.
6. of → with : deal with는 '다루다'라는 뜻
7. more → 삭제 : simpler가 simple의 비교급이므로 more를 붙여서는 안 된다.
8. of → 삭제 : because 다음에는 주어+동사, because of 다음에는 명사(구)가 온다.
9. hunt → hunting : stop ~ing는 '~하는 것을 막다'라는 뜻
10. specie → species : species는 셀 수 있는 명사로 복수 명사로 쓴다.
11. implement → implementing : by~ing는 '~함으로써'의 뜻으로 by 다음에 동명사가 와야 한다.
12. legal → illegal : 불법거래라고 해야 논리에 맞다. 이걸 놓치면 절대 안 된다!
13. hunts → hunt : 주어는 poachers이므로 복수 동사인 hunt를 쓴다.

틀린 개수 : 총 13개

Sample Answer

> **Question** Nowadays many species of animals and plants are in danger of becoming extinct. What do you think the reasons are? What can you suggest as a solution?

Animal and plant species throughout the world are being threatened by extinction at an alarming rate. All of us should bear some responsibility for this worrying trend, and that also means everyone has a role to play in confronting the crisis facing these species.

There are two main reasons why so many species are in danger of extinction these days. The most serious one is probably environmental degradation and pollution. Humans have spread across the globe and disturbed the ecological balance through processes such as urbanisation, agricultural development and deforestation, leaving fewer natural habitats for animals and plants to flourish in. In addition, poaching continues to be a major threat to certain species in some parts of the world, including elephants in Africa. We often hear in the news how these magnificent animals have fallen prey to poachers who are able to raise considerable funds by selling ivory from their tusks.

Although solving these problems is not easy, there are feasible steps which we can take. Striking a balance between urban development and nature conservation would be the first action. Listening to the advice of environmentalists and adopting a more eco-friendly attitude when we set up an urban plan project could be far less likely to exploit animals and plants whether directly or indirectly. Dealing with poaching might seem simpler because all we have to do is stop hunting endangered species and avoid buying rare animal organs. By implementing a policy of prohibiting the illegal trade and improving the living conditions of poachers who hunt for a living we could conserve the numbers.

In conclusion, it is clear that there are various reasons for the threat of extinction faced by various species of animals and plants, and both individual and government efforts are needed to tackle this phenomenon.

word counts : 298 words

우리말 해석

전세계의 동식물 종들은 놀랄만한 속도로 멸종의 위협을 받고 있다. 우리 모두는 이러한 걱정스런 추세에 어느 정도 책임 져야 하며 그것은 또한 모두가 이러한 종들이 직면한 위기에 맞설 수 있도록 역할을 해야 한다는 의미이다.

왜 너무나 많은 종이 요즘 멸종의 위험에 처했는지에 대한 두 가지 주된 이유가 있다. 가장 심각한 이유는 아마도 환경 악화와 오염일 것이다. 인류는 지구상에 널리 분포하여 살아왔고, 동식물이 번성할 수 있는 자연 서식지를 거의 남겨두지 않고, 도시화와 농업개발 그리고 산림벌채와 같은 과정을 통해 생태학적 균형을 무너뜨렸다. 게다가, 아프리카의 코끼리를 포함해 밀렵은 세계 일부 지역에서 특정 종에게 가장 중대한 위협으로 지속되고 있다. 우리는 어떻게 이 거대한 동물들이 그것들의 어금니에서 얻어낸 상아를 팔아서 엄청난 자금을 거둬들일 수 있는 밀렵꾼들의 먹이로 전락했는지에 대해 종종 뉴스에서 듣는다.

비록 이러한 문제들을 해결하는 게 쉽진 않지만 우리가 취할 수 있는 실행 가능한 방법들이 있다. 도시 개발과 자연보호 사이의 균형을 맞추는 것이 그 첫 번째 조치가 될 것이다. 우리가 도시 계획 프로젝트를 세울 때 환경론자들의 조언을 듣고 좀 더 친환경적인 태도를 채택한다면 직접적이든 간접적이든 동식물을 착취할 가능성이 훨씬 더 낮다. 밀렵을 다루는 것은 더 간단해 보일지 모르는데, 왜냐하면 우리 모두가 해야 할 일은 멸종위기에 처한 종들을 사냥하는 것을 멈추고, 희귀 동물의 장기를 사는 것을 피하면 되기 때문이다. 불법거래를 금지하고 사냥으로 생계를 이어가는 밀렵꾼들의 생활환경을 개선하는 정책을 이행함으로써, 우리는 이 개체 수를 지킬 수 있을 것이다.

결론적으로, 다양한 동식물의 종들이 직면한 멸종 위기에 대해 여러 가지 이유가 있는 것은 분명하고 이런 현상을 방지하기 위해 개인과 정부 모두의 노력이 요구된다.

불법 Review

앞에서 배운 내용을 바탕으로 다음 빈칸을 영어로 작성해 보자.

Animal and plant species throughout the world are being threatened by extinction _____ (1. 놀랄만한 속도로). All of us should bear some responsibility for this worrying trend, and that also means everyone has a role to play in confronting _____ (2. 이러한 종들이 직면한 위기).

_____ (3. 두 가지 주된 이유가 있다) why so many species are in danger of extinction these days. The most serious one is probably _____ (4. 환경 악화와 오염). Humans have spread across the globe and disturbed _____ (5. 생태학적 균형) through processes such as _____ (6. 도시화와 농업개발 그리고 산림벌채), leaving fewer natural habitats for animals and plants to flourish in. In addition, poaching continues to be a major threat to certain species in some parts of the world, including elephants in Africa. We often hear in the news how these magnificent animals have fallen prey to poachers who are able to raise considerable funds by selling ivory from their tusks.

Although solving these problems is not easy, there are feasible steps which we can take. Striking a balance between _____ (7. 도시 개발) and _____ (8. 자연보호) would be the first action. Listening to _____ (9. 환경론자들의 조언) and adopting a more eco-friendly attitude when we set up an urban plan project could be far less likely to exploit animals and plants whether directly or indirectly. Dealing with poaching might seem simpler because all we have to do is stop hunting endangered species and avoid buying _____ (10. 희귀 동물의 장기). By implementing a policy of prohibiting the illegal trade and improving the living conditions of poachers who hunt for a living we could conserve the numbers.

In conclusion, it is clear that there are various reasons for the threat of extinction faced by various species of animals and plants, and _____ (11. 개인과 정부 모두의 노력) are needed to tackle this phenomenon.

Answer
1. at an alarming rate / 2. the crisis facing these species / 3. There are two main reasons
4. environmental degradation and pollution / 5. the ecological balance
6. urbanisation, agricultural development and deforestation / 7. urban development
8. nature conservation / 9. the advice of environmentalists / 10. rare animal organs
11. both individual and government efforts

Day 9 Natural Environment & Wildlife 불법 포인트 정리

임상실험	clinical trials	환경 악화와 오염	environmental degradation and pollution
동물 실험	animal testing	(여러 장소로) 퍼뜨리다	spread
최소화하다	minimize	전세계에서	across the globe
목표로 하다	aim	방해하다, 훼방 놓다	disturb
화장용 제품	cosmetic products	생태학적 균형	the ecological balance
성분	ingredients	도시화	urbanisation
유럽 연합	the European Union	농업개발	agricultural development
동물 애호가들	animal lovers	산림벌채	deforestation
실험	experiments	자연 서식지	natural habitats
권리	right	밀렵	poaching
연구하다	conduct research	거대한	magnificient
인공적인	artificial	먹이	prey
자유	freedom	밀렵꾼	poachers
반박하다	counter	어금니	tusks
서식지 감소	habitat loss	상아	ivory
생존	survival	실행 가능한	feasible
나무를 쓰러뜨리다	push down trees	A와 B의 균형을 맞추다	strike a balance between A and B
서식지 파괴	habitat destruction	도시 개발	urban development
인간의 활동	human activities	자연보호	nature conservation
~로부터 위협을 받는	under threat from ~	환경론자들	environmentalists
(동식물의) 종	species	친환경적인	eco-friendly
멸종 위기에 처해 있는	in danger of becoming extinct	착취하다	exploit
멸종	extinction	희귀 동물의 장기	rare animal organs
놀랄만한 속도로	at an alarming rate	이행하다, 시행하다	implement
~에 대해 책임을 지다	bear responsibility for	멸종 위기	the threat of extinction
위기	crisis		

Day 10 Earth & Space 지구와 우주

Question

Some people think governments should spend as much money as possible exploring outer space. Others argue they should spend the money for poor people. Discuss both views and give your own opinion.

어떤 사람들은 정부가 가능한 한 많은 돈을 우주 탐험에 써야 한다고 생각한다. 반면 정부는 가난한 사람들을 위해 그 돈을 써야 한다고 주장하는 사람들도 있다. 양쪽의 견해를 논하고 당신의 주장을 제시하라.

 빈출 문제

1. Some people say that a huge amount of money spent on space exploration is a complete waste. To what extent do you agree or disagree with this opinion?

2. Although in the 20th century human beings landed on the moon surprisingly, it has made little difference to our daily lives. Do you agree or disagree with this statement?

3. Space travel to the moon will soon be accessible to the general public. Do you agree or disagree with this statement?

4. Space exploration is beneficial for mankind. Do you agree or disagree with this statement?

1. 어떤 사람들은 우주 탐험에 막대한 돈을 쓰는 것이 완전히 낭비라고 생각한다. 당신은 이 의견에 얼마만큼 동의하는가? 또는 동의하지 않는가?

2. 비록 20세기에 놀랍게도 인간이 달에 착륙했지만, 이것은 우리의 일상을 거의 변화시키지 않았다. 당신은 이 말에 동의하는가? 또는 동의하지 않는가?

3. 달나라 여행은 일반 대중들에게도 곧 가능해질 것이다. 당신은 이 말에 동의하는가? 또는 동의하지 않는가?

4. 우주 탐험은 인간에게 이롭다. 당신은 이 말에 동의하는가? 또는 동의하지 않는가?

 브레인스토밍

1) 우주 탐사는 지구에 있는 모든 사람들의 삶에 극적인 변화를 가져다 줄 것이다.
   우주 탐사 : space exploration / 극적인 변화 : a dramatic change

2) 우주를 탐사하는 것은 어떤 필수 광물질을 찾는 커다란 기회를 준다.
   필수 광물질 : essential minerals

3) 우주 탐사는 모험과 관련되어 있고, 대부분의 사람들은 모험과 도전을 받아들이는 것 그리고 불가능한 일을 가능하게 만드는 것을 정말로 좋아한다.
   모험 : adventure / 관련되어 있다 : be associated with / 불가능한 일 : impossibilities

4) 우주 연구에 많은 돈을 쓰는 것 대신에 우리는 그 돈을 몇몇 후진국들의 가난을 감소시키는 데 쓸 수 있다.
   대신에 : instead of / 후진국들 : underdeveloped nations

5) 우주 탐사는 우주 기술과 천문학을 포함하기 때문에 단지 우주로 여행하는 데에도 사실상 엄청난 자본이 요구된다.
   천문학 : astronomy / 엄청난 자본 : a big amount of capital

6) 돈 문제를 떠나서 우주를 탐험하는 것은 우주 공간으로 여행하는 우주 비행사의 생명을 위협할 수 있다.
~ 떠나서 : aside from / 우주 비행사 : astronauts

7) 비용에 기초해서 우주 탐사와 여행의 가치를 측정하는 것은 극도로 어렵다.
비용에 기초해서 : based on cost / 측정하다, 추산하다 : gauge

8) 우주를 탐험하는 것은 진보를 위해 필요한 지식을 준다.
진보 : advancement

9) 우주 비행사들과 과학자들은 우주에 있는 생명체와 이것이 인간에게 미치는 영향에 대해 계속해서 연구하고 있다.

10) 우리의 금융 자원과 시간을 우리 행성과 주민들에게 주력하는 것이 좀 더 건설적인 접근일지도 모른다.
금융 자원 : monetary resources / 주민들 : inhabitants / 건설적인 접근 : a constructive approach

11) 어떤 사람들은 국가적 우주 프로그램의 단점은 이점을 훨씬 능가한다고 생각한다.
훨씬 능가하다 : far outweigh

12) 우주 여행과 탐험의 가장 큰 우려 중의 하나는 우주를 오염시키는 가능성이다.
가능성 : possibility

13) 우리는 목적 없이 우주를 떠다니는 오래된 위성들과 장비 파편들 그리고 로켓 발사 추진체로 우주를 파괴시키고 있다.
목적 없이 : aimlessly / 떠다니다 : float / 위성들 : satellites / 장비 파편들 : pieces of equipment
로켓 발사 추진체 : rocket launch boosters

14) 우주에 대한 우리의 임무는 우리의 경제의 현재 상태를 고려할 때 비용 효과적이지 않다.
임무 : missions / 현재 상태 : the current state / 비용 효과적인 : cost effective

15) 우주와 관련된 발견은 의학, 교통, 환경과 농업 자원 관리, 컴퓨터 기술 그리고 산업 생산력이 진전되는 것을 도왔다.

산업 생산력 : industrial productivity

Answer

1) Space exploration will bring a dramatic change to the life of every individual on Earth.
2) Exploring space gives a great chance to find out some essential minerals.
3) Space exploration is associated with adventure and most people really love adventure, accepting challenges and making impossibilities possible.
4) Instead of spending a lot of money on space research, we can use the money to reduce the poverty in some of the underdeveloped nations.
5) Since space exploration involves space technology and astronomy, it usually requires a big amount of capital just to travel to space.
6) Aside from money matters, exploring space can risk the life of astronauts who travel into outer space.
7) It is extremely hard to gauge the value of space exploration and travel based on cost.
8) Exploring space gives us the knowledge we need for advancement.
9) Astronauts and scientists are continually studying life in space and the effects it has on humans.
10) Focusing our monetary resources and time on our own planet and its inhabitants might be a more constructive approach.
11) Some people feel that the disadvantages of a national space program far outweigh the benefits.
12) One of the biggest concerns about space travel and exploration is the possibility of polluting space.
13) We are destroying space with the old satellites, pieces of equipment, and rocket launch boosters that float aimlessly around the universe.
14) Our missions to space are not cost effective, especially considering the current state of our economy.
15) Discoveries related to space have helped advance medicine, transportation, environmental and agricultural resource management, computer technology, and industrial productivity.

 실전문제

You should spend about 40 minutes on this task.
Write about the following topic :

> Some people think governments should spend as much money as possible exploring outer space. Others argue they should spend the money for poor people. Discuss both views and give your own opinion.

Give reasons for your answer and include any relevant examples from your own knowledge or experience.

Write at least 250 words.

 **1단계** 문제 정독, 문제 유형 파악, 브레인스토밍 (0 ~ 5분)

| Question | Some people think governments should spend as much money as possible exploring outer space. Others argue they should spend the money for poor people. Discuss both views and give your own opinion. |

문제 정독
어떤 사람들은 정부가 가능한 한 많은 돈을 우주 탐험에 써야 한다고 생각한다. 반면 정부는 가난한 사람들을 위해 그 돈을 써야 한다고 주장하는 사람들도 있다. 양쪽의 견해를 논하고 당신의 주장을 제시하라.

as ~ as possible : 가능한 한
explore : 탐험하다, 탐사하다
outer space : = space, cosmos, universe 우주

문제 유형 파악

1-2. Discuss both views and give your own opinion. 유형

Brainstorming

Topic : 정부가 우주 탐험에 지출하는 많은 돈	
Some People : 정부가 우주 탐험에 많은 돈을 쓰는 것은 정당하다.	Others : 정부는 가난한 사람들을 위해 그 돈을 써야 한다.
1. 미스터리하고 매력적임 mysterious and fascinating → 우주의 비밀을 풀 수 있음 unlock the secrets of the universe 2. 인류의 장기간 생존을 보장 ensure the long-term survival of humanity → 더 이상 지구에 사람이 살 수 없게 된다면 우리에게 구제책을 제공 offer us salvation if Earth was ever to become uninhabitable	1. 빈부격차 강조 highlight the gap between the rich and the poor → 인도에서는 상당수의 국민들이 빈곤에 허덕임 in India, a significant portion of its people live in impoverishment 2. 우리 중 누가 행성 간의 일에 돈을 쓰기를 선택할 것인지 의심스러워 보임 it seems doubtful that any of us would choose to spend money on inter-planetary pursuits → 빈곤의 희생자들의 상황을 고려하지 못함 fails to consider the circumstances of the victims of poverty

* 아이디어의 수도 같고 영어로 쓸 수 있는 말도 비슷하다면, 좀 더 설득력 있게 논리적으로 접근할 수 있는 쪽을 내 의견으로 한다. 이 에세이에서는 others의 주장, '정부는 가난한 사람들을 위해 그 돈을 써야 한다.'를 내 주장으로 삼았다.

2단계 서론 (Introduction) (6~10분) : 두 문장으로 작성

Question	Some people think governments should spend as much money as possible exploring outer space. Others argue they should spend the money for poor people. Discuss both views and give your own opinion.

단계	Question	서론 작성
1단계 Paraphrasing	**토픽 :** Some people think governments should spend as much money as possible exploring outer space. Others argue they should spend the money for poor people.	**Paraphrasing :** When it comes to considering billions of US dollars spent on space exploration by countries worldwide, there is a growing debate over whether we should aim to resolve issues like poverty before focusing too much on this space race.
2단계 Answering	**질문 :** Discuss both views and give your own opinion.	**Answering : Others에 동의할 경우** Although broadening our horizons is important, ultimately the people of our own planet should be our priority.

Introduction
When it comes to considering billions of US dollars spent on space exploration by countries worldwide, there is a growing debate over whether we should aim to resolve issues like poverty before focusing too much on this space race. Although broadening our horizons is important, ultimately the people of our own planet should be our priority.

billions of : 수십억의
space exploration : 우주 탐사(탐험)

resolve issues : 문제를 해결하다
focus on : ~에 초점을 맞추다

우리말 해석
전세계 국가들에 의해 수십억 미국 달러가 우주 탐사에 쓰여지는 것에 관해서 말하자면, 이 우주 개발 경쟁에 지나치게 집중하기 전에 빈곤과 같은 문제들을 해결하는 것을 목표로 해야 할지 여부에 대한 논쟁이 커지고 있다. 우리의 시야를 넓히는 것도 중요하지만, 궁극적으로 우리 (자신의) 행성 사람들이 우선시 되어야 한다.

3단계　본론 1 (Body 1) (11~20분) : 나와 다른 의견 = Some people (정부가 우주 탐험에 많은 돈을 쓰는 것은 정당하다)

Question	Some people think governments should spend as much money as possible exploring outer space. Others argue they should spend the money for poor people. Discuss both views and give your own opinion.

Body 1은 1단계에서 브레인스토밍한 'Some people'의 주장을 바탕으로 작성한다.

1단계	Topic Sentence	Those in favour of spending as much money as possible exploring outer space would point out the virtues of better understanding our cosmos.
2단계 (1)	Supporting Sentence (1)	*mysterious and fascinating* There are few subjects more mysterious and fascinating than this field.
3단계 (1)	Supporting Sentence or Specific Example (1)	*unlock the secrets of the universe* The more we are able to study outer space, the likelier we are to unlock the secrets of the universe.
2단계 (2)	Supporting Sentence (2)	*ensure the long-term survival of humanity* In addition, space exploration could ensure the long-term survival of humanity.
3단계 (2)	Supporting Sentence or Specific Example (2)	*offer us salvation if Earth was ever to become uninhabitable* The development of space stations or even the ability to colonise other planets could offer us salvation if Earth was ever to become uninhabitable due to climate change or other factors.

Body 1

Those in favour of spending as much money as possible exploring outer space would point out the virtues of better understanding our cosmos. There are few subjects more mysterious and fascinating than this field. The more we are able to study outer space, the likelier we are to unlock the secrets of the universe. In addition, space exploration could ensure the long-term survival of humanity. The development of space stations or even the ability to colonise other planets could offer us salvation if Earth was ever to become uninhabitable due to climate change or other factors.

those in favour of~ : ~에 찬성하는 사람들
virtues : 장점들
fascinating : 매력적인
the more S+V, the likelier S+V : 더욱 ~할수록, 더욱 ~하게 될 가능성이 크다
unlock : 풀다
the long-term survival of humanity : 인류의 장기간 생존
space stations : 우주 정거장
colonise : 식민지화 하다
salvation : 구원, 구제책
uninhabitable : 사람이 살 수 없는, 주거하기 부적절한
due to : ~ 때문에
climate change : 기후 변화

우리말 해석

우주 공간 탐사에 가능한 많은 돈을 쓰는 것을 찬성하는 사람들은 우리의 우주에 대한 더 나은 이해를 장점으로 꼽을 것이다. 이 분야보다 더 미스터리하고 매력적인 주제는 거의 없다. 우리가 우주 공간에 대해 더 많은 연구를 할 수 있게 될수록 우리는 더욱 우주의 비밀을 풀 수 있게 될 가능성이 크다. 게다가, 우주 탐사는 인류의 장기간 생존을 보장할 수 있다. 만일 지구가 기후 변화나 다른 요인들로 인해 더 이상 사람이 살 수 없게 된다면, 우주 정거장의 개발이나 심지어 다른 행성을 식민지화 할 수 있는 능력이 우리에게 구제책을 제공할 수 있을 것이다.

4 단계   본론 2 (Body 2) (21~30분) : 내 의견 = Others (정부는 가난한 사람들을 위해 그 돈을 써야 한다)

Question	Some people think governments should spend as much money as possible exploring outer space. Others argue they should spend the money for poor people. Discuss both views and give your own opinion.

Body 2는 1단계에서 브레인스토밍한 'Others'의 주장을 바탕으로 작성한다.

1단계	Topic Sentence	There are still urgent matters which require immediate steps, like looking after the poor.
2단계 (1)	Supporting Sentence (1)	*highlight the gap between the rich and the poor* There are few endeavours that highlight the gap between the rich and the poor more clearly than space exploration.
3단계 (1)	Supporting Sentence or Specific Example (1)	*in India, a significant portion of its people live in impoverishment* India, for example, is planning a hugely expensive voyage to Mars when a significant portion of its people live in impoverishment.
2단계 (2)	Supporting Sentence (2)	*it seems doubtful that any of us would choose to spend money on inter-planetary pursuits* On a personal level, it seems doubtful that any of us would choose to spend money on inter-planetary pursuits if we could instead use it to drastically improve the lives of our loved ones.
3단계 (2)	Supporting Sentence or Specific Example (2)	*fails to consider the circumstances of the victims of poverty* So the justification for exploring space appears to rely on an outlook that fails to consider the circumstances of the victims of poverty.

Body 2

There are still urgent matters which require immediate steps, like looking after the poor. There are few endeavours that highlight the gap between the rich and the poor more clearly than space exploration. India, for example, is planning a hugely expensive voyage to Mars when a significant portion of its people live in impoverishment. On a personal level, it seems doubtful that any of us would choose to spend money on inter-planetary pursuits if we could instead use it to drastically improve the lives of our loved ones. So the justification for exploring space appears to rely on an outlook that fails to consider the circumstances of the victims of poverty.

urgent matters : 긴급한 문제들
immediate steps : 즉각적인 조치들
look after : 돌보다
endeavours : 시도들
highlight : 강조하다
the gap between the rich and the poor : 빈부격차
voyage : 비행(바다 혹은 우주로의 긴 여행)
impoverishment : = poverty, 빈곤(화)
inter-planetary pursuits : 행성 간의 일
drastically : 대폭, 과감하게
justification : 정당화
outlook : 전망
circumstances : 상황들
victims : 희생자들

우리말 해석

가난한 사람들을 돌보는 것처럼 즉각적인 조치를 필요로 하는 긴급한 문제들이 여전히 존재한다. 우주 탐사보다 더 분명하게 빈부격차를 강조하는 시도는 거의 없다. 예를 들어, 인도는 상당수의 국민들이 빈곤에 허덕이고 있을 때 화성으로의 엄청나게 비싼 비행을 계획 중이다. 개인적 수준에서는 만약 우리가 사랑하는 사람들의 삶을 대폭 개선하도록 대신 그 돈을 사용할 수 있다면, 우리 중 누가 행성 간의 일에 돈을 쓰기를 선택할 것인지 의심스러워 보인다. 그래서 우주 탐사에 대한 정당화는 빈곤의 희생자들의 상황을 고려하지 못한 전망에 의존하는 듯 보인다.

5 단계 결론 (Conclusion) (31~35분) : 본문에 제시한 내 주장 요약하며 다시 한 번 강조

Question	Some people think governments should spend as much money as possible exploring outer space. Others argue they should spend the money for poor people. Discuss both views and give your own opinion.

결론 작성 시, 먼저 문제 유형을 파악한 후, 'Conclusion Template'의 표현을 인용한다. (See p58)

문제 유형 파악	1-2) Discuss both views and give your own opinion.
Conclusion Template 인용	In conclusion, there are convincing arguments both for and against…(토픽), but I am convinced that… 본론에서 제시한 내 주장 간단히 요약

결론을 작성하기 전, 서론과 본론 2에서 Others의 의견(정부는 가난한 사람들을 위해 그 돈을 써야 한다)에 동의했는지 다시 한 번 확인하자!

Conclusion

In conclusion, there are convincing arguments both for and against spending as much money as possible on outer space exploration, **but I am convinced that** the expenditure should be directed towards people in need.

expenditure : 비용
directed towards : ~로 향하다
people in need : 도움이 필요한 사람들

우리말 해석
결론적으로 우주 공간 탐사에 가능한 많은 돈을 사용하는 것에 대해 찬성과 반대를 하는 설득력 있는 주장들이 있지만, 나는 이 비용은 도움이 필요한 사람들에게 향해져야 한다고 확신한다.

6 단계 교정 (Self-correction) (36~40분) : 내용의 일관성 및 문법 검토

다음 Body 2의 내용을 교정해 보자. 틀린 부분은 총 몇 개일까?

교정 전 (직접 문장 부호를 이용하여 틀린 부분을 교정해 보자.)

There is still urgent matters which require immediate steps, like looking of the poor. there are a few endeavours that highlight the gap between the rich or the poor more clearly then space exploration. India, for example, is planning a hugely expensive voyage to mars when a significant portion of its people live in impoverishment.

On a personal level, it seem doubtful that any of us would choose to spend moneys on inter-planetary pursuits if we could instead use it to drastically improve the lives of our loved ones. So the justification for exploring space appear to rely to a outlook that fails to consider the circumstances of the victims of poverty.

교정

> There is still urgent matters which require immediate steps, like looking of the poor. there are a few endeavours that highlight the gap between the rich or the poor more clearly then space exploration. India, for example, is planning a hugely expensive voyage to mars when a significant portion of its people live in impoverishment.
>
> On a personal level, it seem doubtful that any of us would choose to spend moneys on inter-planetary pursuits if we could instead use it to drastically improve the lives of our loved ones. So the justification for exploring space appear to rely to a outlook that fails to consider the circumstances of the victims of poverty.

교정 표시:
- are (is → are)
- after (of → after)
- T (there → There)
- of (a 삭제)
- and (or → and)
- than (then → than)
- M (mars → Mars)
- seems (seem → seems)
- money (moneys → money)
- appears (appear → appears)
- on (to → on)
- an (a → an)

1. is → are : matters가 복수다.
2. of → after : look after는 '돌보다'라는 뜻
3. t → T : 문장의 첫 글자는 반드시 대문자로 시작한다.
4. a → 삭제 : a few는 긍정(조금 있는), few는 부정(거의 없는)이고 여기서는 부정으로 써야 논리에 맞다. 이걸 놓치면 절대 안 된다!
5. or → and : the gap between the rich and the poor는 '빈부격차'라는 뜻
6. then → than : then은 '그리고 나서', than은 비교급과 함께 사용하는 '~보다'라는 뜻
7. mars → Mars : 행성 이름의 첫 글자는 대문자로 쓴다.
8. 붙여쓰기 : 위의 글은 Body 2 단락이다. 단락이 바뀌지 않는 한, 줄을 바꿔 쓰지 않는다.
9. seem → seems : 주어는 it이므로 단수 동사인 seems를 쓴다.
10. moneys → money : money는 셀 수 없는 명사이므로 ~s를 붙일 수 없다.
11. appear → appears : 주어는 justification이므로 단수 동사인 appears를 쓴다.
12. to → on : rely on은 '~에 의존하다'라는 뜻
13. a → an : 모음(a/i/u/e/o)으로 발음이 시작되는 단어 outlook[aʊtlʊk] 앞에는 a가 아닌 an으로 쓰고 말한다.

틀린 개수 : 총 13개

Sample Answer

> **Question**
>
> Some people think governments should spend as much money as possible exploring outer space. Others argue they should spend the money for poor people. Discuss both views and give your own opinion.

When it comes to considering billions of US dollars spent on space exploration by countries worldwide, there is a growing debate over whether we should aim to resolve issues like poverty before focusing too much on this space race. Although broadening our horizons is important, ultimately the people of our own planet should be our priority.

Those in favour of spending as much money as possible exploring outer space would point out the virtues of better understanding our cosmos. There are few subjects more mysterious and fascinating than this field. The more we are able to study outer space, the likelier we are to unlock the secrets of the universe. In addition, space exploration could ensure the long-term survival of humanity. The development of space stations or even the ability to colonise other planets could offer us salvation if Earth was ever to become uninhabitable due to climate change or other factors.

There are still urgent matters which require immediate steps, like looking after the poor. There are few endeavours that highlight the gap between the rich and the poor more clearly than space exploration. India, for example, is planning a hugely expensive voyage to Mars when a significant portion of its people live in impoverishment. On a personal level, it seems doubtful that any of us would choose to spend money on inter-planetary pursuits if we could instead use it to drastically improve the lives of our loved ones. So the justification for exploring space appears to rely on an outlook that fails to consider the circumstances of the victims of poverty.

In conclusion, there are convincing arguments both for and against spending as much money as possible on outer space exploration, but I am convinced that the expenditure should be directed towards people in need.

word counts : 297 words

우리말 해석

전세계 국가들에 의해 수십억 미국 달러가 우주 탐사에 쓰여지는 것에 관해서 말하자면, 이 우주 개발 경쟁에 지나치게 집중하기 전에 빈곤과 같은 문제들을 해결하는 것을 목표로 해야 할지 여부에 대한 논쟁이 커지고 있다. 우리의 시야를 넓히는 것도 중요하지만, 궁극적으로 우리 (자신의) 행성 사람들이 우선시 되어야 한다.

우주 공간 탐사에 가능한 많은 돈을 쓰는 것을 찬성하는 사람들은 우리의 우주에 대한 더 나은 이해를 장점으로 꼽을 것이다. 이 분야보다 더 미스터리하고 매력적인 주제는 거의 없다. 우리가 우주 공간에 대해 더 많은 연구를 할 수 있게 될수록 우리는 더욱 우주의 비밀을 풀 수 있게 될 가능성이 크다. 게다가, 우주 탐사는 인류의 장기간 생존을 보장할 수 있다. 만일 지구가 기후 변화나 다른 요인들로 인해 더 이상 사람이 살 수 없게 된다면, 우주 정거장의 개발이나 심지어 다른 행성을 식민지화 할 수 있는 능력이 우리에게 구제책을 제공할 수 있을 것이다.

가난한 사람들을 돌보는 것처럼 즉각적인 조치를 필요로 하는 긴급한 문제들이 여전히 존재한다. 우주 탐사보다 더 분명하게 빈부격차를 강조하는 시도는 거의 없다. 예를 들어, 인도는 상당수의 국민들이 빈곤에 허덕이고 있을 때 화성으로의 엄청나게 비싼 비행을 계획 중이다. 개인적 수준에서는 만약 우리가 사랑하는 사람들의 삶을 대폭 개선하도록 대신 그 돈을 사용할 수 있다면, 우리 중 누가 행성 간의 일에 돈을 쓰기를 선택할 것인지 의심스러워 보인다. 그래서, 우주 탐사에 대한 정당화는 빈곤의 희생자들의 상황을 고려하지 못한 전망에 의존하는 듯 보인다.

결론적으로 우주 공간 탐사에 가능한 많은 돈을 사용하는 것에 대해 찬성과 반대를 하는 설득력 있는 주장들이 있지만, 나는 이 비용은 도움이 필요한 사람들에게 향해져야 한다고 확신한다.

불법 Review

앞에서 배운 내용을 바탕으로 다음 빈칸을 영어로 작성해 보자.

When it comes to considering _____ (1. 수십억 미국 달러) spent on space exploration by countries worldwide, there is a growing debate over whether we should aim to _____ (2. 문제들을 해결하다) like poverty before focusing too much on this space race. Although _____ (3. 우리의 시야를 넓히는 것) is important, ultimately the people of our own planet should be our priority.

_____ (4. ~에 찬성하는 사람들) spending as much money as possible exploring outer space would point out the virtues of better understanding our cosmos. _____ (5. 거의 없다) subjects more mysterious and fascinating than this field. The more we are able to study outer space, the likelier we are to _____ (6. 우주의 비밀을 풀다). In addition, space exploration could ensure the long-term survival of humanity. The development of space stations or even the ability to colonise other planets could offer us salvation if Earth was ever to become uninhabitable due to _____ (7. 기후 변화) or other factors.

There are still urgent matters which require _____ (8. 즉각적인 조치들), like looking after the poor. There are few endeavours that _____ (9. 빈부격차를 강조하다) more clearly than space exploration. India, for example, is planning a hugely expensive voyage to Mars when a significant portion of its people live in impoverishment. On a personal level, it seems doubtful that any of us would choose to spend money on inter-planetary pursuits if we could instead use it to drastically improve the lives of our loved ones. So the justification for exploring space appears to rely on an outlook that fails to consider _____ (10. 빈곤의 희생자들의 상황들).

In conclusion, there are convincing arguments both for and against spending as much money as possible on outer space exploration, but I am convinced that the expenditure should be directed towards _____ (11. 도움이 필요한 사람들).

Answer 1. billions of US dollars / 2. resolve issues / 3. broadening our horizons / 4. Those in favour of 5. There are few / 6. unlock the secrets of the universe / 7. climate change / 8. immediate steps 9. highlight the gap between the rich and the poor / 10. the circumstances of the victims of poverty 11. people in need

Day 10 Earth & Space 불법 포인트 정리

우주 탐사	space exploration	수십억의	billions of
극적인 변화	a dramatic change	문제를 해결하다	resolve issues
필수 광물질	essential minerals	~에 초점을 맞추다	focus on
모험	adventure	~에 찬성하는 사람들	those in favour of~
관련되어 있다	be associated with	장점들	virtues
불가능한 일	impossibilities	매력적인	fascinating
대신에	instead of	더욱 ~할수록, 더욱 ~ 하게 될 가능성이 크다	the more S+V, the likelier S+V
후진국들	underdeveloped nations	풀다	unlock
천문학	astronomy	인류의 장기간 생존	the long-term survival of humanity
엄청난 자본	a big amount of capital	우주 정거장	space stations
~ 떠나서	aside from	식민지화 하다	colonise
우주 비행사	astronauts	구원, 구제책	salvation
비용에 기초해서	based on cost	사람이 살 수 없는, 주거하기 부적절한	uninhabitable
측정하다, 추산하다	gauge	~ 때문에	due to
진보	advancement	기후 변화	climate change
금융 자원	monetary resources	긴급한 문제들	urgent matters
주민들	inhabitants	즉각적인 조치들	immediate steps
건설적인 접근	a constructive approach	돌보다	look after
훨씬 능가하다	far outweigh	시도들	endeavours
가능성	possibility	강조하다	highlight
목적 없이	aimlessly	빈부격차	the gap between the rich and the poor
떠다니다	float	비행(바다 혹은 우주로의 긴 여행)	voyage
위성들	satellites	빈곤(화)	Impoverishment / poverty
장비 파편들	pieces of equipment	행성 간의 일	inter-planetary pursuits
로켓 발사 추진체	rocket launch boosters	대폭, 과감하게	drastically
임무	missions	정당화	justification
현재 상태	the current state	전망	outlook
비용 효과적인	cost effective	상황들	circumstances
산업 생산력	industrial productivity	희생자들	victims
가능한 한	as ~ as possible	비용	expenditure
탐험하다, 탐사하다	explore	~로 향하다	directed towards
우주	outer space / space / cosmos universe	도움이 필요한 사람들	people in need

Day 11 Building & Design 빌딩과 디자인

| Question | Many people prefer to rent a house rather than buying one. Describe the advantages and disadvantages of renting a house.

많은 사람들이 집을 사는 것보다 임대하는 것을 더 선호한다. 주택 임대의 장단점을 논하라. |

 빈출 문제

1. Many old buildings are protected by law. Why is it important to maintain old buildings? How do we maintain them?

2. Some people say that the design of newly constructed buildings in big cities should be controlled by governments. Others insist that there should be no regulation to design the buildings. Discuss both views and give your own opinion.

3. Some people prefer to live in a traditional house. Others prefer to live in a modern apartment building? Discuss both views and give your own opinion.

4. In the past, buildings often reflected the culture of a society but today all modern buildings look alike. Therefore cities throughout the world are becoming more and more similar. What do you think the reasons are? Is it a positive or negative development?

1. 오래된 많은 건물들이 법에 의해 보호되고 있다. 오래된 건물들을 유지하는 일이 왜 중요한가? 그 건물들을 어떻게 유지할 수 있는가?

2. 어떤 사람들은 대도시에 새롭게 건설되는 건물의 디자인을 정부가 규제해야 한다고 말한다. 반면 이러한 건물 디자인에 규제가 없어야 한다고 주장하는 사람들도 있다. 양쪽의 견해를 논하고 당신의 주장을 제시하라.

3. 어떤 사람들은 전통적인 주택에 사는 것을 선호한다. 반면 현대식 아파트에 사는 것을 선호하는 사람들도 있다. 양쪽의 견해를 논하고 당신의 주장을 제시하라.

4. 과거의 건물들은 사회 문화를 반영하는 경우가 많았지만 오늘날에는 모든 현대식 건물들이 매우 비슷하다. 그러므로 전세계의 도시들은 점점 비슷해지고 있다. 그 원인은 무엇이라고 생각하는가? 이것은 긍정적인 발전인가? 아니면 부정적인 발전인가?

 **STEP2 브레인스토밍**

1) 역사적 건물들은 한 국가의 유산의 일부이다.
   유산 : heritage

2) 오래된 건물들은 종종 예술 작품들로 간주되고 이 건물들은 해외 관광객들을 끌어들인다.
   예술 작품들 : works of art / 해외 관광객들 : overseas tourists

3) 정부는 역사적 건물들을 유지하는 데 돈을 써야 한다.

4) 현대 건물들은 반드시 친환경적으로 디자인되어야 한다.
   친환경적인 : environmentally friendly

5) 현대적 단열은 집을 좀 더 에너지 효율적으로 만들 수 있고, 난방비를 줄이는 데 도움을 줄 수 있다.
   단열 : insulation / 에너지 효율적 : energy-efficient / 난방비 : heating bills

6) 상당히 낮은 대출 금리와 아파트 월세의 향상은 일부 사람들에게 주택소유에 뛰어들도록 이끌었다.
　　낮은 대출 금리 : low mortgage rates / 주택소유 : homeownership / 뛰어들다 : dive into

7) 만약 어떤 사람이 직업적으로 안정되지 않았거나 가까운 미래에 이사 갈 기회가 있다면, 집이나 아파트를 임대하는 것이 훨씬 더 좋다.
　　자리잡다 : settle into

8) 주택소유는 모두를 위한 것이 아니지만, 매력적일 수 있는 재정적 감정적 장점들이 있다.
　　매력적인, 유혹적인 : enticing

9) 일단 어떤 사람이 집을 소유하는 것에 전념한다면, 그들은 좀 더 그들의 지역 사회에 참여할 수 있게 될 가능성이 커지는 데, 그들은 수년간 거기에 살 것을 알기 때문이다.
　　~에 전념하다 : commit to+(동)명사 / 지역 사회 : community / 참여하다 : be involved in

10) 시간이 지나면 집의 가치가 상승할 것이라는 보장이 없다.
　　시간이 지나면 : over time / 보장 : guarantee

11) 역사적 구조물들은 우리나라의 역사에 대한 통찰력을 제공하고 수세기 전 사람들은 어떠한 삶을 살았는지를 보여준다.
　　통찰력 : an insight / 수세기 전 : many centuries ago

12) 실질적인 측면에서 많은 오래된 건물들은 한 나라에 중요한 수입을 제공하는데 많은 관광객들이 엄청나게 방문하기 때문이다.
　　실질적인 측면에서 : on a practical level / 수입 : income / 엄청나게 (많은 수) : in great numbers

13) 역사적 건물들은 오늘날 도시의 필수적인 부분이고 그 건물들의 보존은 기초 건축의 한 요소이다.
　　필수적인 : integral / 보존 : preservation

14) 역사적 건축물에 대한 작업은 미래를 위한 가치 있는 유산을 제공하는 동시에 과거를 존중하는 것이다.
   가치 있는 유산 : a worthy legacy

15) 오래된 건축물들은 특히 화재 피해를 잘 입는다.
   화재 피해 : fire damage / ~경향이 있는, 당하기 쉬운 : prone to

Answer

1) Historic buildings are part of a country's heritage.
2) Old buildings are often considered to be works of art and they attract overseas tourists.
3) Governments should spend money on maintaining historic buildings.
4) Modern buildings should be designed to be environmentally friendly.
5) Modern insulation can make houses more energy-efficient and then help to reduce heating bills.
6) Extremely low mortgage rates and rising apartment rents have led some people to dive into homeownership.
7) If some people are not settled into their career or could have an opportunity to relocate in the near future, renting a house or flat is much better.
8) Homeownership is not for everyone, but there are some financial and emotional advantages that can be enticing.
9) Once some people commit to owning a home, they are more likely to become more involved in their community because they know they will be there for years.
10) There is no guarantee that houses will increase in value over time.
11) Historic structures provide an insight into the history of our countries and show us how people many centuries ago lived their lives.
12) On a practical level, many old buildings provide an important income to a country as many tourists visit them in great numbers.
13) Historic buildings are an integral part of today's cities and their preservation is an element of basic architecture.
14) Work on historic constructions is about respecting the past while providing a worthy legacy for the future.
15) Old constructions are particularly prone to fire damage.

실전문제

You should spend about 40 minutes on this task.
Write about the following topic :

> Many people prefer to rent a house rather than buying one. Describe the advantages and disadvantages of renting a house.

Give reasons for your answer and include any relevant examples from your own knowledge or experience.

Write at least 250 words.

 **문제 정독, 문제 유형 파악, 브레인스토밍 (0 ~ 5분)**

Question	Many people prefer to rent a house rather than buying one. Describe the advantages and disadvantages of renting a house.

문제 정독
많은 사람들이 집을 사는 것보다 임대하는 것을 더 선호한다. 주택 임대의 장단점을 논하라.

rent : 임대하다

문제 유형 파악

2-2. Discuss the advantages and the disadvantages of 토픽. 유형

* 장단점을 논하라고 했기 때문에, 어느 쪽이 더 많다고 결론을 내려서는 안 된다. Body 1에는 장점을, Body 2에는 단점을 비슷한 분량으로 적고, 결론에는 '장점도 있지만 단점도 있다'라고 쓴다.

Brainstorming

Topic : 주택 임대	
Advantages : 주택 임대의 장점	Disadvantages : 주택 임대의 단점
1. 너무 많은 (돈의) 투입 없이 해결책 제공 provide a solution without too much commitment → 주택을 구입하는 것은 많은 돈을 지불해야 함 purchasing a home involves paying a large amount of money 2. 세입자가 그들이 사는 집의 장기적 마모를 책임질 필요가 없음 tenants are not responsible for the long-term wear and tear of their home → 집을 유지하는 것은 엄청난 비용이 될 수 있음 maintaining a building can become extremely expensive	1. 자신의 주택이나 아파트가 실질적으로 자신들의 집이 아닌 것처럼 느낌 feel like their house or flat is not really their own home → 정착할 수 있는 곳을 소유하기를 꿈꿈 dream of having a place where we can settle 2. 보통 그 이상의 돈을 매달 내야 하는 상황에 처함 usually end up paying more monthly → 결국 그들 소유의 부동산을 사기 위한 충분한 돈을 저축할 수 있었기를 바라게 될 것임 end up wishing they could save enough to buy their own property

* 장점과 단점의 아이디어 수는 같아야 한다.

2 단계 서론 (Introduction) (6~10분) : 두 문장으로 작성

| Question | Many people prefer to rent a house rather than buying one. Describe the advantages and disadvantages of renting a house. |

단계	Question	서론 작성
1단계 Paraphrasing	토픽 : Many people prefer to rent a house rather than buying one.	Paraphrasing : A lot of us choose not to get on the property ladder and instead just rent our homes.
2단계 Answering	질문 : Describe the advantages and disadvantages of renting a house.	Answering : 장단점 간단히 언급 There are pros and cons of both choices and money is a big factor on both sides of the argument.

Introduction
A lot of us choose not to get on the property ladder and instead just rent our homes. There are pros and cons of both choices and money is a big factor on both sides of the argument.

property ladder : 자산 사다리 (개인 또는 한 가정이 일생 동안 가격이 싼 주택에서 보다 비싼 주택으로 옮겨가는 과정)
pros and cons : 장단점들

우리말 해석
우리 중 많은 사람들은 자산 사다리를 올라가는 것이 아니라 대신 단지 집을 임대하는 것을 선택한다. 양쪽 선택에 장단점이 있고 돈은 이 논쟁의 양쪽 모두에게 커다란 요인이 된다.

 **3단계** 본론 1 (Body 1) (11~20분) : **Advantages** (주택 임대의 장점)

> **Question** Many people prefer to rent a house rather than buying one. Describe the advantages and disadvantages of renting a house.

Body 1은 1단계에서 브레인스토밍한 'Advantages'를 바탕으로 작성한다.

1단계	Topic Sentence	There are a couple of benefits of renting a house.
2단계 (1)	Supporting Sentence (1)	*provide a solution without too much commitment* For those who are concerned about the financial risks of buying a house or flat, renting can provide a solution without too much commitment.
3단계 (1)	Supporting Sentence or Specific Example (1)	*purchasing a home involves paying a large amount of money* Needless to say purchasing a home involves paying a large amount of money up front as well as then being tied to a mortgage in most cases, and a fall in house prices can be disastrous if a homeowner needs to sell.
2단계 (2)	Supporting Sentence (2)	*tenants are not responsible for the long-term wear and tear of their home* Another advantage of renting is that tenants are not responsible for the long-term wear and tear of their home.
3단계 (2)	Supporting Sentence or Specific Example (2)	*maintaining a building can become extremely expensive* Every building falls into disrepair at some point, and maintaining a building over many years can become extremely expensive.

Body 1

There are a couple of benefits of renting a house. For those who are concerned about the financial risks of buying a house or flat, renting can provide a solution without too much commitment. Needless to say purchasing a home involves paying a large amount of money up front as well as then being tied to a mortgage in most cases, and a fall in house prices can be disastrous if a homeowner needs to sell. Another advantage of renting is that tenants are not responsible for the long-term wear and tear of their home. Every building falls into disrepair at some point, and maintaining a building over many years can become extremely expensive.

commitment : (돈의) 투입
needless to say : 말할 필요도 없이
up front : 선불로
tied to : ~와 관련 있는
a mortgage : 대출
disastrous : 재앙인

tenants : 세입자들(↔ landlords, landladies)
be responsible for : ~에 대해 책임지다
wear and tear : 마모
fall into disrepair : 파손되다, 황폐해지다
maintain : 유지하다

우리말 해석

주택 임대에는 몇 가지 장점이 있다. 주택이나 아파트를 구입하는 데 재정적 위험을 걱정하는 사람들에게는 임대가 너무 많은 (돈의) 투입 없이 해결책을 제공할 수 있다. 말할 필요도 없이 주택을 구입하는 것은 대부분의 경우 대출과 관련 있을 뿐만 아니라, 선불로 큰 액수의 돈을 지불해야 하고, 그리고 또한 주택 소유자들이 팔고자 한다면 집값의 하락은 재앙이 될 수 있다. 임대의 또 다른 장점은 세입자가 그들이 사는 집의 장기적 마모를 책임질 필요가 없다는 것이다. 모든 건물은 어느 시점에 이르면 파손되고 수년 동안 집을 유지하는 것은 엄청난 비용이 될 수 있다.

 **본론 2 (Body 2) (21~30분) : Disadvantages** (주택 임대의 단점)

> **Question** Many people prefer to rent a house rather than buying one. Describe the advantages and disadvantages of renting a house.

Body 2는 1단계에서 브레인스토밍한 'Disadvantages'를 바탕으로 작성한다.

1단계	Topic Sentence	However, we should consider its negative side as well.
2단계 (1)	Supporting Sentence (1)	*feel like their house or flat is not really their own home* People who rent can sometimes feel like their house or flat is not really their own home.
3단계 (1)	Supporting Sentence or Specific Example (1)	*dream of having a place where we can settle* Many of us surely dream of having a place where we can settle regardless of what is happening to the economy, whether it be an old-fashioned cottage in the countryside or a modern flat in a high-rise building.
2단계 (2)	Supporting Sentence (2)	*usually end up paying more monthly* The other big disadvantage of renting is the cost of living because even though it can be an easier financial decision in the short term, people usually end up paying more monthly.
3단계 (2)	Supporting Sentence or Specific Example (2)	*end up wishing they could save enough to buy their own property* Tenants can end up giving a significant portion of their salaries to their landlords and end up wishing they could save enough to buy their own property.

Body 2

However, we should consider its negative side as well. People who rent can sometimes feel like their house or flat is not really their own home. Many of us surely dream of having a place where we can settle regardless of what is happening to the economy, whether it be an old-fashioned cottage in the countryside or a modern flat in a high-rise building. The other big disadvantage of renting is the cost of living because even though it can be an easier financial decision in the short term, people usually end up paying more monthly. Tenants can end up giving a significant portion of their salaries to their landlords and end up wishing they could save enough to buy their own property.

settle : 정착하다
regardless of : ~에 상관없이
whether it be A or B : 양보의 부사절로 'A든 B든 간에'
old-fashioned : 구식의
cottage : 작은 집
in the countryside : 시골에서
a high-rise building : 고층 빌딩
the cost of living : 생활비
end up : 결국 (어떤 처지에) 처하게 되다
property : 부동산, 자산

우리말 해석

하지만 우리는 이것의 부정적인 측면 또한 고려해야 한다. 임대한 사람들은 때로 자신의 주택이나 아파트가 실질적으로 자신들의 집이 아닌 것처럼 느낀다. 우리들 중 많은 사람들은 틀림없이 시골의 오래된 작은 집이든, 고층 빌딩의 현대식 아파트든 간에, 경제사정에 상관없이 우리가 정착할 수 있는 곳을 소유하기를 꿈꾼다. 임대의 다른 큰 단점은 생활비인데 왜냐하면 임대가 단기적으로는 더 쉬운 재정적 결정일 수 있지만, 사람들은 보통 그 이상의 돈을 매달 내야 하는 상황에 처하기 때문이다. 세입자들은 월급의 상당부분을 집주인에게 주게 될 것이고, 결국 그들 소유의 부동산을 사기 위한 충분한 돈을 저축할 수 있었기를 바라게 될 것이다.

 **5 단계** 결론 (Conclusion) (31~35분) : 본문에 제시한 내 주장 요약하며 다시 한 번 강조

> **Question**
> Many people prefer to rent a house rather than buying one. Describe the advantages and disadvantages of renting a house.

결론 작성 시, 먼저 문제 유형을 파악한 후, 'Conclusion Template'의 표현을 인용한다. (See p58)

문제 유형 파악	2-2) Discuss the advantages and the disadvantages of 토픽. 유형
Conclusion Template 인용	In conclusion, although there are benefits(drawbacks) of … (토픽), its drawbacks(benefits) also should not be ignored because … 본문에 제시한 장점과 단점 간단히 요약

결론에서 절대로 해결책을 제시해서는 안 된다.

> **Conclusion**
> **In conclusion, although there are benefits of** renting a home such as a lower financial burden and maintenance cost, **the drawbacks should not be ignored because** ultimately people can find financial and emotional security in owning a house.

* 상황에 따라 템플릿을 살짝 변형해도 좋다.

financial burden : 재정적 부담
maintenance cost : 유지 비용
financial and emotional security : 재정적 감정적 안정

> **우리말 해석**
> 결론적으로 비록 낮은 재정적 부담과 유지 비용처럼 주택 임대의 장점들이 있지만, 그 단점들을 간과해서는 안 되는데 왜냐하면 결국에는 사람들이 주택을 소유하는 데에서 재정적 감정적 안정을 찾을 수 있기 때문이다.

6 단계 교정 (Self-correction) (36~40분) : 내용의 일관성 및 문법 검토

다음 Body 2의 내용을 교정해 보자. 틀린 부분은 총 몇 개일까?

교정 전 (직접 문장 부호를 이용하여 틀린 부분을 교정해 보자.)

however, We should consider its negative side as well. People who rents can sometimes feel like their house or flat is not really their own home. Many of us surely dream of having a place where we can settles regardless of what is happening to the economy, whether it be a old-fashioned cottage in the countryside or a modern flat in a high-rise building.

The other big disadvantage of renting are the cost of live because even though it can be an easier financial decision in the short term, people usually ends up paying more monthly. Tenants can end up giving a significant portion of their salaries to their landlords and end up wishing they could save enough to buy their own property.

교정

~~h~~**H**owever, ~~W~~**w**e should consider its negative side as well. People who ~~rents~~ **rent** can sometimes feel like their house or flat is not really their own home. Many of us surely dream of having a place where we can ~~settles~~ **settle** regardless of what is happening to the economy, whether it be ~~a~~ **an** old-fashioned cottage in the countryside or a modern flat in a high-rise building. The other big disadvantage of renting ~~are~~ **is** the cost of ~~live~~ **living** because even though it can be an easier financial decision in the short term, people usually ~~ends~~ **end** up paying more monthly. Tenants can end up giving a significant portion of their salaries to their landlords and end up wishing they could save enough to buy their own property.

1. h → H : 문장의 첫 글자는 반드시 대문자로 시작한다.
2. W → w : 갑자기 대문자를 문장 중간에 쓰지 않는다(고유명사 예외).
3. rents → rent : 관계 대명사의 주격 who는 앞의 people을 의미하므로 복수 동사인 rent를 쓴다.
4. settles → settle : 조동사 can 다음에는 동사 원형을 쓴다.
5. a → an : 모음(a/i/u/e/o)으로 발음이 시작되는 단어 old[ould] 앞에는 a가 아닌 an으로 쓰고 말한다.
6. 붙여쓰기 : 위의 글은 Body 2 단락이다. 단락이 바뀌지 않는 한, 줄을 바꿔 쓰지 않는다.
7. are → is : 주어인 disadvantage가 단수이므로 단수 동사인 is를 쓴다.
8. live → living : the cost of living은 '삶의 질'이라는 뜻. 전치사 of 다음에는 (동)명사를 쓴다.
9. ends → end : 주어인 people이 복수이므로 복수 동사인 end를 쓴다.

틀린 개수 : 총 9개

Sample Answer

Question Many people prefer to rent a house rather than buying one. Describe the advantages and disadvantages of renting a house.

A lot of us choose not to get on the property ladder and instead just rent our homes. There are pros and cons of both choices and money is a big factor on both sides of the argument.

There are a couple of benefits of renting a house. For those who are concerned about the financial risks of buying a house or flat, renting can provide a solution without too much commitment. Needless to say purchasing a home involves paying a large amount of money up front as well as then being tied to a mortgage in most cases, and a fall in house prices can be disastrous if a homeowner needs to sell. Another advantage of renting is that tenants are not responsible for the long-term wear and tear of their home. Every building falls into disrepair at some point, and maintaining a building over many years can become extremely expensive.

However, we should consider its negative side as well. People who rent can sometimes feel like their house or flat is not really their own home. Many of us surely dream of having a place where we can settle regardless of what is happening to the economy, whether it be an old-fashioned cottage in the countryside or a modern flat in a high-rise building. The other big disadvantage of renting is the cost of living because even though it can be an easier financial decision in the short term, people usually end up paying more monthly. Tenants can end up giving a significant portion of their salaries to their landlords and end up wishing they could save enough to buy their own property.

In conclusion, although there are benefits of renting a home such as a lower financial burden and maintenance cost, the drawbacks should not be ignored because ultimately people can find financial and emotional security in owning a house.

word counts : 313 words

우리말 해석

우리 중 많은 사람들은 자산 사다리를 올라가는 것이 아니라 대신 단지 집을 임대하는 것을 선택한다. 양쪽 선택에 장단점이 있고 돈은 이 논쟁의 양쪽 모두에게 커다란 요인이 된다.

주택 임대에는 몇 가지 장점이 있다. 주택이나 아파트를 구입하는 데 재정적 위험을 걱정하는 사람들에게는 임대가 너무 많은 (돈의) 투입 없이 해결책을 제공할 수 있다. 말할 필요도 없이 주택을 구입하는 것은 대부분의 경우 대출과 관련 있을 뿐만 아니라, 선불로 큰 액수의 돈을 지불해야 하고, 그리고 또한 주택 소유자들이 팔고자 한다면 집값의 하락은 재앙이 될 수 있다. 임대의 또 다른 장점은 세입자가 그들이 사는 집의 장기적 마모를 책임질 필요가 없다는 것이다. 모든 건물은 어느 시점에 이르면 파손되고 수년 동안 집을 유지하는 것은 엄청난 비용이 될 수 있다.

하지만 우리는 이것의 부정적인 측면 또한 고려해야 한다. 임대한 사람들은 때로 자신의 주택이나 아파트가 실질적으로 자신들의 집이 아닌 것처럼 느낀다. 우리들 중 많은 사람들은 틀림없이 시골의 오래된 작은 집이든, 고층 빌딩의 현대식 아파트든 간에, 경제사정에 상관없이 우리가 정착할 수 있는 곳을 소유하기를 꿈꾼다. 임대의 다른 큰 단점은 생활비인데 왜냐하면 임대가 단기적으로는 더 쉬운 재정적 결정일 수 있지만, 사람들은 보통 그 이상의 돈을 매달 내야 하는 상황에 처하기 때문이다. 세입자들은 월급의 상당부분을 집주인에게 주게 될 것이고, 결국 그들 소유의 부동산을 사기 위한 충분한 돈을 저축할 수 있었기를 바라게 될 것이다.

결론적으로 비록 낮은 재정적 부담과 유지 비용처럼 주택 임대의 장점들이 있지만, 그 단점들을 간과해서는 안 되는데 왜냐하면 결국에는 사람들이 주택을 소유하는 데에서 재정적 감정적 안정을 찾을 수 있기 때문이다.

불법 Review

앞에서 배운 내용을 바탕으로 다음 빈칸을 영어로 작성해 보자.

A lot of us choose not to get on _____ (1. 자산 사다리) and instead just rent our homes. There are pros and cons of both choices and money is a big factor on both sides of the argument.

There are a couple of benefits of renting a house. For those who are concerned about _____ (2. 재정적 위험들) of buying a house or flat, renting can provide a solution without _____ (3. 너무 많은 돈의 투입). Needless to say purchasing a home involves paying a large amount of money _____ (4. 선불로) as well as then being tied to a mortgage in most cases, and a fall in house prices can be disastrous if a homeowner needs to sell. Another advantage of renting is that tenants are not responsible for _____ (5. 장기적 마모) of their home. Every building falls into disrepair at some point, and maintaining a building over many years can become extremely expensive.

However, we should consider its negative side as well. People who rent can sometimes feel like their house or flat is not really their own home. Many of us surely dream of having a place where we can settle regardless of what is happening to the economy, whether it be an old-fashioned cottage in the countryside or _____ (6. 고층 빌딩의 현대식 아파트). The other big disadvantage of renting is the cost of living because even though it can be an easier financial decision _____ (7. 단기적으로), people usually end up paying more monthly. _____ (8. 세입자들) can end up giving a significant portion of their salaries to their landlords and end up wishing they could save enough to buy their own property.

In conclusion, although there are benefits of renting a home such as _____ (9. 낮은 재정적 부담) and maintenance cost, the drawbacks should not be ignored because ultimately people can find _____ (10. 재정적 감정적 안정) in owning a house.

Answer 1. the property ladder / 2. the financial risks / 3. too much commitment / 4. up front
5. the long-term wear and tear / 6. a modern flat in a high-rise building / 7. in the short term
8. Tenants / 9. a lower financial burden / 10. financial and emotional security

Day 11 Building & Design 불법 포인트 정리

유산	heritage	임대하다	rent
예술 작품들	works of art	자산 사다리	property ladder
해외 관광객들	overseas tourists	장단점들	pros and cons
친환경적인	environmentally friendly	(돈의) 투입	commitment
단열	insulation	말할 필요도 없이	needless to say
에너지 효율적	energy-efficient	선불로	up front
난방비	heating bills	~와 관련 있는	tied to
낮은 대출 금리	low mortgage rates	대출	a mortgage
주택소유	homeownership	재앙인	disastrous
뛰어들다	dive into	세입자들	tenants ↔ landlords, landladies
자리잡다	settle into	~에 대해 책임지다	be responsible for
매력적인, 유혹적인	enticing	마모	wear and tear
~에 전념하다	commit to+(동)명사	파손되다, 황폐해지다	fall into disrepair
지역 사회	community	유지하다	maintain
참여하다	be involved in	정착하다	settle
시간이 지나면	over time	~에 상관없이	regardless of
보장	guarantee	A든 B든 간에	whether it be A or B
통찰력	an insight	구식의	old-fashioned
수세기 전	many centuries ago	작은 집	cottage
실질적인 측면에서	on a practical level	시골에서	in the countryside
수입	income	고층 빌딩	a high-rise building
엄청나게 (많은 수)	in great numbers	생활비	the cost of living
필수적인	integral	결국 (어떤 처지에) 처하게 되다	end up
보존	preservation	부동산, 자산	property
가치 있는 유산	a worthy legacy	재정적 부담	financial burden
화재 피해	fire damage	유지 비용	maintenance cost
~경향이 있는, 당하기 쉬운	prone to	재정적 감정적 안정	financial and emotional security

Day 12 IT 정보기술
(Information Technology)

Question	Teenagers are spending too much time on computers and this will lead to a severe problem in their mental and physical health. Do you agree or disagree with this statement? 십대들은 컴퓨터에 너무나 많은 시간을 할애하고 있고 이것은 그들의 정신적, 신체적 건강에 심각한 문제를 초래할 것이다. 당신은 이 말에 동의하는가? 또는 동의하지 않는가?

 빈출 문제

1. When a nation develops its technology, the traditional skills and ways of life die out. This is because it is pointless to keep them alive. Do you agree or disagree with this statement?

2. Using a computer every day can have more negative than positive effects on children. Do you agree or disagree with this statement?

3. People are relying considerably on computers. These machines are used in businesses, medical care and even crime. What areas will they be used for in the future? Is this dependence on computers beneficial?

4. In the near future people who cannot deal with computers will not be able to get a job. Do you agree or disagree with this statement?

1. 국가의 과학기술이 발전할 때, 그 나라의 전통 기술과 삶의 방식은 사라진다. 왜냐하면 그것들을 유지하는 것은 무의미하기 때문이다. 당신은 이 말에 동의하는가? 또는 동의하지 않는가?

2. 매일 컴퓨터를 사용하는 것은 아이들에게 긍정적인 영향보다는 부정정적인 영향을 더 많이 끼친다. 당신은 이 말에 동의하는가? 또는 동의하지 않는가?

3. 사람들은 컴퓨터에 상당히 의존하고 있다. 컴퓨터는 산업, 의료, 범죄에까지 이용되고 있다. 미래에는 컴퓨터가 어떤 분야에 사용될 것인가? 컴퓨터에 의존하는 것은 이로운가?

4. 머지않아 컴퓨터를 다루지 못하는 사람들은 일자리를 구할 수 없을 것이다. 당신은 이 말에 동의하는가? 또는 동의하지 않는가?

 브레인스토밍

1) 일부 컴퓨터 게임들은 사람을 죽이거나, 범죄를 저지르는 걸 포함하므로 이러한 게임 웹사이트에는 나이 제한이 있어야 한다.
   범죄를 저지르다 : commit crimes / 나이 제한 : age limits

2) 인터넷은 통제되는 것이 필요한데 많은 웹사이트들이 더 많은 인터넷 사용자들을 끌어들이기 위해 폭력적이고 선정적인 이미지를 보여주기 때문이다.
   통제하다 : control / 폭력적이고 선정적인 이미지 : violent or sexual images

3) 사람들은 인터넷을 통해 자신의 집에서 편안하게 상품과 서비스를 살 수 있다.
   편안함 : comfort

4) 부모들은 그들의 자녀가 온라인에서 무엇을 보는지 통제하기 어렵다고 느낀다.
   ~하는 것이 어렵다고 느끼다 : find it difficult to +V

5) 너무 많은 웹사이트들로 좋은 정보를 찾는 건 어렵다.

6) 범죄자들은 사람들의 돈을 훔치기 위해 인터넷을 점점 더 사용한다.
　　범죄자들 : criminals / 훔치다 : steal

7) 우리는 어떤 언어로든 전세계 어떤 국가의 뉴스라도 온라인으로 읽을 수 있다.

8) 사람들은 여전히 신문이나 책을 사는데 그들 중의 일부는 스크린으로 읽는 것을 좋아하지 않기 때문이다.

9) 고용주들은 지금 세대 졸업생들은 뛰어난 IT 기술을 갖췄다고 당연하게 기대한다.
　　당연하게 : as a matter of course

10) 컴퓨터에 기반을 둔 직업들을 위해 구직자들은 여러 가지 프로그래밍 언어들을 알고 이용할 수 있어야 할 필요가 있다.
　　컴퓨터에 기반을 둔 직업들 : computer-oriented professions / 구직자들 : job seekers

11) 거의 모든 직업들은 지금 컴퓨터 하드웨어와 소프트웨어의 기본적 이해를 요구하는데 특히 워드 프로세싱과 이메일이다.
　　거의 모든 : almost all / 기본적 이해 : basic understanding

12) 컴퓨터는 아이들이 그들의 수학적 사고, 문제 해결 능력 그리고 비판적 사고를 향상시키는 데 도움을 준다.
　　수학적 사고 : mathematical thinking / 문제 해결 능력 : problem solving skills / 비판적 사고 : critical thinking

13) 컴퓨터를 오랫동안 사용하는 아이들은 컴퓨터 시력 증후군이 발생할 더 높은 위험에 처한다.
　　컴퓨터 시력 증후군 : computer vision syndrome

14) 아이의 신체적 발달은 컴퓨터 앞에서 너무나 많은 시간을 보내면서 방해받을지도 모른다.
　　컴퓨터 앞에서 : in front of a computer / 방해하다 : hinder

15) 인터넷 접속은 아이들이 좀 더 창의적이고 말을 잘하게 되는데 도움을 줄 수 있다.
   인터넷 접속 : Internet access / 창의적인 : creative / 말을 잘하는 : communicative

---

Answer

1) Some computer games involve killing people or committing crimes, therefore there should be age limits for these game websites.
2) The Internet needs to be controlled because many websites show violent or sexual images to attract more Internet users.
3) People can buy goods and services from the comfort of their homes through the Internet.
4) Parents find it difficult to control what their children see online.
5) With so many websites it is difficult to search for good information.
6) Criminals increasingly use the Internet to steal people's money.
7) We can read the news online in any language from any country in the world.
8) People still buy newspapers and books because some of them do not like reading from a screen.
9) Employers expect this generation's graduates to have strong IT skills as a matter of course.
10) For computer-oriented professions job seekers need to know and be able to use several programming languages.
11) Almost all jobs now require some basic understanding of computer hardware and software, especially word processing and emails.
12) Computers help children improve their mathematical thinking, problem solving skills and critical thinking.
13) Children who use computers for a long time are at a higher risk of developing computer vision syndrome.
14) A child's physical development may be hindered by spending too much time in front of a computer.
15) Internet access can help children become more creative and communicative.

 실전문제

You should spend about 40 minutes on this task.
Write about the following topic :

> Teenagers are spending too much time on computers and this will lead to a severe problem in their mental and physical health. Do you agree or disagree with this statement?

Give reasons for your answer and include any relevant examples from your own knowledge or experience.

Write at least 250 words.

| 1 단계 | 문제 정독, 문제 유형 파악, 브레인스토밍 (0 ~ 5분) |

| Question | Teenagers are spending too much time on computers and this will lead to a severe problem in their mental and physical health. Do you agree or disagree with this statement? |

문제 정독
십대들은 컴퓨터에 너무나 많은 시간을 할애하고 있고 이것은 그들의 정신적, 신체적 건강에 심각한 문제를 초래할 것이다. 당신은 이 말에 동의하는가? 또는 동의하지 않는가?

teenagers의 동의어 : teenage children
adolescents / young people
* 문제에 있는 단어를 그대로 여러 번 에세이에 쓰면 감점이다. 키워드의 동의어를 외워서 풍부한 어휘력을 보여줘야 한다. 아이엘츠에서는 동의어의 폭이 넓다. 100% 똑같은 단어가 아니더라도 의미상 비슷하다면 동의어로 사용해도 괜찮다.

spend 시간 on : ~에 시간을 보내다
lead to : 초래하다
severe : 심각한
mental and physical health : 정신적 신체적 건강

문제 유형 파악
1-1. Do you agree or disagree? 유형

Brainstorming

Topic : 십대의 장시간 컴퓨터 사용은 정신적 신체적 건강에 심각한 문제를 초래함	
Agree : 정신적 건강에 미치는 문제	Agree : 신체적 건강에 미치는 문제
1. 컴퓨터의 장점을 취할 수 있는 동기부여 결핍 lack the motivation to take advantage of computers → 영화와 드라마를 보고, 채팅이나 게임을 함 watching movies and dramas, chatting or playing games 2. 숙제와 다른 취미생활을 하는 것을 그만둠 stop doing homework or alternative hobbies → 그들의 일반적 동기부여와 인지 발달이 느려질 수 있음 their general motivation and cognitive development can be slowed	1. 오랜 시간 앉아 있거나 누워 있음 sit or lie down for a long time → 몸 상태가 안 좋아지고 심지어 비만이 됨 become unfit and even obese 2. 수면부족 a lack of sleep → 안구건조증, 손가락과 손목에 발생하는 반복성 긴장 장애 repetitive strain injuries to their fingers and wrists as well as dry eyes

* 반드시 정신적 건강과 신체적 건강 두 가지 모두를 언급해야 한다.
** 이 에세이에서는 내 의견(Agree)만 다루었는데 남의 의견(Disagree)까지 다룰 경우 분량이 너무 많아지기 때문이다.

2단계　서론 (Introduction) (6~10분) : 두 문장으로 작성

Question	Teenagers are spending too much time on computers and this will lead to a severe problem in their mental and physical health. Do you agree or disagree with this statement?

단계	Question	서론 작성
1단계 Paraphrasing	토픽 : Teenagers are spending too much time on computers and this will lead to a severe problem in their physical and mental health.	**Paraphrasing :** Parents often worry about the negative effects of computer use on their teenage children because they spend so much of their leisure time on PCs, laptops and tablets.
2단계 Answering	질문 : Do you agree or disagree with this statement?	**Answering: Agree일 경우** I share their concerns because the current generation of adolescents is more exposed to technology than ever before.

Introduction
Parents often worry about the negative effects of computer use on their teenage children because they spend so much of their leisure time on PCs, laptops and tablets. I share their concerns because the current generation of adolescents is more exposed to technology than ever before.

worry about : ~에 대해 걱정하다　　concerns : 고민들, 걱정들
leisure time : 여가시간　　　　　　generation : 세대 (한 세대는 30년을 의미)

우리말 해석
부모들은 종종 그들의 십대 아이들의 컴퓨터 사용에 있어 부정적인 영향을 걱정하는데 아이들이 컴퓨터와 노트북 그리고 태블릿에 여가시간을 너무 많이 할애하기 때문이다. 나는 부모들의 고민에 공감하는데 현재 청소년 세대가 이전보다 더 기술에 노출되어 있기 때문이다.

3 단계 본론 1 (Body 1) (11~20분) : 내 의견 = **Agree** (십대의 장시간 컴퓨터 사용이 정신적 건강에 미치는 문제)

> **Question** Teenagers are spending too much time on computers and this will lead to a severe problem in their mental and physical health. Do you agree or disagree with this statement?

Body 1은 1단계에서 브레인스토밍한 'Agree'의 '정신적 건강에 미치는 문제'를 바탕으로 작성한다.

1단계	Topic Sentence	Spending too much time using these smart machines can be harmful to a teenager's mental health.
2단계 (1)	Supporting Sentence (1)	*lack the motivation to take advantage of computers* Although computers do offer practical benefits such as allowing teenagers wider access to study materials and e-books, many young people lack the motivation to take advantage of these.
3단계 (1)	Supporting Sentence or Specific Example (1)	*watching movies and dramas, chatting or playing games* Instead, research suggests teenagers spend most of their computer time watching movies and dramas, chatting or playing games.
2단계 (2)	Supporting Sentence (2)	*stop doing homework or alternative hobbies* While these aspects of computer use might not be harmful in the short term, problems begin to appear when adolescents stop doing homework or alternative hobbies such as outdoor sports.
3단계 (2)	Supporting Sentence or Specific Example (2)	*their general motivation and cognitive development can be slowed* In these cases teenagers may feel bored when doing anything away from their computers, and their general motivation and cognitive development can be slowed by a kind of brain fog caused by spending too much time focused on virtual activities.

Body 1

Spending too much time using these smart machines can be harmful to a teenager's mental health. Although computers do offer practical benefits such as allowing teenagers wider access to study materials and e-books, many young people lack the motivation to take advantage of these. Instead, research suggests teenagers spend most of their computer time watching movies and dramas, chatting or playing games. While these aspects of computer use might not be harmful in the short term, problems begin to appear when adolescents stop doing homework or alternative hobbies such as outdoor sports. In these cases teenagers may feel bored when doing anything away from their computers, and their general motivation and cognitive development can be slowed by a kind of brain fog caused by spending too much time focused on virtual activities.

practical benefits : 실질적 이득
study materials : 학습 자료
e-books : 전자책
motivation : 동기
take advantage of~ : ~를 이용하다
research : 연구조사
outdoor sports : 야외 운동
cognitive development : 인지 발달
brain fog : 뇌 안개(머리가 혼란스럽고 안개같이 뿌예서 분명하게 생각하거나 표현하지 못하는 상태)
virtual : 가상의

우리말 해석

이러한 스마트 기기들을 사용하는 데 너무 많은 시간을 소비하는 것은 십대의 정신건강에 해가 될 수 있다. 비록 컴퓨터가 십대들이 학습 자료와 전자책을 폭넓게 접할 수 있게 해주는 실질적 이득을 제공하기도 하지만, 많은 젊은이들은 이러한 장점을 이용할 수 있는 동기부여가 결핍되어 있다. 그 대신, 연구조사는 십대들이 영화와 드라마를 보고, 채팅이나 게임을 하는데 컴퓨터 사용시간의 대부분을 보낸다고 제시한다. 컴퓨터 사용의 이러한 측면은 단기적으로는 해가 되지 않지만, 문제는 청소년들이 숙제나 야외 운동과 같은 다른 취미생활을 하는 것을 그만둘 때 나타나기 시작한다. 이런 경우 십대들은 어떤 일을 하든 컴퓨터와 떨어지면 지루하다고 느낄지도 모르고, 지나치게 많은 시간을 가상 활동에 집중하며 보냄으로써 그들의 일반적 동기부여와 인지 발달은 일종의 뇌 안개(brain fog) 현상에 의해 느려질 수 있다.

4단계 본론 2 (Body 2) (21〜30분) : 내 의견 = **Agree** (십대의 장시간 컴퓨터 사용이 신체적 건강에 미치는 문제)

> **Question**
> Teenagers are spending too much time on computers and this will lead to a severe problem in their mental and physical health. Do you agree or disagree with this statement?

Body 2는 1단계에서 브레인스토밍한 'Agree'의 '신체적 건강에 미치는 문제'를 바탕으로 작성한다.

1단계	Topic Sentence	Teenagers' physical as well as mental health can be negatively affected if they devote most of their attention to computers.
2단계 (1)	Supporting Sentence (1)	*sit or lie down for a long time* This is because they usually sit or lie down for a long time while using these devices.
3단계 (1)	Supporting Sentence or Specific Example (1)	*become unfit and even obese* Adolescents are likely to become unfit and even obese if they do not get up and do physical exercise on a regular basis.
2단계 (2)	Supporting Sentence (2)	*a lack of sleep* Moreover we increasingly hear about teenagers becoming addicted to computer games and chat programs, and this can lead to a lack of sleep as a consequence of late-night use.
3단계 (2)	Supporting Sentence or Specific Example (2)	*repetitive strain injuries to their fingers and wrists as well as dry eyes* In addition, the repetitive actions involved in using a computer can cause repetitive strain injuries to their fingers and wrists as well as dry eyes.

Body 2

Teenagers' physical as well as mental health can be negatively affected if they devote most of their attention to computers. This is because they usually sit or lie down for a long time while using these devices. Adolescents are likely to become unfit and even obese if they do not get up and do physical exercise on a regular basis. Moreover we increasingly hear about teenagers becoming addicted to computer games and chat programs, and this can lead to a lack of sleep as a consequence of late-night use. In addition, the repetitive actions involved in using a computer can cause repetitive strain injuries to their fingers and wrists as well as dry eyes.

lie down : 눕다
unfit : 몸 상태가 안 좋은
obese : 비만인
on a regular basis : 정기적으로
a lack of sleep : 수면부족
as a consequence of : ~의 결과로서
late-night : 심야의

repetitive : 반복적인
repetitive strain injuries : 반복성 긴장 장애(장시간의 반복된 작업으로 인한 손상. 컴퓨터 키보드나 마우스를 이용한 작업 등 긴장된 상태에서 장시간 반복 작업을 할 때 손이나 손목, 어깨 등에 발생하는 손상)
wrist : 손목
dry eyes : 안구 건조증

우리말 해석

십대들의 정신 건강뿐만 아니라 신체도 그들이 컴퓨터에 그들의 주의력을 거의 다 쏟아붓는다면 부정적인 영향을 받을 것이다. 이것은 십대들이 이러한 기기를 사용하는 동안 오랜 시간 앉아 있거나 누워 있기 때문이다. 청소년들은 만약 정기적으로 일어나서 신체적 운동을 하지 않으면 몸 상태가 안 좋아지고 심지어 비만이 될 가능성이 높다. 게다가 우리는 컴퓨터 게임과 채팅 프로그램에 중독된 십대들에 대해 갈수록 더 듣고 있고, 이는 늦은 밤까지 사용한 결과로 인해 수면부족을 초래할 수 있다. 또한 컴퓨터의 사용에 수반되는 반복적인 행동들은 안구건조증뿐만 아니라 손가락과 손목에 발생하는 반복성 긴장 장애의 원인이 될 수 있다.

5 단계 결론 (Conclusion) (31~35분) : 본문에 제시한 내 주장 요약하며 다시 한 번 강조

Question	Teenagers are spending too much time on computers and this will lead to a severe problem in their mental and physical health. Do you agree or disagree with this statement?

결론 작성 시, 먼저 문제 유형을 파악한 후, 'Conclusion Template'의 표현을 인용한다. (See p58)

문제 유형 파악	1-1) Do you agree or disagree? 유형
Conclusion Template 인용	For the reasons mentioned above, I totally agree(disagree) with the opinion because… 본문에 제시한 내 주장 간단히 요약

결론을 작성하기 전, 서론과 본론 1&2에서 Agree(십대의 장시간 컴퓨터 사용은 정신적 신체적 건강에 심각한 문제를 초래함)라고 했는지 다시 한 번 확인하자!

Conclusion
For the reasons mentioned above, I totally agree that we should aim to limit the amount of time teenagers spend on computers.

* 상황에 따라 템플릿을 살짝 변형해도 좋다.

limit : 제한하다
the amount of time : 시간의 양

우리말 해석
위에서 언급한 이런 이유들 때문에, 나는 우리가 십대들이 컴퓨터에 소비하는 시간의 양을 제한하는 데 목표를 두어야 한다는 의견에 전적으로 동의한다.

6 단계 교정 (Self-correction) (36~40분) : 내용의 일관성 및 문법 검토

다음 Body 2의 내용을 교정해 보자. 틀린 부분은 총 몇 개일까?

교정 전 (직접 문장 부호를 이용하여 틀린 부분을 교정해 보자.)

Teenagers' Physical as well as mental health can be negatively effected if they devote most of their attention to computers.

This is because of they usually sit or lie down for a long time while using this devices.

Adolescents is likely to become unfit and even obese if they does not get up and do physical exercise in a regular basis. Moreover we increasingly hears about teenagers becoming addicted to computer game and chat programs, and this can lead to a lack of sleep as a consequence of late-night use. In addition, the repetitive actions involved in using a computer can causes repetitive strain injuries to their fingers and wrists as well as dry eyes.

교정

Teenagers' ~~P~~[p]hysical as well as mental health can be negatively ~~effected~~[affected] if they devote most of their attention to computers. This is because ~~of~~ they usually sit or lie down for a long time while using ~~this~~[these] devices. Adolescents ~~is~~[are] likely to become unfit and even obese if they ~~does~~[do] not get up and do physical exercise ~~in~~[on] a regular basis. Moreover we increasingly ~~hears~~[hear] about teenagers becoming addicted to computer ~~game~~[games] and chat programs, and this can lead to a lack of sleep as a consequence of late-night use. In addition, the repetitive actions involved in using a computer can ~~causes~~[cause] repetitive strain injuries to their fingers and wrists as well as dry eyes.

1. P → p : 갑자기 대문자를 문장 중간에 쓰지 않는다(고유명사 예외).
2. effected → affected : effect는 '영향'이라는 명사, affect는 '영향을 주다'라는 동사다.
3. 붙여쓰기 : 위의 글은 Body 2 단락이다. 단락이 바뀌지 않는 한, 줄을 바꿔 쓰지 않는다.
4. of → 삭제 : because 다음에는 주어+동사, because of 다음에는 명사(구)가 온다.
5. this → these : this는 '이것'이라는 단수 지시 대명사, these는 '이것들'이라는 복수 지시 대명사
6. is → are : 주어인 Adolescents가 복수이므로 복수 동사 are를 쓴다.
7. does → do : does는 단수 조동사, do는 복수 조동사
8. in → on : on a regular basis는 '정기적으로'라는 뜻
9. hears → hear : 주어인 we가 복수이므로 복수 동사 hear을 쓴다.
10. game → games : games는 셀 수 있는 명사로 복수로 쓴다.
11. causes → cause : 조동사 can 다음에는 동사 원형을 쓴다.

틀린 개수 : 총 11개

Sample Answer

> **Question** Teenagers are spending too much time on computers and this will lead to a severe problem in their mental and physical health. Do you agree or disagree with this statement?

Parents often worry about the negative effects of computer use on their teenage children because they spend so much of their leisure time on PCs, laptops and tablets. I share their concerns because the current generation of adolescents is more exposed to technology than ever before.

Spending too much time using these smart machines can be harmful to a teenager's mental health. Although computers do offer practical benefits such as allowing teenagers wider access to study materials and e-books, many young people lack the motivation to take advantage of these. Instead, research suggests teenagers spend most of their computer time watching movies and dramas, chatting or playing games. While these aspects of computer use might not be harmful in the short term, problems begin to appear when adolescents stop doing homework or alternative hobbies such as outdoor sports. In these cases teenagers may feel bored when doing anything away from their computers, and their general motivation and cognitive development can be slowed by a kind of brain fog caused by spending too much time focused on virtual activities.

Teenagers' physical as well as mental health can be negatively affected if they devote most of their attention to computers. This is because they usually sit or lie down for a long time while using these devices. Adolescents are likely to become unfit and even obese if they do not get up and do physical exercise on a regular basis. Moreover we increasingly hear about teenagers becoming addicted to computer games and chat programs, and this can lead to a lack of sleep as a consequence of late-night use. In addition, the repetitive actions involved in using a computer can cause repetitive strain injuries to their fingers and wrists as well as dry eyes.

For the reasons mentioned above, I totally agree that we should aim to limit the amount of time teenagers spend on computers.

word counts : 314 words

우리말 해석

부모들은 종종 그들의 십대 아이들의 컴퓨터 사용에 있어 부정적인 영향을 걱정하는데 아이들이 컴퓨터와 노트북 그리고 태블릿에 여가시간을 너무 많이 할애하기 때문이다. 나는 부모들의 고민에 공감하는데 현재 청소년 세대가 이전보다 더 기술에 노출되어 있기 때문이다.

이러한 스마트 기기들을 사용하는 데 너무 많은 시간을 소비하는 것은 십대의 정신건강에 해가 될 수 있다. 비록 컴퓨터가 십대들이 학습 자료와 전자책을 폭넓게 접할 수 있게 해주는 실질적 이득을 제공하기도 하지만, 많은 젊은이들은 이러한 장점을 이용할 수 있는 동기부여가 결핍되어 있다. 그 대신, 연구조사는 십대들이 영화와 드라마를 보고, 채팅이나 게임을 하는데 컴퓨터 사용시간의 대부분을 보낸다고 제시한다. 컴퓨터 사용의 이러한 측면은 단기적으로는 해가 되지 않지만, 문제는 청소년들이 숙제나 야외 운동과 같은 다른 취미생활을 하는 것을 그만둘 때 나타나기 시작한다. 이런 경우 십대들은 어떤 일을 하든 컴퓨터와 떨어지면 지루하다고 느낄지도 모르고, 지나치게 많은 시간을 가상 활동에 집중하며 보냄으로써 그들의 일반적 동기부여와 인지 발달은 일종의 뇌 안개(brain fog) 현상에 의해 느려질 수 있다.

십대들의 정신 건강뿐만 아니라 신체도 그들이 컴퓨터에 그들의 주의력을 거의 다 쏟아붓는다면 부정적인 영향을 받을 것이다. 이것은 십대들이 이러한 기기를 사용하는 동안 오랜 시간 앉아 있거나 누워 있기 때문이다. 청소년들은 만약 정기적으로 일어나서 신체적 운동을 하지 않으면 몸 상태가 안 좋아지고 심지어 비만이 될 가능성이 높다. 게다가 우리는 컴퓨터 게임과 채팅 프로그램에 중독된 십대들에 대해 갈수록 더 듣고 있고, 이는 늦은 밤까지 사용한 결과로 인해 수면부족을 초래할 수 있다. 또한 컴퓨터의 사용에 수반 되는 반복적인 행동들은 안구건조증뿐만 아니라 손가락과 손목에 발생하는 반복성 긴장 장애의 원인이 될 수 있다.

위에서 언급한 이런 이유들 때문에, 나는 우리가 십대들이 컴퓨터에 소비하는 시간의 양을 제한하는 데 목표를 두어야 한다는 의견에 전적으로 동의한다.

불법 Review

앞에서 배운 내용을 바탕으로 다음 빈칸을 영어로 작성해 보자.

Parents often _____ (1. ~에 대해 걱정하다) the negative effects of computer use on their teenage children because they spend so much of their leisure time on PCs, laptops and tablets. I share their concerns because _____ (2. 현재 청소년 세대) is more exposed to technology than ever before.

Spending too much time using _____ (3. 이러한 스마트 기기들) can be harmful to _____ (4. 십대의 정신건강). Although computers do offer practical benefits such as allowing teenagers wider access to study materials and e-books, many young people lack the motivation to take advantage of these. Instead, research suggests teenagers spend most of their computer time watching movies and dramas, chatting or playing games. While these aspects of computer use might not be harmful in the short term, problems begin to appear when adolescents stop doing homework or alternative hobbies such as outdoor sports. In these cases teenagers may feel bored when doing anything away from their computers, and their general motivation and _____ (5. 인지 발달) can be slowed by a kind of _____ (6. 뇌 안개) caused by spending too much time focused on virtual activities.

Teenagers' physical as well as mental health can be negatively affected if they devote most of their attention to computers. This is because they usually _____ (7. 오랜 시간 앉아 있거나 누워 있다) while using these devices. Adolescents are likely to become unfit and even obese if they do not get up and do physical exercise on a regular basis. Moreover we increasingly hear about teenagers becoming addicted to computer games and chat programs, and this can lead to _____ (8. 수면부족) as a consequence of late-night use. In addition the repetitive actions involved in using a computer can cause _____ (9. 반복성 긴장 장애) to their fingers and wrists as well as _____ (10. 안구 건조증).

For the reasons mentioned above, I totally agree that we should aim to limit the amount of time teenagers spend on computers.

Answer 1. worry about / 2. the current generation of adolescents / 3. these smart machines
4. a teenager's mental health / 5. cognitive development / 6. brain fog
7. sit or lie down for a long time / 8. a lack of sleep / 9. repetitive strain injuries / 10. dry eyes

Day 12 IT(Information Technology) 불법 포인트 정리

범죄를 저지르다	commit crimes	~에 대해 걱정하다	worry about
나이 제한	age limits	여가시간	leisure time
통제하다	control	고민들, 걱정들	concerns
폭력적이거나 선정적인 이미지	violent or sexual images	세대 (한 세대는 30년을 의미)	generation
편안함	comfort	실질적 이득	practical benefits
~하는 것이 어렵다고 느끼다	find it difficult to +V	학습 자료	study materials
범죄자들	criminals	전자책	e-books
훔치다	steal	동기	motivation
당연하게	as a matter of course	~를 이용하다	take advantage of~
컴퓨터에 기반을 둔 직업들	computer-oriented professions	연구, 조사	research
구직자들	job seekers	야외 운동	outdoor sports
거의 모든	almost all	인지 발달	cognitive development
기본적 이해	basic understanding	뇌 안개	brain fog
수학적 사고	mathematical thinking	가상의	virtual
문제 해결 능력	problem solving skills	눕다	lie down
비판적 사고	critical thinking	몸 상태가 안 좋은	unfit
컴퓨터 시력 증후군	computer vision syndrome	비만인	obese
컴퓨터 앞에서	in front of a computer	정기적으로	on a regular basis
방해하다	hinder	수면부족	a lack of sleep
인터넷 접속	Internet access	~의 결과로서	as a consequence of
창의적인	creative	심야의	late-night
말을 잘하는	communicative	반복적인	repetitive
십대들	teenagers / teenage children adolescents / young people	반복성 긴장 장애	repetitive strain injuries
~에 시간을 보내다	spend 시간 on	손목	wrist
초래하다	lead to	안구 건조증	dry eyes
심각한	severe	제한하다	limit
정신적 신체적 건강	mental and physical health	시간의 양	the amount of time

Day 13 Shopping & Party 쇼핑과 파티

Question	Young people are strongly influenced by fashion, such as clothing or hairstyle. Is it a positive or negative development? 젊은 사람들은 옷이나 머리스타일 같은 패션의 영향을 강하게 받는다. 이것은 긍정적인 발전인가? 부정적인 발전인가?

 빈출 문제

1. Spending a lot of money on holding wedding parties, birthday parties and other celebrations is just a waste of money. Do you agree or disagree with this statement?

2. Online shopping is booming. How could this trend influence our environment and business?

3. Some people feel that we now place too much importance on money and possessions. Others believe that this trend has played an important role in improving our lives. Discuss both views and give your own opinion.

4. Fashion trends are difficult to follow because they are changing too fast. Some people believe that we do not have to follow them and that we should dress in what we like and feel comfortable in. To what extent do you agree or disagree with this opinion?

1. 결혼식, 생일 파티 그리고 다른 축하 행사들은 돈 낭비일 뿐이다. 당신은 이 말에 동의하는가? 또는 동의하지 않는가?

2. 온라인 쇼핑이 붐을 일으키고 있다. 이러한 경향은 우리의 환경과 산업에 어떠한 영향을 미칠 수 있는가?

3. 사람들은 오늘날 우리가 돈과 재산을 너무나 중요시한다고 생각한다. 반면 이런 트렌드가 생활을 향상시키는 데 중요한 역할을 한다고 주장하는 사람들도 있다. 양쪽의 견해를 논하고 당신의 주장을 제시하라.

4. 패션 트렌드는 너무나 빠르게 바뀌어서 따라가기 어렵다. 어떤 사람들은 패션을 따라갈 필요 없이, 입고 싶은 대로 편하게 입어야 한다고 주장한다. 당신은 이 의견에 얼마만큼 동의하는가? 또는 동의하지 않는가?

STEP2 브레인스토밍

1) 사회는 점점 물질만능주의가 되어가고 사람들은 좀 더 많은 돈을 벌기를 갈망한다.
   물질만능주의의 : materialistic / 갈망하다 : aspire to

2) 우리는 부와 물질적 소유를 행복과 성공과 연관짓는다.
   부 : wealth / 물질적 소유 : material possessions / A와 B를 연관짓다 : connect A with B

3) 현대 사회에서 샤넬이나 메르세데스 같은 고가 명품들은 신분의 상징이 되었다.
   고가 명품들 : high-priced luxury goods / 신분의 상징 : status symbols

4) 광고는 새로운 욕망과 필요를 만들고 우리가 신상품을 사도록 설득한다.
   욕망과 필요 : desires and needs / 신상품, 최신 유행 제품 : the latest styles / 설득하다 : persuade

5) 소비문화는 고용을 창출하고 빈곤을 감소시키는 데 도움을 준다.
   소비(문화) : consumerism / 고용 : employment

6) 소비 지상주의 사회는 더 많은 쓰레기를 만들고 더 많은 천연 자원을 사용한다.
   소비 지상주의의 : consumerist / 천연 자원 : natural resources

7) 소비문화는 (한 번 쓰고 쉽게) 버리는 문화를 만들고 환경을 훼손하는 원인이 된다.
   (한 번 쓰고 쉽게) 버리는 문화 : a throw-away culture / 훼손하다 : damage

8) 회사에서 프로젝트를 처음 시작할 때 여는 파티는 썰렁한 분위기를 깨고 팀 멤버들이 서로 더 잘 알 수 있도록 돕는 좋은 기회이다.
   처음 시작하는 : kick-off / 썰렁한 분위기를 깨다 : break the ice

9) 파티는 종종 좋은 추억을 남기는데 우리 모두는 아이였을 때 생일파티에 대한 행복한 추억을 가지고 있기 때문이다.
   좋은 추억을 남기다 : leave good memories

10) 파티는 파티에서 스스로 불편하다고 느끼는 내성적인 사람들에게는 어렵다.
    내성적인 사람들 : introverted people

11) 생일이나 결혼 같은 축하 행사들은 우리의 사회 생활을 풍부하게 하고, 우리의 문화를 표현하며 우리를 가족과 친구들과 더 가깝게 만들어 준다.
    축하 행사들 : celebrations / 풍부하게 하다 : enrich / 표현하다 : express

12) 함께 축하하는 것은 손님들 간에 화합을 이룰 수 있고 친척들과 친구들과 계속 연락할 수 있는 좋은 방법일 수 있다.
    화합 : cohesion / 계속 연락하다 : keep in touch with

13) 호화스러운 축하 행사들은 높은 비용을 수반할 수 있는데 행사 주최자들을 빚더미에 허덕이게도 할 수도 있다.
    호화스러운 : lavish / 수반하다 : come with / 빚더미에 : in debt

14) 우리는 손님들에게 강한 인상을 남기고 과시하려고 노력하는 것 대신에 가능한 예산 안에서 비용을 쓰는 것을 목표로 해야 한다.

강한 인상을 남기다 : impress / 과시하다 : show off / 예산 : budget

15) 어떤 나라에서는 커플들이 그들의 결혼식 비용을 지불하기 위해 많은 빚을 지는 것이 일반적이다.

많은 빚을 지다 : incur a lot of debt

Answer

1) Society becomes increasingly materialistic and people aspire to earn more money.
2) We connect wealth and material possessions with happiness and success.
3) In modern society, high-priced luxury goods like Chanel or Mercedes have become status symbols.
4) Advertising creates new desires and needs and persuades us to buy the latest styles.
5) Consumerism creates employment and it helps to reduce poverty.
6) Consumerist societies create more waste and they use more natural resources.
7) Consumerism creates a throw-away culture and causes damage to the environment.
8) Project kick-off parties in companies are a good chance to break the ice and help team members get to know each other better.
9) Parties often leave good memories because we all have happy memories of our birthday parties when we were a child.
10) Parties are hard on introverted people who find themselves uncomfortable in parties.
11) Celebrations such as birthdays and marriages enrich our social lives, express our culture and bring us closer to family and friends.
12) Celebrating together can create cohesion among guests and it can be a good way to keep in touch with relatives and friends.
13) Lavish celebrations can come with high costs, even leaving the hosts in debt.
14) We should aim to keep the cost within the available budget instead of trying to impress guests and show off.
15) In some countries it is common for couples to incur a lot of debt to pay for their weddings.

 실전문제

You should spend about 40 minutes on this task.
Write about the following topic :

> Young people are strongly influenced by fashion, such as clothing or hairstyle. Is it a positive or negative development?

Give reasons for your answer and include any relevant examples from your own knowledge or experience.

Write at least 250 words.

 **1 단계** 문제 정독, 문제 유형 파악, 브레인스토밍 (0 ~ 5분)

Question Young people are strongly influenced by fashion, such as clothing or hairstyle. Is it a positive or negative development?

문제 정독
젊은 사람들은 옷이나 머리스타일 같은 패션의 영향을 강하게 받는다. 이것은 긍정적인 발전인가? 부정적인 발전인가?

 be influenced by : ~에 의해 영향 받다

문제 유형 파악

2-1. Is it a positive or negative development? 유형

Brainstorming

Topic : 젊은 사람들은 패션의 영향을 강하게 받음	
Positive development : 긍정적 발전	Negative development : 부정적 발전
1. 매력적으로 보임 look attractive → 멋있게 보이는 사람들을 모방, 외모로 사람을 판단 imitate those who look good, judge people by appearance 2. 더욱 사회에 귀속감을 가짐 be more engaged in society → 소외감이나 외로움을 느낄 가능성이 낮음 less likely to feel excluded or lonely	1. 다른 사람들의 눈에 멋지게 보이고자 하는 강박관념 obsessed with looking good in the eyes of others → 자의식과 허영 self-consciousness and vanity 2. 윤리와 타협 compromising their ethics → 가혹행위 여부를 고려하지 않고 모피 제품 구매 buying a fur adornment without considering the torture

* 아이디어의 수도 같고 영어로 쓸 수 있는 말도 비슷하다면, 좀 더 설득력 있게 논리적으로 접근할 수 있는 쪽을 내 의견으로 한다. 이 에세이에서는 negative development, '젊은 사람들이 패션의 영향을 강하게 받는 것은 부정적인 발전이다.'를 내 주장으로 삼았다.

2단계 | 서론 (Introduction) (6~10분) : 두 문장으로 작성

Question	Young people are strongly influenced by fashion, such as clothing or hairstyle. Is it a positive or negative development?

단계	Question	서론 작성
1단계 Paraphrasing	**토픽 :** Young people are strongly influenced by fashion, such as clothing or hairstyle.	**Paraphrasing :** Fashion has always had a strong influence on young people because most of them are concerned about how others view them.
2단계 Answering	**질문 :** Is it a positive or negative development?	**Answering : Negative development일 경우** Although this trend does have some superficial benefits for those youngsters in question, they should guard themselves against insecurity.

Introduction
Fashion has always had a strong influence on young people because most of them are concerned about how others view them. Although this trend does have some superficial benefits for those youngsters in question, they should guard themselves against insecurity.

superficial : 표면적인, 피상적인
youngsters : 젊은 사람들
in question : 문제의
insecurity : 불안감

우리말 해석
유행은 항상 젊은 사람들에게 강력한 영향력을 미쳤는데 왜냐하면 그들 중 대부분은 다른 사람들이 자신을 어떻게 보는지에 대해 신경쓰기 때문이다. 비록 이러한 유행은 문제의 (당사자인) 그 젊은이에게 몇 가지 외적인 이득을 주기도 하지만, 그들은 불안감에 대항해 스스로를 보호해야 한다.

 **본론 1 (Body 1) (11~20분) : 나와 다른 의견 = Positive** (패션의 영향을 크게 받는 것은 긍정적)

Question Young people are strongly influenced by fashion, such as clothing or hairstyle. Is it a positive or negative development?

Body 1은 1단계에서 브레인스토밍한 'Positive'를 바탕으로 작성한다.

1단계	Topic Sentence	It seems positive that the young are fascinated by fashion.
2단계 (1)	Supporting Sentence (1)	*look attractive* First of all, young people who take an interest in their appearance by following the latest fashions are more likely to look attractive.
3단계 (1)	Supporting Sentence or Specific Example (1)	*imitate those who look good, judge appearance* This is because people are naturally inclined to imitate those who look good, and most of us judge people by appearance to a certain extent whether we like to admit it or not.
2단계 (2)	Supporting Sentence (2)	*be more engaged in society* In addition, fashion is an expression of culture and so it can encourage younger people to be more engaged in society.
3단계 (2)	Supporting Sentence or Specific Example (2)	*less likely to feel excluded or lonely* By being interested in new trends they are less likely to feel excluded or lonely and that is a positive effect.

Body 1

It seems positive that the young are fascinated by fashion. First of all, young people who take an interest in their appearance by following the latest fashions are more likely to look attractive. This is because people are naturally inclined to imitate those who look good, and most of us judge appearance to a certain extent whether we like to admit it or not. In addition, fashion is an expression of culture and so it can encourage younger people to be more engaged in society. By being interested in new trends they are less likely to feel excluded or lonely and that is a positive effect.

be fascinated by : ~에 매료되다, ~에 마음을 다 뺏기다
the latest fashions : 최신 유행들
be inclined to : ~에 마음이 기울다, ~하는 경향이 있다
imitate : = copy, mimic, 모방하다
judge people by appearance : 외모로 사람을 판단하다
to a certain extent : 어느 정도
admit : 인정하다
be engaged in : 속하다, 참가하다
feel excluded : 소외감을 느끼다

> **우리말 해석**
> 젊은 사람들이 유행에 매료되는 것은 긍정적으로 보인다. 우선 최신 유행을 따르며 자신들의 외모에 관심을 갖는 젊은 사람들은 매력적으로 보일 가능성이 더 크다. 이것은 사람들은 자연스럽게 멋있게 보이는 사람들을 모방하는 경향이 있고, 우리 대부분이 인정하고 싶어하든 아니든 어느 정도 외모로 사람을 판단하기 때문이다. 게다가 유행은 문화의 표현이며, 따라서 이는 젊은 사람들이 더욱 사회에 귀속감을 가지도록 할 수 있을 것이다. 새로운 유행에 대해 관심을 가짐으로써 그들은 소외감이나 외로움을 느낄 가능성이 낮고 그것은 긍정적인 영향이 될 것이다.

4 단계 본론 2 (Body 2) (21~30분) : 내 의견 = Negative (패션의 영향을 크게 받는 것은 부정적)

Question	Young people are strongly influenced by fashion, such as clothing or hairstyle. Is it a positive or negative development?

Body 2는 1단계에서 브레인스토밍한 'Negative'를 바탕으로 작성한다.

1단계	Topic Sentence	However, we should not neglect the negative side of this trend.
2단계 (1)	Supporting Sentence (1)	*obsessed with looking good in the eyes of others* Young people who are strongly influenced by fashionistas and celebrities, as opposed to taking a healthy interest in their appearance, are at risk of becoming obsessed with looking good in the eyes of others.
3단계 (1)	Supporting Sentence or Specific Example (1)	*self-consciousness and vanity* Self-consciousness and vanity are harmful to the spirit.
2단계 (2)	Supporting Sentence (2)	*compromising their ethics* Moreover young people might even find themselves compromising their ethics in order to keep up with their peers.
3단계 (2)	Supporting Sentence or Specific Example (2)	*buying a fur adornment without considering the torture* An example of this would be an animal lover who would never otherwise harm a creature buying a fur adornment without considering the torture involved in the manufacture of such a product.

Body 2

However, we should not neglect the negative side of this trend. Young people who are strongly influenced by fashionistas and celebrities, as opposed to taking a healthy interest in their appearance, are at risk of becoming obsessed with looking good in the eyes of others. Self-consciousness and vanity are harmful to the spirit. Moreover young people might even find themselves compromising their ethics in order to keep up with their peers. An example of this would be an animal lover who would never otherwise harm a creature buying a fur adornment without considering the torture involved in the manufacture of such a product.

fashionistas : 패셔니스타
celebrities : 유명 인사들
as opposed to + 동(명사) : ~와는 대조적으로,
　~이 아니라
obsessed with : 강박관념에 시달리는, ~에 사로잡힌
self-consciousness : 자의식(인간이 자기 자신을 타
　인으로부터 구별하고, 자기 자신의 인격, 행동, 사상,
　감정, 의욕 등에 대하여 의식적으로 열중하는 것)

vanity : 허영
compromise : 타협하다
ethics : 윤리, 도덕
an animal lover : 동물 애호가
adornment : 장식, 장식품
torture : 고문, 가혹행위
manufacture : 제조

우리말 해석

하지만 우리는 이러한 유행의 부정적인 측면을 무시해서는 안 된다. 자신의 외모에 건강한 관심을 갖는 것과는 반대로, 패셔니스타와 유명인사들에게 강하게 영향을 받는 젊은 사람들은 다른 사람들의 눈에 멋지게 보이고자 하는 강박관념을 가지게 될 위험성이 있다. 자의식과 허영은 정신에 해롭다. 더욱이 젊은 사람들은 그들의 또래들을 따라잡기 위해 윤리와 스스로 타협할지도 모른다. 이러한 실례로 그 생산품의 제조과정에 가혹행위 여부를 고려하지 않고 모피 제품을 사면서 다른 상황에서 생명체에 어떤 해도 끼치지 않는다는 동물 애호가들을 들 수 있을 것이다.

5 단계 결론 (Conclusion) (31~35분) : 본문에 제시한 내 주장 요약하며 다시 한 번 강조

> **Question**
> Young people are strongly influenced by fashion, such as clothing or hairstyle. Is it a positive or negative development?

결론 작성 시, 먼저 문제 유형을 파악한 후, 'Conclusion Template'의 표현을 인용한다. (See p58)

문제 유형 파악	2-1) Is it a positive or negative development? 유형
Conclusion Template 인용	For the reasons mentioned above, I would argue that the benefits(drawbacks) of… (토픽) outweigh its drawbacks(benefits) because… 본론에 제시한 장점(단점) 간략히 요약

결론을 작성하기 전, 서론과 본론 2에서 Negative, '젊은 사람들이 패션의 영향을 크게 받는 것은 부정적'이라고 했는지 다시 한 번 확인하자!

> **Conclusion**
> **For the reasons mentioned above, I would argue that the benefits of** young people being strongly influenced by fashion **are outweighed by the drawbacks** of this trend **because** they should be aiming to find satisfaction from within and through meaningful activities.

* 상황에 따라 템플릿을 살짝 변형해도 좋다.

satisfaction : 만족
from within : 내면으로부터
meaningful : 의미 있는

우리말 해석
위에서 언급한 이러한 이유들 때문에, 나는 유행에 강하게 영향을 받는 젊은 사람들의 장점은 단점에 의해 압도 당하게 될 것이라 주장하는데 왜냐하면 그들은 의미 있는 행동들과 내면으로부터 만족을 찾고자 노력해야 할 것이기 때문이다.

6 단계 교정 (Self-correction) (36~40분) : 내용의 일관성 및 문법 검토

다음 Body 2의 내용을 교정해 보자. 틀린 부분은 총 몇 개일까?

교정 전 (직접 문장 부호를 이용하여 틀린 부분을 교정해 보자.)

However, We should not neglect the negative side of this trend. Young people who is strongly influenced by fashionistas and celebrities, as opposed to take a healthy interest in their appearance, is at risk of becoming obsessed with looking good in the eyes of others.

Self-consciousness and vanity are harmful to the spirit. moreover young people might even find themselves compromising their ethics in order to keeping up with their peers.

A example of this would be an animal lover who would naver otherwise harm a creature buying a fur adornment without consider the torture involved in the manufacture of such a product.

교정

However, ~~We~~ (w) should not neglect the negative side of this trend. Young people who ~~is~~ (are) strongly influenced by fashionistas and celebrities, as opposed to ~~take~~ (taking) a healthy interest in their appearance, ~~is~~ (are) at risk of becoming obsessed with looking good in the eyes of others. Self-consciousness and vanity are harmful to the spirit. ~~moreover~~ (M) young people might even find themselves compromising their ethics in order to ~~keeping~~ (keep) up with their peers. ~~A~~ (An) example of this would be an animal lover who would ~~naver~~ (never) otherwise harm a creature buying a fur adornment without ~~consider~~ (considering) the torture involved in the manufacture of such a product.

1. W → w : 갑자기 대문자를 문장 중간에 쓰지 않는다(고유명사 예외).
2. is → are : 주어인 people이 복수이므로 복수 동사인 are를 쓴다.
3. take → taking : as opposed to + 동(명사)
4. is → are : 주어인 people이 복수이므로 복수 동사인 are를 쓴다.
5. 붙여쓰기 : 위의 글은 Body 2 단락이다. 단락이 바뀌지 않는 한, 줄을 바꿔 쓰지 않는다.
6. m → M : 문장의 첫 글자는 반드시 대문자로 시작한다.
7. keeping → keep : in order to + 동사 원형
8. A → An : 모음(a/i/u/e/o)으로 발음이 시작되는 단어 example[ɪgzaːmpl] 앞에는 a가 아닌 an으로 쓰고 말한다.
9. naver → never : '네이버'가 아니다. 스펠링 주의!
10. consider → considering : 전치사 without 다음에는 (동)명사를 쓴다.

틀린 개수 : 총 10개

Sample Answer

Question Young people are strongly influenced by fashion, such as clothing or hairstyle. Is it a positive or negative development?

Fashion has always had a strong influence on young people because most of them are concerned about how others view them. Although this trend does have some superficial benefits for those youngsters in question, they should guard themselves against insecurity.

It seems positive that the young are fascinated by fashion. First of all, young people who take an interest in their appearance by following the latest fashions are more likely to look attractive. This is because people are naturally inclined to imitate those who look good, and most of us judge people by appearance to a certain extent whether we like to admit it or not. In addition, fashion is an expression of culture and so it can encourage younger people to be more engaged in society. By being interested in new trends they are less likely to feel excluded or lonely and that is a positive effect.

However, we should not neglect the negative side of this trend. Young people who are strongly influenced by fashionistas and celebrities, as opposed to taking a healthy interest in their appearance, are at risk of becoming obsessed with looking good in the eyes of others. Self-consciousness and vanity are harmful to the spirit. Moreover young people might even find themselves compromising their ethics in order to keep up with their peers. An example of this would be an animal lover who would never otherwise harm a creature buying a fur adornment without considering the torture involved in the manufacture of such a product.

For the reasons mentioned above, I would argue that the benefits of young people being strongly influenced by fashion are outweighed by the drawbacks of this trend because they should be aiming to find satisfaction from within and through meaningful activities.

word counts : 292 words

우리말 해석

유행은 항상 젊은 사람들에게 강력한 영향력을 미쳤는데 왜냐하면 그들 중 대부분은 다른 사람들이 자신을 어떻게 보는지에 대해 신경쓰기 때문이다. 비록 이러한 유행은 문제의 (당사자인) 그 젊은이에게 몇 가지 외적인 이득을 주기도 하지만, 그들은 불안감에 대항해 스스로를 보호해야 한다.

젊은 사람들이 유행에 매료되는 것은 긍정적으로 보인다. 우선 최신 유행을 따르며 자신들의 외모에 관심을 갖는 젊은 사람들은 매력적으로 보일 가능성이 더 크다. 이것은 사람들은 자연스럽게 멋있게 보이는 사람들을 모방하는 경향이 있고, 우리 대부분이 인정하고 싶어하든 아니든 어느 정도 외모로 사람을 판단하기 때문이다. 게다가 유행은 문화의 표현이며, 따라서 이는 젊은 사람들이 더욱 사회에 귀속감을 가지도록 할 수 있을 것이다. 새로운 유행에 대해 관심을 가짐으로써 그들은 소외감이나 외로움을 느낄 가능성이 낮고 그것은 긍정적인 영향이 될 것이다.

하지만 우리는 이러한 유행의 부정적인 측면을 무시해서는 안 된다. 자신의 외모에 건강한 관심을 갖는 것과는 반대로, 패션니스타와 유명인사들에게 강하게 영향을 받는 젊은 사람들은 다른 사람들의 눈에 멋지게 보이고자 하는 강박관념을 가지게 될 위험성이 있다. 자의식과 허영은 정신에 해롭다. 더욱이 젊은 사람들은 그들의 또래들을 따라잡기 위해 윤리와 스스로 타협할지도 모른다. 이러한 실례로 그 생산품의 제조과정에 가혹행위 여부를 고려하지 않고 모피 제품을 사면서 다른 상황에서 생명체에 어떤 해도 끼치지 않는다는 동물 애호가들을 들 수 있을 것이다.

위에서 언급한 이러한 이유들 때문에, 나는 유행에 강하게 영향을 받는 젊은 사람들의 장점은 단점에 의해 압도 당하게 될 것이라 주장하는데 왜냐하면 그들은 의미 있는 행동들과 내면으로부터 만족을 찾고자 노력해야 할 것이기 때문이다.

불법 Review

앞에서 배운 내용을 바탕으로 다음 빈칸을 영어로 작성해 보자.

Fashion has always had _____ (1. 강력한 영향력) on young people because most of them are concerned about how others view them. Although this trend does have some _____ (2. 외적인 이득) for those youngsters in question, they should guard themselves against insecurity.

It seems positive that the young _____ (3. ~에 매료되다) fashion. First of all, young people who take an interest in their appearance _____ (4. 최신 유행을 따르며) are more likely to look attractive. This is because people are naturally _____ (5. 모방하는 경향이 있고) those who look good, and most of us _____ (6. 외모로 사람을 판단하다) to a certain extent whether we like to admit it or not. In addition, fashion is an expression of culture and so it can encourage younger people to be more engaged in society. By being interested in new trends they _____ (7. 소외감이나 외로움을 느낄 가능성이 낮다) and that is a positive effect.

However, we should not neglect the negative side of this trend. Young people who are strongly influenced by _____ (8. 패셔니스타와 유명인사들), as opposed to taking a healthy interest in their appearance, are at risk of becoming obsessed with looking good in the eyes of others. _____ (9. 자의식과 허영) are harmful to the spirit. Moreover young people might even find themselves compromising their ethics in order to keep up with their peers. An example of this would be _____ (10. 동물 애호가) who would never otherwise harm a creature buying a fur adornment without considering the torture involved in the manufacture of such a product.

For the reasons mentioned above, I would argue that the benefits of young people being strongly influenced by fashion are outweighed by the drawbacks of this trend because they should be aiming to find satisfaction _____ (11. 내면으로부터) and through meaningful activities.

Answer 1. a strong influence / 2. superficial benefits / 3. are fascinated by / 4. by following the latest fashions
5. inclined to imitate / 6. judge people by appearance / 7. are less likely to feel excluded or lonely
8. fashionistas and celebrities / 9. Self-consciousness and vanity / 10. an animal lover / 11. from within

Day 13 Shopping & Party 불법 포인트 정리

물질만능주의의	materialistic	많은 빚을 지다	incur a lot of debt
갈망하다	aspire to	~에 의해 영향받다	be influenced by
부	wealth	표면적인, 피상적인	superficial
물질적 소유	material possessions	젊은 사람들	youngsters
A와 B를 연관짓다	connect A with B	문제의	in question
고가 명품들	high-priced luxury goods	불안감	insecurity
신분의 상징	status symbols	~에 매료되다, ~에 마음을 다 뺏기다	be fascinated by
욕망과 필요	desires and needs	최신 유행들	the latest fashions
신상품, 최신 유행 제품	the latest styles	~에 마음이 기울다, ~하는 경향이 있다	be inclined to
설득하다	persuade	모방하다	imitate / copy / mimic
소비(문화)	consumerism	외모로 사람을 판단하다	judge people by appearance
고용	employment	어느 정도	to a certain extent
소비 지상주의의	consumerist	인정하다	admit
천연 자원	natural resources	속하다, 참가하다	be engaged in
(한 번 쓰고 쉽게) 버리는 문화	a throw-away culture	소외감을 느끼다	feel excluded
훼손하다	damage	패셔니스타	fashionistas
처음 시작하는	kick-off	유명 인사들	celebrities
썰렁한 분위기를 깨다	break the ice	~와는 대조적으로, ~이 아니라	as opposed to + 동(명사)
좋은 추억을 남기다	leave good memories	강박관념에 시달리는, ~에 사로잡힌	obsessed with
내성적인 사람들	introverted people	자의식	self-consciousness
축하 행사들	celebrations	허영	vanity
풍부하게 하다	enrich	타협하다	compromise
표현하다	express	윤리, 도덕	ethics
화합	cohesion	동물 애호가	an animal lover
계속 연락하다	keep in touch with	장식, 장식품	adornment
호화스러운	lavish	고문, 가혹행위	torture
수반하다	come with	제조	manufacture
빚더미에	in debt	만족	satisfaction
강한 인상을 남기다	impress	내면으로부터	from within
과시하다	show off	의미 있는	meaningful
예산	budget		

Day 14 International Relations & Urbanisation

국제관계와 도시화

Question

The world population is dramatically increasing. This is causing problems for developed countries as well as underdeveloped nations. Explain the problems of overpopulation, and suggest some possible solutions.

세계 인구는 엄청나게 증가하고 있다. 이것은 선진국뿐만 아니라 후진국에서도 문제를 일으키고 있다. 인구과잉의 문제점을 설명하고 가능한 해결책을 제시하라.

 빈출 문제

1. Even rich countries have poor people and each country has different ways of helping the poor. What are the reasons for poverty? What can the government and individuals do to help the poor?

2. Some people insist that giving aid to poorer nations has more negative effects than positives ones. To what extent do you agree or disagree with this opinion?

3. Today, the quality of life in large cities is decreasing. Discuss the causes and solutions.

4. Many people leave the countryside for the greater opportunities of work and education in big cities. What are some benefits and drawbacks of urbanisation for both people and the environment?

1. 부자나라에도 가난한 사람들이 있고 나라마다 그들을 돕는 방법이 다르다. 가난의 이유는 무엇인가? 가난한 사람들을 돕기 위해 정부와 개인은 무엇을 해야 하는가?

2. 어떤 사람들은 가난한 나라에 도움을 주는 것은 긍정적인 영향보다 부정적인 영향이 더 많다고 주장한다. 당신은 이 의견에 얼마만큼 동의하는가? 또는 동의하지 않는가?

3. 오늘날 대도시의 삶의 질은 떨어지고 있다. 원인과 해결책을 논하라.

4. 대도시에서 더 많은 직업과 교육의 기회를 얻기 위해서 많은 사람들이 시골을 떠난다. 도시화가 사람과 환경에 미치는 혜택과 폐해는 무엇인가?

 **STEP2 브레인스토밍**

1) 도시화는 도시가 사람이 너무 많은 것과 지나친 부동산 가격 그리고 테러리스트의 공격에 취약성이 증가되는 것을 경험할 수 있기 때문에 삶의 질 감소를 초래한다.
   사람이 너무 많은 것, 초만원 : overcrowding / 지나친 부동산 가격 : exorbitant property prices / 취약성 : vulnerability

2) 대중교통에 대한 더 큰 투자는 교통 혼잡을 덜어줄 것이다.
   투자 : investment / 교통 혼잡 : traffic congestion / 덜어주다 : ease

3) 대도시에서 대중교통을 이용하는 것은 공기 오염을 줄일 것이고 (거기에 사는) 사람들의 안녕을 향상시킬 가능성이 있다.
   공기 오염 : air pollution / 안녕(편안히 잘 지내는 것) : well-being

4) 폭력적인 테러리스트의 공격에 대응하기 위해서 도시는 CCTV 설치에 착수할 수 있다.
   대응하다 : counter / CCTV 설치 : CCTV installations / 착수하다 : embark on

5) 부유한 도시는 대규모 인구 유입을 이끈다.
   대규모 인구 유입 : large population inflows

6) 대도시의 생활비는 시골 지역에 비해 훨씬 높다.
　　시골 지역 : in rural areas

7) 도시에서의 삶은 극도로 스트레스를 받을 수 있는 데 교통 혼잡과 범죄와 같은 다양한 문제들이 있기 때문이다.
　　극도로 스트레스를 받다 : be extremely stressful

8) 도시에 사는 사람들은 공동체 의식이 부족하므로 그들은 그들의 이웃조차 알지 못한다.
　　공동체 의식 : a sense of community

9) 어떤 사람들은 가난한 나라의 정부에 단순히 재정적 원조를 주는 것은 잘못된 생각이라고 말한다.
　　재정적 원조를 주다 : give financial aid

10) 부자인 나라에서 받은 원조는 가난한 국가의 요구를 맞추기 쉽지 않을지도 모른다.
　　요구를 맞추다 : meet demands

11) 재정적 도움은 가난한 정부들에 의해 잘못 사용될 수 있다.
　　~에 의해 잘못 사용되다 : be misused by

12) 어떠한 후진국에서는 부패한 정치가들은 더 부자가 되는 반면 그들의 시민들은 고통을 계속 겪는다.
　　부패한 정치가들 : corrupt politicians

13) 선진국은 단지 돈을 기부하는 것 대신에 후진국에 투자하는 방법을 찾는 것이 중요하다.
　　돈을 기부하다 : donate money

14) 세계화 시대에 세상은 점점 더 가깝게 연관되어 가고 있다.
　　세계화 시대에 : in this era of globalisation

15) 많은 나라들은 경제적인 이유로 더 가난한 나라들을 돕는데 기부자들(기부 국가들)은 석유 같은 물자의 공급을 통제하기를 원할지도 모르기 때문이다.

기부자들 : donors / 물자 : commodities

Answer

1) Urbanisation leads to a decrease in the quality of life as the city can experience overcrowding, exorbitant property prices, and increased vulnerability to terrorist attacks.
2) Greater investment in public transport would ease traffic congestion.
3) Using public transport in major cities would reduce air pollution, and possibly improve the well-being of the population.
4) To counter violent terrorist attacks, cities could embark on CCTV installations.
5) A wealthy city attracts large population inflows.
6) The cost of living in big cities is much higher than in rural areas.
7) Life in cities can be extremely stressful because there are various problems like traffic congestion and crime.
8) People living in cities lack a sense of community therefore they do not even know their neighbours.
9) Some people say that simply giving financial aid to governments of poor countries is a bad idea.
10) The aid given by richer countries may not easily meet the demands of poor nations.
11) Financial help could be misused by poor governments.
12) In some underdeveloped countries, corrupt politicians have become richer whereas their citizens continue to suffer.
13) It is important for advanced countries to find ways to invest in less advanced nations, instead of just donating money.
14) In this era of globalisation, the world is becoming more and more closely linked.
15) Many countries help poorer ones for economic reasons because the donors may want to control the supply of commodities such as oil.

실전문제

You should spend about 40 minutes on this task.
Write about the following topic :

> The world population is dramatically increasing. This is causing problems for developed countries as well as underdeveloped nations. Explain the problems of overpopulation, and suggest some possible solutions.

Give reasons for your answer and include any relevant examples from your own knowledge or experience.

Write at least 250 words.

 **1단계** 문제 정독, 문제 유형 파악, 브레인스토밍 (0 ~ 5분)

| Question | The world population is dramatically increasing. This is causing problems for developed countries as well as underdeveloped nations. Explain the problems of overpopulation, and suggest some possible solutions. |

문제 정독

세계 인구는 엄청나게 증가하고 있다. 이것은 선진국뿐만 아니라 후진국에서도 문제를 일으키고 있다. 인구과잉의 문제점을 설명하고 가능한 해결책을 제시하라.

 overpopulation : 인구과잉

문제 유형 파악

3-2. Problems and Solutions 유형

Brainstorming

Topic : 인구 과잉은 전세계에 문제가 되고 있다.	
Problems : 인구과잉의 문제점들	Solutions : 인구과잉의 해결책들
1. 천연 자원은 한정되어 있음 natural resources are limited → 가격 상승함, 생활비 인상 prices rise, an increase in the cost of living 2. 전염병이 유행할 수 있음 infectious diseases can also flourish → 인구 밀집지역에서 악화됨 exacerbated within dense populations	1. 출산율 낮추기 lowering its birth rate → 산아 제한 방법, 증가된 생활비 birth control methods, increased living costs 2. 이민 제한, 인구가 덜 밀집된 지역으로 이주 근로자들을 끌어들이기 restricting immigration, pooling migrant workers in less crowded areas → 자국 시민들의 문화 보호와 국제 사회의 인권 존중 protecting their own citizens' culture and respecting the human rights of the international community

* 문제점과 해결책의 분량은 비슷하거나, 해결책이 조금 더 많은 것이 좋다.

2단계 서론 (Introduction) (6~10분) : 두 문장으로 작성

Question	The world population is dramatically increasing. This is causing problems for developed countries as well as underdeveloped nations. Explain the problems of overpopulation, and suggest some possible solutions.

단계	Question	서론 작성
1단계 Paraphrasing	토픽 : The world population is dramatically increasing. This is causing problems for developed countries as well as underdeveloped nations.	**Paraphrasing** : Population growth continues to explode across the world.
2단계 Answering	질문 : Explain the problems of overpopulation, and suggest some possible solutions.	**Answering** : 문제와 해결책 간단히 언급 Governments face the challenge of addressing the problems associated with this global trend.

introduction
Population growth continues to explode across the world. Governments face the challenge of addressing the problems associated with this global trend.

- explode : 폭발적으로 증가하다
- address : 고심하다

우리말 해석
인구 증가는 전세계에 걸쳐 폭발적으로 증가하는 것을 지속하고 있다. 정부는 이런 세계적인 추세와 연계된 문제들을 고심해야 하는 도전에 직면해 있다.

3 단계　본론 1 (Body 1) (11~20분) : Problems (인구과잉의 문제점들)

> **Question**　The world population is dramatically increasing. This is causing problems for developed countries as well as underdeveloped nations. Explain the problems of overpopulation, and suggest some possible solutions.

Body 1은 1단계에서 브레인스토밍한 'Problems'를 바탕으로 작성한다.

1단계	Topic Sentence	One major issue with overpopulation is scarcity.
2단계 (1)	Supporting Sentence (1)	*natural resources are limited* Natural resources are limited and if there are more people occupying the same space it puts pressure on the supply of basic goods and services.
3단계 (1)	Supporting Sentence or Specific Example (1)	*prices rise, an increase in the cost of living* According to the principles of economics, when supply is limited prices rise and so overpopulation leads to an increase in the cost of living.
2단계 (2)	Supporting Sentence (2)	*infectious diseases can also flourish* Infectious diseases can also flourish in crowded cities and towns because so many people live and work close to each other.
3단계 (2)	Supporting Sentence or Specific Example (2)	*exacerbated within dense populations* Some of the most devastating plague and influenza outbreaks in the history of mankind were exacerbated within dense populations.

Body 1

One major issue with overpopulation is scarcity. Natural resources are limited and if there are more people occupying the same space it puts pressure on the supply of basic goods and services. According to the principles of economics, when supply is limited prices rise and so overpopulation leads to an increase in the cost of living. Infectious diseases can also flourish in crowded cities and towns because so many people live and work close to each other. Some of the most devastating plague and influenza outbreaks in the history of mankind were exacerbated within dense populations.

scarcity : 부족, 결핍
occupy : 점유하다, 차지하다
put pressure on : ~에 압력을 가하다
the principles of economics : 경제원칙
infectious diseases : 전염병
flourish : 번창하다
devastating : 파괴적인

plague : 전염병
influenza : 인플루엔자, 유행성 감기
outbreaks : (질병, 전쟁의) 발생, 발발
mankind : 인류
exacerbate : (질병, 문제를) 악화시키다
dense : 밀집한

우리말 해석

인구과잉에 있어 주된 문제는 부족이다. 천연자원은 한정되어 있고 만약 같은 공간을 점유한 사람들이 더 많다면, 이것은 기본적인 물자와 서비스의 공급에 압력을 가한다. 경제원칙에 따라, 공급이 제한되면 가격이 오르고 그래서 인구과잉은 생활비의 인상을 초래한다. 전염성 질병이 혼잡한 도시와 마을에 유행할 수 있는데 너무 많은 사람들이 서로 가깝게 살고 일하기 때문이다. 인류 역사에서 일부 가장 파괴적인 전염병과 인플루엔자의 발발은 인구 밀집지역에서 악화되었다.

4단계 본론 2 (Body 2) (21~30분) : Solutions (인구과잉의 해결책들)

> **Question** The world population is dramatically increasing. This is causing problems for developed countries as well as underdeveloped nations. Explain the problems of overpopulation, and suggest some possible solutions.

Body 2는 1단계에서 브레인스토밍한 'Solutions'를 바탕으로 작성한다.

1단계	Topic Sentence	In tackling these problems governments need to understand the main causes of overpopulation, which include a high birth rate and immigration.
2단계 (1)	Supporting Sentence (1)	*lowering its birth rate* China's one-child policy might have provoked outrage around the world, but it has eased the country's population concerns by lowering its birth rate.
3단계 (1)	Supporting Sentence or Specific Example (1)	*birth control methods, increased living costs* In other nations, most governments are more likely to rely on increased living costs to dissuade couples from having too many children as well as making birth control methods.
2단계 (2)	Supporting Sentence (2)	*restricting immigration, pooling migrant workers in less crowded areas* Policymakers also have the option of dealing with overpopulation by restricting immigration, and pooling migrant workers in less crowded areas.
3단계 (2)	Supporting Sentence or Specific Example (2)	*protecting their own citizens' culture and respecting the human rights of the international community* Governments going down this route should tread the fine line between protecting their own citizens' culture and respecting the human rights of the international community.

Body 2

In tackling these problems governments need to understand the main causes of overpopulation, which include a high birth rate and immigration. China's one-child policy might have provoked outrage around the world, but it has eased the country's population concerns by lowering its birth rate. In other nations, most governments are more likely to rely on increased living costs to dissuade couples from having too many children as well as making birth control methods. Policymakers also have the option of dealing with overpopulation by restricting immigration, and pooling migrant workers in less crowded areas. Governments going down this route should tread the fine line between protecting their own citizens' culture and respecting the human rights of the international community.

a high birth rate : 높은 출산율
immigration : 이민
provoke : 유발하다
outrage : 격분
dissuade from : 단념시키다
birth control : 산아 제한
policymakers : 정책을 만드는 사람들

have an option : 선택권을 갖다
pool : 모으다
migrant workers : 이주 노동자
go down : 실패하다
tread a fine line : 아슬아슬한 곡예를 하다
the human rights : 인권

우리말 해석

이러한 문제들을 막기 위해서 정부는 높은 출산율과 이민을 포함하여 인구과잉의 주요 원인을 이해할 필요가 있다. 중국의 한 자녀 정책이 세계적으로 격분을 유발한 듯하지만, 이것은 출산율을 낮춤으로써 그 나라의 인구에 대한 고충을 완화시켰다. 다른 국가에서는 대부분의 정부가 커플들에게 산아 제한 방법을 실시하는 것뿐만 아니라 지나치게 많은 아이들을 낳는 것을 단념시키기 위해 증가된 생활비에 의존하는 경향이 있다. 정책을 만드는 사람들은 또한 이민을 제한하고 인구가 덜 밀집된 지역으로 이주 근로자들을 끌어들임으로써 인구과잉을 다루는 선택권을 갖는다. 이러한 방법에 실패한 정부는 자국 시민들의 문화 보호하는 것과 국제 사회의 인권을 존중하는 것 사이에서 아슬아슬한 곡예를 해야 한다.

 **5 단계** 결론 (Conclusion) (31~35분) : 본문에 제시한 내 주장 요약하며 다시 한 번 강조

| Question | The world population is dramatically increasing. This is causing problems for developed countries as well as underdeveloped nations. Explain the problems of overpopulation, and suggest some possible solutions. |

결론 작성 시, 먼저 문제 유형을 파악한 후, 'Conclusion Template'의 표현을 인용한다. (See p58)

문제 유형 파악	3-2) Problems and Solutions
Conclusion Template 인용	In conclusion, it is clear that there are various problems for…(토픽), steps are needed to tackle this phenomenon.

3-2 유형의 결론을 작성할 때 문제와 해결책을 구체적으로 작성하게 되면 자칫 결론이 너무 길어질 수 있기 때문에 포괄적으로 작성한다.

Conclusion

In conclusion, it is clear that there are various problems associated with overpopulation, therefore enforcing birth control and inducing proper immigration policies **are needed to tackle the phenomenon.**

* 상황에 따라 템플릿을 살짝 변형해도 좋다.

enforce : 시행하다
induce : 도입하다

우리말 해석
결론적으로, 인구과잉과 관련된 다양한 문제들이 있으므로 이 현상을 막기 위해 산아 제한을 실시하고 적절한 이민 정책을 도입하는 것이 필요하다.

6 단계 교정 (Self-correction) (36~40분) : 내용의 일관성 및 문법 검토

다음 Body 2의 내용을 교정해 보자. 틀린 부분은 총 몇 개일까?

교정 전 (직접 문장 부호를 이용하여 틀린 부분을 교정해 보자.)

in tackling these problems governments need to understanding the main causes of overpopulation, which include a high birth rate and immigration. china's one-child policy might have provoked outrage around the world, but it has eased the country's population concerns by lowering its birth rate.

In other nations, Most government are more likely to rely on increased living costs to dissuade couples from having too many childs as well as making birth control methods.

Policymakers also have the option of dealing to overpopulation by restricting immigration, and pooling migrant workers in more crowded areas. Governments going down this route should tread the fine line between protecting their own citizens' culture and respecting the human rights of the international community.

교정

~~i~~ **I** tackling these problems governments need to ~~understanding~~ **understand** the main causes of overpopulation, which include a high birth rate and immigration. ~~c~~ **C**hina's one-child policy might have provoked outrage around the world, but it has eased the country's population concerns by lowering its birth rate.

~~In other nations,~~ ~~M~~**m**ost ~~government~~ **governments** are more likely to rely on increased living costs to dissuade couples from having too many ~~childs~~ **children** as well as making birth control methods. Policymakers also have the option of dealing ~~to~~ **with** overpopulation by restricting immigration, and pooling migrant workers in ~~more~~ **less** crowded areas. Governments going down this route should tread the fine line between protecting their own citizens' culture and respecting the human rights of the international community.

1. i → I : 문장의 첫 글자는 반드시 대문자로 시작한다.
2. understanding → understand : need to + 동사 원형
3. c → C : china는 도자기, China는 중국이다. 또한 문장의 첫 글자는 반드시 대문자로 시작해야 한다.
4. 붙여쓰기 : 위의 글은 Body 2 단락이다. 단락이 바뀌지 않는 한, 줄을 바꿔 쓰지 않는다.
5. M → m : 콤마(,) 다음에는 소문자로 쓴다.
6. government → governments : 앞에 '대부분(most)'이라는 복수를 의미하는 단어가 있으므로 복수 형태로 쓴다.
7. childs → children : child의 복수는 children이다.
8. to → with : deal with는 '다루다'라는 뜻
9. more → less : 인구가 '덜' 밀집된 지역이라고 해야 논리에 맞다. 이걸 놓치면 절대 안 된다!

틀린 개수 : 총 9개

Sample Answer

> **Question**
>
> The world population is dramatically increasing. This is causing problems for developed countries as well as underdeveloped nations. Explain the problems of overpopulation, and suggest some possible solutions.

Population growth continues to explode across the world. Governments face the challenge of addressing the problems associated with this global trend.

One major issue with overpopulation is scarcity. Natural resources are limited and if there are more people occupying the same space it puts pressure on the supply of basic goods and services. According to the principles of economics, when supply is limited prices rise and so overpopulation leads to an increase in the cost of living. Infectious diseases can also flourish in crowded cities and towns because so many people live and work close to each other. Some of the most devastating plague and influenza outbreaks in the history of mankind were exacerbated within dense populations.

In tackling these problems governments need to understand the main causes of overpopulation, which include a high birth rate and immigration. China's one-child policy might have provoked outrage around the world, but it has eased the country's population concerns by lowering its birth rate. In other nations, most governments are more likely to rely on increased living costs to dissuade couples from having too many children as well as making birth control methods. Policymakers also have the option of dealing with overpopulation by restricting immigration, and pooling migrant workers in less crowded areas. Governments going down this route should tread the fine line between protecting their own citizens' culture and respecting the human rights of the international community.

In conclusion, it is clear that there are various problems associated with overpopulation, therefore enforcing birth control and inducing proper immigration policies are needed to tackle the phenomenon.

word counts : 263 words

우리말 해석

인구 증가는 전세계에 걸쳐 폭발적으로 증가하는 것을 지속하고 있다. 정부는 이런 세계적인 추세와 연계된 문제들을 고심해야 하는 도전에 직면해 있다.

인구과잉에 있어 주된 문제는 부족이다. 천연자원은 한정되어 있고 만약 같은 공간을 점유한 사람들이 더 많다면, 이것은 기본적인 물자와 서비스의 공급에 압력을 가한다. 경제원칙에 따라, 공급이 제한되면 가격이 오르고 그래서 인구과잉은 생활비의 인상을 초래한다. 전염성 질병이 혼잡한 도시와 마을에 유행할 수 있는데 너무 많은 사람들이 서로 가깝게 살고 일하기 때문이다. 인류 역사에서 일부 가장 파괴적인 전염병과 인플루엔자의 발발은 인구 밀집지역에서 악화되었다.

이러한 문제들을 막기 위해서 정부는 높은 출산율과 이민을 포함하여 인구과잉의 주요 원인을 이해할 필요가 있다. 중국의 한 자녀 정책이 세계적으로 격분을 유발한 듯 하지만, 이것은 출산율을 낮춤으로써 그 나라의 인구에 대한 고충을 완화시켰다. 다른 국가에서는 대부분의 정부가 커플들에게 산아 제한 방법을 실시하는 것뿐만 아니라 지나치게 많은 아이들을 낳는 것을 단념시키기 위해 증가된 생활비에 의존하는 경향이 있다. 정책을 만드는 사람들은 또한 이민을 제한하고 인구가 덜 밀집된 지역으로 이주 근로자들을 끌어들임으로써 인구과잉을 다루는 선택권을 갖는다. 이러한 방법에 실패한 정부는 자국 시민들의 문화 보호하는 것과 국제 사회의 인권을 존중하는 것 사이에서 아슬아슬한 곡예를 해야 한다.

결론적으로, 인구과잉과 관련된 다양한 문제들이 있으므로 이 현상을 막기 위해 산아 제한을 실시하고 적절한 이민정책을 도입하는 것이 필요하다.

불법 Review

앞에서 배운 내용을 빈칸으로 다음 빈칸을 영어로 작성해 보자.

_____ (1. 인구 증가) continues to explode across the world. Governments face the challenge of addressing the problems associated with this global trend.

One major issue with overpopulation is _____ (2. 부족). Natural resources are limited and if there are more people occupying the same space it _____ (3. ~에 압력을 가하다)the supply of basic goods and services. According to the principles of economics, when supply is limited prices rise and so overpopulation leads to an increase in the cost of living. Infectious diseases can also flourish in crowded cities and towns because so many people live and work close to each other. Some of the most devastating plague and _____ (4. 인플루엔자의 발발) in the history of mankind were exacerbated within dense populations.

In tackling these problems governments need to understand the main causes of overpopulation, which include _____ (5. 높은 출산율과 이민). China's one-child policy might have provoked outrage around the world, but it has eased the country's population concerns by lowering its birth rate. In other nations, most governments are more likely to rely on increased living costs to dissuade couples from having too many children as well as making _____ (6. 산아 제한 방법들). Policymakers also have the option of dealing with overpopulation _____ (7. 이민을 제한함으로써), and pooling migrant workers in less crowded areas. Governments going down this route should _____ (8. 아슬아슬한 곡예를 하다) between protecting their own citizens' culture and respecting _____ (9. 인권) of the international community.

In conclusion, it is clear that there are various problems associated with overpopulation, and enforcing birth control and _____ (10. 적절한 이민정책을 도입함으로써) are needed to tackle the phenomenon.

Answer   1. Population growth / 2. scarcity / 3. puts pressure on / 4. influenza outbreaks
5. a high birth rate and immigration / 6. birth control methods / 7. by restricting immigration
8. tread a fine line / 9. the human rights / 10. inducing proper immigration policies

STEP5 Day 14 International Relations & Urbanisation 불법 포인트 정리

사람이 너무 많은 것, 초만원	overcrowding	점유하다, 차지하다	occupy
지나친 부동산 가격	exorbitant property prices	~에 압력을 가하다	put pressure on
취약성	vulnerability	경제원칙	the principles of economics
투자	investment	전염병	infectious diseases
교통 혼잡	traffic congestion	번창하다	flourish
덜어주다	ease	파괴적인	devastating
공기 오염	air pollution	전염병	plague
안녕(편안히 잘 지내는 것)	well-being	인플루엔자, 유행성 감기	influenza
대응하다	counter	(질병, 전쟁의)발생, 발발	outbreaks
CCTV 설치	CCTV installations	인류	mankind
착수하다	embark on	(질병, 문제를) 악화시키다	exacerbate
대규모 인구 유입	large population inflows	밀집한	dense
시골 지역	in rural areas	높은 출산율	a high birth rate
극도로 스트레스를 받다	be extremely stressful	이민	immigration
공동체 의식	a sense of community	유발하다	provoke
재정적 원조를 주다	give financial aid	격분	outrage
요구를 맞추다	meet demands	단념시키다	dissuade from
~에 의해 잘못 사용되다	be misused by	산아 제한	birth control
부패한 정치가들	corrupt politicians	정책을 만드는 사람들	policymakers
돈을 기부하다	donate money	선택권을 갖다	have an option
세계화 시대에	in this era of globalisation	모으다	pool
기부자들	donors	이주 노동자	migrant workers
물자	commodities	실패하다	go down
인구과잉	overpopulation	아슬아슬한 곡예를 하다	tread a fine line
폭발적으로 증가하다	explode	인권	the human rights
고심하다	address	시행하다	enforce
부족, 결핍	scarcity	도입하다	induce

Day 15 Environmental Pollution 환경오염

Question

Global warming is one of the most serious issues that the world is facing today. Explain the main causes of global warming and suggest some measures that individuals and governments can take to tackle the problem.

지구 온난화는 오늘날 세계가 직면하고 있는 가장 심각한 문제들 중 하나이다. 지구 온난화의 주된 원인을 설명하고 개인과 정부가 이 문제를 막기 위해 취할 수 있는 조치를 제시하라.

 빈출 문제

1. Scientists are warning of the danger of climate change. Some people say that governments should take full responsibility for solving this problem. Others insist that it is the responsibility of the people and they should change their lifestyle. Discuss both views and give your own opinion.

2. Nowadays environmental problems are too big to be managed by individual persons or individual countries. In other words, it is an international problem. Do you agree or disagree with this statement?

3. Deforestation is a serious problem and it may lead to the extinction of animals and mankind. Do you agree or disagree with this statement?

4. Technology is a cause of environmental pollution. Some say that we should not use it and make our lives simple. Others believe that we should use it to tackle the problem. Discuss both views and give your own opinion.

1. 과학자들은 기후 변화의 위험을 경고하고 있다. 어떤 사람들은 정부가 이 문제를 해결하는 데 전적으로 책임을 져야 한다고 말한다. 반면 이것이 개개인의 책임이고 사람들이 삶의 방식을 바꿔야 한다고 주장하는 사람들도 있다. 양쪽의 견해를 논하고 당신의 주장을 제시하라.

2. 오늘날 환경문제는 너무나 커서 개인이나 한 국가가 해결할 수 없다. 다시 말해 이것은 국제적인 문제이다. 당신은 이 말에 동의하는가? 또는 동의하지 않는가?

3. 산림 벌채는 심각한 문제이고 동물과 인간의 멸종을 초래할지도 모른다. 당신은 이 말에 동의하는가? 또는 동의하지 않는가?

4. 기술은 환경오염의 원인이다. 어떤 사람들은 기술을 사용하지 말고 단순한 삶을 살아야 한다고 말한다. 반면 기술을 사용해서 환경오염을 막아야 한다고 주장하는 사람들도 있다. 양쪽의 견해를 논하고 당신의 주장을 제시하라.

 STEP2 브레인스토밍

1) 이산화탄소와 같은 가스는 태양으로부터의 열을 가두고 이것은 지구의 온도를 상승시키는 원인이 된다.
   이산화탄소 : carbon dioxide, CO_2 / 가두다 : trap / 지구의 온도 : global temperatures

2) 인간의 활동은 온실 가스의 상승에 주된 요인이다.
   온실 가스 : greenhouse gases

3) 차량은 공기를 오염시키는 배기 가스를 배출한다.
   차량 : vehicles / 배기 가스 : exhaust gas

4) 지구 온난화는 우리 행성에 심각한 영향을 미칠 것이다.
   지구 온난화 : global warming

5) 기온이 상승하는 것은 극지방의 만년설과 빙하를 녹이는 원인이 될 것이다.
   극지방의 만년설과 빙하 : the polar ice caps and glaciers / 녹이다 : melt

6) 홍수와 가뭄 같은 자연 재해들은 좀 더 흔하게 될지도 모른다.
홍수와 가뭄 : floods and droughts / 자연 재해 : natural disasters

7) 석유와 석탄 같은 화석 연료는 다 떨어지고 있다.
화석 연료 : fossil fuels / 다 떨어지다, 다 쓰다 : run out

8) 정부는 공장에서 나오는 배출물을 제한하는 법을 도입해야 한다.
법을 도입하다 : introduce laws

9) 정부는 운전자들과 항공사에 환경세를 부과해야 한다.
~에 환경세를 부과하다 : impose green taxes on

10) 개인들은 운전하기보다는 대중교통을 이용하고 포장이 덜 된 제품을 선택할 수 있다.
포장이 덜 된 제품 : products with less packaging

11) 재사용하고 재활용함으로써 우리는 쓰레기 매립지로 가는 쓰레기의 양을 줄이는 데 도움을 줄 수 있다.
재사용과 재활용 : reusing and recycling / 쓰레기 매립지 : landfill

12) 많은 공장들은 그들의 쓰레기를 태우거나 땅속에 묻어서 없앤다.
태우다 : burn / 땅속 : under the ground / 묻다 : bury / 없애다 : get rid of

13) 환경에 대해 무관심한 사람들은 그들의 태도를 바꿔야 한다.
무관심한 : careless / 태도 : attitude

14) 철도 시스템은 여러 가지 면에서 가장 효율적인데, 일반적으로 버스보다 승객 한 명당 더 낮은 탄소를 배출하고 더 적은 연료를 사용한다.
승객 한 명당 : per passenger

15) 오염물질은 사람뿐만 아니라 기후와 다른 생명체들에게도 영향을 끼친다.
오염물질 : pollutants

Answer

1) Gases such as carbon dioxide trap heat from the sun and this causes global temperatures to rise.
2) Human activity is a major factor in the rise of greenhouse gases.
3) Vehicles release exhaust gas which pollutes the air.
4) Global warming will have a significant impact on our planet.
5) Rising temperatures will cause melting of the polar ice caps and glaciers.
6) Natural disasters like floods and droughts may become more common.
7) Fossil fuels like oil and coal are running out.
8) Governments should introduce laws to limit emissions from factories.
9) Governments should impose green taxes on drivers and airline companies.
10) Individuals can take public transport rather than driving and choose products with less packaging.
11) By reusing and recycling, we can help to reduce the amount of waste going into landfills.
12) Many factories get rid of their trash by burning or burying it under the ground.
13) People who are careless about the environment should change their attitude.
14) Train systems are the most efficient in many ways, typically emitting less carbon and using less fuel per passenger than buses.
15) Pollutants affect not only people, but also the climate and other creatures.

실전문제

You should spend about 40 minutes on this task.
Write about the following topic :

> Global warming is one of the most serious issues that the world is facing today. Explain the main causes of global warming and suggest some measures that individuals and governments can take to tackle the problem.

Give reasons for your answer and include any relevant examples from your own knowledge or experience.

Write at least 250 words.

1 단계 문제 정독, 문제 유형 파악, 브레인스토밍 (0 ~ 5분)

Question Global warming is one of the most serious issues that the world is facing today. Explain the main causes of global warming and suggest some measures that individuals and governments can take to tackle the problem.

문제 정독
지구 온난화는 오늘날 세계가 직면하고 있는 가장 심각한 문제들 중 하나이다. 지구 온난화의 주된 원인을 설명하고 개인과 정부가 이 문제를 막기 위해 취할 수 있는 조치를 제시하라.

global warming : 지구 온난화

문제 유형 파악
3-1. Reasons and Solutions 유형
* reason과 cause는 동의어로 봐도 좋다.

Brainstorming

Topic : 지구 온난화는 가장 심각한 문제들 중 하나이다.	
Reasons : 지구 온난화의 주된 원인들	Solutions : 개인과 정부가 취할 수 있는 조치들
1. 온실 가스의 존재 the existence of greenhouse gases → 태양에서 발생한 열이 지구 표면에서 다시 반사 heat from the sun to be reflected back to Earth's surface 2. 인간의 활동 human activities → 화석 연료의 연소 the burning of fossil fuels	1. 개인 : 집에서 에너지 소비를 줄이는 것 cutting down our energy consumption at home → 개인의 탄소 발자국 줄이기 reduce our individual carbon footprint 2. 정부 : 보다 깨끗한 대체 에너지 자원을 개발 develop cleaner alternative energy sources → 친환경적인 기업과 시민들에게 혜택을 제공 offering incentives to businesses and citizens to be eco-friendly

* 이유와 해결책을 각각 연관성 있게 작성하되 개인과 정부가 취할 수 있는 조치를 각각 제시해야 한다.

2단계 서론 (Introduction) (6~10분) : 두 문장으로 작성

Question	Global warming is one of the most serious issues that the world is facing today. Explain the main causes of global warming and suggest some measures that individuals and governments can take to tackle the problem.

단계	Question	서론 작성
1단계 Paraphrasing	**토픽 :** Global warming is one of the most serious issues that the world is facing today.	**Paraphrasing :** Many people are devoting their time and research to tackling the potentially disastrous problem of global warming.
2단계 Answering	**질문 :** Explain the main causes of global warming and suggest some measures that governments and individuals can take to tackle the problem.	**Answering :** 이유와 해결책 간단히 언급 All of us can play a role in reducing mankind's contribution to this process by changing our attitudes towards energy production and use.

Introduction
Many people are devoting their time and research to tackling the potentially disastrous problem of global warming. All of us can play a role in reducing mankind's contribution to this process by changing our attitudes towards energy production and use.

devote A to B : A를 B하는데 헌신하다, 쏟다
potentially : 잠재적으로
disastrous : 재앙의, 형편없는
contribution : 원인 제공, 기여

우리말 해석
많은 사람들은 그들의 시간과 연구를 지구 온난화의 잠재적인 재앙적 문제를 막기 위해 쏟고 있다. 우리 모두는 에너지 생산과 사용에 대한 우리의 태도를 바꿈으로써 이러한 과정에 미친 인류의 원인 제공을 줄이는 데 역할을 할 수 있다.

3단계   본론 1 (Body 1) (11~20분) : Reasons (지구 온난화의 주된 원인들)

> **Question**   Global warming is one of the most serious issues that the world is facing today. Explain the main causes of global warming and suggest some measures that individuals and governments can take to tackle the problem.

Body 1은 1단계에서 브레인스토밍한 'Reasons'를 바탕으로 작성한다.

1단계	Topic Sentence	There are a couple of reasons why global warming occurs.
2단계 (1)	Supporting Sentence (1)	*the existence of greenhouse gases* The main cause is the existence of greenhouse gases, such as CO_2, in our atmosphere.
3단계 (1)	Supporting Sentence or Specific Example (1)	*heat from the sun to be reflected back to Earth's surface* The presence of these gases allows heat from the sun to be reflected back to Earth's surface, which is known as the greenhouse effect.
2단계 (2)	Supporting Sentence (2)	*human activities* While some academics suggest this is a natural phenomenon, the general consensus is that human activities are exacerbating the situation.
3단계 (2)	Supporting Sentence or Specific Example (2)	*the burning of fossil fuels* For example, it is believed that the burning of fossil fuels during the production of energy to meet the world's electricity needs has led to the release of too much CO_2, speeding up global warming and climate change.

Body 1

There are a couple of reasons why global warming occurs. The main cause is the existence of greenhouse gases, such as CO_2, in our atmosphere. The presence of these gases allows heat from the sun to be reflected back to Earth's surface, which is known as the greenhouse effect. While some academics suggest this is a natural phenomenon, the general consensus is that human activities are exacerbating the situation. For example, it is believed that the burning of fossil fuels during the production of energy to meet the world's electricity needs has led to the release of too much CO_2, speeding up global warming and climate change.

existence, presence : 존재
atmosphere : 대기
surface : 표면
be known as : ~로 알려지다
the greenhouse effect : 온실 효과
academics : 교수들

the general consensus : 전반전 합의
exacerbate : 악화시키다
fossil fuels : 화석 연료
release : 배출
speed up : 가속화시키다, 속도를 올리다

우리말 해석
지구 온난화가 발생하는 데에는 두 가지 이유가 있다. 주된 원인은 우리의 대기 중에 있는 이산화탄소와 같은 온실 가스의 존재가 원인이다. 이러한 가스의 존재는 온실 효과로 알려진, 태양에서 발생한 열이 지구 표면에서 다시 반사되는 것을 가능하게 한다. 일부 교수들은 이를 자연현상이라고 제안하는 반면에, 전반적인 합의는 인간의 활동이 이 상황을 악화시킨다는 것이다. 예를 들어, 세계의 전력 필요량을 충족시키기 위해 에너지를 생산하는 동안 발생하는 화석 연료의 연소는, 지구 온난화와 기후 변화를 가속화시킬 지나치게 많은 이산화탄소의 배출을 초래했다.

 본론 2 (Body 2) (21~30분) : **Solutions** (개인과 정부가 취할 수 있는 조치들)

| Question | Global warming is one of the most serious issues that the world is facing today. Explain the main causes of global warming and suggest some measures that individuals and governments can take to tackle the problem. |

Body 2는 1단계에서 브레인스토밍한 'Solutions'를 바탕으로 작성한다.

1단계	Topic Sentence	Although solving these problems is not easy, there are feasible steps which individuals and governments can take.
2단계 (1)	Supporting Sentence (1)	*cutting down our energy consumption at home* Cutting down our energy consumption at home is the first step.
3단계 (1)	Supporting Sentence or Specific Example (1)	*reduce our individual carbon footprint* This is why we often hear about campaigns to reduce our individual carbon footprint by unplugging home appliances that we are not using.
2단계 (2)	Supporting Sentence (2)	*develop cleaner alternative energy sources* But governments also have a big responsibility to develop cleaner alternative energy sources such as solar, wind or tide power.
3단계 (2)	Supporting Sentence or Specific Example (2)	*offering incentives to businesses and citizens to be eco-friendly* They can discourage the excessive release of pollutants by offering incentives to businesses and citizens to be eco-friendly in every aspect of our lives from transportation to lighting at the same time.

Body 2

Although solving these problems is not easy, there are feasible steps which individuals and governments can take. Cutting down our energy consumption at home is the first step. This is why we often hear about campaigns to reduce our individual carbon footprint by unplugging home appliances that we are not using. But governments also have a big responsibility to develop cleaner alternative energy sources such as solar, wind or tide power. They can discourage the excessive release of pollutants by offering incentives to businesses and citizens to be eco-friendly in every aspect of our lives from transportation to lighting at the same time.

cut down : 줄이다
energy consumption : 에너지 소비
carbon footprint : 탄소 발자국(이산화탄소의 배출량)
unplug home appliances : 가전 기기의
　전기 코드를 빼다
alternative energy sources : 대체 에너지 자원
tide power : 조력 에너지
pollutants : 오염물질

우리말 해석
문제를 해결하는 게 쉽진 않지만, 개인과 정부가 취할 수 있는 실행 가능한 방법들이 있다. 집에서 에너지 소비를 줄이는 것이 첫 번째 단계이다. 이것이 우리가 사용하지 않는 가전 기기의 전기 코드를 빼면서 개인의 탄소 발자국(이산화탄소의 배출량)을 줄이는 캠페인에 관해 자주 듣는 이유이다. 그러나 정부 또한 태양, 풍력 혹은 조력 에너지 같이 보다 깨끗한 대체 에너지 자원을 개발할 커다란 책임을 갖는다. 동시에 정부는 교통수단에서 조명까지 우리의 생활 일상의 모습에서 친환경적인 기업과 시민들에게 혜택을 제공함으로써 과도한 오염물질의 배출을 막을 수 있을 것이다.

5 단계 결론 (Conclusion) (31~35분) : 본문에 제시한 내 주장 요약하며 다시 한 번 강조

> **Question**
> Global warming is one of the most serious issues that the world is facing today. Explain the main causes of global warming and suggest some measures that individuals and governments can take to tackle the problem.

결론 작성 시, 먼저 문제 유형을 파악한 후, 'Conclusion Template'의 표현을 인용한다. (See p58)

문제 유형 파악	3-1) Reasons and Solutions
Conclusion Template 인용	In conclusion, it is clear that there are various reasons for…(토픽), steps are needed to tackle this phenomenon.

3-1 유형의 결론을 작성할 때 문제와 해결책을 구체적으로 작성하게 되면 자칫 결론이 너무 길어질 수 있기 때문에 포괄적으로 작성한다.

> **Conclusion**
> **In conclusion, it is clear that there are various reasons for** global warming, and we should all put pressure on ourselves and politicians to work towards dealing with **this phenomenon**.

* 상황에 따라 템플릿을 살짝 변형해도 좋다.

politicians : 정치가들

> **우리말 해석**
> 결론적으로, 지구 온난화에는 다양한 이유가 있다는 것이 분명하며, 우리는 우리 자신과 정치가들이 이 현상을 처리하도록 모든 압력을 행사해야 한다.

6 단계   교정 (Self-correction) (36~40분) : 내용의 일관성 및 문법 검토

다음 Body 2의 내용을 교정해 보자. 틀린 부분은 총 몇 개일까?

교정 전 (직접 문장 부호를 이용하여 틀린 부분을 교정해 보자.)

Although solving these problems is not easy, but there are feasible steps which individuals and goverments can take. Cutting down our energy consumption at home is the first step. This is why we often hears about campaigns to reduce our individual carbon footprint by unplugging home appliances that we are not using. But governments also has a big responsibility to develop more cleaner alternative energy sources such as solar, wind or tide power. They can discourage the excessive release of pollutants by offering incentives to businesses and citizens to be eco-friendly in every aspects of our lives from transportation to lighting at a same time.

교정

Although solving these problems is not easy, ~~but~~ there are feasible steps which individuals and ~~goverments~~ [governments] can take. Cutting down our energy consumption at home is the first step. This is why we often ~~hears~~ [hear] about campaigns to reduce our individual carbon footprint by unplugging home appliances that we are not using. But governments also ~~has~~ [have] a big responsibility to develop ~~more~~ cleaner alternative energy sources such as solar, wind or tide power. They can discourage the excessive release of pollutants by offering incentives to businesses and citizens to be eco-friendly in every ~~aspects~~ [aspect] of our lives from transportation to lighting at ~~a~~ [the] same time.

1. but → 삭제 : although 자체에 but의 뜻을 포함하고 있기 때문에 절대로 but을 써서는 안 된다.
2. goverments → governments : 상당히 많은 학생들이 실수하는 스펠링! n을 빠뜨리지 말자!
3. 붙여쓰기 : 위의 글은 Body 2 단락이다. 단락이 바뀌지 않는 한, 줄을 바꿔 쓰지 않는다.
4. hears → hear : 주어 we는 복수이므로 복수 동사 hear을 쓴다.
5. has → have : 주어 governments가 복수이므로 복수 동사 have를 쓴다.
6. more → 삭제 : cleaner가 clean의 비교급이므로 more를 붙여서는 안 된다.
7. aspects → aspect : every 다음에는 단수 명사를 쓴다.
8. a → the : at the same time은 '동시에'라는 뜻. same 앞에는 보통 the를 쓴다.

틀린 개수 : 총 8개

Sample Answer

> **Question**
>
> Global warming is one of the most serious issues that the world is facing today. Explain the main causes of global warming and suggest some measures that individuals and governments can take to tackle the problem.

Many people are devoting their time and research to tackling the potentially disastrous problem of global warming. All of us can play a role in reducing mankind's contribution to this process by changing our attitudes towards energy production and use.

There are a couple of reasons why global warming occurs. The main cause is the existence of greenhouse gases, such as CO_2, in our atmosphere. The presence of these gases allows heat from the sun to be reflected back to Earth's surface, which is known as the greenhouse effect. While some academics suggest this is a natural phenomenon, the general consensus is that human activities are exacerbating the situation. For example, it is believed that the burning of fossil fuels during the production of energy to meet the world's electricity needs has led to the release of too much CO_2, speeding up global warming and climate change.

Although solving these problems is not easy, there are feasible steps which individuals and governments can take. Cutting down our energy consumption at home is the first step. This is why we often hear about campaigns to reduce our individual carbon footprint by unplugging home appliances that we are not using. But governments also have a big responsibility to develop cleaner alternative energy sources such as solar, wind or tide power. They can discourage the excessive release of pollutants by offering incentives to businesses and citizens to be eco-friendly in every aspect of our lives from transportation to lighting at the same time.

In conclusion, it is clear that there are various reasons for global warming, and we should all put pressure on ourselves and politicians to work towards dealing with this phenomenon.

word counts : 280 words

우리말 해석

많은 사람들은 그들의 시간과 연구를 지구 온난화의 잠재적인 재앙적 문제를 막기 위해 쏟고 있다. 우리 모두는 에너지 생산과 사용에 대한 우리의 태도를 바꿈으로써 이러한 과정에 미친 인류의 원인 제공을 줄이는 데 역할을 할 수 있다.

지구 온난화가 발생하는 데에는 두 가지 주된 이유가 있다. 주된 원인은 우리의 대기 중에 있는 이산화탄소와 같은 온실 가스의 존재가 원인이다. 이러한 가스의 존재는 온실 효과로 알려진, 태양에서 발생한 열이 지구 표면에서 다시 반사되는 것을 가능하게 한다. 일부 교수들은 이를 자연현상이라고 제안하는 반면에, 전반적인 합의는 인간의 활동이 이 상황을 악화시킨다는 것이다. 예를 들어, 세계의 전력 필요량을 충족시키기 위해 에너지를 생산하는 동안 발생하는 화석 연료의 연소는, 지구 온난화와 기후 변화를 가속화시킬 지나치게 많은 이산화탄소의 배출을 초래했다.

문제를 해결하는 게 쉽진 않지만, 개인과 정부가 취할 수 있는 실행 가능한 방법들이 있다. 집에서 에너지 소비를 줄이는 것이 첫 번째 단계이다. 이것이 우리가 사용하지 않는 가전 기기의 전기 코드를 빼면서 개인의 탄소 발자국(이산화탄소의 배출량)을 줄이는 캠페인에 관해 자주 듣는 이유이다. 그러나 정부 또한 태양, 풍력 혹은 조력 에너지 같이 보다 깨끗한 대체 에너지 자원을 개발할 커다란 책임을 갖는다. 동시에 정부는 교통수단에서 조명까지 우리의 생활 일상의 모습에서 친환경적인 기업과 시민들에게 혜택을 제공함으로써 과도한 오염물질의 배출을 막을 수 있을 것이다.

결론적으로, 지구 온난화에는 다양한 이유가 있다는 것이 분명하며, 우리는 우리 자신과 정치가들이 이 현상을 처리하도록 모든 압력을 행사해야 한다.

불법 Review

앞에서 배운 내용을 바탕으로 다음 빈칸을 영어로 작성해 보자.

Many people are devoting their time and research to tackling the potentially disastrous problem of _____ (1. 지구 온난화). All of us can play a role in reducing mankind's contribution to this process by changing our attitudes towards energy production and use.

There are a couple of reasons why global warming occurs. The main cause is _____ (2. 온실 가스의 존재), such as CO_2, in our atmosphere. The presence of these gases allows heat from the sun to be reflected back to _____ (3. 지구의 표면), which is known as the greenhouse effect. While some academics suggest this is a natural phenomenon, the general consensus is that human activities are _____ (4. 이러한 상황을 악화시키다). For example, it is believed that _____ (5. 화석 연료의 연소) during the production of energy to meet the world's electricity needs has led to the release of too much CO_2, speeding up global warming and _____ (6. 기후 변화).

Although solving these problems is not easy, there are feasible steps which individuals and governments can take. Cutting down our energy consumption at home is the first step. This is why we often hear about campaigns to reduce our individual _____ (7. 탄소 발자국) by unplugging home appliances that we are not using. But governments also have a big responsibility to develop _____ (8. 보다 깨끗한 대체 에너지 자원) such as solar, wind or tide power. They can discourage _____ (9. 과도한 오염물질의 배출) by offering incentives to businesses and citizens to be eco-friendly in every aspect of our lives from transportation to lighting at the same time.

In conclusion, it is clear that there are various reasons for global warming, and we should all put pressure on ourselves and _____ (10. 정치가들) to work towards dealing with this phenomenon.

Answer 1. global warming / 2. the existence of greenhouse gases / 3. Earth's surface
4. exacerbating the situation / 5. the burning of fossil fuels / 6. climate change
7. carbon footprint / 8. cleaner alternative energy sources
9. the excessive release of pollutants / 10. politicians

Day 15 Environmental Pollution 불법 포인트 정리

이산화탄소	carbon dioxide / CO₂	오염물질	pollutants
가두다	trap	지구 온난화	global warming
지구의 온도	global temperatures	A를 B하는데 헌신하다, 쏟다	devote A to B
온실 가스	greenhouse gases	잠재적으로	potentially
차량	vehicles	재앙의, 형편없는	disastrous
배기 가스	exhaust gas	원인 제공, 기여	contribution
극지방의 만년설과 빙하	the polar ice caps and glaciers	존재	existence, presence
녹이다	melt	대기	atmosphere
홍수와 가뭄	floods and droughts	표면	surface
자연 재해	natural disasters	~로 알려지다	be known as
화석 연료	fossil fuels	온실 효과	the greenhouse effect
다 떨어지다, 다 쓰다	run out	교수들	academics
법을 도입하다	introduce laws	전반적 합의	the general consensus
~에 환경세를 부과하다	impose green taxes on	악화시키다	exacerbate
포장이 덜 된 제품	products with less packaging	화석 연료	fossil fuels
재사용과 재활용	reusing and recycling	배출	release
쓰레기 매립지	landfills	가속화시키다, 속도를 올리다	speed up
태우다	burn	줄이다	cut down
땅속	under the ground	에너지 소비	energy consumption
묻다	bury	탄소 발자국	carbon footprint
없애다	get rid of	가전 기기의 전기 코드를 빼다	unplug home appliances
무관심한	careless	대체 에너지 자원	alternative energy sources
태도	attitude	조력 에너지	tide power
승객 한 명당	per passenger	정치가들	politicians

Day 16 The Energy Crisis 에너지 위기

Question

We are faced with a severe energy shortage these days. Explain the main causes of this problem, and suggest some possible solutions.

오늘날 우리는 심각한 에너지 부족 문제에 직면했다. 이 문제의 주된 원인을 설명하고 가능한 해결책을 제시하라.

 빈출 문제

1. Increasing the price of energy is one of the best ways to tackle the energy crisis. Do you agree or disagree with this statement?

2. Nuclear power provides cheap and clean energy. The benefits of nuclear technology far outweigh the drawbacks. Do you agree or disagree with this statement?

3. Governments should make more efforts to develop alternative energy. Do you agree or disagree with this statement?

4. Some people think that planning for the future such as developing alternative energy and protecting the environment is just a waste of time. They believe it is more important to focus on the present. To what extent do you agree or disagree with this opinion?

1. 에너지 가격 인상은 에너지 위기를 막는 가장 좋은 방법 중 하나다. 당신은 이 말에 동의하는가? 또는 동의하지 않는가?

2. 원자력은 저렴하고 깨끗한 에너지를 제공한다. 원자력 기술의 혜택은 단점을 훨씬 능가한다. 당신은 이 말에 동의하는가? 또는 동의하지 않는가?

3. 정부는 대체에너지 개발에 더 많은 노력을 기울여야 한다. 당신은 이 말에 동의하는가? 또는 동의하지 않는가?

4. 어떤 사람들은 대체 에너지 개발이나 환경보호 같은 미래 계획이 시간 낭비에 불과하다고 생각한다. 그들은 현재에 초점을 맞추는 것이 더 중요하다고 믿는다. 당신은 이 의견에 얼마만큼 동의하는가? 또는 동의하지 않는가?

 **브레인스토밍**

1) 소비자들은 과대 포장된 제품을 사는 것을 피해야 한다.
   과대 포장된 제품 : over-packaged goods

2) 쓰레기를 버리기 전에 분리해야 한다.
   버리다 : throw away / 분리하다 : separate

3) 줄이고, 재사용하고 재활용하는 환경의 3개의 'R'을 배울 때이다.
   3개의 R : the three R's

4) 좀 더 많은 원자력 발전소를 짓는 데에는 몇 가지 장점이 있다.
   원자력 발전소 : nuclear power stations

5) 원자력은 지속 가능한 에너지 자원이고 천연자원을 낭비하지 않으면서 전기를 생산하는 데 사용될 수 있다.
   지속 가능한 : sustainable / 전기, 전력 : electricity

6) 원자력 발전소는 화석 연료 발전소보다 훨씬 깨끗하고 저렴하다.
   화석 연료 발전소 : fossil fuel power stations

7) 원자력에 반대하는 사람들은 발전소의 안전성에 대해 걱정한다.
   반대자들 : opponents

8) 새로운 원자력 발전소를 짓는 것은 인기가 없는데 아무도 발전소 근처에 살기를 원하지 않기 때문이다.

9) 핵폐기물 처리는 심각한 문제인데 현재로는 방사능 물질의 오염을 제거할 방법이 없기 때문이다.
   핵폐기물 처리 : nuclear waste disposal / 방사능 물질 : radioactive material / 오염(물질)을 제거하다 : decontaminate

10) 몇몇 국가들은 원자력을 높은 오일과 가스 가격의 해결책으로 고려하고 있다.

11) 상대적으로 막대한 설립 비용에도 불구하고 대체에너지원은 결국 비용 효율적이고 지속적이라고 입증되고 있다.
    설립 비용 : setup costs / 결국 : in the long run

12) 녹색 에너지원은 확실히 무한하기 때문에 우리는 어느 날 이 자원들이 궁극적으로 고갈될 것을 걱정하지 않는다.
    무한한 : endless / 고갈시키다, 다 써버리다 : exhaust / 걱정하다 : worry

13) 핵반응은 눈 깜짝할 순간에 커다란 에너지를 방출할 수 있다.
    핵반응 : nuclear reactions / 눈 깜짝할 순간 : in a split second

14) 방사성 폐기물은 무해한 수준까지 줄어드는 데 수천 년이나 그 이상이 걸린다.
    방사성 폐기물 : radioactive waste / 무해한 : harmless / 수천 년이나 그 이상 : thousands of years or even longer

15) 발전 설비의 노화된 기반 시설은 에너지 부족의 또 다른 이유이다.
노화된 기반 시설 : aging infrastructure

Answer

1) Consumers should avoid buying over-packaged goods.
2) Before throwing away our trash, we should separate it.
3) It is time to learn the three R's of the environment: reduce, reuse and recycle.
4) There are several benefits to building more nuclear power stations.
5) Nuclear power is a sustainable energy source and it can be used to produce electricity without wasting natural resources.
6) Nuclear power stations are much cleaner and less expensive than fossil fuel power stations.
7) Opponents of nuclear power worry about the safety of power stations.
8) The building of new nuclear power stations is unpopular because nobody wants to live near the stations.
9) Nuclear waste disposal is a severe problem because there is currently no way to decontaminate radioactive material.
10) Some countries are considering nuclear power as a solution to high oil and gas prices.
11) Despite relatively large setup costs, alternative energy sources are proving to be cost-effective and sustainable in the long run.
12) As green energy sources are definitely endless, we do not worry that one day they will ultimately exhaust.
13) Nuclear reactions can release great energy in a split second.
14) Radioactive waste takes thousands of years or even longer to be reduced to a harmless level.
15) Aging infrastructure of power generating equipment is another reason for energy shortages.

 실전문제

You should spend about 40 minutes on this task.
Write about the following topic :

> We are faced with a severe energy shortage these days. Explain the main causes of this problem, and suggest some possible solutions.

Give reasons for your answer and include any relevant examples from your own knowledge or experience.

Write at least 250 words.

 **1 단계** 문제 정독, 문제 유형 파악, 브레인스토밍 (0 ~ 5분)

Question We are faced with a severe energy shortage these days. Explain the main causes of this problem, and suggest some possible solutions.

문제 정독
오늘날 우리는 심각한 에너지 부족 문제에 직면했다. 이 문제의 주된 원인을 설명하고 가능한 해결책을 제시하라.

severe : 심각한

문제 유형 파악

3-1. Reasons and Solutions 유형

* reason과 cause는 동의어로 봐도 좋다.

Brainstorming

Topic : 심각한 에너지 부족 문제	
Reasons : 에너지 부족의 이유들	Solutions : 에너지 부족의 해결책들
1. 다양한 에너지 제품과 공공요금의 비용 상승 forced up the cost of various energy products and utilities → 일부 국가, 이런 상황이 더욱 악화되는데 전적으로 수입에 의존하기 때문 some countries, this situation is worsened because they rely entirely on imports 2. 에너지가 소비되는 속도 the speed at which energy is being consumed → 전보다 더 많은 에너지 사용 using more energy than ever before	1. 국민들에게 전력 사용을 제한하도록 권고 urging people to limit electricity use → 효율적으로 에너지를 절약하는 방법을 사람들에게 교육할 캠페인 campaigns to educate people on how to be efficient and save energy 2. 대체 에너지 자원 alternative energy sources → 원자력이 가장 현실적인 답 nuclear power is the most realistic answer

* 이유와 해결책을 각각 연관성 있게 작성한다.

2 단계   서론 (Introduction) (6~10분) : 두 문장으로 작성

	Question	서론 작성
Question	We are faced with a severe energy shortage these days. Explain the main causes of this problem, and suggest some possible solutions.	

단계	Question	서론 작성
1단계 Paraphrasing	**토픽 :** We are faced with a severe energy shortage these days.	**Paraphrasing :** The threat of an energy shortage has become a critical issue for those of us who rely on it in our daily lives.
2단계 Answering	**질문 :** Explain the main causes of this problem, and suggest some possible solutions.	**Answering : 이유와 해결책 간단히 언급** Dwindling resources and excessive consumption mean we are faced with blackouts and rising energy costs, but at least there are some solutions on the horizon.

Introduction
The threat of an energy shortage has become a critical issue for those of us who rely on it in our daily lives. Dwindling resources and excessive consumption mean we are faced with blackouts and rising energy costs, but at least there are some solutions on the horizon.

an energy shortage : 에너지 부족
critical : 심각한, 중대한
in our daily lives : 일상생활에서

dwindling : 점점 줄어드는
blackouts : 정전
on the horizon : 조짐이 보이는, 장래에 일어날 것 같은

우리말 해석
에너지 부족의 위협은 일상생활에서 그것에 의존하는 우리들에게는 심각한 문제가 되고 있다. 점점 줄어드는 자원과 과도한 소비는 우리가 정전과 에너지 비용의 상승에 직면했다는 의미지만, 적어도 수면 위로 떠오르는 몇 가지 해결책이 있다.

 본론 1 (Body 1) (11~20분) : **Reasons** (에너지 부족의 이유들)

> **Question** We are faced with a severe energy shortage these days. Explain the main causes of this problem, and suggest some possible solutions.

Body 1은 1단계에서 브레인스토밍한 'Reasons'를 바탕으로 작성한다.

1단계	Topic Sentence	A major factor behind this escalating concern is the increasing scarcity of fossil fuels such as coal.
2단계 (1)	Supporting Sentence (1)	*forced up the cost of various energy products and utilities* This has forced up the cost of various energy products and utilities.
3단계 (1)	Supporting Sentence or Specific Example (1)	*some countries, this situation is worsened because they rely entirely on imports* For some countries this situation is worsened because they rely entirely on imports to meet their gas, oil and fuel needs.
2단계 (2)	Supporting Sentence (2)	*the speed at which energy is being consumed* Another aspect to consider is the speed at which energy is being consumed due to overpopulation and urbanisation.
3단계 (2)	Supporting Sentence or Specific Example (2)	*using more energy than ever before* Our planet is struggling to meet the demands of its people, who are using more energy than ever before, from the petrol needed to fuel our cars to the gas required to heat our homes.

Body 1

A major factor behind this escalating concern is the increasing scarcity of fossil fuels such as coal. This has forced up the cost of various energy products and utilities. For some countries this situation is worsened because they rely entirely on imports to meet their gas, oil and fuel needs. Another aspect to consider is the speed at which energy is being consumed due to overpopulation and urbanisation. Our planet is struggling to meet the demands of its people, who are using more energy than ever before, from the petrol needed to fuel our cars to the gas required to heat our homes.

behind : 뒤에
utilities : 공공요금(가스·전기·수도 등의 사용 요금)
worsen : 악화시키다
meet a need(demand) : 수요를 맞추다
struggle to : 고군분투하다, 애쓰다

> **우리말 해석**
> 이 가속화 되고 있는 우려의 배후의 주요 원인은 석탄과 같은 화석 연료의 증가하는 부족(현상)이다. 이것은 다양한 에너지 제품과 공공요금의 비용을 상승시켰다. 일부 국가들에서는 이런 상황이 더욱 악화되고 있는데 가스, 석유, 석탄의 수요를 충족시키기 위해 전적으로 수입에 의존하기 때문이다. 고려해볼 또 다른 측면은 인구과잉과 도시화로 인해 에너지가 소비되는 속도이다. 우리 지구는, 우리의 차에 공급할 기름부터 집을 난방하는 데 필요한 가스까지, 전보다 더 많은 에너지를 사용하고 있는 사람들의 수요를 충족시키기 위해 고군분투하고 있다.

 **본론 2 (Body 2) (21~30분) : Solutions** (에너지 부족의 해결책들)

> **Question** We are faced with a severe energy shortage these days. Explain the main causes of this problem, and suggest some possible solutions.

Body 2는 1단계에서 브레인스토밍한 'Solutions'를 바탕으로 작성한다.

1단계	Topic Sentence	The most immediate solution is to reduce consumption.
2단계 (1)	Supporting Sentence (1)	*urging people to limit electricity use* Many governments do issue warnings during the peak seasons of summer and winter urging people to limit electricity use.
3단계 (1)	Supporting Sentence or Specific Example (1)	*campaigns to educate people on how to be efficient and save energy* Such alerts can also serve as an opportunity to carry out campaigns to educate people on how to be efficient and save energy in their homes and business operations.
2단계 (2)	Supporting Sentence (2)	*alternative energy sources* But many experts would say that we need a drastic shift to alternative energy sources if we are to avoid continued shortages.
3단계 (2)	Supporting Sentence or Specific Example (2)	*nuclear power is the most realistic answer* As yet nuclear power is the most realistic answer because it is readily available to those with the relevant technology, and despite security and radiation worries it is more effective than other abundant options like solar and wind power.

Body 2

The most immediate solution is to reduce consumption. Many governments do issue warnings during the peak seasons of summer and winter urging people to limit electricity use. Such alerts can also serve as an opportunity to carry out campaigns to educate people on how to be efficient and save energy in their homes and business operations. But many experts would say that we need a drastic shift to alternative energy sources if we are to avoid continued shortages. As yet nuclear power is the most realistic answer because it is readily available to those with the relevant technology, and despite security and radiation worries it is more effective than other abundant options like solar and wind power.

immediate : 즉각적인
issue warnings : 주의보를 발령하다, 경고하다
urge A to B : A에게 B하도록 촉구하다
carry out campaigns : 캠페인을 벌이다
business operations : 사업장
drastic : 과감한
as yet : 아직까지
nuclear power : 원자력
readily available : 손쉽게 이용할 수 있는
despite : ~에도 불구하고
radiation : 방사능
abundant : 풍부한

> **우리말 해석**
> 가장 즉각적인 해결책은 소비를 줄이는 것이다. 많은 정부들은 여름과 겨울의 (전력) 성수기에 국민들에게 전력 사용을 제한하도록 권고하는 주의보를 발령한다. 그러한 주의보는 또한 가정과 사업장에서 효율적으로 에너지를 절약하는 방법을 사람들에게 교육할 캠페인을 벌일 수 있는 기회를 제공할 수 있다. 그러나 많은 전문가들은 우리가 계속되는 부족을 피하려면 대체 에너지 자원으로의 과감한 전환이 필요하다고 말할 것이다. 아직까지는 원자력이 가장 현실적인 답인데 그것과 관련된 기술을 손쉽게 이용할 수 있고, 안전성과 방사능에 대한 걱정에도 불구하고 태양력과 풍력 같은 다른 무수한 선택들보다 더 효과적이기 때문이다.

 **5 단계** 결론 (Conclusion) (31~35분) : 본문에 제시한 내 주장 요약하며 다시 한 번 강조

> **Question** We are faced with a severe energy shortage these days. Explain the main causes of this problem, and suggest some possible solutions.

결론 작성 시, 먼저 문제 유형을 파악한 후, 'Conclusion Template'의 표현을 인용한다. (See p58)

문제 유형 파악	3-1) Reasons and Solutions
Conclusion Template 인용	In conclusion, it is clear that there are various reasons for…(토픽), steps are needed to tackle this phenomenon.

3-1 유형의 결론을 작성할 때 이유와 해결책을 구체적으로 작성하게 되면 자칫 결론이 너무 길어질 수 있기 때문에 포괄적으로 작성한다.

> **Conclusion**
> **In conclusion, it is clear that there are various reasons for** the current severe energy shortage, and we need to carefully consider how we source energy as well as how we lead our own lifestyles to **tackle this phenomenon**.

* 상황에 따라 템플릿을 살짝 변형해도 좋다.

source energy : 에너지를 공급받다

> **우리말 해석**
> 결론적으로 현재의 심각한 에너지 부족에는 다양한 이유가 있는 것이 분명하고, 우리는 이러한 현상을 막기 위해 우리 자신들의 생활방식을 이끌 방법뿐만 아니라 우리가 에너지를 공급받을 방법도 주의 깊게 고려해야 할 필요가 있다.

6 단계 교정 (Self-correction) (36~40분) : 내용의 일관성 및 문법 검토

다음 Body 2의 내용을 교정해 보자. 틀린 부분은 총 몇 개일까?

교정 전 (직접 문장 부호를 이용하여 틀린 부분을 교정해 보자.)

---

the most immediate solution is to reduce consumption. Many government do issue warnings during the peak seasons of summer and winter urging people to limit electricity use.

Such alerts can also serve as a opportunity to carry out campaigns to educate people on how to be efficient and save energy in their homes and business operations. But many expert would say that we needs a drastic shift to alternative energy sources if we are to avoid continued shortages. As yet nuclear power is a most realistic answer because of it is readily available to those with the relevant technology, and despite of security and radiation worries it is more effective then other abundant options like solar and wind power.

교정

the most immediate solution is to reduce consumption. Many government do issue warnings during the peak seasons of summer and winter urging people to limit electricity use.

Such alerts can also serve as a opportunity to carry out campaigns to educate people on how to be efficient and save energy in their homes and business operations. But many expert would say that we needs a drastic shift to alternative energy sources if we are to avoid continued shortages. As yet nuclear power is a most realistic answer because of it is readily available to those with the relevant technology, and despite of security and radiation worries it is more effective then other abundant options like solar and wind power.

1. t → T : 문장의 첫 글자는 반드시 대문자로 시작한다.
2. government → governments : many + 복수 명사
3. 붙여쓰기 : 위의 글은 Body 2 단락이다. 단락이 바뀌지 않는 한, 줄을 바꿔 쓰지 않는다.
4. a → an : 모음(a/i/u/e/o)으로 발음이 시작되는 단어 opportunity [àpərtjúːnəti] 앞에는 a가 아닌 an으로 쓰고 말한다.
5. expert → experts : many + 복수 명사
6. needs → need : 주어인 we가 복수이므로 복수 동사인 need를 쓴다.
7. a → the : 최상급을 의미하는 most 앞에는 the를 쓴다.
8. of → 삭제 : because 다음에는 주어+동사, because of 다음에는 명사(구)가 온다.
9. of → 삭제 : despite는 '~에도 불구하고'의 뜻, despite of라는 말은 없다.
10. then → than : then은 '그리고 나서', than은 비교급과 함께 사용하는 '~보다'라는 뜻

틀린 개수 : 총 10개

Sample Answer

Question: We are faced with a severe energy shortage these days. Explain the main causes of this problem, and suggest some possible solutions.

The threat of an energy shortage has become a critical issue for those of us who rely on it in our daily lives. Dwindling resources and excessive consumption mean we are faced with blackouts and rising energy costs, but at least there are some solutions on the horizon.

A major factor behind this escalating concern is the increasing scarcity of fossil fuels such as coal. This has forced up the cost of various energy products and utilities. For some countries this situation is worsened because they rely entirely on imports to meet their gas, oil and fuel needs. Another aspect to consider is the speed at which energy is being consumed due to overpopulation and urbanisation. Our planet is struggling to meet the demands of its people, who are using more energy than ever before, from the petrol needed to fuel our cars to the gas required to heat our homes.

The most immediate solution is to reduce consumption. Many governments do issue warnings during the peak seasons of summer and winter urging people to limit electricity use. Such alerts can also serve as an opportunity to carry out campaigns to educate people on how to be efficient and save energy in their homes and business operations. But many experts would say that we need a drastic shift to alternative energy sources if we are to avoid continued shortages. As yet nuclear power is the most realistic answer because it is readily available to those with the relevant technology, and despite security and radiation worries it is more effective than other abundant options like solar and wind power.

In conclusion, it is clear that there are various reasons for the current severe energy shortage, and we need to carefully consider how we source energy as well as how we lead our own lifestyles to tackle this phenomenon.

word counts : 307 words

우리말 해석

에너지 부족의 위협은 일상생활에서 그것에 의존하는 우리들에게는 심각한 문제가 되고 있다. 점점 줄어드는 자원과 과도한 소비는 우리가 정전과 에너지 비용의 상승에 직면했다는 의미지만, 적어도 수면 위로 떠오르는 몇 가지 해결책이 있다.

이 가속화 되고 있는 우려의 배후의 주요 원인은 석탄과 같은 화석 연료의 증가하는 부족(현상)이다. 이것은 다양한 에너지 제품과 공공요금의 비용을 상승시켰다. 일부 국가들에서는 이런 상황이 더욱 악화되고 있는데 가스, 석유, 석탄의 수요를 충족시키기 위해 전적으로 수입에 의존하기 때문이다. 고려해볼 또 다른 측면은 인구과잉과 도시화로 인해 에너지가 소비되는 속도이다. 우리 지구는, 우리의 차에 공급할 기름부터 집을 난방하는 데 필요한 가스까지, 전보다 더 많은 에너지를 사용하고 있는 사람들의 수요를 충족시키기 위해 고군분투하고 있다.

가장 즉각적인 해결책은 소비를 줄이는 것이다. 많은 정부들은 여름과 겨울의 (전력) 성수기에 국민들에게 전력 사용을 제한하도록 권고하는 주의보를 발령한다. 그러한 주의보는 또한 가정과 사업장에서 효율적으로 에너지를 절약하는 방법을 사람들에게 교육할 캠페인을 벌일 수 있는 기회를 제공할 수 있다. 그러나 많은 전문가들은 우리가 계속되는 부족을 피하려면 대체 에너지 자원으로의 과감한 전환이 필요하다고 말할 것이다. 아직까지는 원자력이 가장 현실적이 답인데 그것과 관련된 기술을 손쉽게 이용할 수 있고, 안전성과 방사능에 대한 걱정에도 불구하고 태양력과 풍력 같은 다른 무수한 선택들보다 더 효과적이기 때문이다.

결론적으로 현재의 심각한 에너지 부족에는 다양한 이유가 있는 것이 분명하고, 우리는 이러한 현상을 막기 위해 우리 자신들의 생활방식을 이끌 방법뿐만 아니라 우리가 에너지를 공급받을 방법도 주의 깊게 고려해야 할 필요가 있다.

불법 Review

앞에서 배운 내용을 바탕으로 다음 빈칸을 영어로 작성해 보자.

_____ (1. 에너지 부족의 위협) has become a critical issue for those of us who rely on it _____ (2. 일상생활에서). Dwindling resources and excessive consumption mean we are faced with blackouts and rising energy costs, but at least there are some solutions on the horizon.

A major factor behind this escalating concern is the increasing scarcity of fossil fuels such as coal. This has forced up the cost of various energy products and utilities. For some countries this situation is worsened because they rely entirely on imports to meet their gas, oil and fuel needs. Another aspect to consider is the speed at which energy is being consumed _____ (3. 인구과잉과 도시화로 인해). Our planet is struggling to meet the demands of its people, who are using more energy than ever before, from the petrol needed to fuel our cars to the gas required to heat our homes.

_____ (4. 가장 즉각적인 해결책) is to reduce consumption. Many governments do issue warnings during the peak seasons of summer and winter urging people to _____ (5. 전력 사용을 제한하다). Such alerts can also serve as an opportunity to carry out campaigns to educate people on how to be efficient and save energy in their homes and business operations. But many experts would say that we need a drastic shift to _____ (6. 대체 에너지 자원) if we are to avoid continued shortages. As yet _____ (7. 원자력) is the most realistic answer because it is readily available to those with the relevant technology, and _____ (8. 안전성과 방사능에 대한 걱정에도 불구하고) it is more effective than other abundant options like solar and wind power.

In conclusion, it is clear that there are various reasons for _____ (9. 현재의 심각한 에너지 부족), and we need to carefully consider how we source energy as well as how we lead our own lifestyles to tackle this phenomenon.

Answer 1. The threat of an energy shortage / 2. in our daily lives / 3. due to overpopulation and urbanisation
4. The most immediate solution / 5. limit electricity use / 6. alternative energy sources
7. nuclear power / 8. despite security and radiation worries / 9. the current severe energy shortage

Day 16 The Energy Crisis 불법 포인트 정리

과대 포장된 제품	over-packaged goods	심각한, 중대한	critical
버리다	throw away	일상생활에서	in our daily lives
분리하다	separate	점점 줄어드는	dwindling
3개의 R	the three R's	정전	blackouts
원자력 발전소	nuclear power stations	조짐이 보이는, 장래에 일어날 것 같은	on the horizon
지속 가능한	sustainable	뒤에	behind
전기, 전력	electricity	공공요금	utilities
화석 연료 발전소	fossil fuel power stations	악화시키다	worsen
반대자들	opponents	수요를 맞추다	meet a need(demand)
핵폐기물 처리	nuclear waste disposal	고군분투하다, 애쓰다	struggle to
방사능 물질	radioactive material	즉각적인	immediate
오염(물질)을 제거하다	decontaminate	주의보를 발령하다, 경고하다	issue warnings
무한한	endless	A에게 B하도록 촉구하다	urge A to B
고갈시키다, 다 써버리다	exhaust	캠페인을 벌이다	carry out campaigns
걱정하다	worry	사업장	business operations
핵반응	nuclear reactions	과감한	drastic
눈 깜짝할 순간	in a split second	아직까지	as yet
방사성 폐기물	radioactive waste	원자력	nuclear power
무해한	harmless	손쉽게 이용할 수 있는	readily available
수천 년이나 그 이상	thousands of years or even longer	~에도 불구하고	despite
노화된 기반 시설	aging infrastructure	방사능	radiation
심각한	severe	풍부한	abundant
에너지 부족	an energy shortage	에너지를 공급받다	source energy

Day 17 Economy & Business 경제와 산업

Question

A number of people are changing careers several times during their working lives. Why do people change careers? Is it a positive or negative development for society?

많은 사람들이 일을 하는 동안 직업을 여러 번 바꾸고 있다. 사람들은 왜 직업을 바꾸는가? 이것은 사회를 위한 긍정적인 발전인가? 또는 부정적인 발전인가?

 빈출 문제

1. We are surrounded by a lot of advertisements and it is unavoidable in everyday life. Some people say that advertising is positive in our lives while others insist it is negative. Discuss both views and give your own opinion.

2. The high sales of popular consumer goods reflect the power of advertising. However, the products are not the real needs of the buyer. To what extent do you agree or disagree with this opinion?

3. People in poor countries are happier than people in developed nations. Do you agree or disagree with this statement?

4. Increasing the amount of salaries is the only way to make employees work harder and to enhance the productivity. Do you agree or disagree with this statement?

1. 우리는 많은 광고에 둘러싸여 있고, 이러한 상황은 일상에서 피할 수 없다. 어떤 사람들은 광고가 생활에 긍정적이라고 말하는 반면, 이를 부정적이라고 주장하는 사람들도 있다. 양쪽의 견해를 논하고 당신의 주장을 제시하라.

2. 인기 있는 소비재의 높은 판매량은 광고의 힘을 보여준다. 하지만 소비자가 이런 제품들을 정말로 필요로 하는 것은 아니다. 당신은 이 의견에 얼마만큼 동의하는가? 또는 동의하지 않는가?

3. 후진국 사람들은 선진국 사람들보다 행복하다. 당신은 이 말에 동의하는가? 또는 동의하지 않는가?

4. 직원들을 더 열심히 일하게 만들고 생산성을 높이는 유일한 방법은 월급을 인상하는 것이다. 당신은 이 말에 동의하는가? 또는 동의하지 않는가?

STEP2 브레인스토밍

1) 돈은 직업을 결정할 때 중요한 고려사항이다.
   중요한 고려사항 : the key consideration

2) 어떤 사람들에게는 직장 내 인간 관계가 직업을 선택할 때 상당히 중요하다.
   인간 관계 : personal relationships

3) 좋은 관리자나 친절한 동료들과 일하는 것은 근로자들의 행복 수준과 전반적 삶의 질에 큰 차이를 만들 수 있다.
   동료들 : colleagues

4) 우리들 중 일부는 도움이 필요한 사람들을 위해 직업을 선택한다.
   도움이 필요한 사람들 : people in need

5) 비록 월급이 사람들의 직업 선택에 영향을 주지만, 나는 돈이 다른 동기요인들을 능가한다고 생각하지 않는다.
   동기요인들 : motivators

6) 회사들은 광고를 통해서 그들의 제품과 서비스에 대해 알린다.
   알리다 : inform

7) 광고는 아이들의 감성 지능을 향상시키는 데 도움을 주는 데 광고가 종종 재미있고, 예술적이며 시사하는 바가 많기 때문이다.
   감성 지능 : emotional intelligence / 시사하는 바가 많은 : thought-provoking

8) 아이들은 광고에 의해 쉽게 영향을 받을 수 있고, 그들은 부모를 조르면서 압력을 가하는 경향이 있다.
   조르다 : pester

9) 광고는 필요하지만 아이들을 보호하기 위해서 통제되는 것이 필요하다.
   통제하다 : control

10) 평균 행복 수준과 평균 소득 사이에는 믿을 수 없을 정도로 높은 상관관계가 있다.
    믿을 수 없을 정도로 : incredibly / 상관관계 : correlation

11) 선진국의 일반적인 생각은 아프리카에 사는 사람들은 가난하지만 행복하다 이다.
    일반적인 생각 : a common belief

12) 광고의 목적은 소비자들에게 언제 신제품이 이용 가능하게 되는지 알려주는 것이다.
    광고의 목적 : the purpose of advertising / 이용 가능하게 되다 : become available

13) 쇼핑객들은 광고가 필요하고 그들은 쇼핑하러 갈 때 좋은 결정을 내릴 수 있다.
    쇼핑객들 : shoppers / 쇼핑하러 가다 : go shopping

14) 비록 가격은 항상 변동하지만, 우리는 광고를 통해서 최신 가격이 무엇인지를 알 수 있다.

15) 사람들은 보통 일생 동안 7개의 직업을 가지고 이 수치는 증가하고 있다.

Answer

1) Money is the key consideration when deciding on a career.
2) For some people, personal relationships in a workplace are extremely important when choosing a job.
3) Working with a good manager or friendly colleagues can make a huge difference to workers' levels of happiness and general quality of life.
4) Some of us choose a career helping people in need.
5) Although salaries impact people's choice of profession, I do not think money outweighs other motivators.
6) Companies inform customers about their goods and services through advertisements.
7) Advertisements help to improve children's emotional intelligence because they are often funny, artistic or thought-provoking.
8) Children can be easily influenced by advertisements and they tend to put pressure on their parents by pestering them.
9) Advertising is necessary but it needs to be controlled to protect children.
10) There is an incredibly high correlation between average levels of happiness and average incomes.
11) A common belief in rich countries is that people in Africa are poor but happy.
12) The purpose of advertising is to tell consumers when new products become available.
13) Shoppers need advertising so they can make good decisions when they go shopping.
14) Although prices change all the time, we can see what the latest prices are through advertisements.
15) People normally have seven careers in their lifetime and the number is growing.

 실전문제

You should spend about 40 minutes on this task.
Write about the following topic :

> A number of people are changing careers several times during their working lives. Why do people change careers? Is it a positive or negative development for society?

Give reasons for your answer and include any relevant examples from your own knowledge or experience.

Write at least 250 words.

1 단계 문제 정독, 문제 유형 파악, 브레인스토밍 (0 ~ 5분)

Question	A number of people are changing careers several times during their working lives. Why do people change careers? Is it a positive or negative development for society?

문제 정독

많은 사람들이 일을 하는 동안 직업을 여러 번 바꾸고 있다. 사람들은 왜 직업을 바꾸는가? 이것은 사회를 위한 긍정적인 발전인가? 또는 부정적인 발전인가?

a number of : 많은
careers : 직업들

문제 유형 파악

3-1. Reasons and Solutions 유형과 2-1. Is it a positive or negative development?의 혼합 유형

* Body 1은 3-1 유형의 Body 1(이유들), Body 2는 2-1 유형의 Body 2(내 주장)에 맞춰 작성하고, 결론은 2-1 유형을 따른다.
** 저자가 분류한 기본 유형이 95%, 혼합 유형은 약 5% 내외로 출제된다. 혼합 유형이라고 해도 기본 유형의 변형이기 때문에 기본 유형을 잘 익히면 당황하지 않고 충분히 논리적으로 작성할 수 있다.

Brainstorming

Topic : 많은 사람들이 일을 하는 동안 직업을 여러 번 바꾸고 있다.	
Reasons : 사람들이 직업을 바꾸는 이유	Positive Development : 사회를 위한 긍정적인 발전
1. 현대의 불안감 a modern restlessness → 더 나은 월급과 향상된 삶의 질 추구 seeking a better salary and an improved quality of life 2. 더 많은 창의력을 표현하고 더 큰 성취감을 갈망 express more creativity and desire a greater sense of fulfilment → 일상에 지루함을 느낌 bored with our daily routines	1. 인간의 기본적 인권을 보장 guarantee people's fundamental human rights → 복지국가 건설의 필수 요소 the essential factor of building a welfare state 2. 사회는 폭넓고 다양한 기술을 쌓은 사람들에게서 이득을 취함 society benefits from people building a wide variety of skills → 경제 성장의 잠재력 the economic growth potential

* Body 2에는 '사회'를 위한 긍정적인 발전에 초점을 맞춘다. 내 의견과 다른 부정적 발전에 대해서까지 작성하면 자칫 분량이 너무 길어질 수 있기 때문에 내 의견만 제시한다.

2단계 서론 (Introduction) (6~10분) : 두 문장으로 작성

Question	A number of people are changing careers several times during their working lives. Why do people change careers? Is it a positive or negative development for society?

단계	Question	서론 작성
1단계 Paraphrasing	토픽 : A number of people are changing careers several times during their working lives.	Paraphrasing : In recent years many of us pursue a variety of career paths rather than sticking with just one industry.
2단계 Answering	질문 : Why do people change careers? Is it a positive or negative development for society?	Answering : 이유와 장점 간단히 언급 This development is generally positive because we all enjoy greater freedom and our society derives benefit from us as a result.

Introduction

In recent years many of us pursue a variety of career paths rather than sticking with just one industry. This development is generally positive because we all enjoy greater freedom and our society derives benefit from us as a result.

우리말 해석

요즘 우리들 중 다수는 오직 한 산업 분야를 고수하기 보다는 오히려 다양한 진로를 추구한다. 이러한 발달은 대체로 긍정적인데 우리 모두가 더 큰 자유를 만끽하고 결과적으로 우리 사회는 우리에게서 이득을 취하기 때문이다.

3 단계 본론 1 (Body 1) (11~20분) : Reasons (사람들이 직업을 바꾸는 이유)

> **Question**
>
> A number of people are changing careers several times during their working lives. Why do people change careers? Is it a positive or negative development for society?

Body 1은 1단계에서 브레인스토밍한 'Reasons'를 바탕으로 작성한다.

1단계	Topic Sentence	We often change careers several times in our lifetime due to a variety of reasons as follows.
2단계 (1)	Supporting Sentence (1)	*a modern restlessness* First of all, a modern restlessness that influences many aspects of our lives would be the first reason.
3단계 (1)	Supporting Sentence or Specific Example (1)	*seeking a better salary and an improved quality of life* This impatience drives some of us to be bolder in seeking a better salary and an improved quality of life.
2단계 (2)	Supporting Sentence (2)	*express more creativity and desire a greater sense of fulfilment* We also want to express more creativity and desire a greater sense of fulfilment by changing a job.
3단계 (2)	Supporting Sentence or Specific Example (2)	*bored with our daily routines* We are more likely to become bored with our daily routines.

Body 1

We often change careers several times in our lifetime due to a variety of reasons as follows. First of all, a modern restlessness that influences many aspects of our lives would be the first reason. This impatience drives some of us to be bolder in seeking a better salary and an improved quality of life. We also want to express more creativity and desire a greater sense of fulfilment by changing a job. We are more likely to become bored with our daily routines.

as follows : 다음과 같이
a modern restlessness : 현대의 불안감
impatience : 조바심, 조급함
drive A to B : A가 B 하도록 몰고 가다
bolder : 더 용감한
creativity : 창의력
a sense of fulfilment : 성취감
daily routines : 반복되는 일상

우리말 해석
우리는 종종 다음과 같은 다양한 이유들 때문에 일생 동안 여러 번 직업을 바꾼다. 우선, 우리 삶의 많은 측면에 영향을 주는 현대의 불안감이 첫 번째 이유이다. 이러한 조바심은 우리 중 일부를 더 나은 월급과 향상된 삶의 질을 얻기 위해 더욱 용감해지도록 만든다. 우리 중 일부는 또한 직업을 바꿈으로써 더 많은 창의력을 표현하길 원하고 더 큰 성취감을 갈망한다. 우리는 반복되는 일상에 지루함을 느끼게 될 가능성이 크다.

4 단계 본론 2 (Body 2) (21~30분) : 내 의견 = Positive (사회를 위한 긍정적인 발전)

> **Question** A number of people are changing careers several times during their working lives. Why do people change careers? Is it a positive or negative development for society?

Body 2는 1단계에서 브레인스토밍한 'Positive'를 바탕으로 작성한다.

1단계	Topic Sentence	I am in favour of people being able to change their career as many times as they wish.
2단계 (1)	Supporting Sentence (1)	*guarantee people's fundamental human rights* This is because that will guarantee people's fundamental human rights and then make the society much happier and healthier.
3단계 (1)	Supporting Sentence or Specific Example (1)	*the essential factor of building a welfare state* This social atmosphere is the essential factor of building a welfare state which everyone pursues.
2단계 (2)	Supporting Sentence (2)	*society benefits from people building a wide variety of skills* In addition, society benefits from people building a wide variety of skills in the career change process.
3단계 (2)	Supporting Sentence or Specific Example (2)	*the economic growth potential* The most important point is the economic growth potential because employees are more likely to be more productive in jobs they enjoy.

Body 2

I am in favour of people being able to change their career as many times as they wish. This is because that will guarantee people's fundamental human rights and then make the society much happier and healthier. This social atmosphere is the essential factor of building a welfare state which everyone pursues. In addition, society benefits from people building a wide variety of skills in the career change process. The most important point is the economic growth potential because employees are more likely to be more productive in jobs they enjoy.

in favour of : ~에 찬성하는, 호의적인
human rights : 인권
a welfare state : 복지 국가
career change : 이직
the economic growth potential : 경제 성장 잠재력
productive : 생산적인

> **우리말 해석**
> 나는 원하는 만큼 많이 직업을 바꿀 수 있는 사람들에 찬성한다. 이것은 인간의 기본적 인권을 보장하고 사회를 훨씬 더 행복하고 건강하게 만들 것이기 때문이다. 이러한 사회적 분위기는 우리가 추구하는 복지 국가 건설의 필수 요소이다. 게다가 사회는 이러한 이직 과정을 통해 폭넓고 다양한 기술을 쌓은 사람들에게서 이득을 취한다. 가장 중요한 점은 경제 성장의 잠재력인데, 근로자들이 자신들이 즐기는 일에서 보다 더 생산적일 가능성이 크기 때문이다.

5 단계 결론 (Conclusion) (31~35분) : 본문에 제시한 내 주장 요약하며 다시 한 번 강조

| Question | A number of people are changing careers several times during their working lives. Why do people change careers? Is it a positive or negative development for society? |

결론 작성 시, 먼저 문제 유형을 파악한 후, 'Conclusion Template'의 표현을 인용한다. (See p58)

문제 유형 파악	2-1) Is it a positive or negative development?
Conclusion Template 인용	For the reasons mentioned above, I would argue that the benefits(drawbacks) of… (토픽) outweigh its drawbacks(benefits) because… 본론에 제시한 장점(단점) 간략히 요약

결론을 작성하기 전, 서론과 본론 2에서 Positive, '사람들이 여러 번 직업을 바꾸는 것은 사회를 위한 긍정적인 발전이다.'이라고 했는지 다시 한 번 확인하자!

Conclusion

For the reasons mentioned above, I would argue that the benefits of a society in which people change careers several times **outweigh its drawbacks because** protecting human rights and encouraging economic growth are the basis of setting up a welfare state.

* 상황에 따라 템플릿을 살짝 변형해도 좋다.

the basis of : ~의 기본

우리말 해석
위에서 언급한 이러한 이유들 때문에 나는 사람들이 여러 번 직업을 바꾸는 사회의 장점이 그 단점을 능가한다고 주장하는데 인권을 보호하고 경제 성장을 장려하는 것이 복지 국가 설립의 기초이기 때문이다.

6 단계 교정 (Self-correction) (36~40분) : 내용의 일관성 및 문법 검토

다음 Body 2의 내용을 교정해 보자. 틀린 부분은 총 몇 개일까?

교정 전 (직접 문장 부호를 이용하여 틀린 부분을 교정해 보자.)

I am in favour to people being able to changing their career as many time as they wishs.

This is because that will guarantee people's fundamental human rights and then make the society much more happier and healthier. This social atmosphere is the essential factor of building a welfare state which everyone pursue.

In addition, Society benefits from people building a wide variety of skill in the career change process. The most important point is the economic growth potential because employees is more likely to be more productive in jobs they enjoys.

교정

> I am in favour ~~to~~ **of** people being able to ~~changing~~ **change** their career as many ~~time~~ **times** as they ~~wishs~~ **wish**.
>
> This is because that will guarantee people's fundamental human rights and then make the society much ~~more~~ happier and healthier. This social atmosphere is the essential factor of building a welfare state which everyone ~~pursue~~ **pursues**.
>
> In addition, ~~S~~**s**ociety benefits from people building a wide variety of ~~skill~~ **skills** in the career change process. The most important point is the economic growth potential because employees ~~is~~ **are** more likely to be more productive in jobs they ~~enjoys~~ **enjoy**.

1. to → of : in favour of는 '~에 찬성하는, 호의적인'의 뜻
2. changing → change : be able to + 동사 원형
3. time → times : many + 복수 명사
4. wishs → wish : 주어인 they가 복수이므로 복수 동사인 wish를 쓴다. 단수 주어가 나올 땐, wishes라고 쓴다.
5. more → 삭제 : happier가 happy의 비교급이므로 more를 붙여서는 안 된다.
6. pursue → pursues : 주어인 everyone이 단수이므로 단수 동사인 pursues를 쓴다.
7. 붙여쓰기 : 위의 글은 Body 2 단락이다. 단락이 바뀌지 않는 한, 줄을 바꿔 쓰지 않는다.
8. S → s : 콤마(,) 다음에는 소문자로 쓴다.
9. skill → skills : a variety of + 복수 명사
10. is → are : 주어인 employees가 복수이므로 복수 동사인 are를 쓴다.
11. enjoys → enjoy : 주어인 they가 복수이므로 복수 동사인 enjoy를 쓴다.

틀린 개수 : 총 11개

Sample Answer

> **Question**: A number of people are changing careers several times during their working lives. Why do people change careers? Is it a positive or negative development for society?

In recent years many of us pursue a variety of career paths rather than sticking with just one industry. This development is generally positive because we all enjoy greater freedom and our society derives benefit from us as a result.

We often change careers several times in our lifetime due to a variety of reasons as follows. First of all, a modern restlessness that influences many aspects of our lives would be the first reason. This impatience drives some of us to be bolder in seeking a better salary and an improved quality of life. We also want to express more creativity and desire a greater sense of fulfilment by changing a job. We are more likely to become bored with our daily routines.

I am in favour of people being able to change their career as many times as they wish. This is because that will guarantee people's fundamental human rights and then make the society much happier and healthier. This social atmosphere is the essential factor of building a welfare state which everyone pursues. In addition, society benefits from people building a wide variety of skills in the career change process. The most important point is the economic growth potential because employees are more likely to be more productive in jobs they enjoy.

For the reasons mentioned above, I would argue that the benefits of a society in which people change careers several times outweigh its drawbacks because protecting human rights and encouraging economic growth are the basis of setting up a welfare state.

word counts : 256 words

우리말 해석

요즘 우리들 중 다수는 오직 한 산업 분야를 고수하기 보다는 오히려 다양한 진로를 추구한다. 이러한 발달은 대체로 긍정적인데 우리 모두가 더 큰 자유를 만끽하고 결과적으로 우리 사회는 우리에게서 이득을 취하기 때문이다.

우리는 종종 다음과 같은 다양한 이유들 때문에 일생 동안 여러 번 직업을 바꾼다. 우선, 우리 삶의 많은 측면에 영향을 주는 현대의 불안감이 첫 번째 이유이다. 이러한 조바심은 우리 중 일부를 더 나은 월급과 향상된 삶의 질을 얻기 위해 더욱 용감해지도록 만든다. 우리 중 일부는 또한 직업을 바꿈으로써 더 많은 창의력을 표현하길 원하고 더 큰 성취감을 갈망한다. 우리는 반복되는 일상에 지루함을 느끼게 될 가능성이 크다.

나는 원하는 만큼 많이 직업을 바꿀 수 있는 사람들에 찬성한다. 이것은 인간의 기본적 인권을 보장하고 사회를 훨씬 더 행복하고 건강하게 만들 것이기 때문이다. 이러한 사회적 분위기는 우리가 추구하는 복지 국가 건설의 필수 요소이다. 게다가 사회는 이러한 이직 과정을 통해 폭넓고 다양한 기술을 쌓은 사람들에게서 이득을 취한다. 가장 중요한 점은 경제 성장의 잠재력인데, 근로자들이 자신들이 즐기는 일에서 보다 더 생산적일 가능성이 크기 때문이다.

위에서 언급한 이러한 이유들 때문에 나는 사람들이 여러 번 직업을 바꾸는 사회의 장점이 그 단점을 능가한다고 주장하는데 인권을 보호하고 경제 성장을 장려하는 것이 복지 국가 설립의 기초이기 때문이다.

불법 Review

앞에서 배운 내용을 바탕으로 다음 빈칸을 영어로 작성해 보자.

In recent years many of us pursue a variety of career paths rather than _____ (1. 고수하는 것) just one industry. This development is generally positive because we all _____ (2. 더 큰 자유를 만끽하다) and our society derives benefit from us as a result.

We often change careers several times in our lifetime due to a variety of reasons as follows. First of all, _____ (3. 현대의 불안감) that influences many aspects of our lives would be the first reason. This impatience drives some of us to be bolder in seeking a better salary and _____ (4. 향상된 삶의 질). We also want to express more creativity and desire _____ (5. 더 큰 성취감) by changing a job. We are more likely to become bored with our _____ (6. 반복되는 일상).

I am _____ (7. ~에 호의적인) people being able to change their career as many times as they wish. This is because that will guarantee people's _____ (8. 기본적 인권) and then make the society much happier and healthier. This social atmosphere is the essential factor of building a welfare state which everyone pursues. In addition, society benefits from people building a wide variety of skills in the career change process. The most important point is _____ (9. 경제 성장의 잠재력) because employees are more likely to be more productive in jobs they enjoy.

For the reasons mentioned above, I would argue that the benefits of a society in which people change careers several times outweigh its drawbacks because protecting human rights and encouraging economic growth are the basis of _____ (10. 복지 국가 설립).

Answer 1. sticking with / 2. enjoy greater freedom / 3. a modern restlessness / 4. an improved quality of life
5. a greater sense of fulfilment / 6. daily routines / 7. in favour of / 8. fundamental human rights
9. the economic growth potential / 10. setting up a welfare state

Day 17 Economy & Business 불법 포인트 정리

중요한 고려사항	the key consideration	많은	a number of
인간 관계	personal relationships	직업들	careers
동료들	colleagues	다음과 같이	as follows
도움이 필요한 사람들	people in need	현대의 불안감	a modern restlessness
동기요인들	motivators	조바심, 조급함	impatience
알리다	inform	A가 B 하도록 몰고 가다	drive A to B
감성지능	emotional intelligence	더 용감한	bolder
시사하는 바가 많은	thought-provoking	창의력	creativity
조르다	pester	성취감	a sense of fulfilment
통제하다	control	반복되는 일상	daily routines
믿을 수 없을 정도로	incredibly	~에 찬성하는, 호의적인	in favour of
상관관계	correlation	인권	human rights
일반적인 생각	a common belief	복지 국가	a welfare state
광고의 목적	the purpose of advertising	이직	career change
이용 가능하게 되다	become available	경제 성장 잠재력	the economic growth potential
쇼핑객들	shoppers	생산적인	productive
쇼핑하러 가다	go shopping	~의 기본	the basis of

Day 18 The Government & Law 정부와 법

Question

Many criminals re-offend after they have been released from prison. Why do some of them continue to commit crimes? What measures can be taken to tackle this problem?

많은 범죄자들이 교도소에서 풀려난 후 다시 범죄를 저지른다. 왜 그들 중 일부는 계속해서 범죄를 저지르는 것일까? 이러한 문제를 막기 위해 취할 수 있는 조치는 무엇인가?

 빈출 문제

1. Without capital punishment our lives are less secure and crimes increase continuously. Do you agree or disagree with this statement?

2. Some people say that long imprisonment of criminals is the only way to reduce crime rates. Others believe there should be alternative ways. Discuss both views and give your own opinion.

3. Some people say that there should be fixed punishments for each type of crime. Others argue that the circumstances and motivation of an individual crime should always be taken into account when deciding on the punishment. Discuss both views and give your own opinion.

4. Some people say that criminals should be sent to prison. Others insist that they should do something else as a punishment. Discuss both views and give your own opinion.

1. 사형제도가 없으면 우리의 삶은 덜 안전하고 범죄는 계속해서 증가할 것이다. 당신은 이 말에 동의하는가? 또는 동의하지 않는가?

2. 어떤 사람들은 범죄자들의 장기 징역이 범죄율을 낮출 수 있는 유일한 방법이라고 말한다. 반면 다른 대안이 있을 것이라고 믿는 사람들도 있다. 양쪽의 견해를 논하고 당신의 주장을 제시하라.

3. 어떤 사람들은 각 범죄의 유형에 정해진 형량이 있어야 한다고 말한다. 반면 처벌을 내릴 때 각 범죄의 상황과 동기를 항상 고려해야 한다고 주장하는 사람들도 있다. 양쪽의 견해를 논하고 당신의 주장을 제시하라.

4. 어떤 사람들은 범죄자들을 감옥으로 보내야 한다고 말한다. 반면 범죄자들이 처벌로써 다른 무언가를 해야 한다고 말하는 사람들도 있다. 양쪽의 견해를 논하고 당신의 주장을 제시하라.

 브레인스토밍

1) 정부는 기후 변화와 건강식 같은 이슈에 대한 사람들의 의식을 높일 수 있다.
   건강식 : healthy eating / 의식을 높이다 : raise awareness

2) 정부는 건강관리와 교육 같은 공공 서비스를 제공한다.
   건강관리 : healthcare / 공공 서비스 : public services

3) 경찰의 임무는 범죄자를 잡고 사회를 더욱 안전하게 만드는 것이다.
   범죄자를 잡다 : catch criminals

4) 벌금은 경범죄를 위한 처벌로써 사용된다.
   벌금 : fines / 경범죄 : minor crimes

5) 어떤 범죄자들은 사회에 위협이 되기 때문에, 그들은 다른 시민들의 안전을 보장하기 위해 교도소에 수감되어야 한다.
   위협이 되다 : pose a threat / 보장하다 : ensure / 교도소에 수감되다 : be put in prison

6) 범죄 기록은 범죄자들이 직업을 구하기 더욱 어렵게 만든다.
   범죄 기록 : a criminal record

7) 재소자들은 감옥에서 직업 교육과 훈련을 받는다.
   재소자들 : prisoners / 직업 교육과 훈련 : vocational education and training

8) 어떤 사람들은 사형이 범죄를 막을 유일한 방법이라고 말한다.
   사형 : capital punishment

9) 나는 사형제도에 반대하는데 무고한 사람들이 부당하게 유죄를 선고받거나 처형될 수 있기 때문이다.
   무고한 사람들 : innocent people / 부당하게 : wrongly / 유죄를 선고하다 : convict / 처형하다 : execute

10) 재소자들을 처형하는 것은 폭력적인 문화를 만들고 보복을 조장한다.
    보복, 복수 : revenge

11) 우리는 다른 사람의 목숨을 빼앗을 권리가 없다.
    다른 사람의 목숨을 빼앗다 : take another human life

12) 지역 봉사 활동은 수감에 드는 비용을 피하는 데 사용될 수 있다.
    지역 봉사 활동 : community service / 수감 : imprisonment

13) 지역 봉사 활동의 장점 중의 하나는 교도소의 과밀에 대한 해결책이 될 수 있다는 것이다.

14) 어떤 수감자들은 미니 냉장고, 평면 스크린 티비 그리고 개인 욕실까지 갖춰진 독방에서 지낸다.
    수감자들 : inmates / 독방 : a private cell

15) 노르웨이의 수감 제도는 인간의 기본권과 존경에 초점을 맞춘다.

노르웨이의 : Norwegian

Answer

1) Governments can raise people's awareness of issues such as climate change and healthy eating.
2) Governments provide public services like healthcare and education.
3) The job of the police is to catch criminals and make communities safer.
4) Fines are used as punishment for minor crimes.
5) As some criminals pose a threat to society, they should be put in prison to ensure the safety of other citizens.
6) A criminal record makes finding a job more difficult for criminals.
7) Prisoners receive vocational education and training in prison.
8) Some people say that capital punishment is the only way to deter crime.
9) I am against capital punishment because innocent people could be wrongly convicted and executed.
10) Executing prisoners creates a violent culture and encourages revenge.
11) We have no right to take another human life.
12) Community service can be used to avoid the cost of imprisonment.
13) One of the advantages of community service is that it could be a solution to prison overcrowding.
14) Some inmates stay in a private cell equipped with a mini fridge, a flat screen TV, and even a private bathroom.
15) The Norwegian prison system focuses on human rights and respect.

 실전문제

You should spend about 40 minutes on this task.
Write about the following topic :

> Many criminals re-offend after they have been released from prison. Why do some of them continue to commit crimes? What measures can be taken to tackle this problem?

Give reasons for your answer and include any relevant examples from your own knowledge or experience.

Write at least 250 words.

1 단계 문제 정독, 문제 유형 파악, 브레인스토밍 (0 ~ 5분)

Question	Many criminals re-offend after they have been released from prison. Why do some of them continue to commit crimes? What measures can be taken to tackle this problem?

문제 정독
많은 범죄자들이 교도소에서 풀려난 후 다시 범죄를 저지른다. 왜 그들 중 일부는 계속해서 범죄를 저지르는 것일까? 이러한 문제를 막기 위해 취할 수 있는 조치는 무엇인가?

re-offend : 다시 범죄를 저지르다
release : 풀어주다, 석방하다
commit crimes : 범죄를 저지르다

문제 유형 파악

3-1. Reasons and Solutions 유형

Brainstorming

Topic : 많은 범죄자들이 교도소에서 풀려난 후 다시 범죄를 저지른다.	
Reasons : 계속해서 범죄를 저지르는 이유들	Solutions : 이러한 문제를 막기 위한 조치들
1. 재정적으로 자립할 수 없음 cannot support themselves financially → 같은 이유로 다시 범죄를 저지름 re-offend for the same reason 2. 부적절한 갱생제도 the inadequate rehabilitation of prisoners → 나중에 더 심각한 범죄에 가담하도록 조장 encouraged to participate in more serious crimes later	1. 정부는 갱생에 더 많은 투자를 할 필요가 있음 authorities need to invest more in rehabilitation → 재소자들은 새로운 기술을 배워야 함 prison inmates should be learning new skills 2. 취약한 범죄자들은 지원받을 필요가 있음 vulnerable criminals need to be supported → 편안한 생활을 즐기면 재범을 저지를 가능성 훨씬 낮음 far less likely to re-offend if they enjoy a comfortable lifestyle 3. 판사들은 더 관대한 선고를 고려해야 함 judges should consider more lenient sentences → 교도소 환경 이외의 곳에서 갱생을 더욱 잘할지도 모름 might achieve more from rehabilitation outside of a prison environment

* 이유와 해결책을 각각 연관성 있게 작성한다.

2단계 서론 (Introduction) (6~10분) : 두 문장으로 작성

Question	Many criminals re-offend after they have been released from prison. Why do some of them continue to commit crimes? What measures can be taken to tackle this problem?

단계	Question	서론 작성
1단계 Paraphrasing	**토픽 :** Many criminals re-offend after they have been released from prison.	**Paraphrasing :** The question of how to effectively rehabilitate criminals so that they do not continue to break the law has been a long-standing issue for justice systems around the world.
2단계 Answering	**질문 :** Why do some of them continue to commit crimes? What measures can be taken to tackle this problem?	**Answering : 이유와 해결책 간단히 언급** Understanding the reasons why some former convicts re-offend is vital to solving the problem.

Introduction

The question of how to effectively rehabilitate criminals so that they do not continue to break the law has been a long-standing issue for justice systems around the world. Understanding the reasons why some former convicts re-offend is vital to solving the problem.

rehabilitate : 갱생 치료를 하다, 사회 복귀를 돕다
break the law : 법률을 위반하다
a long-standing issue : 오래 지속된 논란거리
justice systems : 사법 제도
convicts : 재소자

우리말 해석
어떻게 효율적으로 범죄자들의 사회 복귀를 도와서 그 결과 그들이 법을 위반하는 것을 지속할 수 없게 하느냐의 문제는 전세계 사법 제도의 오래 지속된 논란거리였다. 왜 몇몇 기존의 재소자들이 다시 범죄를 저지르는지 그 이유를 이해하는 것이 이 문제를 푸는 데 중요하다.

3단계 　 본론 1 (Body 1) (11~20분) : Reasons (계속해서 범죄를 저지르는 이유들)

> **Question** Many criminals re-offend after they have been released from prison. Why do some of them continue to commit crimes? What measures can be taken to tackle this problem?

Body 1은 1단계에서 브레인스토밍한 'Reasons'를 바탕으로 작성한다.

1단계	Topic Sentence	Multiple factors explain why individuals break the law repeatedly.
2단계 (1)	Supporting Sentence (1)	*cannot support themselves financially* Some people commit crimes out of desperation because they cannot support themselves financially.
3단계 (1)	Supporting Sentence or Specific Example (1)	*re-offend for the same reason* If they return to poverty after prison, then they might re-offend for the same reason.
2단계 (2)	Supporting Sentence (2)	*the inadequate rehabilitation of prisoners* Another issue is the inadequate rehabilitation of prisoners.
3단계 (2)	Supporting Sentence or Specific Example (2)	*encouraged to participate in more serious crimes later* A major problem in some countries is that minor criminals actually join gangs while in prison and are encouraged to participate in more serious crimes later.

Body 1

Multiple factors explain why individuals break the law repeatedly. Some people commit crimes out of desperation because they cannot support themselves financially. If they return to poverty after prison, then they might re-offend for the same reason. Another issue is the inadequate rehabilitation of prisoners. A major problem in some countries is that minor criminals actually join gangs while in prison and are encouraged to participate in more serious crimes later.

repeatedly : 반복적으로
out of desperation : 자포자기로
rehabilitation : 갱생 제도
minor criminals : 경범죄자들

우리말 해석

복합적인 요인들이 왜 개인이 반복적으로 법을 어기는지를 설명한다. 어떤 사람들은 재정적으로 자립할 수가 없기 때문에 자포자기로 범죄를 저지른다. 만약 그들이 출소 후 가난으로 되돌아간다면, 그리고 나서 그들은 같은 이유로 다시 범죄를 저지르게 될지도 모른다. 또 다른 문제는 죄수들에 대한 부적절한 갱생 제도이다. 몇몇 국가에서의 가장 큰 문제가 경범죄자들이 감옥에 있는 동안 실제로 갱단에 가입하고 나중에 더 심각한 범죄에 가담하도록 조장된다는 것이다.

4단계 본론 2 (Body 2) (21~30분) : Solutions (이러한 문제를 막기 위한 조치들)

> **Question** Many criminals re-offend after they have been released from prison. Why do some of them continue to commit crimes? What measures can be taken to tackle this problem?

Body 2는 1단계에서 브레인스토밍한 'Solutions'를 바탕으로 작성한다.

1단계	Topic Sentence	Greater resources and attention are required to solve these issues.
2단계 (1)	Supporting Sentence (1)	*authorities need to invest more in rehabilitation* Firstly, authorities need to invest more in rehabilitation, so that prison is not just about punishment or revenge for victims of crime.
3단계 (1)	Supporting Sentence or Specific Example (1)	*prison inmates should be learning new skills* Instead of joining gangs or spending their days in boredom, prison inmates should be learning new skills and understanding the consequences of their crimes.
2단계 (2)	Supporting Sentence (2)	*vulnerable criminals need to be supported* Also, vulnerable criminals need to be supported through welfare systems.
3단계 (2)	Supporting Sentence or Specific Example (2)	*far less likely to re-offend if they enjoy a comfortable lifestyle* A former convict is far less likely to re-offend if they can enjoy a relatively comfortable lifestyle.
2단계 (3)	Supporting Sentence (3)	*judges should consider more lenient sentences* Moreover, judges should consider more lenient sentences when the benefits of incarceration appear to be limited.
3단계 (3)	Supporting Sentence or Specific Example (3)	*might achieve more from rehabilitation outside of a prison environment* Minor criminals with a history of juvenile delinquency, for example, might achieve more from rehabilitation outside of a prison environment.

Body 2

Greater resources and attention are required to solve these issues. Firstly, authorities need to invest more in rehabilitation, so that prison is not just about punishment or revenge for victims of crime. Instead of joining gangs or spending their days in boredom, prison inmates should be learning new skills and understanding the consequences of their crimes. Also, vulnerable criminals need to be supported through welfare systems. A former convict is far less likely to re-offend if they can enjoy a relatively comfortable lifestyle. Moreover, judges should consider more lenient sentences when the benefits of incarceration appear to be limited. Minor criminals with a history of juvenile delinquency, for example, might achieve more from rehabilitation outside of a prison environment.

punishment : 처벌
revenge for victims of crime : 범죄 피해자들을 향한 보복
boredom : 지루함
prison inmates : 재소자들
vulnerable : 취약한, 형편이 어려운

welfare systems : 복지 제도
judges : 판사들
lenient sentences : 관대한 선고, 형량
incarceration : 감금, 투옥
juvenile delinquency : 청소년 범죄

우리말 해석

더 큰 자원과 관심이 이러한 문제를 해결하기 위해 요구된다. 첫째 정부는 갱생에 더 많은 투자를 할 필요가 있는데, 그 결과 수감이 단지 처벌이나 범죄 피해자들을 향한 보복이 아니게 된다. 갱단에 가입하거나 감금 생활을 지루하게 보내는 대신 재소자들은 새로운 기술을 배우고 자신들이 저지른 범죄의 결과를 이해해야 한다. 또한, 취약한 범죄자들은 사회복지 제도를 통해 지원받을 필요가 있다. 전과자들은 상대적으로 편안한 생활을 즐길 수 있다면 재범을 저지를 가능성이 훨씬 낮다. 더욱이, 판사들은 감금의 이점이 한정적으로 보일 때, 더 관대한 선고를 고려해야 한다. 청소년 범죄 기록을 가진 경범죄자는 예를 들면 교도소 환경 이외의 곳에서 갱생을 더욱 잘할지도 모른다.

5 단계　결론 (Conclusion) (31~35분) : 본문에 제시한 내 주장 요약하며 다시 한 번 강조

Question	Many criminals re-offend after they have been released from prison. Why do some of them continue to commit crimes? What measures can be taken to tackle this problem?

결론 작성 시, 먼저 문제 유형을 파악한 후, 'Conclusion Template'의 표현을 인용한다. (See p58)

문제 유형 파악	3-1) Reasons and Solutions
Conclusion Template 인용	In conclusion, it is clear that there are various reasons for…(토픽), steps are needed to tackle this phenomenon.

3-1 유형의 결론을 작성할 때 문제와 해결책을 구체적으로 작성하게 되면 자칫 결론이 너무 길어질 수 있기 때문에 포괄적으로 작성한다.

Conclusion

In conclusion, it is clear that there are various reasons why criminals re-offend after they have been released from prison, and punishment alone is not sufficient to deter them.

* 상황에 따라 템플릿을 살짝 변형해도 좋다.

sufficient : 충분한

deter : 단념시키다

우리말 해석

결론적으로, 범죄자가 교도소에서 풀려났을 때 다시 범죄를 저지르는 데에는 다양한 이유가 있는 것이 분명하고 처벌 그 자체가 그들을 단념시키기에는 충분치 못하다.

6 단계 교정 (Self-correction) (36~40분) : 내용의 일관성 및 문법 검토

다음 Body 2의 내용을 교정해 보자. 틀린 부분은 총 몇 개일까?

교정 전 (직접 문장 부호를 이용하여 틀린 부분을 교정해 보자.)

More greater resources and attention are required to solve these issue. Firstly, authorities need to invest more in rehabilitation, so that prison is not just about punishment or revenge for victims of crime. Instead of join gangs or spending their days in boredom, prison inmates should be learning new skills and understanding the consequences of their crimes.

Also, Vulnerable criminals need to be supported through welfare systems. A former convict is far more likely to re-offend if they can enjoys a relatively comfortable lifestyle.

Moreover, judges should consider more lenient sentences when the benefits of incarceration appear to be limited. Minor criminals with a history of juvenile delinquency, for example, might achieve more from rehabilitation outside of a prison enviroment.

교정

~~More~~ greater [G] resources and attention are required to solve these ~~issue~~ [issues]. Firstly, authorities need to invest more in rehabilitation, so that prison is not just about punishment or revenge for victims of crime. Instead of ~~join~~ [joining] gangs or spending their days in boredom, prison inmates should be learning new skills and understanding the consequences of their crimes.

Also, ~~V~~[v]ulnerable criminals need to be supported through welfare systems. A former convict is far ~~more~~ [less] likely to re-offend if they can ~~enjoys~~ [enjoy] a relatively comfortable lifestyle.

Moreover, judges should consider more lenient sentences when the benefits of incarceration appear to be limited. Minor criminals with a history of juvenile delinquency, for example, might achieve more from rehabilitation outside of a prison ~~enviroment~~ [environment].

1. More → 삭제 : greater가 great의 비교급이므로 more를 붙여서는 안 된다.
2. g → G : More를 삭제한 후 greater은 Greater로 G를 대문자로 바꾼다.
3. issue → issues : these + 복수 명사
4. join → joining : 전치사 of 다음에는 (동)명사를 쓴다.
5. 붙여쓰기 : 위의 글은 Body 2 단락이다. 단락이 바뀌지 않는 한, 줄을 바꿔 쓰지 않는다.
6. V → v : 콤마(,) 다음에는 소문자로 쓴다.
7. more → less : 재범을 저지를 가능성이 훨씬 '낮다'라고 해야 논리에 맞다. 이걸 놓치면 절대 안 된다!
8. enjoys → enjoy : 전치사 can 다음에는 동사 원형을 쓴다.
9. enviroment → environment : 상당히 많은 학생들이 실수하는 스펠링! n을 빠뜨리지 말자!

틀린 개수 : 총 9개

Sample Answer

Question	Many criminals re-offend after they have been released from prison. Why do some of them continue to commit crimes? What measures can be taken to tackle this problem?

The question of how to effectively rehabilitate criminals so that they do not continue to break the law has been a long-standing issue for justice systems around the world. Understanding the reasons why some former convicts re-offend is vital to solving the problem.

Multiple factors explain why individuals break the law repeatedly. Some people commit crimes out of desperation because they cannot support themselves financially. If they return to poverty after prison, then they might re-offend for the same reason. Another issue is the inadequate rehabilitation of prisoners. A major problem in some countries is that minor criminals actually join gangs while in prison and are encouraged to participate in more serious crimes later.

Greater resources and attention are required to solve these issues. Firstly, authorities need to invest more in rehabilitation, so that prison is not just about punishment or revenge for victims of crime. Instead of joining gangs or spending their days in boredom, prison inmates should be learning new skills and understanding the consequences of their crimes. Also, vulnerable criminals need to be supported through welfare systems. A former convict is far less likely to re-offend if they can enjoy a relatively comfortable lifestyle. Moreover, judges should consider more lenient sentences when the benefits of incarceration appear to be limited. Minor criminals with a history of juvenile delinquency, for example, might achieve more from rehabilitation outside of a prison environment.

In conclusion, it is clear that there are various reasons why criminals re-offend after they have been released from prison, and punishment alone is not sufficient to deter them.

word counts : 262 words

우리말 해석

어떻게 효율적으로 범죄자들의 사회 복귀를 도와서 그 결과 그들이 법을 위반하는 것을 지속할 수 없게 하느냐의 문제는 전세계 사법 제도의 오래 지속된 논란거리였다. 왜 몇몇 기존의 재소자들이 다시 범죄를 저지르는지 그 이유를 이해하는 것이 이 문제를 푸는 데 중요하다.

복합적인 요인들이 왜 개인이 반복적으로 법을 어기는지를 설명한다. 어떤 사람들은 재정적으로 자립할 수가 없기 때문에 자포자기로 범죄를 저지른다. 만약 그들이 출소 후 가난으로 되돌아간다면, 그리고 나서 그들은 같은 이유로 다시 범죄를 저지르게 될지도 모른다. 또 다른 문제는 죄수들에 대한 부적절한 갱생 제도이다. 몇몇 국가에서의 가장 큰 문제가 경범죄자들이 감옥에 있는 동안 실제로 갱단에 가입하고 나중에 더 심각한 범죄에 가담하도록 조장된다는 것이다.

더 큰 자원과 관심이 이러한 문제를 해결하기 위해 요구된다. 첫째 정부는 갱생에 더 많은 투자를 할 필요가 있는데, 그 결과 수감이 단지 처벌이나 범죄 피해자들을 향한 보복이 아니게 된다. 갱단에 가입하거나 감금 생활을 지루하게 보내는 대신 재소자들은 새로운 기술을 배우고 자신들이 저지른 범죄의 결과를 이해해야 한다. 또한, 취약한 범죄자들은 사회복지 제도를 통해 지원받을 필요가 있다. 전과자들은 상대적으로 편안한 생활을 즐길 수 있다면 재범을 저지를 가능성이 훨씬 낮다. 더욱이, 판사들은 감금의 이점이 한정적으로 보일 때, 더 관대한 선고를 고려해야 한다. 청소년 범죄 기록을 가진 경범죄자는 예를 들면 교도소 환경 이외의 곳에서 갱생을 더욱 잘할지도 모른다.

결론적으로, 범죄자가 교도소에서 풀려났을 때 다시 범죄를 저지르는 데에는 다양한 이유가 있는 것이 분명하고 처벌 그 자체가 그들을 단념시키기에는 충분치 못하다.

불법 Review

앞에서 배운 내용을 바탕으로 다음 빈칸을 영어로 작성해 보자.

The question of how to effectively rehabilitate criminals so that they do not continue to _____ (1. 법을 위반하다) has been _____ (2. 오래 지속된 논란거리) for justice systems around the world. Understanding the reasons why some former convicts re-offend is vital to solving the problem.

Multiple factors explain why individuals break the law repeatedly. Some people commit crimes _____ (3. 자포자기로) because they cannot support themselves financially. If they return to poverty after prison, then they might re-offend for the same reason. Another issue is _____ (4. 죄수들에 대한 부적절한 갱생 제도). A major problem in some countries is that _____ (5. 경범죄자들) actually join gangs while in prison and are encouraged to participate in more serious crimes later.

Greater resources and attention are required to solve these issues. Firstly, authorities need to invest more in rehabilitation, so that prison is not just about _____ (6. 처벌) or revenge for victims of crime. Instead of joining gangs or spending their days in boredom, prison inmates should be learning new skills and understanding the consequences of their crimes. Also, vulnerable criminals need to be supported _____ (7. 복지 제도를 통해서). A former convict is far less likely to re-offend if they can enjoy a relatively comfortable lifestyle. Moreover, judges should consider more _____ (8. 관대한 선고) when the benefits of incarceration appear to be limited. Minor criminals with a history of _____ (9. 청소년 범죄), for example, might achieve more from rehabilitation outside of a prison environment.

In conclusion, it is clear that there are various reasons why criminals re-offend after they have been released from prison, and punishment alone is not sufficient to _____ (10. 단념시키다) them.

Answer 1. break the law / 2. a long-standing issue / 3. out of desperation
4. the inadequate rehabilitation of prisoners / 5. minor criminals / 6. punishment
7. through welfare systems / 8. lenient sentences / 9. juvenile delinquency / 10. deter

Day 18 The Government & Law 불법 포인트 정리

건강식	healthy eating	다시 범죄를 저지르다	re-offend
의식을 높이다	raise awareness	풀어주다, 석방하다	release
건강관리	healthcare	범죄를 저지르다	commit crimes
공공 서비스	public services	갱생 치료를 하다, 사회 복귀를 돕다	rehabilitate
범죄자를 잡다	catch criminals	법률을 위반하다	break the law
벌금	fines	오래 지속된 논란거리	a long-standing issue
경범죄	minor crimes	사법 제도	justice systems
위협이 되다	pose a threat	재소자	convicts
보장하다	ensure	반복적으로	repeatedly
교도소에 수감되다	be put in prison	자포자기로	out of desperation
범죄 기록	a criminal record	갱생 제도	rehabilitation
재소자들	prisoners	경범죄자들	minor criminals
직업 교육과 훈련	vocational education and training	처벌	punishment
사형	capital punishment	범죄 피해자들을 향한 보복	revenge for victims of crime
무고한 사람들	innocent people	지루함	boredom
부당하게	wrongly	재소자들	prison inmates
유죄를 선고하다	convict	취약한, 형편이 어려운	vulnerable
처형하다	execute	복지 제도	welfare systems
보복, 복수	revenge	판사들	judges
다른 사람의 목숨을 빼앗다	take another human life	관대한 선고, 형량	lenient sentences
지역 봉사 활동	community service	감금, 투옥	incarceration
수감	imprisonment	청소년 범죄	juvenile delinquency
수감자들	inmates	충분한	sufficient
독방	a private cell	단념시키다	deter
노르웨이의	Norwegian		

Day 19 Mass Media, 대중매체, 영화와 연극
Movie & Play

Question

News editors decide what to broadcast on television and what to print in newspapers. What factors influence their decisions? Should they select more good news than bad news?

뉴스 편집장은 TV에 무엇을 방영할 것인지, 신문에 무엇을 기재할 것인지를 결정한다. 어떤 요소들이 그들의 결정에 영향을 미치는가? 그들은 좋은 뉴스를 나쁜 뉴스보다 더 많이 선정해야 하는가?

 빈출 문제

1. A detailed description of a crime will impact the general public and cause a number of social problems. Some people argue that the media should be strictly controlled. To what extent do you agree or disagree with this view?

2. The government should control the scenes of violence and pornography in films and on television in order to prevent youth crime. Do you agree or disagree with this statement?

3. Some people say that television programs are of no value for children. To what extent do you agree or disagree with this view?

4. Some people say that the privacy of celebrities should be protected. Others believe that an invasion of their private lives is the price of their fame. Discuss both views and give your own opinion.

1. 범죄에 대한 자세한 설명은 일반 대중에게 영향을 미칠 것이고 많은 사회적 문제들의 원인이 될 것이다. 어떤 사람들은 미디어가 반드시 엄격하게 통제되어야 한다고 주장한다. 당신은 이 의견에 얼마만큼 동의하는가? 또는 동의하지 않는가?

2. 정부는 청소년 범죄를 예방하기 위해서 영화와 TV의 폭력적이고 선정적인 장면들을 통제해야 한다. 당신은 이 말에 동의하는가? 또는 동의하지 않는가?

3. 어떤 사람들은 TV 프로그램이 아이들에게 가치가 없다고 말한다. 당신은 이 의견에 얼마만큼 동의하는가? 또는 동의하지 않는가?

4. 어떤 사람들은 유명인사들의 사생활을 보호해야 한다고 말한다. 반면 그들이 사생활을 침해받는 것이 명성에 대한 대가라고 주장하는 사람들도 있다. 양쪽의 견해를 논하고 당신의 주장을 제시하라.

 브레인스토밍

1) 범죄는 대부분의 뉴스 프로그램의 가장 중요한 주제들 중의 하나다.
   가장 중요한 주제들 : the main subjects

2) 대중 매체는 더 많은 시청자와 독자를 끌기 위해 폭력적이고 선정적인 기사에 초점을 맞춘다.
   대중 매체 : mass media / 폭력적이고 선정적인 : violent and sensational

3) 대중 매체는 그들의 시청자를 늘리기 위해 범죄 기사를 보도하지만 이것은 대중들 사이에 범죄에 대한 공포를 초래한다.
   범죄에 대한 공포 : fear of crime

4) 우리는 티비에 나오는 폭력적인 장면들로부터 아이들을 보호하기 위해 검열해야 한다.
   검열하다 : censor

5) 인터넷은 통제될 필요가 있는데 몇몇 컴퓨터 게임들은 사람들을 죽이고 범죄를 저지르는 것을 포함하고 있기 때문이다.

6) 웹사이트나 컴퓨터 게임뿐만 아니라 티비 프로그램에도 나이 제한이 있어야 한다.
   나이 제한 : age limits

7) 부모는 그들의 아이들이 티비와 인터넷에서 무엇을 보는지 확인하는 책임을 져야 한다.
   책임지다 : take responsibility for

8) CCTV 카메라는 우리를 보호하고 범죄자들을 단념시키기 위해 많은 공공 장소에 설치되었다.
   공공 장소 : public places / 설치하다 : install

9) 티비를 보는 것은 직장에서 힘든 하루를 보낸 후 긴장을 풀고 쉬는, 많은 사람들의 가장 좋아하는 취미이다.
   긴장을 풀고 쉬다 : wind [wáind] down, 발음 주의!

10) CCTV의 사용은 확대되어가고 있고 어떤 사람들은 이러한 감시가 우리의 사생활을 침해한다고 주장한다.
   감시 : surveillance / ~의 사생활을 침해하다 : intrude upon one's privacy

11) 티비 프로그램들은 재미있고 즐거울 뿐만 아니라 유익하고 교육적이다.
   재미있고 즐거운 : entertaining and enjoyable / 유익하고 교육적인 : informative and educational

12) 어떤 전문가들은 티비에서의 폭력성과 현실 세계에서의 범죄율을 연관짓는다.
   현실 세계에서 : in the real world / A와 B를 연관짓다 : link A with B

13) 많은 유명인사들은 그들이 하는 일보다 그들의 화려한 생활 방식으로 잘 알려져 있다.
   유명인사들 : celebrities / 화려한 생활방식 : glamorous lifestyles / ~로 잘 알려지다 : be well known for

14) 몇몇 유명 연예인들은 아이들에게 긍정적인 역할 모델로써 행동한다.
유명 연예인들 : famous entertainers / 긍정적인 역할 모델 : positive role models

15) 우리의 삶에서 대중 매체의 영향을 벗어나는 것은 더욱 어려워지고 있다.
벗어나다 : escape

Answer
1) Crime is one of the main subjects of most news programs.
2) Mass media focus on violent and sensational stories to attract more viewers or readers.
3) The media report crime stories in order to increase their audience but this leads to fear of crime among the public.
4) We should censor to protect children from violent images on TV.
5) The Internet needs to be controlled because some computer games involve killing people or committing crimes.
6) There should be age limits for TV programs as well as websites and computer games.
7) Parents should take responsibility for checking what their children watch on TV or the Internet.
8) Closed-circuit television (CCTV) cameras have been installed in many public places to protect us and deter criminals.
9) Watching television is many people's favourite hobby to wind down after a hard day at work.
10) The use of CCTV is becoming widespread and some people argue that this surveillance intrudes upon our privacy.
11) Television programs are not only entertaining and enjoyable but also informative and educational.
12) Some experts link violence on television with crime rates in the real world.
13) A lot of celebrities are well known for their glamorous lifestyles rather than for the work they do.
14) Some famous entertainers act as positive role models for children.
15) It is becoming more difficult to escape the influence of the media on our lives.

실전문제

You should spend about 40 minutes on this task.
Write about the following topic :

> News editors decide what to broadcast on television and what to print in newspapers. What factors influence their decisions? Should they select more good news than bad news?

Give reasons for your answer and include any relevant examples from your own knowledge or experience.

Write at least 250 words.

1 단계 문제 정독, 문제 유형 파악, 브레인스토밍 (0 ~ 5분)

Question	News editors decide what to broadcast on television and what to print in newspapers. What factors influence their decisions? Should they select more good news than bad news?

문제 정독
뉴스 편집장은 TV에 무엇을 방영할 것인지, 신문에 무엇을 기재할 것인지를 결정한다. 어떤 요소들이 그들의 결정에 영향을 미치는가? 그들은 좋은 뉴스를 나쁜 뉴스보다 더 많이 선정해야 하는가?

news editors : 뉴스 편집장들
broadcast : 방송하다

문제 유형 파악

3-1. Reasons and Solutions 유형과 2-1. Is it a positive or negative development?의 혼합 유형

* 뉴스 선정에 영향을 주는 요소를 편집자들이 특정 뉴스를 선정하는 이유로 생각해도 좋다.
** Body 1은 3-1 유형의 Body 1(이유들), Body 2는 2-1 유형의 Body 2(내 주장)에 맞춰 작성하고, 결론은 2-1 유형을 따른다.
*** 저자가 분류한 기본 유형이 95%, 혼합 유형은 약 5% 내외로 출제된다. 혼합 유형이라고 해도 기본 유형의 변형이기 때문에 기본 유형을 잘 익히면 당황하지 않고 충분히 논리적으로 작성할 수 있다.

Brainstorming

Topic : 뉴스 편집장은 TV에 무엇을 방영할 것인지, 신문에 무엇을 기재할 것인지를 결정한다.	
Factors : 편집장의 결정에 영향을 미치는 요소들	Good news : 좋은 뉴스를 더 많이 선정해야 함
1. 더 많은 신문을 판매, 수요 창출 sell more newspapers, generate demand → 시선을 사로잡는 헤드라인 선정, 타블로이드 신문 choose attention-grabbing headlines, tabloid newspapers 2. 자신의 정치적 의견에 영향 받음 influenced by their own political opinions → 편파적인 언론으로 이끎 leads to biased journalism	1. 뉴스는 결코 진실을 왜곡해서는 안 됨 news should never distort the truth → 최근의 에볼라 공포 the recent Ebola scare 2. 사람들을 우울하게 만듦 make people feel depressed → 시청자들과 독자들에게 제공하는 가치로 이야기를 평가해야 함 should assess stories for the value they offer viewers and readers

* Body 2에는 '좋은 뉴스'를 선정해야 한다에 초점을 맞춘다. 내 의견과 다른 '나쁜 뉴스'를 선정해야 한다까지 작성하면 자칫 분량이 너무 길어질 수 있기 때문에 내 의견만 제시한다.

2 단계 서론 (Introduction) (6~10분) : 두 문장으로 작성

Question	News editors decide what to broadcast on television and what to print in newspapers. What factors influence their decisions? Should they select more good news than bad news?

단계	Question	서론 작성
1단계 Paraphrasing	토픽 : News editors decide what to broadcast on television and what to print in newspapers.	**Paraphrasing** : Nowadays there is growing skepticism about the media's role in delivering news because editors are often accused of highlighting negative stories in order to attract more attention.
2단계 Answering	질문 : What factors influence their decisions? Should they select more good news than bad news?	**Answering : Good news일 경우** Therefore, I would believe that they should deliver more good news for the public.

Introduction
Nowadays there is growing skepticism about the media's role in delivering news because editors are often accused of highlighting negative stories in order to attract more attention. Therefore, I would believe that they should deliver more good news for the public.

scepticism : 회의론
be accused of : ~로 비난받다

우리말 해석
요즘 뉴스를 전달하는 미디어의 역할에 대한 회의론이 커지고 있는데 편집자들이 더 많은 관심을 끌기 위해 부정적인 이야기를 강조해서 종종 비난받기 때문이다. 그러므로 나는 그들은 대중을 위해 좋은 뉴스를 더 많이 전달해야 한다고 생각한다.

3 단계　본론 1 (Body 1) (11~20분) : Factors (편집장의 결정에 영향을 미치는 요소들)

> **Question**　News editors decide what to broadcast on television and what to print in newspapers. What factors influence their decisions? Should they select more good news than bad news?

Body 1단계에서 브레인스토밍한 'Factors'를 바탕으로 작성한다.

1단계	Topic Sentence	A number of factors influence news editors when they are selecting stories.
2단계 (1)	Supporting Sentence (1)	*sell more newspapers, generate demand* Their ultimate goal is to attract a bigger audience and to sell more newspapers. After all, television stations and newspaper publishers need to generate demand just like in any other industry.
3단계 (1)	Supporting Sentence or Specific Example (1)	*choose attention-grabbing headlines, tabloid newspapers* As a result, editors often choose attention-grabbing headlines to stand out among their competitors. Tabloid newspapers are especially prone to covering sensational or bad news, which can seem more compelling than feel-good stories.
2단계 (2)	Supporting Sentence (2)	*influenced by their own political opinions* Some news editors may also be influenced by their own political opinions.
3단계 (2)	Supporting Sentence or Specific Example (2)	*leads to biased journalism* This leads to biased journalism, although it can still appeal to viewers and readers who share similar views.

Body 1

A number of factors influence news editors when they are selecting stories. Their ultimate goal is to attract a bigger audience and to sell more newspapers. After all, television stations and newspaper publishers need to generate demand just like in any other industry. As a result, editors often choose attention-grabbing headlines to stand out among their competitors. Tabloid newspapers are especially prone to covering sensational or bad news, which can seem more compelling than feel-good stories. Some news editors may also be influenced by their own political opinions. This leads to biased journalism, although it can still appeal to viewers and readers who share similar views.

generate demand : 수요를 창출하다
attention-grabbing : 시선을 사로잡는
stand out : 눈에 띄다, 두드러지다
competitors : 경쟁자들
be prone to : ~하기 쉽다, 경향이 있다
cover : 취재하다
sensational : 선정적인
compelling : (너무나 흥미로워서) 주목하지 않을 수 없는, 눈을 뗄 수 없는
biased : 편파적인, 치우친

우리말 해석

뉴스 편집자들이 이야기를 선정할 때 수많은 요인들이 그들에게 영향을 미친다. 그들의 궁극적인 목표는 더 많은 독자를 끌어들여 더 많은 신문을 판매하는 것이다. 결국, TV 방송국과 신문 발행인들은 여타 산업들과 마찬가지로 수요를 창출해야 할 필요가 있다. 그 결과 편집자들은 종종 그들의 경쟁자들 사이에서 눈에 띄기 위해 시선을 사로잡는 헤드라인을 선정한다. 타블로이드 신문은 특히 기분 좋은 이야기보다 좀 더 눈을 뗄 수 없는 선정적이거나 나쁜 소식을 취재하려는 경향이 있다. 일부 뉴스 편집자들은 또한 그들 자신의 정치적 의견에 영향을 받을지도 모른다. 이는 비록 비슷한 견해를 공유하는 시청자나 독자에게는 여전히 호소할 수 있지만, 편파적인 언론으로 이끈다.

 **본론 2 (Body 2) (21~30분) : 내 의견 = Good news** (좋은 뉴스를 더 많이 선정해야 함)

Question	News editors decide what to broadcast on television and what to print in newspapers. What factors influence their decisions? Should they select more good news than bad news?

Body 2는 1단계에서 브레인스토밍한 'Good news'를 바탕으로 작성한다.

1단계	Topic Sentence	While I agree that stories should be presented in as interesting a way as possible, editors should be fair and responsible. They have the opportunity to both shape public opinion and influence political decisions with serious consequences, including countries going to war.
2단계 (1)	Supporting Sentence (1)	*news should never distort the truth* News should never distort the truth or deliberately encourage public panic.
3단계 (1)	Supporting Sentence or Specific Example (1)	*the recent Ebola scare* The recent Ebola scare led to widespread fear about the virus in Korea, even though there was no justification for it.
2단계 (2)	Supporting Sentence (2)	*make people feel depressed* Also, negative news may have the potential to draw a lot of attention, but it can make people feel depressed.
3단계 (2)	Supporting Sentence or Specific Example (2)	*should assess stories for the value they offer viewers and readers* Editors should assess stories for the value they offer viewers and readers rather than simply for the interest they stir up.

Body 2

While I agree that stories should be presented in as interesting a way as possible, editors should be fair and responsible. They have the opportunity to both shape public opinion and influence political decisions with serious consequences, including countries going to war. News should never distort the truth or deliberately encourage public panic. The recent Ebola scare led to widespread fear about the virus in Korea, even though there was no justification for it. Also, negative news may have the potential to draw a lot of attention, but it can make people feel depressed. Editors should assess stories for the value they offer viewers and readers rather than simply for the interest they stir up.

as interesting a way as possible : 가능한 한 흥미로운 방식으로
shape public opinion : 여론을 형성하다
go to war : 전쟁에 나가다
distort : 왜곡하다
deliberately : 의도적으로, 고의적으로
panic = scare = fear : 공황, 공포
justification : 타당성
feel depressed : 우울함을 느끼다
stir up : 자극하다, 선동하다

우리말 해석

나는 이야기들이 가능한 한 흥미로운 방식으로 표현되어야 한다는 데 동의하지만 편집자들은 공정하고 책임감이 있어야 한다. 그들은 여론을 형성하는 기회와, 전쟁에 나가는 나라들을 포함해서 심각한 결과를 초래할 정치적 결정에 영향력을 끼칠 기회 두 가지를 모두 가지고 있다. 뉴스는 결코 진실을 왜곡하거나 대중을 의도적으로 공황상태에 빠뜨려서는 안 된다. 최근의 에볼라 공포는 그것에 대한 타당성 없이 한국에서 바이러스 공포로 널리 확산되었다. 또한 부정적인 뉴스는 많은 관심을 이끌어낼 잠재력이 있을지도 모르지만 사람들을 우울하게 만들 수 있다. 편집자들은 사람들을 자극하는 단순한 흥미거리보다 오히려 그들이 시청자들과 독자들에게 제공하는 가치로 이야기를 평가하여야 한다.

5 단계   결론 (Conclusion) (31~35분) : 본문에 제시한 내 주장 요약하며 다시 한 번 강조

| Question | News editors decide what to broadcast on television and what to print in newspapers. What factors influence their decisions? Should they select more good news than bad news? |

결론 작성 시, 먼저 문제 유형을 파악한 후, 'Conclusion Template'의 표현을 인용한다. (See p58)

문제 유형 파악	2-1) Is it a positive or negative development?
Conclusion Template 인용	For the reasons mentioned above, I would argue that the benefits(drawbacks) of… (토픽) outweigh its drawbacks(benefits) because… 본론에 제시한 장점(단점) 간략히 요약

결론을 작성하기 전, 서론과 본론 2에서 Good news, '좋은 뉴스를 더 많이 선정해야 한다.'라고 했는지 다시 한 번 확인하자!

> **Conclusion**
> **For the reasons mentioned above, I would argue that** news editors should focus on selecting positive stories because they should serve the public more than themselves or their organisations.

* 상황에 따라 템플릿을 살짝 변형해도 좋다.

serve the public : 대중을 위해 일하다

> **우리말 해석**
> 위에서 언급한 이유들 때문에, 나는 뉴스 편집자들은 긍정적인 이야기를 선택하는 데 초점을 맞춰야 한다고 생각하는데 그들은 자신이나 조직이 아닌 대중을 위해 일해야 하기 때문이다.

6 단계   교정 (Self-correction) (36~40분) : 내용의 일관성 및 문법 검토

다음 Body 2의 내용을 교정해 보자. 틀린 부분은 총 몇 개일까?

교정 전 (직접 문장 부호를 이용하여 틀린 부분을 교정해 보자.)

> While i agree that stories should be presented in as interesting a way in possible, editors should be fair and responsibility. They have the opportunity to both shape public opinion and influence political decisions with serious consequences, including countries going on war.
>
> News never should distort the truth or deliberately encourage public panic. The recent ebola scare led to widespread fear about the virus in korea, even though there was no justification for it. Also, negative news may have the potential to draw a lot of attention, but it can make people feeling depressed. Editors should assess stories for the value they offer viewers and readers rather than simply for the interest they stirs up.

교정

> While i agree that stories should be presented in as interesting a way in possible, editors should be fair and responsibility. They have the opportunity to both shape public opinion and influence political decisions with serious consequences, including countries going on war.
> News never should distort the truth or deliberately encourage public panic. The recent ebola scare led to widespread fear about the virus in korea, even though there was no justification for it. Also, negative news may have the potential to draw a lot of attention, but it can make people feeling depressed. Editors should assess stories for the value they offer viewers and readers rather than simply for the interest they stirs up.

교정 표시:
- i → I
- in → as
- responsibility → responsible
- on → to
- (붙여쓰기)
- never should → should never
- ebola → Ebola
- korea → Korea
- feeling → feel
- stirs → stir

1. i → I : 1인칭 주어 'I'는 언제 어디서나 대문자로 쓴다. 이 세상에서 가장 소중한 사람은 바로 나(I)이니까!
2. in → as : as ~ as possible은 '가능한 한'의 뜻
3. responsibility → responsible : be 동사 다음에 형용사를 쓴다. 또한 and 앞의 fair가 형용사인데 보통 품사가 같은 단어들을 and로 나열한다.
4. on → to : go to war는 '전쟁에 나가다'의 뜻
5. 붙여쓰기 : 위의 글은 Body 2 단락이다. 단락이 바뀌지 않는 한, 줄을 바꿔 쓰지 않는다.
6. never should → should never : 순서 주의! 빈도 부사 never는 조동사 다음에 온다.
7. ebola → Ebola : 전염병의 이름은 고유명사로 첫 글자를 대문자로 쓴다.
8. korea → Korea : 나라 이름은 고유명사로 첫 글자를 대문자로 쓴다.
9. feeling → feel : make + 목적어 + 동사원형
10. stirs → stir : 주어인 they가 복수이므로 복수 동사인 stir를 쓴다.

틀린 개수 : 총 10개

Sample Answer

> **Question**: News editors decide what to broadcast on television and what to print in newspapers. What factors influence their decisions? Should they select more good news than bad news?

Nowadays there is growing skepticism about the media's role in delivering news because editors are often accused of highlighting negative stories in order to attract more attention. Therefore, I would believe that they should deliver more good news for the public.

A number of factors influence news editors when they are selecting stories. Their ultimate goal is to attract a bigger audience and to sell more newspapers. After all, television stations and newspaper publishers need to generate demand just like in any other industry. As a result, editors often choose attention-grabbing headlines to stand out among their competitors. Tabloid newspapers are especially prone to covering sensational or bad news, which can seem more compelling than feel-good stories. Some news editors may also be influenced by their own political opinions. This leads to biased journalism, although it can still appeal to viewers and readers who share similar views.

While I agree that stories should be presented in as interesting a way as possible, editors should be fair and responsible. They have the opportunity to both shape public opinion and influence political decisions with serious consequences, including countries going to war. News should never distort the truth or deliberately encourage public panic. The recent Ebola scare led to widespread fear about the virus in Korea, even though there was no justification for it. Also, negative news may have the potential to draw a lot of attention, but it can make people feel depressed. Editors should assess stories for the value they offer viewers and readers rather than simply for the interest they stir up.

For the reasons mentioned above, I would argue that news editors should focus on selecting positive stories because they should serve the public more than themselves or their organisations.

word counts : 291 words

우리말 해석

요즘 뉴스를 전달하는 미디어의 역할에 대한 회의론이 커지고 있는데 편집자들이 더 많은 관심을 끌기 위해 부정적인 이야기를 강조해서 종종 비난 받기 때문이다. 그러므로 나는 그들은 대중을 위해 좋은 뉴스를 더 많이 전달해야 한다고 생각한다.

뉴스 편집자들이 이야기를 선정할 때 수많은 요인들이 그들에게 영향을 미친다. 그들의 궁극적인 목표는 더 많은 독자를 끌어들여 더 많은 신문을 판매하는 것이다. 결국, TV 방송국과 신문 발행인들은 여타 산업들과 마찬가지로 수요를 창출해야 할 필요가 있다. 그 결과 편집자들은 종종 그들의 경쟁자들 사이에서 눈에 띄기 위해 시선을 사로잡는 헤드라인을 선정한다. 타블로이드 신문은 특히 기분 좋은 이야기보다 좀 더 눈을 뗄 수 없는 선정적이거나 나쁜 소식을 취재하려는 경향이 있다. 일부 뉴스 편집자들은 또한 그들 자신의 정치적 의견에 영향을 받을지도 모른다. 이는 비록 비슷한 견해를 공유하는 시청자나 독자에게는 여전히 호소할 수 있지만, 편파적인 언론으로 이끈다.

나는 이야기들이 가능한 한 흥미로운 방식으로 표현되어야 한다는 데 동의하지만 편집자들은 공정하고 책임감이 있어야 한다. 그들은 여론을 형성하는 기회와, 전쟁에 나가는 나라들을 포함해서 심각한 결과를 초래할 정치적 결정에 영향력을 끼칠 기회 두 가지를 모두 가지고 있다. 뉴스는 결코 진실을 왜곡하거나 대중을 의도적으로 공황상태에 빠뜨려서는 안 된다. 최근의 에볼라 공포는 그것에 대한 타당성 없이 한국에서 바이러스 공포로 널리 확산되었다. 또한 부정적인 뉴스는 많은 관심을 이끌어낼 잠재력이 있을지도 모르지만 사람들을 우울하게 만들 수 있다. 편집자들은 사람들을 자극하는 단순한 흥미거리보다 오히려 그들이 시청자들과 독자들에게 제공하는 가치로 이야기를 평가하여야 한다.

위에서 언급한 이유들 때문에, 나는 뉴스 편집자들은 긍정적인 이야기를 선택하는 데 초점을 맞춰야 한다고 생각하는데 그들은 자신이나 조직이 아닌 대중을 위해 일해야 하기 때문이다.

불법 Review

앞에서 배운 내용을 바탕으로 다음 빈칸을 영어로 작성해 보자.

Nowadays there is growing _____ (1. 회의론) about the media's role in delivering news because editors _____ (2. 종종 비난을 받다) highlighting negative stories in order to attract more attention. Therefore, I would believe that they should deliver more good news for _____ (3. 대중들).

A number of factors influence news editors when they are selecting stories. Their ultimate goal is to attract a bigger audience and to sell more newspapers. After all, television stations and newspaper publishers need to _____ (4. 수요를 창출하다) just like in any other industry. As a result, editors often choose _____ (5. 시선을 사로잡는 헤드라인들) to stand out among their competitors. Tabloid newspapers are especially prone to covering sensational or bad news, which can seem more compelling than feel-good stories. Some news editors may also be influenced by their own political opinions. This leads to _____ (6. 편파적인 언론), although it can still appeal to viewers and readers who share similar views.

While I agree that stories should be presented in _____ (7. 가능한 한 흥미로운 방식으로), editors should be fair and responsible. They have the opportunity to both shape public opinion and influence political decisions with serious consequences, including countries _____ (8. 전쟁에 나가다). News should never distort the truth or _____ (9. 의도적으로) encourage public panic. The recent Ebola scare led to widespread fear about the virus in Korea, even though there was no justification for it. Also, negative news may have the potential to draw a lot of attention, but it can make people feel depressed. Editors should assess stories for the value they offer _____ (10. 시청자들과 독자들) rather than simply for the interest they stir up.

For the reasons mentioned above, I would argue that news editors should focus on selecting positive stories because they should serve the public more than themselves or their organisations.

Answer 1. scepticism / 2. are often accused of / 3. the public / 4. generate demand
5. attention-grabbing headlines / 6. biased journalism / 7. as interesting a way as possible
8. going to war / 9. deliberately / 10. viewers and readers

Day 19 Mass Media, Movie & Play 불법 포인트 정리

가장 중요한 주제들	the main subjects	방송하다	broadcast
대중 매체	mass media	회의론	scepticism
폭력적이고 선정적인	violent and sensational	~로 비난받다	be accused of
범죄에 대한 공포	fear of crime	수요를 창출하다	generate demand
검열하다	censor	시선을 사로잡는	attention-grabbing
나이 제한	age limits	눈에 띄다, 두드러지다	stand out
설치하다	install	경쟁자들	competitors
책임지다	take responsibility for	~하기 쉽다, 경향이 있다	be prone to
공공 장소	public places	취재하다	cover
긴장을 풀고 쉬다	wind[wáind] down, 발음주의!	선정적인	sensational
감시	surveillance	(너무나 흥미로워서) 주목하지 않을 수 없는, 눈을 뗄 수 없는	compelling
~의 사생활을 침해하다	intrude upon one's privacy	편파적인, 치우친	biased
재미있고 즐거운	entertaining and enjoyable	가능한 한 흥미로운 방식으로	as interesting a way as possible
유익하고 교육적인	informative and educational	여론을 형성하다	shape public opinion
현실 세계에서	in the real world	전쟁에 나가다	go to war
A와 B를 연관짓다	link A with B	왜곡하다	distort
유명인사들	celebrities	의도적으로, 고의적으로	deliberately
화려한 생활방식	glamorous lifestyles	공황, 공포	panic = scare = fear
~로 잘 알려지다	be well known for	타당성	justification
유명 연예인들	famous entertainers	우울함을 느끼다	feel depressed
긍정적인 역할 모델	positive role models	자극하다, 선동하다	stir up
벗어나다	escape	대중을 위해 일하다	serve the public
뉴스 편집장들	news editors		

Day 20 Art 예술

Question

Sports stars earn large amounts of money and are often given media coverage. Meanwhile, the arts such as music, artwork and plays are neglected. Is it a positive or negative development?

스포츠 스타들은 상당히 많은 돈을 벌고 매스컴에 자주 등장한다. 반면 음악, 미술 그리고 연극 같은 예술은 무시된다. 이것은 긍정적인 발전인가? 부정적인 발전인가?

 빈출 문제

1. The Internet has provided us with the easy downloadable versions of most books. Some people say that the Internet books can completely replace paper ones sooner or later. To what extent do you agree or disagree with this opinion?

2. There are many different types of music in the world and the music industry is becoming bigger. Why do we need music? Is it a positive or negative development?

3. The traditional music of a country is more important than the international music that can be heard everywhere nowadays. Do you agree or disagree with this statement?

4. Today people pay more attention to artists such as writers and painters and have less interest in scientists. Is it a positive or negative development?

1. 인터넷은 대부분의 책을 쉽게 다운로드 할 수 있는 버전으로 제공하고 있다. 어떤 사람들은 조만간 인터넷 도서가 종이책을 완벽하게 대체할 수 있다고 주장한다. 당신은 이 의견에 얼마만큼 동의하는가? 또는 동의하지 않는가?

2. 세상에는 많은 종류의 음악이 있고 음악 산업은 더욱 커지고 있다. 왜 음악이 우리에게 필요한가? 이것은 긍정적인 발전인가? 부정적인 발전인가?

3. 한 나라의 전통 음악은 오늘날 어디에서나 들을 수 있는 국제적인 음악보다 더 중요하다. 당신은 이 말에 동의하는가? 또는 동의하지 않는가?

4. 오늘날 사람들은 작가나 화가 같은 예술가들에게 더 많은 관심을 갖고 과학자에게는 관심을 덜 갖는다. 이것은 긍정적인 발전인가? 부정적인 발전인가?

 **브레인스토밍**

1) 오늘날 몇몇 스포츠 스타들은 돈과 명예에 대해서만 신경 쓴다.
   ~에 대해 신경 쓰다 : be concerned about

2) 몇몇 운동 선수들은 어떤 희생을 치르더라도 이기기 위해서 스테로이드 같은 금지 약물을 복용한 혐의로 기소된다.
   운동 선수들 : athletes / 어떤 희생을 치르더라도 : at any cost / 금지 약물을 복용하다 : take banned drugs
   기소되다 : be accused of

3) 스포츠는 직업이라기 보다는 여가 활동이 되어야 함으로 사람들은 즐거움과 건강의 이유로 스포츠 활동을 해야 한다.
   여가 활동 : leisure activities

4) 어떤 사람들은 참여하는 것이 이기는 것보다 더 중요하다고 믿는다.

5) 프로 스포츠는 다른 산업들과 같으므로 사람들은 그들의 재능을 연봉을 버는데 이용할 수 있어야 한다.
   프로 스포츠 : professional sports / 재능 : talents / 연봉을 벌다 : earn a salary

6) 유명한 운동 선수들은 상당히 많은 돈을 받을 만한데 그들은 전세계 수백만의 사람들을 즐겁게 해주기 때문이다.
   받을 만하다 : deserve / 수백만의 사람들 : millions of people / 즐겁게 해 주다 : entertain

7) 경쟁은 인간의 선천적 본능이고 스포츠는 경쟁의 안전한 형태이다.
   선천적 본능 : a natural instinct / 경쟁 : competition

8) 스포츠 팀의 지지자들은 어떤 공동체에 대해 소속감을 느낀다.
   지지자들 : supporters / 소속감 : a sense of belonging

9) 축구 선수들은 단순히 공을 차는 것으로써 엄청난 연봉을 번다.
   공을 차다 : kick a ball

10) 전통 음악은 현대 음악보다 더 중요하다.
    전통 음악 : traditional music / 현대 음악 : modern music

11) 전통 음악은 한 나라의 문화와 관습 그리고 역사를 표현한다.
    표현하다 : express

12) 교육이나 의료 그리고 안전과 같은 공공 서비스는 한 국가를 제대로 운영하는 데 매우 중요한 반면 창의적인 예술가들의 작품은 사치이다.
    공공 서비스 : public services / 제대로 운영하다 : function properly / 사치 : luxury

13) 예술은 사람들이 일, 아이들 그리고 돈과 같은 삶의 일상적인 문제로부터 벗어나는 것을 가능하게 한다.
    삶의 일상적인 문제들 : life's everyday problems / ~로부터 벗어나다 : escape from

14) 예술은 휴식의 형태로 많은 사람들에게 높이 평가되고 있다.
   휴식의 형태 : a form of relaxation / 높이 평가되다 : be highly valued

15) 예술은 우리의 전반적 안녕을 유지하고 향상시키는 데 필수적 역할을 한다.
   필수적인 : integral

Answer

1) Nowadays some sports stars are only concerned about money and fame.
2) Some athletes are accused of taking banned drugs such as steroids in order to win at any cost.
3) Sports should be leisure activities rather than jobs, therefore people should do sporting activities for enjoyment and health reasons.
4) Some people believe that taking part is more important than winning.
5) Professional sports are the same as any other business, so people should be able to use their talents to earn a salary.
6) Famous athletes deserve a huge amount of money because they entertain millions of people in the world.
7) Competition is a natural instinct in humans and sports are a safe form of competition.
8) Supporters of sports teams feel a sense of belonging to a community.
9) Football players earn enormous salaries by simply kicking a ball.
10) Traditional music is more important than modern music.
11) Traditional music expresses the culture, customs and history of a country.
12) Public services such as education, healthcare and security are vital for a country to function properly, whereas the work of creative artists is a luxury.
13) Art allows people to escape from life's everyday problems such as work, children and money.
14) Art is highly valued by many people as a form of relaxation.
15) Art plays an integral role in maintaining and improving our overall well-being.

실전문제

You should spend about 40 minutes on this task.
Write about the following topic :

> Sports stars earn large amounts of money and are often given media coverage. Meanwhile, the arts such as music, artwork and plays are neglected. Is it a positive or negative development?

Give reasons for your answer and include any relevant examples from your own knowledge or experience.

Write at least 250 words.

1단계 문제 정독, 문제 유형 파악, 브레인스토밍 (0 ~ 5분)

Question	Sports stars earn large amounts of money and are often given media coverage. Meanwhile, the arts such as music, artwork and plays are neglected. Is it a positive or negative development?

문제 정독
스포츠 스타들은 상당히 많은 돈을 벌고 매스컴에 자주 등장한다. 반면 음악, 미술 그리고 연극 같은 예술은 무시된다. 이것은 긍정적인 발전인가? 부정적인 발전인가?

media coverage : 매스컴의 보도

문제 유형 파악

2-1. Is it a positive or negative development? 유형

Brainstorming

Topic : 스포츠 스타들은 상당히 많은 돈을 벌고 매스컴에 자주 등장하지만 예술은 무시된다.	
Positive development : 긍정적 발전	Negative development : 부정적 발전
1. 더 건강한 생활방식을 장려 encourage a healthier lifestyle → 스포츠가 격렬한 신체적 활동을 포함 sports involve intensive physical activities 2. 인간은 스포츠의 완벽함을 동경함 humans have admired sporting perfection → 운동선수들은 더 높은 목표에 도달하는 데 영감을 줌 athletes can inspire us to reach higher goals	1. 즉각적인 만족감을 향해 이동 moving towards instant gratification → 오락에 더 지적이고 교양 있는 접근 more intellectual and cultured approach to entertainment 2. 그들이 재능을 키우는 것을 우리가 막음 we discourage them from developing their talents → 우리가 예술을 감상할 미래의 기회가 줄어듦 reduces future opportunities for us to appreciate the arts → 자유 시장의 부끄러운 폐단 a shameful indictment of the free market

* 아이디어의 수도 같고 영어로 쓸 수 있는 말도 비슷하다면, 좀 더 설득력 있게 논리적으로 접근할 수 있는 쪽을 내 의견으로 한다. 이 에세이에서는 negative development, '스포츠 스타들은 상당히 많은 돈을 벌고 매스컴에 자주 등장하지만 예술은 무시되는 경향은 부정적'을 내 주장으로 삼았다.

2단계 서론 (Introduction) (6~10분) : 두 문장으로 작성

Question	Sports stars earn large amounts of money and are often given media coverage. Meanwhile, the arts such as music, artwork and plays are neglected. Is it a positive or negative development?

단계	Question	서론 작성
1단계 Paraphrasing	토픽 : Sports stars earn large amounts of money and are often given media coverage. Meanwhile, the arts such as music, artwork and plays are neglected.	Paraphrasing : The popularity of sports allows athletes to earn vast amounts of money but skilled artists are ignored.
2단계 Answering	질문 : Is it a positive or negative development?	Answering : Negative development This trend raises the question of why we place so much value on sports stars.

Introduction
The popularity of sports allows athletes to earn vast amounts of money but skilled artists are ignored. This trend raises the question of why we place so much value on sports stars.

popularity : 대중적 인기
raise a question : 문제(의문)를 제기하다
place much value on : ~을 높게 평가하다, 많은 가치를 두다

우리말 해석
스포츠의 대중적 인기는 운동 선수들이 엄청난 액수의 돈을 벌 수 있게 하지만 숙련된 예술가들은 무시당한다. 이러한 경향은 왜 우리가 스포츠 선수들에게 너무 많은 가치를 두는지에 대한 문제를 제기한다.

3단계 본론 1 (Body 1) (11~20분) : 나와 다른 의견 = Positive (운동 선수가 예술가들에 비해 많은 돈을 버는 것은 긍정적)

Question	Sports stars earn large amounts of money and are often given media coverage. Meanwhile, the arts such as music, artwork and plays are neglected. Is it a positive or negative development?

Body 1은 1단계에서 브레인토밍한 'Positive'를 바탕으로 작성한다.

1단계	Topic Sentence	Admittedly, there are some benefits associated with having sports stars as role models.
2단계 (1)	Supporting Sentence (1)	*encourage a healthier lifestyle* They can encourage a healthier lifestyle for both children and adults.
3단계 (1)	Supporting Sentence or Specific Example (1)	*sports involve intensive physical activities* This is because most sports involve intensive physical activities.
2단계 (2)	Supporting Sentence (2)	*humans have admired sporting perfection* Also, humans have admired sporting perfection for thousands of years, such as in ancient Greece and Rome.
3단계 (2)	Supporting Sentence or Specific Example (2)	*athletes can inspire us to reach higher goals* Athletes can inspire us to reach higher goals in our own lives, even if those ambitions have nothing to do with sports.

Body 1

Admittedly, there are some benefits associated with having sports stars as role models. They can encourage a healthier lifestyle for both children and adults. This is because most sports involve intensive physical activities. Also, humans have admired sporting perfection for thousands of years, such as in ancient Greece and Rome. Athletes can inspire us to reach higher goals in our own lives, even if those ambitions have nothing to do with sports.

admittedly : 인정하건대, 틀림없이
intensive physical activities : 격렬한 신체 활동들
sporting perfection : 스포츠의 완벽함(인간이 도달할 수 있는 최고의 성과를 내려고 함)
ambitions : 야망들
have nothing to do with : ~와 관계 없다

우리말 해석

인정하건대, 롤 모델로서 스포츠 선수가 있다는 것과 관련된 몇 가지 이점이 있다. 그들은 아이와 어른 모두에게 더 건강한 생활방식을 장려할 수 있다. 이것은 대부분의 스포츠가 격렬한 신체적 활동을 포함하고 있기 때문이다. 또한 인간은 고대 그리스와 로마에서처럼 수천 년 간 스포츠의 완벽함을 동경해 왔다. 운동선수들은 우리 자신의 삶에서 더 높은 목표에, 비록 그러한 야망이 스포츠와 아무 관련이 없을지라도, 도달하는 데 영감을 줄 수 있다.

4 단계 본론 2 (Body 2) (21~30분) : 내 의견 = **Negative** (운동 선수가 예술가들에 비해 많은 돈을 버는 것은 부정적)

Question	Sports stars earn large amounts of money and are often given media coverage. Meanwhile, the arts such as music, artwork and plays are neglected. Is it a positive or negative development?

Body 2는 1단계에서 브레인스토밍한 'Negative'를 바탕으로 작성한다.

1단계	Topic Sentence	Yet it is sad that we no longer value artists as highly as we used to.
2단계 (1)	Supporting Sentence (1)	*moving towards instant gratification* It probably reflects the way in which many societies have been moving towards instant gratification over an appreciation of life's more subtle beauty.
3단계 (1)	Supporting Sentence or Specific Example (1)	*more intellectual and cultured approach to entertainment* The arts can be just as inspirational as sports, and often they promote a more intellectual and cultured approach to entertainment.
2단계 (2)	Supporting Sentence (2)	*we discourage them from developing their talents* Another problem with neglecting young artists is that we discourage them from developing their talents if they cannot financially support themselves.
3단계 (2)	Supporting Sentence or Specific Example (2)	*reduces future opportunities for us to appreciate the arts* This in turn reduces future opportunities for us to appreciate the arts and it becomes a vicious circle. *a shameful indictment of the free market* At the same time, sports stars continue to earn almost obscene salaries. It is a shameful indictment of the free market that footballers can earn ten times more in a week than most ordinary people in a whole year.

Body 2
Yet it is sad that we no longer value artists as highly as we used to. It probably reflects the way in which many societies have been moving towards instant gratification over an appreciation of life's more subtle beauty. The arts can be just as inspirational as sports, and often they promote a more intellectual and cultured approach to entertainment. Another problem with neglecting young artists is that we discourage them from developing their talents if they cannot financially support themselves. This in turn reduces future opportunities for us to appreciate the arts and it becomes a vicious circle. At the same time, sports stars continue to earn almost obscene salaries. It is a shameful indictment of the free market that footballers can earn ten times more in a week than most ordinary people in a whole year.

instant gratification : 즉각적인 만족감
subtle : 미묘한
inspirational : 영감을 주는
cultured : 교양 있는
in turn : 결국

appreciate : 감상하다
a vicious circle : 악순환
obscene : 터무니없는
a shameful indictment : 부끄러운 폐단

우리말 해석
그러나 우리가 더 이상 과거에 그랬던 것만큼 예술가들의 가치를 높이 평가하지 않는 것은 슬픈 일이다. 이것은 아마도 많은 사회가 인생의 더 미묘한 아름다움을 감상하기보다는 즉각적인 만족감을 향하여 이동하고 있음을 반영하는 것이다. 예술은 스포츠같이 영감을 줄 수 있으며, 종종 오락에 더 지적이고 교양 있는 접근을 추진한다. 젊은 예술가들을 무시하는 또 다른 문제는 만약 그들이 재정적으로 자립할 수 없다면 그들이 재능을 키우는 것을 우리가 막는다는 점이다. 이것은 결국 우리가 예술을 감상할 미래의 기회가 줄어든다는 것이며 악순환이 된다. 동시에 스포츠 스타들은 터무니없는 연봉을 계속 벌어들일 것이다. 축구 선수들이 대다수의 평범한 사람들이 일년 내내 번 것의 열 배 이상을 일주일 만에 벌 수 있다는 것은 자유 시장의 부끄러운 폐단이다.

 **5 단계**　결론 (Conclusion) (31~35분) : 본문에 제시한 내 주장 요약하며 다시 한 번 강조

Question	Sports stars earn large amounts of money and are often given media coverage. Meanwhile, the arts such as music, artwork and plays are neglected. Is it a positive or negative development?

결론 작성 시, 먼저 문제 유형을 파악한 후, 'Conclusion Template'의 표현을 인용한다. (See p58)

문제 유형 파악	2-1) Is it a positive or negative development? 유형
Conclusion Template 인용	For the reasons mentioned above, I would argue that the benefits(drawbacks) of… (토픽) outweigh its drawbacks(benefits) because… 본론에 제시한 장점(단점) 간략히 요약

결론을 작성하기 전, 서론과 본론 2에서 Negative, '스포츠 스타들은 상당히 많은 돈을 벌고 매스컴에 자주 등장하지만 예술은 무시되는 경향은 부정적'이라고 했는지 다시 한 번 확인하자!

> **Conclusion**
> **For the reasons mentioned above, I would argue that the drawbacks of** sports stars' popularity and earning potential over artists **outweigh the benefits because** we have ended up with less balanced cultural and societal values.

* 상황에 따라 템플릿을 살짝 변형해도 좋다.

　end up with : 결국 ~하게 되다

> **우리말 해석**
> 위에서 언급한 이유로 나는 예술가를 넘어서는 스포츠 스타의 인기와 소득의 잠재성의 단점이 장점을 능가한다고 주장하는데 우리가 결국 덜 균형 잡힌 문화와 사회적 가치에 이르렀기 때문이다.

6 단계   교정 (Self-correction) (36~40분) : 내용의 일관성 및 문법 검토

다음 Body 2의 내용을 교정해 보자. 틀린 부분은 총 몇 개일까?

교정 전 (직접 문장 부호를 이용하여 틀린 부분을 교정해 보자.)

yet it is sad that We no longer value artists as highly as we used to. It probably reflect the way in which many society have been moving towards instant gratification over an appreciation of life's more subtle beauty. The arts can be just as inspirational as sports, and often they promotes a more intellectual and cultured approach to entertainment. Another problem with neglecting young artists are that we discourage them from developing their talents if they cannot financially support themselves.

This in turn reduce future opportunities for us to appreciate the arts and it becomes a vicious circle. At a same time, sports stars continue to earning almost obscene salaries. It is a shameful indictment of the free market that footballers can earn ten times more in a week than most ordinary people in a whole year.

교정

~~y~~Y et it is sad that ~~W~~w e no longer value artists as highly as we used to. It probably ~~reflect~~ reflects the way in which many ~~society~~ societies have been moving towards instant gratification over an appreciation of life's more subtle beauty. The arts can be just as inspirational as sports, and often they ~~promotes~~ promote a more intellectual and cultured approach to entertainment. Another problem with neglecting young artists ~~are~~ is that we discourage them from developing their talents if they cannot financially support themselves. This in turn ~~reduce~~ reduces future opportunities for us to appreciate the arts and it becomes a vicious circle. At ~~a~~ the same time, sports stars continue to ~~earning~~ earn almost obscene salaries. It is a shameful indictment of the free market that footballers can earn ten times more in a week than most ordinary people in a whole year.

1. y → Y : 문장의 첫 글자는 반드시 대문자로 시작한다.
2. W → w : 갑자기 대문자를 문장 중간에 쓰지 않는다(고유명사 예외).
3. reflect → reflects : 주어인 It이 단수이므로 단수 동사인 reflects를 쓴다.
4. society → societies : many + 복수 명사
5. promotes → promote : 주어인 they가 복수이므로 복수 동사인 promote를 쓴다.
6. are → is : 주어인 problem이 단수이므로 단수 동사인 is를 쓴다.
7. 붙여쓰기 : 위의 글은 Body 2 단락이다. 단락이 바뀌지 않는 한, 줄을 바꿔 쓰지 않는다.
8. reduce → reduces : 주어인 This가 단수이므로 단수 동사인 reduces를 쓴다.
9. a → the : at the same time은 '동시에'라는 뜻
10. earning → earn : continue to + 동사 원형

틀린 개수 : 총 10개

Sample Answer

> **Question**
>
> Sports stars earn large amounts of money and are often given media coverage. Meanwhile, the arts such as music, artwork and plays are neglected. Is it a positive or negative development?

The popularity of sports allows athletes to earn vast amounts of money but skilled artists are ignored. This trend raises the question of why we place so much value on sports stars.

Admittedly, there are some benefits associated with having sports stars as role models. They can encourage a healthier lifestyle for both children and adults. This is because most sports involve intensive physical activities. Also, humans have admired sporting perfection for thousands of years, such as in ancient Greece and Rome. Athletes can inspire us to reach higher goals in our own lives, even if those ambitions have nothing to do with sports.

Yet it is sad that we no longer value artists as highly as we used to. It probably reflects the way in which many societies have been moving towards instant gratification over an appreciation of life's more subtle beauty. The arts can be just as inspirational as sports, and often they promote a more intellectual and cultured approach to entertainment. Another problem with neglecting young artists is that we discourage them from developing their talents if they cannot financially support themselves. This in turn reduces future opportunities for us to appreciate the arts and it becomes a vicious circle. At the same time, sports stars continue to earn almost obscene salaries. It is a shameful indictment of the free market that footballers can earn ten times more in a week than most ordinary people in a whole year.

For the reasons mentioned above, I would argue that the drawbacks of sports stars' popularity and earning potential over artists outweigh the benefits because we have ended up with less balanced cultural and societal values.

word counts : 277 words

우리말 해석

스포츠의 대중적 인기는 운동 선수들이 엄청난 액수의 돈을 벌 수 있게 하지만 숙련된 예술가들은 무시당한다. 이러한 경향은 왜 우리가 스포츠 선수들에게 너무 많은 가치를 두는지에 대한 문제를 제기한다.

인정하건대, 롤 모델로서 스포츠 선수가 있다는 것과 관련된 몇 가지 이점이 있다. 그들은 아이와 어른 모두에게 더 건강한 생활방식을 장려할 수 있다. 이것은 대부분의 스포츠가 격렬한 신체적 활동을 포함하고 있기 때문이다. 또한 인간은 고대 그리스와 로마에서처럼 수천 년 간 스포츠의 완벽함을 동경해 왔다. 운동선수들은 우리 자신의 삶에서 더 높은 목표에, 비록 그러한 야망이 스포츠와 아무 관련이 없을지라도, 도달하는 데 영감을 줄 수 있다.

그러나 우리가 더 이상 과거에 그랬던 것만큼 예술가들의 가치를 높이 평가하지 않는 것은 슬픈 일이다. 이것은 아마도 많은 사회가 인생의 더 미묘한 아름다움을 감상하기보다는 즉각적인 만족감을 향하여 이동하고 있음을 반영하는 것이다. 예술은 스포츠같이 영감을 줄 수 있으며, 종종 오락에 더 지적이고 교양 있는 접근을 추진한다. 젊은 예술가들을 무시하는 또 다른 문제는 만약 그들이 재정적으로 자립할 수 없다면 그들이 재능을 키우는 것을 우리가 막는다는 점이다. 이것은 결국 우리가 예술을 감상할 미래의 기회가 줄어든다는 것이며 악순환이 된다. 동시에 스포츠 스타들은 터무니없는 연봉을 계속 벌어들일 것이다. 축구 선수들이 대다수의 평범한 사람들이 일년 내내 번 것의 열 배 이상을 일주일 만에 벌 수 있다는 것은 자유 시장의 부끄러운 폐단이다.

위에서 언급한 이유들로 나는 예술가를 넘어서는 스포츠 스타의 인기와 소득의 잠재성의 단점이 장점을 능가한다고 주장하는데 우리가 결국 덜 균형 잡힌 문화와 사회적 가치에 이르렀기 때문이다.

불법 Review

앞에서 배운 내용을 바탕으로 다음 빈칸을 영어로 작성해 보자.

_____ (1. 스포츠의 대중적 인기) allows athletes to earn vast amounts of money but skilled artists are ignored. This trend _____ (2. 문제를 제기하다) of why we place so much value on sports stars.

Admittedly, there are some benefits associated with having sports stars as role models. They can encourage _____ (3. 더 건강한 생활방식) for both children and adults. This is because most sports involve _____ (4. 격렬한 신체적 활동들). Also, humans have admired sporting perfection for thousands of years, such as in ancient Greece and Rome. Athletes can inspire us to reach higher goals in our own lives, even if those ambitions _____ (5. ~와 관련 없다) sports.

Yet it is sad that we no longer value artists as highly as we used to. It probably reflects the way in which many societies have been moving towards _____ (6. 즉각적인 만족감) over an appreciation of life's more subtle beauty. The arts can be just as inspirational as sports, and often they promote a more intellectual and cultured approach to entertainment. Another problem with neglecting young artists is that we discourage them from developing their talents if they cannot financially support themselves. This in turn reduces future opportunities for us to appreciate the arts and it becomes _____ (7. 악순환). At the same time, sports stars continue to earn almost _____ (8. 터무니없는 연봉). It is _____ (9. 부끄러운 폐단) of the free market that footballers can earn ten times more in a week than most ordinary people in a whole year.

For the reasons mentioned above, I would argue that the drawbacks of sports stars' popularity and earning potential over artists outweigh the benefits because we have ended up with less balanced cultural and societal values.

Answer 1. The popularity of sports / 2. raises the question / 3. a healthier lifestyle / 4. intensive physical activities / 5. have nothing to do with / 6. instant gratification / 7. a vicious circle / 8. obscene salaries / 9. a shameful indictment

Day 20 Art 불법 포인트 정리

~에 대해 신경 쓰다	be concerned about	삶의 일상적인 문제들	life's everyday problems
운동 선수들	athletes	~로부터 벗어나다	escape from
어떤 희생을 치르더라도	at any cost	휴식의 형태	a form of relaxation
금지 약물을 복용하다	take banned drugs	높이 평가되다	be highly valued
기소되다	be accused of	필수적인	integral
여가 활동	leisure activities	대중적 인기	popularity
프로 스포츠	professional sports	문제(의문)를 제기하다	raise a question
재능	talents	~을 높게 평가하다, 많은 가치를 두다	place much value on
연봉을 벌다	earn a salary	인정하건대, 틀림없이	admittedly
받을 만하다	deserve	격렬한 신체 활동들	intensive physical activities
수백만의 사람들	millions of people	스포츠의 완벽함	sporting perfection
즐겁게 해 주다	entertain	야망들	ambitions
선천적 본능	a natural instinct	~와 관계 없다	have nothing to do with
경쟁	competition	즉각적인 만족감	instant gratification
지지자들	supporters	미묘한	subtle
소속감	a sense of belonging	영감을 주는	inspirational
공을 차다	kick a ball	교양 있는	cultured
전통 음악	traditional music	결국	in turn
현대 음악	modern music	감상하다	appreciate
표현하다	express	악순환	a vicious circle
공공 서비스	public services	터무니없는	obscene
제대로 운영하다	function properly	부끄러운 폐단	a shameful indictment
사치	luxury	결국 ~하게 되다	end up with

아이엘츠 & 유학 준비는 유학 1위 기업과 함께!

종로유학원
Chongro Overseas Educational Institute

대한민국 1등 안심유학

언론사, 소비자, 전문가들이 선정하는 최고 권위의 브랜드 대상에서
수년간 유학부문 1위를 지키며 명실공히 국가대표 유학원임을 인정받고 있습니다.

올해의 브랜드 대상
16년 연속 수상
주관 | 한국경제신문, 한국소비자포럼

대한민국 국가브랜드 선정
유학원 최초 국가브랜드 선정
주최 | 중앙일보, 후원 | 지식경제부

대학생 선호도 1위 기업
12년 연속 수상
주최 | 한국대학신문

국제교육&박람회 전문가 그룹
ICEF 인증

EnglishUSA
파트너 맴버(2023 ~)

대한민국 대표브랜드 대상
교육/유학부문 1위 수상

문의 | 1577 - 5682

Your journey starts here.

주한영국문화원 **IELTS** 영국문화원 IELTS

Telephone. 02 3702 0601   **Website.** https://www.britishcouncil.kr/exam/ielts

E-mail. exams@britishcouncil.or.kr

Address. 서울특별시 중구 서소문로 11길 19 (정동 34-5 배재정동빌딩B동) 2층 주한영국문화원 (우)04516

시원스쿨LAB × 줄리정 인강

IELTS 불변의 법칙
줄리정 프리패스

베스트셀러 1위 저자 줄리정
대한민국 아이엘츠의 전설!

아이엘츠 대표
스타강사 줄리정 전 강의 포함

아이엘츠 불변의 법칙
베스트셀러 1위 저자 직강

최신 경향 완벽 반영
캠브릿지 공식 교재+강의 포함

전 모듈 대비
기초~실전까지 한 번에

기적의 비법노트
줄리정 VOCA 비법노트 무료

6.5 미달성 시
수강기간 무한연장

지금 시원스쿨 아이엘츠(ielts.siwonschool.com)에서 유료로 수강 가능합니다.
* [1위] 줄리정's IELTS 불변의 법칙 | 2017.01.14 YES24 > IELTS 주간 베스트셀러 1위

시원스쿨 IELTS